ALABAMA

Treasures

A Reading/Language Arts Program

Get Ready for the ARMT
See pages A2-A16

 **Macmillan/McGraw-Hill**

Art credits: A2: Dana Regan. A3: Greg Harris. A7: (t) David Merrell. A7: (b) John Kurtz. A11: Nathan Walker. A14: Nathan Walker. A16: Robert Roper.

Strategy
Make Inferences and Analyze
Figure out something not completely explained in the story.

Focus
Character, Setting, Plot
The setting and characters affect the plot.

ARMT Strategy
Why does Nick's mother protest?

Focus
When does Nick's Mom decide that he is responsible for getting ready on time?

Nick of Time

Nick couldn't seem to arrive on time. His mother protested every time Nick missed the school bus.

Nick was good at other things. He completed his assignments on time. He was always proud of the homework he handed in. He just wasn't good at getting places on time.

Once, Nick set his alarm clock a whole hour before the time he needed to get to school. That day, he forgot to turn the alarm on, and he went running to the bus stop only to see the bus driving away. Another time, he set two alarm clocks. Unfortunately, that night there was a big storm, and the power went out. He missed the bus that day, too. Nick's mom even tried carrying him out of bed to breakfast, but he was so deep asleep that he fell face first into his pancakes. From then on, Nick's mom told him that he was responsible for getting ready for school on time.

Nick had a big test in his next math class. He was worried about arriving late to school again. He did well in math, but he couldn't afford to miss a test.

That night, Nick made sure to eat a healthy dinner. He did not watch television or play video games. He brushed his teeth and got ready for bed.

ARMT Strategy

Think about what Nick does so he will not be late for his test. Tell why you think these actions will or will not work.

That night, Nick fell asleep almost immediately. He had a restful night of sleep.

Nick awoke with a start. "Oh no, I'll be late," he thought. He rushed to get dressed and ran out the door. The house was quiet. "Oh no! I'm so late that Mom already left for work! I must have missed the bus. I better ride my bike to school."

Focus

Where does Nick go after he wakes up?

In a panic, Nick pedaled quickly to school. The road seemed endless. Nick finally arrived. He parked his bike and ran to the front entrance. The door was locked. "I missed my math test!" he cried, and ran to the side entrance.

Nick's math teacher, Mr. Gardner, came out. "Nick! What are you doing here?" asked Mr. Gardner.

Nick tried to think of an excuse for being so late, but no words came out of his mouth.

Mr. Gardner laughed and said, "Nick, go home. You have plenty of time. Nobody wants to come to school on a Saturday!" He felt calm and ready for the day.

ARMT Strategy

How do you think Nick will do on his math test?

Strategy
Generate Questions
Ask yourself questions about what you read.

Focus
Fact and Opinion
Facts are true statements. Opinions are thoughts about a topic.

COMING TO AMERICA

The United States is home to people from all over the world. For many years, people traveled to the United States by ship. The journey was long and hard, but many people hoped to cross America's borders for a better life.

The Statue of Liberty in the New York Harbor is a symbol that welcomes people to the United States. It was given to the United States as a gift from France in 1886. The statue is a tall woman made of copper. She is 151 feet and one inch tall! The statue stands on top of a base that is 154 feet tall. That makes her tall enough to be seen from ships that sail into the harbor.

On her head, Lady Liberty wears a spiked crown. The seven spikes of the crown represent the seven continents and the seven seas around the world. In one hand, she holds a tablet. On the tablet is the date "July 4, 1776" in Roman numerals. In the other hand, she holds a torch high in the air.

ARMT Strategy

Why do you think the Statue of Liberty holds these things in her hands?

The Statue of Liberty is on a small island called Liberty Island. Near Liberty Island is another island, called Ellis Island. Ellis Island was the first stop for people who made the long trip across the Atlantic Ocean in search of the American Dream. The dream was that anyone who worked hard could have a good life in this country. Between 1892 and 1954, more than 12 million people came to America through Ellis Island. Most of these people came from Europe.

For many people, America was a symbol of independence. There were opportunities in America that many people did not have in their home countries. Jobs, education, religious, and political freedom were all reasons that people dreamed of becoming citizens of the United States.

Ask your family members if any of your relatives came to America through the New York Harbor. The Statue of Liberty and Ellis Island are an important part of America's heritage. They represent a time when people from many countries came to the United States in search of a new life.

Focus

Is this statement a fact or an opinion? How do you know?

Focus

Is this statement a fact or an opinion? How do you know?

Strategy
Evaluate
Think about the importance of the information in the text.

Focus
Author's Purpose
Authors write to inform, entertain, or persuade readers.

Focus

What do you think is the author's purpose in writing this passage?

Young Entrepreneurs

Do you have a great idea? Do you want to make some money? Are you an enterprising individual?

If great ideas inspire you to create, you can start your own business. Having your own business is a huge responsibility, but at Young Entrepreneurs, we are here to help. We help kids take their ideas and convert them into businesses. We help you learn the ins and outs of how your idea or service can grow into a successful money-making venture.

Here are some stories of kids who started their own businesses:

Glittering Glamour

Nine year old Jessica of East Lansing, Michigan, enjoyed creating original jewelry designs with glass beads. At first, she gave earrings, necklaces, and bracelets to her friends and family as presents. Soon, people started asking her to design special pieces for them. This satisfying hobby soon turned into Jessica's own jewelry business. She designs and makes all of her jewelry, and she will even gift wrap and ship orders to anywhere in the United States.

Doggie Day Care

Fifteen year old Jamie started his dog day care as a dog walking service in Amherst, Massachusetts. He would earn money after school and on weekends to walk five, six, and even seven dogs at one time! Soon, some of Jamie's neighbors began to ask him if he could walk their dogs every day. Many of Jamie's neighbors worked all day, so Jamie offered to take the dogs out for a walk before he left for school and when he came back, before their owners came home from work. Jamie turned his dog-walking service into a weekend day care service. Jamie still walks the dogs every day, but on weekends, he spends time with the dogs, plays with them, and even helps groom them. Jamie's dog day care has become a popular choice for neighborhood pet owners.

ARMT Strategy

Why does the author include this detail? What does it tell you about Jamie's ability to walk dogs?

Pretty Packages

Every time seven-year-old Mai Lee from St. Louis, Missouri gave people presents, they marveled at the beautiful wrapping and ribbons. She made paper swans, ribbon roses, and colorful gift wrap fans to embellish her gifts. Everyone in her family always asked her to wrap their gifts for them. Mai Lee took this idea and decided to open a Holiday Gift Wrapping stand. During the holiday season, people drop off their packages, and Mai Lee returns them in their beautiful trimmings. Although Mai Lee's busiest time is during the holidays, she is available to wrap gifts throughout the year for birthdays, anniversaries, and other celebrations.

These are just a few of our biggest success stories. Remember, every business starts with an idea. Call and make an appointment to see how you can get started on your kid business today!

Focus

Why does the author choose to tell a few of the biggest success stories?

Strategy
Text Structure
Look at how the author organizes ideas.

Focus
Draw Conclusions
Clues in the text can help you draw conclusions about the topic.

ARMT Strategy

How does the author organize information in this passage?

Focus

What characteristics of wind make it a good alternative to fossil fuels?

Alternative Energy

We need energy to live. All around the globe, fossil fuels are burned for energy. Coal, oil, and natural gas are all fossil fuels that come from the earth. We use them to make electricity. Oil is also used to make gasoline. We use a lot of these fuels. Some fear that we will eventually use up these resources. Also, when we burn fossil fuels, the air gets dirty. Pollution hurts the earth and damages the environment. This in turn harms the homes of people, plants, and animals.

There are other forms of energy that do not burn fossil fuels. These forms of energy do not create pollution. They do not harm the earth. This type of fuel supply will not run out.

One source of energy is the sun. Solar power uses energy from the sun. People on earth only use a small part of the total energy that the sun gives off. Solar panels take light from the sun and turn it into energy. The energy is used to power lights, radios, cars, and homes. Solar power is also used to heat homes and buildings.

Wind is another possible source of energy. Wind is clean. The earth will never run out of it. Wind mills take the force of the wind and change it into electrical power. Electricity that comes from wind can give power to homes, especially in very windy areas.

The natural heat of the earth is also a source of energy. This energy source heats water to make steam. The steam then is used to make electricity. This is a clean way to heat buildings without polluting the environment. Heat from the earth can be used for many good things. It is used in hot springs and spas to help people relieve stress. It can also be used to grow plants in greenhouses. Some places in the United States pump earth-heated water under streets and sidewalks to keep them from freezing. This form of energy is useful not only for farming, but also for winter safety.

Energy comes from many sources. Some types of energy cannot be put back once we use them up. The sun, the wind, and the earth's heat will not go away. They will play a key role in our future. If we make use of these resources, we can do our best to protect our planet.

Focus

In what ways can the earth's heat help us?

Chincoteague Crossing

On Chincoteague Island, Virginia, away from city skyscrapers, lives a breed of wild horses known as the Chincoteague Pony. The ponies are believed to be descendants of wild horses brought to the New World on Spanish ships. One legend tells of a Spanish ship sinking and the wild horses swimming to the island to safety. Others believe that the ponies came from horses that were brought there in the 1600s by farmers who wanted to escape taxes. In either case, since then, these wild horses have found a home on the island sanctuary.

This breed of ponies roams free on Chincoteague and Assateague Islands, off of the coast of Virginia. They spend most of the year roaming the islands, parks, and beaches of Assateague Island. They are smaller and have longer hair than other breeds of horses. A Chincoteague horse grows to the size of a regular pony. The food that these horses eat on the islands tends to be salty, so they drink a lot of fresh water. As a result, their stomachs look swollen. The ponies have threatened the island's marsh habitat because of overfeeding on the marsh grasses.

Every summer, visitors and residents gather for the yearly Pony Swim. There is a lot of commotion as people watch the ponies swim across the channel from Assateague Island to nearby Chincoteague

Island. Some watch the ponies from the crowded beach. Others get a better view from boats on the water. It only takes about five minutes for the ponies to cross the channel. The swim is scheduled during calm waters so that the younger ponies can make it across safely. The ponies are rounded up and sold at an auction. This means that the ponies are sold to the person who bids the most money. The ponies that are not sold swim back to Assateague Island and are set free for another year in the wild. The money that is earned from the auction goes to help the local fire department. They own one of the pony herds. The auction is one way to help control the number of ponies on the island. This protects the resources on the island.

The Pony Swim is a popular event on these remote islands, but visitors can see the wild ponies any time of year. There are daily tours of the islands, and visitors can enjoy other activities, such as bird watching and fishing. But in late summer, the Pony Swim is always the biggest attraction.

ARMT Strategy

Restate the main events of the annual Pony Swim.

Focus

Do you think it is necessary to control the island's pony population? Why or why not?

Benjamin's Birthday Wish List

Benjamin assumed that his brother James would come home from college for his birthday. Every year, James took Benjamin out for ice cream and a movie. Benjamin was looking forward to his time with his brother. More than that, he couldn't wait to see what gift his brother would give him this year.

"What do you want for your birthday, Ben?" James asked on the telephone.

"Lots of stuff," said Ben excitedly. "A new video game, a remote control car, a model ship, a new baseball mitt…"

"Whoa, whoa." James interrupted, trying not to show his disappointment in his little brother.. "You want all that?"

"Sure," said Benjamin. "Isn't that what birthdays are for? I hope I get a lot of stuff on my wish list."

Focus

Why do you think James was disappointed in Benjamin?

James couldn't help but feel annoyed by Benjamin's attitude. He didn't want to make things worse by giving the news that he wouldn't be able to make it home for his little brother's birthday this year. After all, the basketball championships were very important to James. His school was counting on him to help his team bring home the championship trophy.

Benjamin hung up the phone and smiled. He imagined all the other kids green with envy as he steered his remote control car through the streets of his neighborhood.

"Ben, I couldn't help but overhear your conversation," said Benjamin's mother.

"Mom, were you eavesdropping again?" asked Ben.

"No, but I want you to think about your conversation with your brother. There are more important things to wish for than a remote control car," said his mother.

ARMT Strategy

How does the author use conversations between the characters to bring out the theme of the story?

The phone rang again. It was James, giving the bad news to Benjamin that he would not be able to make it home. Benjamin sighed. He would not be able to show his brother how cool the other kids thought he was because of his remote control car.

On the morning of his birthday, Benjamin rushed downstairs to see what gifts awaited him. There was one big package from his parents on the table. "This box is as big as a remote control car," thought Benjamin. He opened the box to find…

…a new sleeping bag that he would use on his school camping trip. Benjamin tried to hide his disappointment and thanked his parents almost too brightly.

That night, while Benjamin and his parents were having cake, his mother asked, "Benjamin, what's wrong? You seem down."

Benjamin did not want to tell his mother that he was disappointed about not getting the car, so he replied, "I'm just tired." He wished that his brother were there. At least they would go to the movies and have ice cream.

Focus

What important lesson did Benjamin learn by the end of the story? What caused this change in Benjamin?

The doorbell rang. Benjamin opened the door to be greeted by his brother James.

"Ready to go to the movies, pal?" said James, holding two movie tickets in his outstretched hands.

At that moment, the remote control car was far away from Benjamin's thoughts.

Paint the Town Red

It is late August. The residents of Buñol, Spain are preparing to paint the town red. Shop owners and residents protect their homes and shops with plastic sheeting. The town will be colored a bright tomato red for the annual food fight known as the Tomatina.

The fight begins after one lucky participant climbs up a greased pole. There is a ham hanging at the top of the pole. When the climber cuts the ham down, the first tomato is thrown. What follows is a shower of ripe juicy tomatoes in the streets of this otherwise tranquil town.

The ripe tomatoes come in large trucks from a nearby region. Before food fighters throw their tomatoes at unsuspecting bystanders, they squish them in their hands to make sure they are juicy and full of pulp. Then, SPLAT! The battle begins. Tomatoes are thrown at anyone or anything that moves. The fight does not last more than an hour, but the streets of Buñol become a sea of red.

Anyone who is outside during the vegetable flinging is sure to get hit by a flying tomato. After the fight ends, fire trucks wash away the tomato pulp, and participants go to the local river to clean up. The town even sets up showers for people to use after the fight!

The Tomatina began in the 1940's. People believe that a group of friends threw tomatoes at each other in the main town square. Nowadays, the Tomatina is part of a week of celebrations and festivals. Tourists from all over the world come to participate.

The town has tried to ban the tomato fight, because officials believed it was getting out of control. The locals, however, protested and continued with the yearly tradition.

Critics of the Tomatina say that it is a waste of food. They maintain that poorer parts of the world could benefit from these tomatoes. Rather than wasting the tomatoes for a frivolous festival, they should be used to help feed hungry nations.

The next time you bite into a ripe red tomato, think of what this piece of produce means to one small town in Spain.

Dinner and a Movie

Welcome to Annette's Mealtime Movies. We are the only restaurant in the area that shows you the latest movie releases and serves dinner at the same time.

Snacks and Appetizers

Enjoy a large bucket of freshly popped, hot, buttery popcorn. Popcorn comes in small, medium, and large.

If you're in the mood for a hot snack, try our hot poppers. Spicy peppers are stuffed with three cheeses and then battered and fried to a deep golden brown.

Are you a veggie lover? We have fresh and crispy vegetable sticks. Carrots, celery, broccoli and red peppers are served with ranch dip.

Entrees

For the big appetite, we have chicken. Roasted gently to perfection, half of a chicken is served with your choice of baked potato or rice.

If burgers are on your mind, we have the burger for you! Our burger is flame broiled and served on a tasty sourdough bun. All hamburgers are served with your choice of fruit salad or French fries.

Spaghetti is never too messy for movies here! Our delicious hand-rolled meatballs rest on top of our heaping pile of spaghetti. This dish is also available in a child's size.

On the lighter side, choose our dinner salad of tossed baby field greens. This crisp salad is topped off with toasted walnuts, fresh pears, goat cheese and our salad dressing. You can also add grilled shrimp or chicken!

Desserts

We offer a large range of sweets and snacks. All of our desserts are baked fresh daily in our own kitchens.

What's Showing

This week, we are pleased to bring you Space Winter, the story of a young family's trip to outer space in the dead of winter.

Please arrive one half hour before show time. All dinner orders will be placed at that time.

David Clark, Parking Lot Planner

"Watch out, Jeff!" David cried as a car reversed in front of them.

"Wow. I didn't even see that," said Jeff.

"Almost every day, the same thing happens," remarked David. "The drivers never pay attention to where they are going. And we're in the school parking lot!"

David was relieved it was the last week of school. He wouldn't have to worry about getting run over all summer. That night, David discussed the problem with his parents.

David's mother was a city planner. When she had a problem to solve, she found it helpful to make drawings. She gave David a big pad of paper, and let him sketch his ideas.

David drew the parking lot and a row of parked cars. The only way for those cars to leave the parking lot was to go in reverse first. That was a problem. Suddenly he had an idea.

David ran downstairs to explain the solution to his mother. She helped him write a letter to the school board.

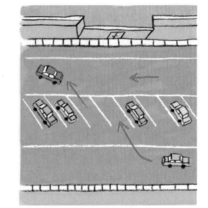

Dear Members of the School Board:

I am a concerned student. In order to leave the school parking lot, cars have to go in reverse. This creates a problem for bicycles, because the drivers do not always look where they are going. Also, there is a lot of traffic because everyone has to wait for the cars to reverse. The situation is dangerous.

I think you should create a one-way travel lane in front of the row of parked cars so the cars do not have to back out. You can make the travel lane safer by posting stop signs. Also, a bike lane would make travel safer for bikers.

I hope that you will consider this solution.

Sincerely,

David Clark, Haven Hill Elementary School

On the first day of school, David prepared for the school parking lot. To his surprise, the school had adopted his idea for the parking lot!

Treasures

A Reading/Language Arts Program

Mc Graw Hill **Macmillan**
McGraw-Hill

Contributors

Time Magazine, Accelerated Reader

learning through listening

Students with print disabilities may be eligible to obtain an accessible, audio version of the pupil edition of this textbook. Please call Recording for the Blind & Dyslexic at 1-800-221-4792 for complete information.

A

The McGraw·Hill Companies

Macmillan McGraw-Hill

Published by Macmillan/McGraw-Hill, of McGraw-Hill Education, a division of The McGraw-Hill Companies, Inc., Two Penn Plaza, New York, New York 10121.

Printed in the United States of America

ISBN-13: 978-0-02-201059-1
ISBN-10: 0-02-201059-9
1 2 3 4 5 6 7 8 9 (027/043) 11 10 09 08 07

Treasures

A Reading/Language Arts Program

Program Authors

Donald R. Bear
Janice A. Dole
Jana Echevarria
Jan E. Hasbrouck
Scott G. Paris
Timothy Shanahan
Josefina V. Tinajero

Mc Graw Hill **Macmillan McGraw-Hill**

Let's Explore

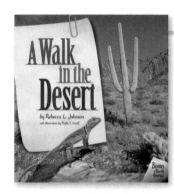

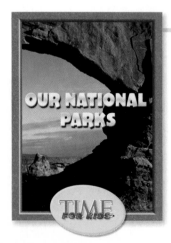

Award Winning Illustrator

Award Winning Selection

TEST PREP

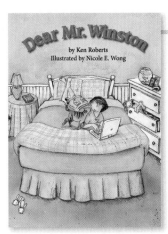

Making a Difference

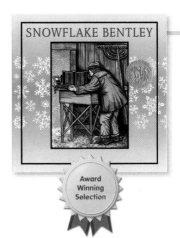

Unit 4

Viewpoints

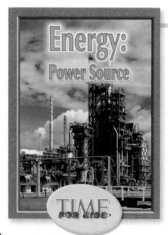

THEME: Whales

THEME: The Sea

Test Strategy: Author and Me

Relationships

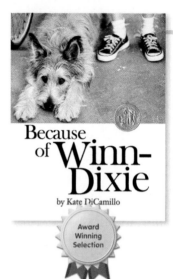

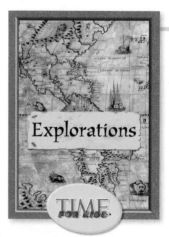

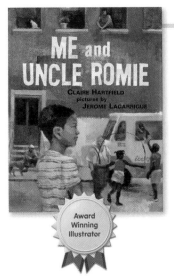

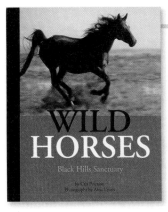

Mysteries

Talk About It

What mysteries could the people in this photograph be investigating?

LOG ON Find out more about mysteries at **www.macmillanmh.com**

17

Vocabulary

assignments	suspicious
consideration	evidence
allergies	consume
accuse	

Dictionary

Unfamiliar Words are words you do not know. You can find the meanings of unfamiliar words in a dictionary. Look up the meaning of *assignment*.

The Case of the

Blurry Board

by Jaime Beaurline

Blurry Vision

After collecting homework **assignments**, Mrs. Morris said, "Jason, would you please read the first problem on the board?"

Jason put on his glasses. "That's weird," he said.

"What's the matter?" Mrs. Morris asked.

"I can't see the board. Everything is blurry," explained Jason.

Mrs. Morris thought a moment. After some **consideration**, she suggested, "Why don't you go see the school nurse? Maybe you have **allergies** to something that's blooming now."

18

Colliding Classmates

Jason walked down the hall. He turned the corner and BAM! He and Susie Hu bumped into each other. Their glasses went flying.

Susie was about to **accuse** Jason of not looking where he was going, but she had been on her way to clean her own glasses.

"That's weird," said Jason, as soon as they had put on their glasses. "Now I can see just fine."

"Me too!" Susie exclaimed.

"Something **suspicious** is going on," said Jason.

Mystery Solved

"Our glasses must have gotten switched when we bumped into each other earlier today," Jason said.

"Hmmm…" said Susie. "What's your proof? I need **evidence**!"

"Look, our glasses are exactly the same," noted Jason.

"You're right!" said Susie. "I'm very glad you solved the mystery. Lunch period is next and I would have hated to **consume** a pencil instead of a pretzel rod!"

Reread for **Comprehension**

Make Inferences and Analyze

Problem and Solution The plot is what happens in a story. The plot often includes a problem and a solution to the problem.

A Problem and Solution Chart can help you make inferences and analyze a story. Reread the selection to find the problem, the actions taken by the characters, and the solution.

Problem
↓
↓
↓
↓
Solution

Comprehension

Genre

A **Mystery** is a story in which the characters and the reader must use clues to find the explanation for a troubling event.

Make Inferences and Analyze

Problem and Solution

As you read, fill in your Problem and Solution Chart.

```
Problem
  ↓
[     ]
  ↓
[     ]
  ↓
[     ]
  ↓
Solution
```

Read to Find Out

Can you solve the mystery before Ramón does?

20

The Mystery of the Missing Lunch

by Johanna Hurwitz

illustrated by Joe Cepeda

Award Winning Author

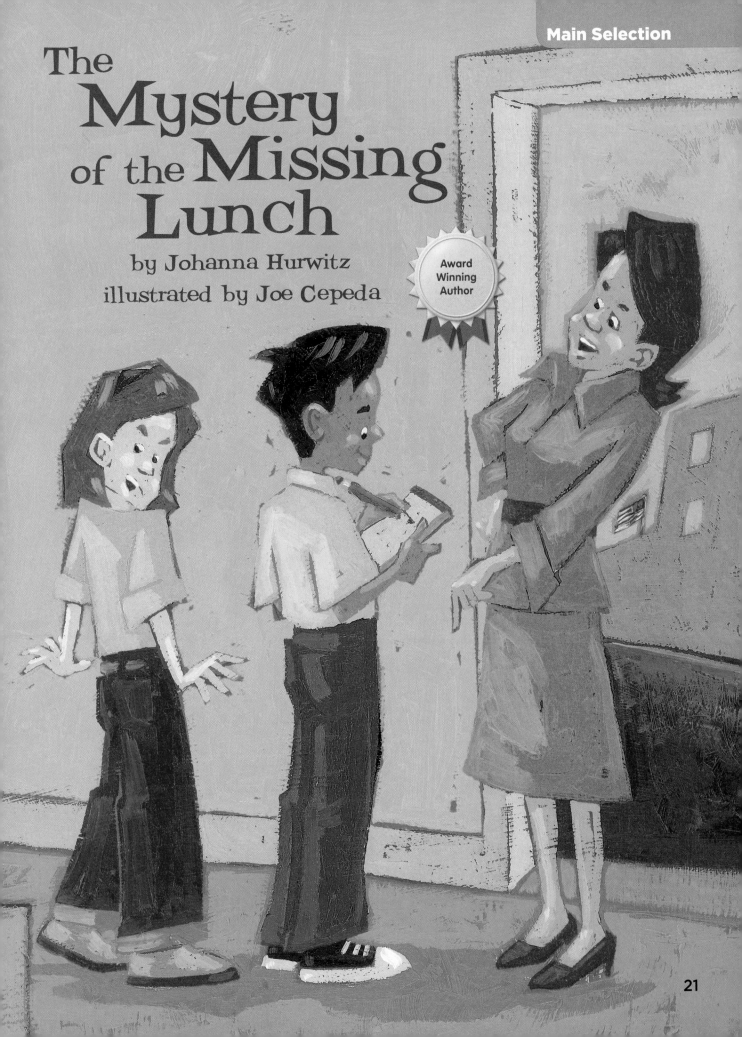

At noon, on the first day of school, a very hungry Ramón García looked for his lunch bag in the coat closet. He searched the shelf above the coat hooks but couldn't find his lunch. "My bag isn't here," he complained.

"Are you sure you brought it?" asked his friend Emily Wilson. "Maybe you left it at home."

Ramón was sure. His mom had made him his favorite sandwich—salami—and he knew he hadn't forgotten it.

"Here's my lunch box," reported Ted Collins between sneezes. Ted had been sneezing all morning. "**Allergies**," he explained, apologetically.

Ramón didn't hear him. He was too angry. "Someone took my salami sandwich!" he said to Emily. "And I'm going to find out who!"

STRATEGY SKILL

Problem and Solution
Ramón has a problem. What does he need to find out?

23

"Maybe it was Jack Crawford," Emily whispered. "He's always hungry."

Ramón took out the little notebook he had bought to write down homework **assignments**. It would be good for keeping track of any clues. Then he went over to Jack. He noticed at once that there was no lunch bag or box on Jack's desk.

"Where's your lunch?" he asked.

"I don't have one," answered Jack.

"Why not?" asked Ramón.

Jack pulled a couple of dollars out of his pocket. "I'm buying today," he said.

Ramón leaned closer to Jack and sniffed deeply. He couldn't smell any salami on his classmate's breath.

"What's that?" asked Emily. She pointed to a brown smudge on Jack's shirt. "It looks like mustard."

"It's just an old paint stain," claimed Jack. "I got it when I helped my dad during the summer. It may look like mustard, but it's called 'golden oak' on the paint can."

"A likely alibi," Ramón muttered to himself. He made a note of the stain on Jack's shirt.

"All right, what's going on here?" asked Mrs. Richmond, their fourth-grade teacher.

"Someone took my lunch," said Ramón.

"Don't look at me," said Jack. "I'm innocent."

Mrs. Richmond clapped her hands. "Everyone in your seats," she shouted. "A lunch is missing. We can't leave for the cafeteria until we find it."

"Awww," grumbled all the students together. By now, everyone was hungry. Ted sneezed three times in succession.

No one knew anything about Ramón's lunch bag. The whole class waited while Mrs. Richmond checked the coat closet, but she didn't find Ramón's lunch.

By this time Ramón was so hungry, his stomach was growling. Mrs. Richmond must have been hungry herself, because she solved the problem by handing Ramón a five dollar bill. "Buy something with this," she told him. "You can pay me back tomorrow. I have a feeling that you left your lunch on the bus. I can't imagine any of your classmates taking it."

Of course, it was a relief that Ramón could buy some food. However, he was 100% certain that he had put the bag in the closet. He was determined to discover who had taken it.

In the cafeteria, while he was eating the soggy tuna fish sandwich he had bought, Ramón wrote again in his notebook. He made a list of all his classmates. Any one of them could be the culprit.

Emily leaned forward to see. "Just because you like salami doesn't mean that everyone else does," she pointed out. "Josh, Tina, and Margaret are vegetarians. They wouldn't eat a salami sandwich."

"You're right," agreed Ramón, crossing out their names. "Sarah thinks salami is smelly. She holds her nose whenever she's around it. And all Max ever eats is peanut butter and jelly," he added. He crossed out their names too. After a minute's **consideration**, he crossed Jack's name off his list.

Ted had been too busy sneezing all morning to secretly **consume** a salami sandwich, Ramón decided. Off went his name too.

"Cross me off the list of suspects, too," said Emily. "I don't even like salami."

So far, out of a class of eighteen, eight were definitely innocent. Then there were Beverly and Grace. Neither of them was tall enough to reach the shelf where Ramón put his lunch. He crossed off their names too. The list of potential suspects kept getting shorter. It got even shorter when Ramón realized that he was one of the eighteen students in the class. And he knew for certain that he had not eaten the salami sandwich.

Ramón sighed deeply. His chances of solving this case were getting slimmer and slimmer.

Then, after lunch, when the students were given quiet time for reading, Ramón went back to the closet to see if he could find any clues that he hadn't noticed earlier. He looked under the book bags but found nothing **suspicious** there.

On his way back to his desk, Ramón passed the library corner. He stopped. What was that scratching sound? Could there be a mouse in the classroom? Mice eat anything.

Looking around, he saw poor Ted was still blowing his nose. Then he spotted something! Pieces of torn brown paper lay on the floor near Ted's desk. Ramón picked them up. Immediately, he noticed that there were ink markings on the papers. He placed them together, like puzzle pieces, to form the picture of a smiley face. Ramón recognized it at once. It was the same smiley face his mom had drawn on his lunch bag that morning!

This was a very important clue. Whoever had taken his lunch had torn up the **evidence**!

Just then, Mr. Gordon, the Assistant Principal, knocked and came into the classroom. "Here's the new computer we ordered for you, Mrs. Richmond." He placed it on the counter.

As he started to leave, Mr. Gordon said, "By the way, has anyone seen a stray cat? She sneaked into the school building a few weeks ago when we were painting, and I think she's still hiding somewhere." The kids looked at each other and shook their heads.

"Please let me know if you do. I want to find her a home," Mr. Gordon added.

Mrs. Richmond looked around with a little chuckle. "I don't see any cat in this room," she said.

At that moment, Ted gave three more loud sneezes.

"Wait a minute," Ramón called out. The biggest clue had been right there under his nose all this time. "Ted, what kind of allergy do you have?" he asked. "Could you be allergic to cats?"

"How did you know?" Ted asked when he stopped blowing his nose.

"Your nose gave it away," said Ramón.

Ted grinned. "I'm very allergic to any animal with fur," he admitted.

Mrs. Richmond turned to Mr. Gordon, "And I was worried that he was allergic to fourth grade!"

Ramón started pulling all the books out of the shelves in the library corner. The other students and Mr. Gordon helped. Sure enough, there behind the mystery books was the solution to the mystery of the missing lunch. Three little kittens were hiding amid the remains of Ramón's salami sandwich.

"But where's the mother cat?" asked Mrs. Richmond.

"She won't be far away from her kittens," Mr. Gordon said.

A loud hiss confirmed his words. On top of the closet stood the anxious mother cat.

"You stole my lunch!" Ramón scolded the cat, but he was smiling. He was pleased that he did not have to **accuse** one of his classmates.

The mother cat jumped off the closet and slipped out the door.

"There she goes!" said Mr. Gordon. "Well, I'll take these kittens to my office until we find good homes for them. Their mama will find them. Cats have a good sense of smell."

"*And* they like salami!" said Ramón.

Problem and Solution
Ramón solved the mystery. Who took his lunch? Why?

Clues About the
Author and Illustrator

Johanna Hurwitz likes to write about everyday boys and girls, like the ones in this story, and their funny adventures. Johanna gets her story ideas from many places. She thinks about children she knew as a librarian and about people and places she's seen on her trips. She also gets ideas from her family, and, as proven in this story, her cats.

Other books by Johanna Hurwitz and Joe Cepeda

Joe Cepeda did not plan on becoming a children's book illustrator. He planned to be an engineer, but then he went back to school to study illustration. Joe thinks that children who want to be artists should spend a lot of time reading and studying math.

LOG ON Find out more about Johanna Hurwitz and Joe Cepeda at **www.macmillanmh.com**

Author's Purpose

What clues can you use to figure out Johanna Hurwitz's purpose for writing *The Mystery of the Missing Lunch*? Did she want to entertain, inform, or persuade? How do you know?

Comprehension Check

Summarize

Use your Problem and Solution Chart to help you summarize *The Mystery of the Missing Lunch.* Describe Ramón's problem and the steps he took to solve it.

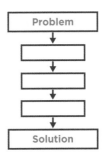

```
┌─────────────┐
│   Problem   │
└─────────────┘
       ↓
┌─────────────┐
│             │
└─────────────┘
       ↓
┌─────────────┐
│             │
└─────────────┘
       ↓
┌─────────────┐
│             │
└─────────────┘
       ↓
┌─────────────┐
│  Solution   │
└─────────────┘
```

Think and Compare

1. Describe one piece of **evidence** Ramón gathered to solve the mystery. How did that piece of evidence help him? **Make Inferences and Analyze: Problem and Solution**

2. Reread the last paragraph on page 28. What conclusion does Ramón draw about Jack? Use story details in your answer. **Analyze**

3. How would you have tried to solve this mystery? Explain. **Apply**

4. Think about Ramón's problem-solving methods. In your opinion, are they effective? Explain your answer. **Evaluate**

5. Read "The Case of the Blurry Board" on pages 18–19. How is Jason's method of solving a problem similar to Ramón's? Use details from both stories in your answer. **Reading/Writing Across Texts**

Science

Genre

Magazine Articles present facts and photographs of the people, places, discoveries, and living things being discussed.

Text Feature

Charts show information in columns and rows.

Content Vocabulary

scientific method	**survey**
secure	**testify**

Putting Together the PIECES of the PUZZLE

by Eric Michaels

e scene investigators are the first people to
he scene of a crime. They search for clues
elp the detectives later decide what probably
and who might be responsible for it. It's
, but these experts are specially trained.
he **scientific method**, a series of specific
hey work.

g the Crime Scene

portant that nothing be disturbed before an
on begins. So the first thing a crime scene
r does is **secure** the crime scene. This
rom being altered in any way.
t step is to simply observe. The investigator
scription of the scene and sketches a floor
cene. Photographs are taken.

Types of Fingerprints

SKILL ✓ Reading a Chart

Read across each row to learn how
common each type of fingerprint is.

Loops		65% of all people
Whorls		30% of all people
Arches		5% of all people

Searching for Evidence

The next step is to search for evidence—physical clues about the crime. This search is done carefully. Hairs and fibers from clothing are gathered. Objects at the scene are dusted with special powder to make any fingerprints show up. Then sticky tape is used to lift the prints off the objects. Fingerprints are important pieces of evidence because they place people at the scene. No two people have the same prints.

Protecting the Evidence

The crime scene investigator must protect evidence as it is gathered. After a piece of evidence is photographed and notes are taken, the evidence is put into a container. It is sealed and labeled to show where it was found. Fingerprints are mounted on cards or special plastic sheets. They will be compared later with those in police records.

After all the evidence is gathered, it's time for a final **survey**, or a last look around. This is to make sure nothing has been overlooked. When the investigator is sure that the search is complete, the crime scene is "released." That means that other people can then enter the area.

Presenting the Findings

A crime scene investigator may help others prepare a court case for the crime. The investigator may also **testify**, or speak about the evidence in court.

Being a crime scene investigator looks exciting on TV. But it takes time, skill, and a lot of scientific knowledge. If a crime scene investigator does the job well, it's likely that the crime will be solved. Then the case can be marked "Closed!"

Connect and Compare

1. Look at the chart on page 39. Which is the most common type of fingerprint? Which type of fingerprint has ridges that rise up in the middle? **Reading a Chart**

2. What information would you use to support the view that a crime scene investigator must be well trained? **Evaluate**

3. Think about this article and "The Mystery of the Missing Lunch." Do you think Ramón would make a good crime scene investigator? Why or why not? **Reading/Writing Across Texts**

 Science Activity

Research how to take someone's fingerprints. Then use an ink pad and index cards to collect classmates' fingerprints. Make a chart of the fingerprints.

 Find out more about fingerprints at **www.macmillanmh.com**

Write About a Problem

I wrote about a problem and how I solved it. Here's my topic sentence.

The other sentences give details about what happened.

What's That Noise?

by Indira S.

Last weekend, all of a sudden, a loud banging woke me up. Thump, thump! I was at Grandma's house in Pennsylvania. I was scared – I thought a bear was trying to get into the house! I thought a light might scare the bear. I put on the lamp, but the thumping got louder.

Then I heard a small woof. I looked over the side of the bed and saw Grandma's dog, Rusty, lying on the floor. The thumping was her tail wagging!

Your Turn

Write a paragraph about a problem you once solved. Be sure to begin your paragraph with a topic sentence that tells what happened. Then include the details of the story in the sentences that follow. Use the Writer's Checklist to check your writing.

Writer's Checklist

 Ideas and Content: Did I include enough details to tell what happened?

 Organization: Did I write a good paragraph that includes a topic sentence and details about what happened in the following sentences?

 Voice: Does my personal narrative tell how I felt?

 Word Choice: Have I chosen the right words to make my story interesting and exciting?

 Sentence Fluency: Did I use complete sentences?

Conventions: Did I use exclamation marks at the end of exclamations?

Adapting to Survive

Talk About It

How is the insect in the photograph adapting to survive? How do you adapt to your surroundings?

LOG ON Find out more about adaptation at **www.macmillanmh.com**

45

Vocabulary

shimmer   climate

eerie   silken

lurk   lumbering

swallows

Context Clues

Surrounding Words can often help you figure out the meaning of unfamiliar words. Find *shimmer* in the story. Use the other words in the sentence to figure out what *shimmer* means.

Living in Alaska

by Marsha Adams

Another World

In some ways, living in Alaska is like living in another world. Winter lasts for about nine months. For more than two months each year, the northern lights that **shimmer** in the sky are the only source of light.

For the people there, it can be **eerie** to go so long without seeing the sun. For the animals, it can be dangerous. Such dim light makes it difficult to see whether predators **lurk** in the shadows, waiting for their next meal. It may be a snowy owl that swoops down on silent wings and **swallows** its prey whole!

Winter Coats

Beavers, sea otters, and other mammals are adapted to survive in the cold Alaskan **climate**. They grow two layers of fur. The thick bottom layer is soft, **silken** fur that helps trap body heat. Longer, coarse hairs that form the outer layer act as a barrier against water, snow, and wind.

The ptarmigan, Alaska's state bird, has a special way to keep warm. It grows feathers down its legs, over its toes, and on the soles of its feet!

A Winter Nap

You won't find **lumbering** black or brown bears when the frigid weather arrives. Bears, mice, and other animals hibernate, or go into a deep sleep, during the winter. When they hibernate, their bodies don't need food or water. Other animals, such as some caterpillars, fish, and houseflies, actually freeze during the winter. Then they thaw out in the spring!

A Low Profile

Arctic plants have their own special traits that help them survive. During the summer months, the dark soil absorbs the sun's heat. So plants grow close to the ground where it's warmer. When snow falls, it protects the plants from the cold winds above.

Reread for Comprehension

Summarize

Main Idea and Details When you summarize what you've read, include the main idea and details. The main idea is the most important point of each paragraph or section. The details give information that supports it.

A Main Idea Chart can help you summarize what you've read. Reread the selection to find the main idea and supporting details.

Main Ideas	Details

Comprehension

Genre

Informational Nonfiction is a detailed composition that sets out to explain something by presenting facts about it.

Summarize

Main Idea and Details

As you read, fill in your Main Idea Chart.

Main Ideas	Details

Read to Find Out

What characteristics allow desert animals to live in such a hot, dry place?

A Walk in the Desert

by Rebecca L. Johnson

with illustrations by Phyllis V. Saroff

Biomes of North America

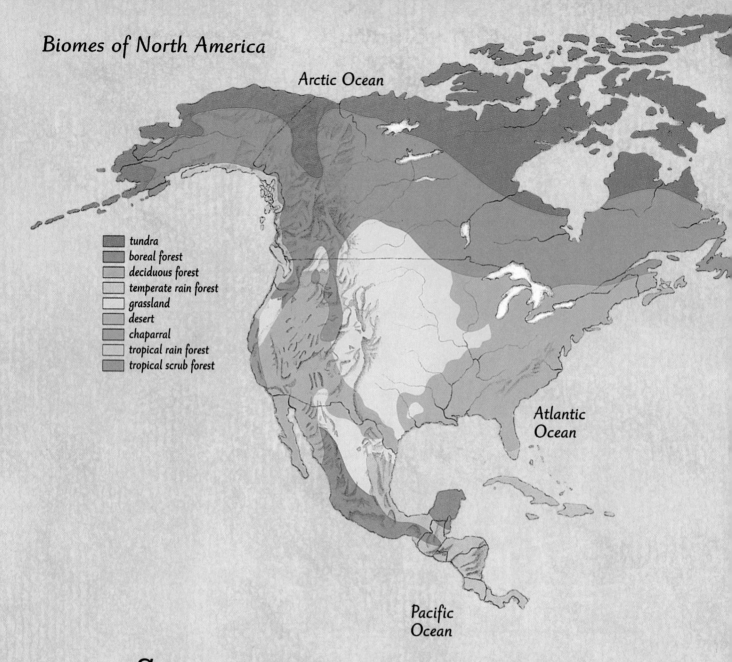

Arctic Ocean

- tundra
- boreal forest
- deciduous forest
- temperate rain forest
- grassland
- desert
- chaparral
- tropical rain forest
- tropical scrub forest

Atlantic Ocean

Pacific Ocean

Sunbeams are flickering over the landscape as the sun rises. A kit fox heads for her den as another day in the desert begins.

Deserts are surrounded by other kinds of landscapes. Scientists call these different land zones biomes. All the plants and animals in a biome form a community. In that community, every living thing depends on other community members for its survival. A biome's **climate**, soil, plants, and animals are all connected this way.

Deserts have a very dry climate. They do get a little rain, but it doesn't come regularly. One storm might drench a desert with several inches of rain in just a few hours. It might not rain again for months—even years.

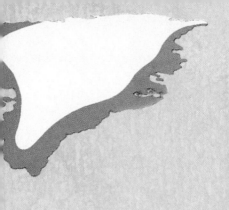

A mother desert tortoise lays her eggs in sandy soil. The sun warms the eggs until they hatch.

Desert plants provide many animals with food and water. Here comes a desert tortoise. It shuffles slowly along and stops often to rest. The tortoise stretches its long neck to nibble a wildflower. Tortoises rarely drink. They get nearly all the water they need from the plants they eat.

Cacti also provide homes for desert animals. Halfway down a nearby saguaro's thick stem, a Gila woodpecker pecks a hole in the juicy flesh. It is making a nest for its eggs. Woodpeckers have nested in this cactus for many years, so they've made many holes in it.

Other creatures have moved into some of the old woodpecker holes. A pair of flycatchers lives in one. Another is home to a hive of honeybees. And peeking out of still another hole is an elf owl. It has white eyebrows and fierce yellow eyes.

60 years old

Saguaro cacti
grow very
slowly. But
they may live
for 200 years.

10 years old

53

A wood rat nibbles on the sweet fruit of a prickly pear cactus.

Not far from the saguaro, you see a very different kind of desert home. Jammed between a dead cactus and a fallen tree is a huge mound of tangled twigs. It's the nest of a wood rat.

Wood rats are also called pack rats. They use anything they can find to build enormous nests. A wood rat's nest might be made of sticks, rocks, leaves, cactus spines, or even bones. It may be as tall as a person and just as wide. The nest protects the wood rat from foxes, hawks, and other predators. It is also a cool place to hide from the hot sun.

STRATEGY SKILL

Main Idea and Details
What is the main idea in the second paragraph?

Many desert animals are nocturnal. They are active only at night, when it is cooler. Nocturnal desert-dwellers spend their days in burrows, dens, and other sheltered places. The kangaroo rat and the kit fox are nocturnal. They stay underground until the sun goes down.

Elf owls are the smallest owls in the world. They are about the size of sparrows.

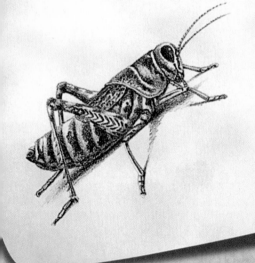

A painted grasshopper uses its long legs to hop from plant to plant—and to escape being eaten.

But some desert animals are active during the day. Insects are on the move everywhere. Columns of ants march across the ground. Colorful beetles crawl up and down stems. Grasshoppers spring from leaf to leaf. Insect-eating spiders are busy, too. They spin **silken** webs among cactus spines.

The sun has climbed higher in the clear blue sky. Can you feel the heat? Desert lizards don't seem to mind. Their tough, scaly skin seals water inside their bodies and keeps them from drying out. Lizards rest on rocks, hunt insects, and cling to cactus stems. In one small patch of desert, you could see tiny skinks, chunky chuckwallas, spiny horned lizards, and **lumbering** Gila monsters.

A horned lizard's spiny scales are a good defense against desert predators.

A roadrunner's feet have two toes that point forward and two that point backward. This shape helps the bird grip the ground when it runs.

Suddenly, something streaks across your path. It's a speedy lizard, and right on its heels is a roadrunner. Roadrunners can fly. But these desert birds prefer to run after lizards and the other small animals they hunt.

Roadrunners have long, strong legs. They can run as fast as many lizards can. In fact, this time the bird is faster. The roadrunner catches the lizard by its tail and **swallows** it in one gulp.

Desert jackrabbits have longer ears than rabbits from other biomes. Long ears release heat and help jackrabbits stay cool.

cottontail rabbit

jackrabbit

Nearby, a jackrabbit looks for plants to nibble. Jackrabbits are even faster than roadrunners. They can outrun almost everything in the desert. They can even outrun coyotes—most of the time!

Coyotes eat rabbits when they can catch them. But they will eat just about anything, from birds and lizards to berries. To find underground water, they dig holes in dry streambeds. Coyotes can survive almost anywhere.

A mother scorpion carries her babies around on her back until they can survive on their own.

By noon, even the coyotes are panting. It's well over 100 degrees. The sun is a fireball overhead. Nearly all the daytime animals move into the shade of rocks and cacti during the hottest part of the day.

A rattlesnake's rattle is made up of a row of large, dry scales.

Take a tip from the animals. Find a place out of the sun to rest. Just be careful where you sit. Scorpions often **lurk** in crevices or under rocks during the day. A scorpion's tail has a stinger filled with poison. Few kinds of scorpions can kill a person. But the sting of any scorpion is very painful.

Watch out for hiding rattlesnakes and coral snakes, too. Their poison is deadly. You don't want to get within striking distance of either one.

Heat waves **shimmer** above the landscape. The leaves of the mesquite trees curl up. Curled leaves lose less water to the hot, dry air. The desert is very quiet. Most of the birds are silent. They seem to be waiting for the sun's fierce heat to fade.

Gradually, the sun moves lower in the sky. As shadows grow longer, the temperature starts to drop. Desert birds begin to sing again. At sunset, coyotes call to each other, barking and yelping. They join voices in an **eerie**, wailing song.

STRATEGY SKILL

Main Idea and Details
Name the main idea on these two pages. Which statements support the main idea?

The hot desert day is over. The cool night is about
to begin. Birds, lizards, and other daytime animals
retreat to snug nests and safe hiding places. There they

Take a Walk with Rebecca

Rebecca L. Johnson grew up in South Dakota. Harsh prairie winters helped her prepare for working with scientists in Antarctica. Ms. Johnson has traveled to Antarctica twice and has written three books on the experience: *Braving the Frozen Frontier*, *Investigating the Ozone Hole*, and *Science on the Ice* (winner of the *Scientific American* Young Readers Award). She has also "walked" in several other biomes—the tundra, the rain forest, the prairie, and others—for the "Biomes of North America" series.

Rebecca studied Biology at Augustana College and has worked as a teacher and a museum curator. She enjoys scuba diving, water color painting, and cross country skiing, and lives in South Dakota with her husband.

LOG ON Find out more about Rebecca L. Johnson at **www.macmillanmh.com**

Author's Purpose

How do you think the author's own experiences influenced her purpose for writing *A Walk in the Desert*? Did she want to explain, inform, entertain, or persuade?

Comprehension Check

Summarize

Use your Main Idea Chart to summarize *A Walk in the Desert.* State the main ideas and the details that support those main ideas.

Main Ideas	Details

Think and Compare

1. What is the main idea of the selection? Find two details that support that main idea. **Summarize: Main Idea and Details**

2. Reread the information about roadrunners on page 58. If roadrunners can fly but prefer to run, what can you conclude about their flying skills? **Analyze**

3. If you were taking a walk in the desert, which of the plants and animals described in this selection would you most want to see? Why? **Apply**

4. How do you think people who live in the desert might adapt to the **climate**? **Apply**

5. Read "Living in Alaska" on pages 46-47. Compare the plants and animals in Alaska's environment with those in the desert. How are they similar? Use details from both selections in your answer. **Reading/Writing Across Texts**

Cinquains

by Polly Peterson

Poetry

A **Cinquain** has five lines of two, four, six, eight, and two syllables. The first line may also be the title.

Literary Elements

Assonance is created by repeating similar vowel sounds in two or more words.

A **Metaphor** is a figure of speech in which two very different objects or ideas are said to be alike.

FAT FROG

Fat frog
Murky as mud
Hides all but his high eyes.
Flash! Flick! Flies cannot flee from that
Fast tongue.

> You can hear assonance in the words "high eyes," which both have the long *i* sound.

White Swans

White swans,
Awkward on land,
Glide through water with ease.
Wide webbed feet grant them the grace of
Dancers.

> The poet creates a metaphor by comparing swans to dancers.

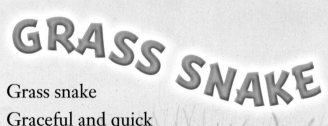

GRASS SNAKE

Grass snake
Graceful and quick
Slithers, slips, slides away —
Disappears quietly as a
Daydream.

Connect and Compare

1. Besides "high eyes," find another example of assonance in one of these cinquains. **Assonance**

2. Which cinquain do you think best captures the animal it describes? Explain. **Analyze**

3. How are the animals in these poems well adapted to their environments? Compare them with animals from *A Walk in the Desert*. **Reading/Writing Across Texts**

 Find out more about cinquains at **www.macmillanmh.com**

Writer's Craft

Precise Words
Good writers choose just the right words to create a clear and accurate picture for readers. Use **precise words** to describe your topic and show how you feel about it.

I wanted to describe zebras with precise words.

I used a thesaurus to find just the right words, such as "steady."

Striped Horse

by Joshua M.

Zebra.
A horse with stripes,
Grazing on grassy plains.
Steady stallions watch over foals.
They sleep.

Your Turn

Write a cinquain to describe
an animal. Think about how the
animal survives. Choose colorful,
precise words that paint a picture.
Use the Writer's Checklist to
check your writing.

Writer's Checklist

 Ideas and Content: Do my details tell how
I feel and what I want to say?

 Organization: Does the organization of ideas
in my poem make sense?

 Voice: Can the reader tell that I care about the
message in my poem?

Word Choice: Did I choose precise words to paint
a picture of the animal?

 Sentence Fluency: Does my poem sound pleasing?

 Conventions: Have I used the right punctuation?

Talk About It

National parks are wonderful places. What things could you learn about at a national park?

LOG ON Find out more about our national parks at **www.macmillanmh.com**

OUR NATIONAL PARKS

Vocabulary

roamed

completed

journey

natural

wildlife

A Prehistoric Park

More than 200 million years ago, dinosaurs **roamed** freely over the Earth. Have you ever wondered what the land was like or what kind of trees there were then? You can see some of these trees today in Arizona! Throughout 28 miles of desert in Petrified Forest National Park, you can see 225-million-year-old fossil trees. Visitors are amazed to see these trees that have turned to stone.

How did it happen? Millions of years ago, water filled with minerals flowed into the area. Over time, the minerals seeped into fallen trees and turned them into rock-hard logs.

Some of these logs are 100 feet long! Today, they create a colorful and amazing sight in Arizona's desert. The petrified logs look like wooden rainbows. The colors range from red, to yellow, to green, to blue, and black and white.

Petrified Forest National Park is one of the world's biggest displays of petrified wood. Nearly one million people visit the park every year to get an up-close look at these fossils of prehistoric trees.

Logs from prehistoric trees have turned to stone in the Petrified National Forest.

King of the Mountain

By the time Scott Cory was 13 years old, he had already scaled two major peaks in California's Yosemite National Park. One was the 2,900-foot "Nose" of El Capitan. The other was the 2,000-foot face of Half Dome. The first time Scott climbed the Nose, it took him three days and two nights. One month later, he **completed** that climb in one day! Later, Scott became the youngest person to climb Half Dome in only one day. The **journey** to the top usually takes three days!

Scott started climbing when he was seven years old. When he's not on the peaks, he hits the gym for push-ups and pull-ups. What's next for this peak pro? Scott wants to climb to the top of the Nose and Half Dome together in just 24 hours. You could say this kid really sets a goal and then climbs for it!

 LOG ON Find out more about Yosemite National Park at **www.macmillanmh.com**

The Top 5 Most Visited National Parks

In 1872, Yellowstone National Park became the first national park in the United States. Since then, more than 383 parks have been added to the list. More than three million people visit these natural, unspoiled places every year. They take thousands of photos of the wildlife. Which parks recently brought in the most visitors in a year? Here's how they ranked.

1. **Great Smoky Mountains National Park, North Carolina and Tennessee**
2. **Grand Canyon National Park, Arizona**
3. **Yosemite National Park, California**
4. **Olympic National Park, Washington**
5. **Rocky Mountain National Park, Colorado**

Comprehension

Genre

A **Nonfiction Article** tells facts about a person, place, or event.

Summarize

Main Idea and Details

The main idea of an article is what it is mostly about. Details give more information about the main idea.

A male and female elk in their new home, the Great Smoky Mountains National Park

Animals Come Home to Our National Parks

How did the return of elk to one national park and gray wolves to another affect the ecosystems of those parks?

National parks protect **wildlife**, history, and culture. Still, hundreds of plants and animals have disappeared from our national parks. That's because their environment has changed, mostly because of human activities.

Today park rangers work to restore the balance of each park ecosystem. They are bringing plants and animals back into their **natural** environments. So far, the programs are working—especially for elk and wolves.

Long Journey Home

It was a cold morning in January when 28 elk had finally **completed** a long **journey**. They had traveled 2,500 miles by truck from Elk Island National Park in Canada to the Great Smoky Mountains National Park in North Carolina. They were the first of 52 elk to be reintroduced into the park.

Ten million elk once **roamed** all over North America. Now there are only about one million. Elk disappeared from North Carolina more than 150 years ago. Many were killed by hunters. Others died as people built farms, towns, and roads where elk used to graze.

Elk munch on trees and bushes, allowing more sunlight into the park so ground-level plants can grow. Smaller animals, like chipmunks, can then flourish. Chipmunks are food for larger animals, like wolves. Without the elk, the park's ecosystem didn't function as well. "We are trying to restore the ecosystem to what it was 200 years ago," said Lawrence Hartman of the National Park Service.

Park workers watch as relocated elk dash for freedom.

Have they achieved their goal? So far, so good. Researchers have been studying the elks' progress. Jennifer Murrow is leading the research. She tracks the elk using special radio collars that are placed around the elks' necks. The collars send signals that show researchers where the elk are and how they are doing.

Researchers also keep track of the number of elk calves that are born each year. In the first year, 11 calves were born in the park. Eight survived, but some were preyed upon by bears. It's all part of the natural balance— and that's exactly what wildlife researchers like to see.

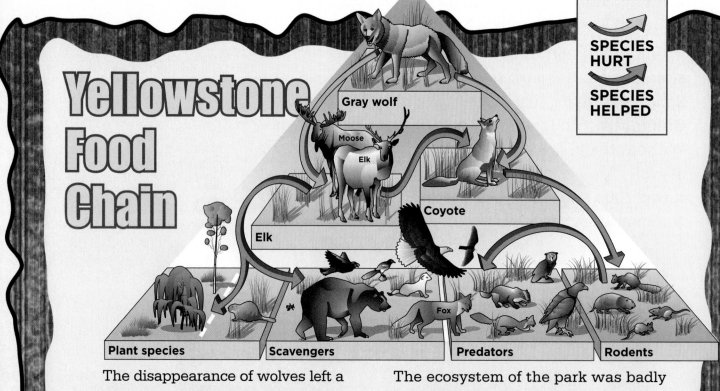

Yellowstone Food Chain

SPECIES HURT
SPECIES HELPED

Gray wolf
Moose
Elk
Coyote
Elk
Fox

Plant species
Scavengers
Predators
Rodents

The disappearance of wolves left a big hole in Yellowstone's ecosystem. Coyotes and elk, which are hunted by wolves, became too numerous. Plants began to disappear because the elk population had grown so large. Foxes, which eat the same rodents as coyotes, were starving because the coyotes were catching most of the prey.

The ecosystem of the park was badly out of balance.

The government wanted to fix the park's ecosystem. They decided to bring back the wolves. The goal was to put nature back into balance. Now, Yellowstone is howling with life once again, and nature is taking its course.

A gray wolf in Yellowstone National Park

Think and Compare

STRATEGY SKILL

1. What animal was returned to Great Smoky Mountains National Park, and what animal was brought back into Yellowstone National Park?

2. How does the disappearance of one animal affect the other animals and plants in an ecosystem?

3. If you could visit any national park in the United States, which one would you choose, and why?

4. Compare the problems a park ranger at Yellowstone might face with those of a ranger in Yosemite or Petrified Forest National Park.

Howling Back to Life

For centuries, packs of wolves lived in the West. When settlers came in the 1800s, they hunted these wild animals. By the 1970s, the wolves had completely disappeared from Yellowstone National Park. They had also become endangered in much of the United States.

In 1995, 31 gray wolves were released into the park. Now, more than a decade later, there are more than five times as many wolves roaming through Yellowstone.

Saving a National Park

Test Strategy

Right There

You can put your finger on the answer. Look for key words in the question. Then find those key words in the selection.

Florida panther

Early settlers declared Florida's Everglades a worthless swamp. In fact it is a unique paradise for thousands of species of plants and animals, forming a delicate food chain. All they need to survive is each other—and a steady supply of precious water.

But humans wanted dry land for homes and crops. They drained water from the Everglades. This started a chain reaction that upset the ecosystem. The Everglades wetlands are now only half their original size. The number of wading birds decreased by 90 percent from 1900 to 2000. All this has made Everglades National Park one of the top ten most endangered parks in the United States.

Now there is a plan to save the Everglades. Engineers will build wells to capture water before it flows out of the Everglades. Then they will pump the water back. Many canals will be removed, allowing water to follow its natural path. The plan may take 50 years to complete. Saving this unique ecosystem is an important goal, no matter how long it takes.

Meet Some Everglades Species

Wood Stork
An endangered species in the Everglades, this tall bird hunts for fish with its long, curved bill.

Manatee
This slow-moving mammal lives in both fresh water and salt water.

Crocodile, Alligator
The Everglades is the only place in the world with both reptiles.

Go On ▶

Directions: Answer the questions.

1. What is a food chain?

   A   unusual species surviving without water

   B   early settlers living off natural resources

   C   plants and animals depending on each other

   D   wetlands that provide food and resources

2. Humans upset the Everglades ecosystem by

   A   hunting animals there.

   B   ignoring it.

   C   draining much of the water there.

   D   making it into a national park.

Tip

Look for key words.

3. The new plan for the Everglades shows that

   A   people want to save it, no matter how long it takes.

   B   people keep wasting natural resources, such as water.

   C   people value new homes over national parks.

   D   engineers will replace the park with canals.

4. Why is the Everglades a "unique paradise"?

5. Explain the main idea of the article. Include the most important details in your response.

Write to a Prompt

In the selection "Animals Come Home to Our National Parks" you read about wolves that have been reintroduced to Yellowstone Park. What effect will this have on the future of the wolves? Do you think they will remain endangered? Use details from the article to support your answer.

I used details to support my main idea.

Giving Wolves a Chance

Wolves were once common in this country, especially in Yellowstone National Park. When large numbers of settlers began to move to the West, they hunted and killed wolves. The wolves disappeared from Yellowstone and became an endangered species.

Wolves were returned to Yellowstone beginning in the 1990s. That means the wolves have a chance to live in their natural habitat. There is food for wolves in Yellowstone, and it has everything they need to survive.

If people leave the wolves alone, they have a chance to survive. Eventually, there will be enough wolves that they will no longer be endangered. That will be good news for the wolves, for Yellowstone, and for people, too.

Writing Prompt

In the selection "Animals Come Home to Our National Parks" you read about elk that were reintroduced to Great Smoky Mountains National Park in North Carolina. Do you think it was a good idea to bring elk back? How will this affect the park? Use details from the article to support your answer.

Writer's Checklist

- ☑ Ask yourself, who is my audience?
- ☑ Think about your purpose for writing.
- ☑ Plan your writing before beginning.
- ☑ Use details to support your main idea.
- ☑ Be sure your ideas are clear and organized.
- ☑ Use your best spelling, grammar, and punctuation.

Astronauts

Talk About It

What do you think is happening in this photograph?

LOG ON Find out more about astronauts at **www.macmillanmh.com**

83

Astronauts in Training

by Benjamin Telicki

Vocabulary

endless   sensible

realistic   protested

universe   paralyzed

astronaut

Dictionary

Using a Dictionary will help you to learn the pronunciation and meaning of a word.

Look up the meaning and pronunciation of *sensible*.

Ana Gomez spotted Larry Waters looking for a table in the cafeteria. "Hi, Larry!" she called out.

Larry smiled and brought his tray over. "Hi, Ana. You're looking especially cheerful this morning," he remarked as he sat.

Ana smiled broadly.

"You got your launch date, didn't you?" Larry exclaimed.

"Yes, I did," Ana replied. "Finally! The wait seemed **endless**. I have been curious about that planet since I was ten and now I'll be on our first mission to Venus. We're leaving ten months from now on April 17, 2016."

"That's **realistic**. You'll have plenty of time to train your crew and they'll have time to review the virtual trip before the actual flight. Congratulations, Ana. It sounds like you would have picked this mission if you had your choice of any planet in the whole **universe**."

"Well," replied Ana, "if I could go anywhere in the solar system, I'd pick Pluto. But that wouldn't be a wise choice for a middle-aged **astronaut**. By the time we're able to go there, I'll be out of the space program! I'll be **sensible** and stick to Venus. What about you, Larry? You applied for the next trip to Mars. It's time you went as the commander."

Larry **protested**. "I wish that were true, but Sergio Casinelli has been ahead of me since we left the academy, and the remote control for his new leg attachment is ready. Sergio's been **paralyzed** since he was a child. He's really looking forward to his walk on Mars. If I'm not mistaken, though, the next trip to Mars is planned for April."

"Wouldn't it be great if we were headed for Earth's nearest neighbors at the same time?"

Reread for **Comprehension**

Make Inferences and Analyze

Character A character's emotions can change often. A character's traits are longer-lasting parts of their personality. You can make inferences about a character's traits from what he or she does, says, feels, or thinks in the story.

A Character Web can help you analyze a character's traits. Reread the selection to find the traits for one of the main characters.

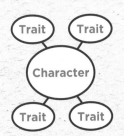

85

Comprehension

Genre

Realistic Fiction is a made-up story that could have happened in real life.

Make Inferences and Analyze

Character

As you read, fill in your Character Web.

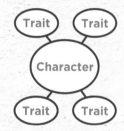

Read to Find Out

How does a trip to the supermarket change Gloria?

The Astronaut and the Onion

BY Ann Cameron

ILLUSTRATED BY

Anna Rich

Award Winning Author

MY MOTHER was making spaghetti sauce. She said, "Gloria, honey, would you go buy me an onion?"

"Sure," I said. She gave me some money, and I went.

The store was crowded with old people holding tightly to their shopping carts, little kids hollering to their parents for candy, and lots of people staring at shopping lists and blocking the aisles.

I ducked around all the carts and went to the back where the vegetables are. From all the onions in the bin, I took the prettiest—a big round one, light tan and shiny, with a silvery glow to its skin.

I carried it to the express checkout and stood at the end of a very long line.

Next to me there was a giant Berkbee's Baby Food display. It was like a wall of glass, and taller than I am. All the little jars were stacked up to look like a castle, with pennants that said "Baby Power" sticking out above the castle doorways and windows. At the top there was a high tower with a red-and-white flag that said "Berkbee's Builds Better Babies!" I started counting the jars, but when I got to 346, I gave up. There must have been at least a thousand.

The checkout line didn't move. To pass the time, I started tossing my onion from hand to hand. I tried to improve and make my throws harder to catch.

A woman wearing a sky-blue jogging suit got in line behind me. She was holding a cereal box. She smiled at me, and I smiled back.

I decided to show her what a really good catcher I am. I made a wild and daring onion throw.

Character

What was wild and daring about Gloria's actions?

I missed the catch. The onion kept going, straight for the middle of the baby food castle. The castle was going to fall!

My folks would have to pay for every broken jar! The store manager would kill me. After that, my folks would bring me back to life to tell me things that would be much worse than death.

I was **paralyzed**. I shut my eyes.

I didn't hear a crash. Maybe I had gone deaf from fright. Or maybe I was in a time warp because of my fear. In fifty years the onion would land, and that would be the end of me.

I felt a tap on my shoulder. If I opened my eyes, I would see the store manager and all the broken jars.

I didn't want to see him. I didn't want to know how bad it was.

There came a tap again, right on the top of my head.

I heard a woman's voice. "I have your onion."

I opened my eyes. The woman in the jogging suit handed the onion to me.

"Lucky I used to play baseball," she said.

"O-o-o-h," I said. I clutched the onion.

"O-o-o-h," I moaned again.

"You're welcome," was all she said.

She had brown eyes with a sparkle in them, and her hair was in shiny black ringlets. She wore blue-green earrings that hung on tiny gold chains. When she tilted her head, her earrings spun around, and I saw they were the Earth—I mean, made to look like the Earth, jeweled with green continents and blue oceans.

"Your earrings are beautiful," I said.

She smiled. "Some friends got them for me," she said, "to remind me of a trip we made."

When she said "trip," her face started to look familiar, but I didn't know why. Then I remembered.

"I've seen you!" I said. "I saw you on TV!"

She smiled. "Could be."

"And you come from right here in town, but you don't live here anymore," I said.

"That's right," she said.

"And you are—aren't you?—Dr. Grace Street, the **astronaut**!"

She tilted her head, and the little Earths on both her ears spun round. "That's me," she said.

I was amazed, because I never thought I would meet a famous person in my life, and yet one was right beside me in the supermarket, and I myself, Gloria Jones, was talking to her, all because of my onion throw.

"We learned about the space station in school last year," I said. "You were up there, orbiting the Earth."

"My team and I were there," Dr. Street said.

"What is space like?"

"You know," she said.

"How could I know?" I said.

"We're always in space," Dr. Street said. "We're in space right now."

"Yes," I said, "but what was it like out there, where you went? Out there it must seem different."

"Do you really want to know?" she asked, and I said yes.

"The most awesome part was when we had to fix things on the outside of the station. We got our jobs done and floated in our space suits, staring out into the **universe**. There were zillions of stars—and space, deep and black, but it didn't seem exactly empty. It seemed to be calling to us, calling us to go on an **endless** journey. And that was very scary.

"So we turned and looked at Earth. We were two hundred miles above it. We saw enormous swirls of clouds and the glow of snowfields at the poles. We saw water like a giant blue cradle for the land. One big ocean, not 'oceans.' The Earth isn't really chopped up into countries, either. Up there you see it is one great big powerful living being that knows a lot, lot more than we do."

"What does it know?" I said.

"It knows how to be Earth," Dr. Street said. "And that's a lot."

I tried to imagine everything she had seen. It gave me a shiver.

"I wish I could see what you saw," I said. "I'd like to be an astronaut. Of course, probably I couldn't."

Dr. Street frowned. "Why do you say 'Probably I couldn't?' "

"Practically nobody gets to do that," I said.

"You might be one of the people who do," she said. "But you'll never do anything you want to do if you keep saying 'Probably I couldn't'."

"But maybe I can't!" I **protested**. I looked down at my onion. I didn't think a very poor onion thrower had a chance to be an astronaut.

Dr. Street looked at my onion, too. "It was a good throw—just a bad catch," she said. "Anyhow—saying 'Maybe I can't' is different. It's okay. It's **realistic**.

"Even 'I can't' can be a good, **sensible** thing to say. It makes life simpler. When you really know you can't do one thing, that leaves you time to try some of the rest. But when you don't even know what you can do, telling yourself 'Probably I couldn't' will stop you before you even start. It's paralyzing. You don't want to be paralyzed, do you?"

"I just was paralyzed," I said. "A minute ago, when I threw my onion. I didn't enjoy it one bit."

"If you don't want to be paralyzed," Dr. Street said, "be careful what you tell yourself—because whatever you tell yourself you're very likely to believe."

I thought about what she said. "If maybe I could be an astronaut," I asked, "how would I get to be one?"

"You need to do well in school," she said. "And you need to tame your fears. Not get rid of them—just tame them."

The line moved forward suddenly, and we moved up. Maybe the people in line behind us thought Dr. Street and I were mother and daughter having a serious conversation, because they left some space around us.

"So how does a person tame fears?"

"By doing things that are difficult, and succeeding," Dr. Street said. "That's how you learn you can count on yourself. That's how you get confidence. But even then, you keep a little bit of fear inside—a fear that keeps you careful."

Character
How do you think Dr. Street felt when she was out in space? How do you know?

The checkout line moved again, and we moved with it.

"Big things are really little," Dr. Street said. "That's a great secret of life."

"How—" I began. But I never got to ask how big things are really little, because I was the first person in line.

The checkout man looked at my onion.

"Young lady, didn't you weigh that?" he asked.

"No, sir," I said.

"Go back to Produce and have it weighed."

So I had to go.

"Goodbye," Dr. Street said.

"Goodbye," I said. On the way to Produce, I looked back at her. She was walking toward the exit with her cereal box. I waved, but she didn't notice.

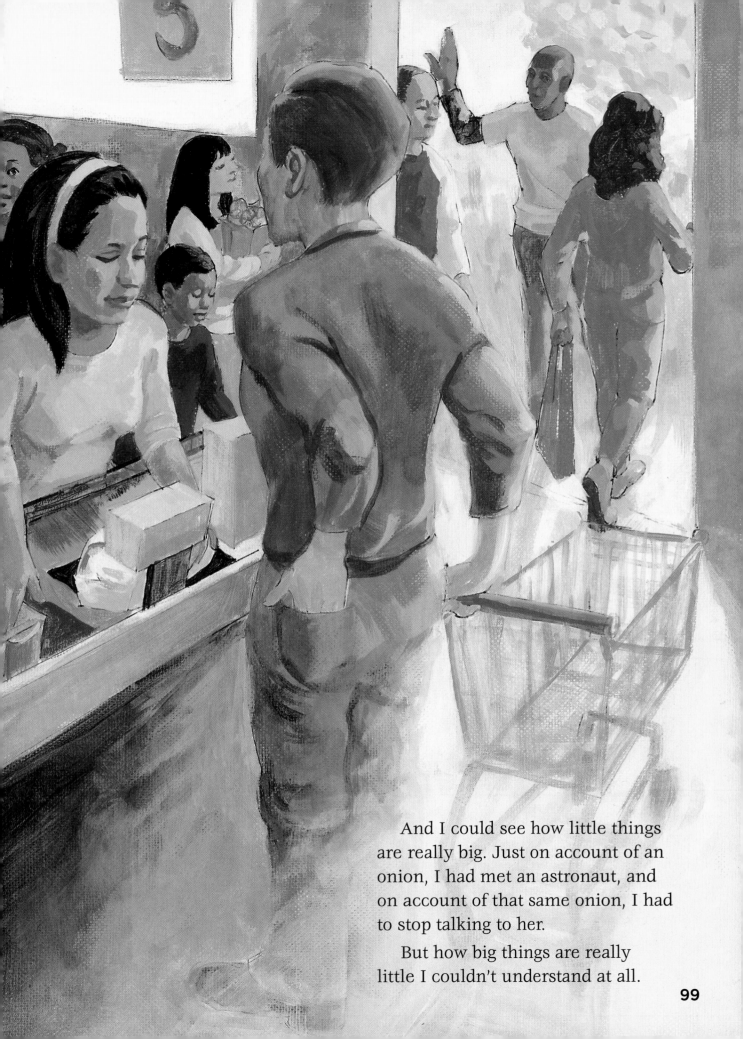

And I could see how little things are really big. Just on account of an onion, I had met an astronaut, and on account of that same onion, I had to stop talking to her.

But how big things are really little I couldn't understand at all.

99

Blast Off with Ann and Anna

Ann Cameron is a well-known writer. When she was a young girl, like Gloria, she was always outside exploring and wondering about the world around her. Ann did not have a TV until she was nine years old. She spent time listening to stories on the radio and reading books. Today Ann still loves nature and books. She lives in Guatemala, near a waterfall and volcanoes.

Other books by Ann Cameron

Anna Rich has always loved to draw. From an early age, her mother saw her talent and encouraged Anna to follow her dream. Her passion for illustration eventually became a full-time job. Good thing, too, because Anna has never considered doing anything else as a career. Anna, a native New Yorker, still lives there with her family.

 Find out more about Ann Cameron and Anna Rich at **www.macmillanmh.com**

Author's Purpose

Think about Ann Cameron's purpose for writing this story. Did she mainly write to inform, persuade, entertain, or explain something to the reader? How do you know?

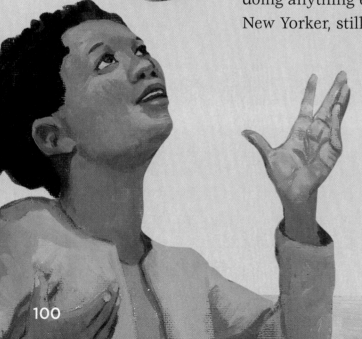

Comprehension Check

STRATEGY SKILL

Summarize

Summarize the plot of *The Astronaut and the Onion*. In your summary include details about Gloria's character.

Think and Compare

STRATEGY SKILL

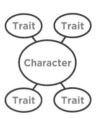

1. How might Gloria's character traits help her become an astronaut? Use the Character Web and story details to support your answer. **Make Inferences and Analyze: Character**

2. Reread page 97. Dr. Grace Street tells Gloria that she still keeps some fear inside of her. What character traits might have helped her overcome that fear? **Analyze**

3. Suppose you meet someone who has a career that interests you. What kind of questions would you ask that person? **Apply**

4. Why does Dr. Street tell Gloria not to be **paralyzed** by her fears? Explain your answer. **Evaluate**

5. Read "Astronauts in Training" on pages 84-85. Compare Ana's character to Dr. Street's character. In what ways are they alike? How are they different? **Reading/Writing Across Texts**

The Solar System

by Thomas Morabito

Our solar system is made up of the Sun, Earth, our moon, seven other planets and their moons, meteors, asteroids, and all the space around them. All eight planets move in **orbits** around the Sun, which is the center of our solar system.

The Sun

The Sun is a medium-size star made up of very hot gases. The temperature of the Sun is almost 10,000°F! The closer a planet is to the Sun, the higher the temperatures are on its surface. The farther away a planet is from the Sun, the lower the temperatures are on its surface.

The Inner Planets

The inner planets are those closest to the Sun. They are made of solid rock.

Mercury

Mercury is the closest planet to the Sun. It is about one-third the size of Earth. Covered with **craters**, it looks a lot like the moon. Mercury has no water and very little air.

Venus

Venus, the second planet from the Sun, is veiled in thick, swirling clouds. About the same size as Earth, Venus is sometimes called a sister planet.

Venus, though, is very different from Earth. It has no oceans and no life. The air is made up of carbon dioxide. This layer traps in heat.

That makes Venus the hottest planet in the solar system. With temperatures of 900°F, Venus is even hotter than Mercury!

Earth

Earth is the third planet from the Sun. In addition to having the most comfortable temperatures, Earth has water and oxygen. As far as we know, Earth is the only planet able to sustain life.

Besides heat, we also get light from the Sun. It takes about 24 hours for Earth to spin, or **rotate**, all the way around. For half of that time, a side of Earth faces the Sun and it is day. At the same time, the other side faces away from the Sun and it is night.

It takes Earth about 365 days to move around the Sun. We call this time period a year.

Distance from the Sun

Reading a Diagram

This diagram shows the distance from the Sun to each of the eight planets in miles and kilometers.

rcury	Venus	Earth	Mars	Jupiter	Saturn	Uranus	Neptune
9,175 km	108,208,930 km	149,597,890 km	227,936,640 km	778,412,020 km	1,426,725,400 km	2,870,972,200 km	4,498,252,900 km
3,095 miles	67,237,910 miles	92,955,820 miles	141,633,260 miles	483,682,810 miles	885,904,700 miles	1,783,939,400 miles	2,795,084,800 miles

Sun

Mars, the planet next farthest from the Sun, is often called the Red Planet. The rocks, soil, and sky are red in color. Before space **exploration**, people thought there might be life on Mars. They thought the lines on Mars's surface were canals made by intelligent life forms. Now we know that Mars has no surface water and no life. Traces of shorelines, riverbeds, and islands may suggest that there was water on Mars at one time. Craters and inactive volcanoes cover most of its surface today.

The Outer Planets

In addition to being farther away from the Sun, these planets are not made of rock. Although they may have solid centers, these planets are made up of gases. They are dark and cold.

Jupiter

Jupiter is the largest planet. If Jupiter were hollow, more than one thousand Earths could fit inside. It is the fifth planet from the Sun and is famous for its great red spot. Scientists believe this spot to be a storm.

Saturn, the sixth planet from the Sun, is the second largest planet. It has thousands of beautiful shiny rings. These rings are made up of chunks of ice, rock, and dust. Saturn is also very windy. Near the equator, the wind blows at speeds of up to 1,100 miles an hour!

Saturn

Uranus

Uranus, the third largest planet, has at least 22 moons. Like Saturn, Uranus has faint gray rings that might be made out of graphite, the black material inside a pencil.

Neptune

Neptune has a great dark spot, about the size of Earth. Neptune's spot, like the one on Jupiter, is thought to be a storm. The winds there are the strongest on any planet. They have been found to reach speeds of 1,200 miles per hour. Neptune has faint rings and eight moons.

A Note About Pluto

Pluto was discovered in 1930 and was called the ninth planet. In 2006, the International Astronomical Union said planets must orbit the Sun, have a nearly round shape, and clear other objects in their orbital neighborhood. Because Pluto's orbit intersects Neptune's, it was renamed a dwarf planet.

Pluto

Connect and Compare

1. Look at the diagram. Which planet is farther away from the Sun—Mars or Neptune? How do you know? **Reading a Diagram**

2. Using information from the article and the latest findings about the solar system, make three observations about the planets. **Synthesize**

3. Think about Gloria from "The Astronaut and the Onion." What do you know about her that tells you Gloria would probably like to visit the solar system? **Reading/Writing Across Texts**

Science Activity

Research the reasons why the International Astronomical Union calls Pluto a "dwarf planet." Draw a diagram of Pluto and its nearest neighbors.

 Find more about space travel at **www.macmillanmh.com**

Write an E-Mail

Writer's Craft

Topic Sentence
Your first sentence, the topic sentence, lets the reader know what you are writing about.

The topic sentence in my e-mail to a friend is about my Space Camp trip.

Details make my e-mail lively and informative.

e-mail

Write | Send | Reply | Print | Delete | Address

TO: Chanell97@example.com

FROM: Taqoya123@example.com

SUBJECT: Space Camp

Dear Chanell,

While I was at Space Camp, I felt what it's like to walk on the moon. At first, I just hopped a bit. Then I bounced high in the air! It was awesome. I hope you and I can leap across the moon together some day for real. Write soon!

Your friend,

Taqoya

Your Turn

Write an e-mail telling about an experience. You may write to a friend or a family member. Be sure to include a topic sentence. Your e-mail should include to whom it is addressed, who is writing, and what it is about. Use the Writer's Checklist to check your writing.

Writer's Checklist

 Ideas and Content: Did my e-mail clearly describe my experience and include interesting details?

Organization: Did my e-mail include a topic sentence telling about my experience?

 Voice: Did the writing show my excitement about the experience?

Word Choice: Did I use strong verbs?

 Sentence Fluency: Did I join related sentences to make complex sentences?

 Conventions: Did I use commas in the greeting and closing? Did I check my spelling?

Talk About It

What is the girl thinking?
What is the frog thinking?

LOG ON Find out more about wildlife at
www.macmillanmh.com

WILDLIFE WATCHERS

Vocabulary

disgusted	cluttered
raft	downstream
scattered	nuzzle

Context Clues

Paragraph Clues are clues within the same paragraph to the meaning of an unfamiliar word. Look for clues within the paragraph where *cluttered* appears to figure out its meaning.

RAFTING— Ready or Not

by Olivia Snow

Dear Diary,

What an amazing day! I never thought rafting could be so much fun. Wait... I should probably back up and explain what I was doing on a raft in the first place.

Today, my family and I started our vacation. We're taking a rafting trip down the Colorado River. I have to admit, it didn't sound like my idea of fun. The thought of getting drenched by the river and sleeping in tents with creepy bugs and spiders kind of **disgusted** me. But, unless I wanted to be left behind, I had to put on my lifejacket and join in.

Lisa, our guide, helped us get our big, rubber **raft** into the river. We joined the others, **scattered** here and there along the river. There were so many, it felt like we were playing bumper boats! Lisa had told us that the river would narrow and we would be a bit **cluttered**. Then the river widened, and the rafts spread out as we were carried in the water's flow **downstream**. At first, I just sat in the raft and listened to my music. But when we picked up speed, I realized my help was needed.

Before long, I was paddling away and enjoying the amazing wildlife overhead and along the shore. We spotted a great blue heron and a coyote. Then we watched a mother beaver **nuzzle** her young gently with her snout. Lisa said that if we looked carefully, we might even see a mountain lion!

I have to admit that when it was time to get off the river and set up camp, I actually felt disappointed. But it gave us a chance to appreciate the beauty of the Grand Canyon. The sunset was amazing. It made the red and gold colors of the canyon walls positively glow.

We'll be back on the river early tomorrow, so I'd better zip up my sleeping bag and get to sleep.

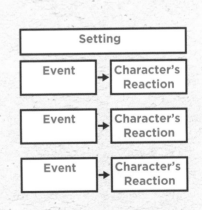

Reread for **Comprehension**

Make Inferences and Analyze
Character, Setting, Plot
Knowing the setting of a story can help readers make inferences and analyze why certain events occur and why characters feel or act the way they do.

A Setting Flow Chart can help you keep track of the setting, character, and events of a story. Reread the selection to learn how the story's setting affects the main character.

Setting	
Event	→ Character's Reaction
Event	→ Character's Reaction
Event	→ Character's Reaction

111

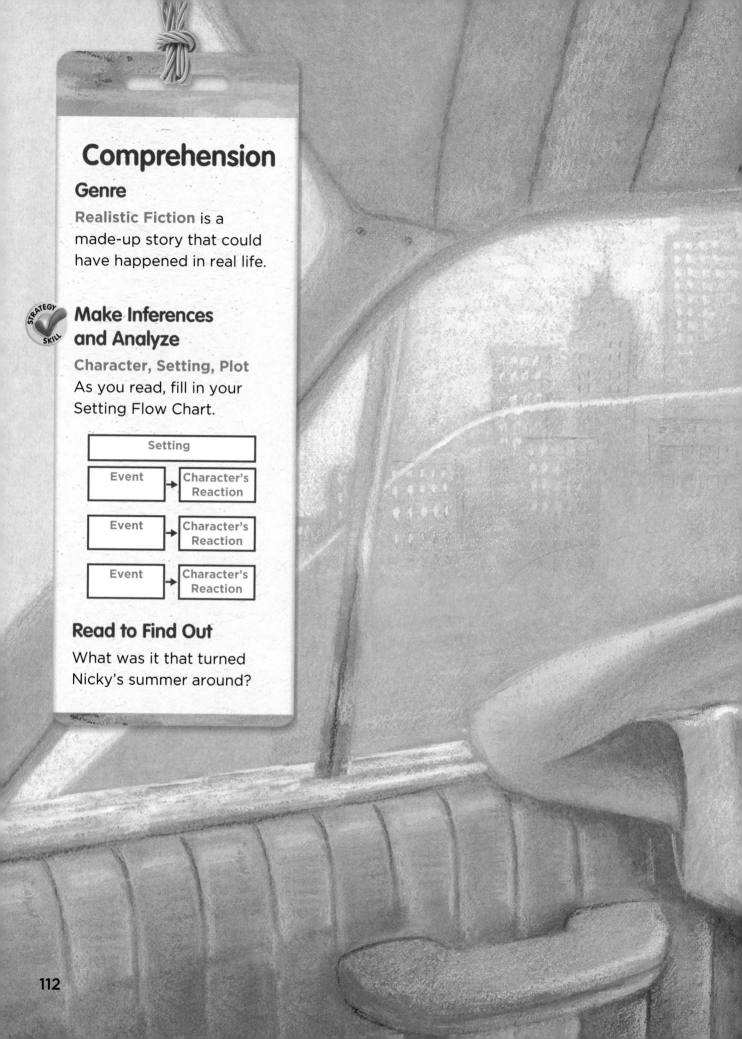

Comprehension

Genre

Realistic Fiction is a made-up story that could have happened in real life.

Make Inferences and Analyze

Character, Setting, Plot
As you read, fill in your Setting Flow Chart.

Setting

Event	→	Character's Reaction

Event	→	Character's Reaction

Event	→	Character's Reaction

Read to Find Out

What was it that turned Nicky's summer around?

THE RAFT

BY JIM LaMarche

"There's nobody to play with," I complained. "She doesn't even have a TV."

Dad grinned. "Well, she's not your normal kind of grandma, I guess," he said. "Calls herself a river rat." He chuckled. "But I promise, she'll find plenty for you to do. And you know I can't take you with me this summer, Nicky. There'll be no kids there, and I'll be spending all my time at the plant."

I felt tears starting again, but I blinked hard and looked out the window.

113

That afternoon, I stood in Grandma's yard and watched my dad drive away. Dust rose up behind our car as it disappeared into the pines.

"Well, we can't stand here all summer," said Grandma. "C'mon, Nicky, it's time for supper."

"Honey or maple syrup on your cornbread?" Grandma asked.

"I don't like cornbread," I mumbled, poking my finger into the syrup pitcher when she wasn't looking.

"If you're going to do that, you'd better wash up first," she said. She had eyes in the back of her head. "Bathroom's through there."

Character, Setting
How do you think Nicky feels about spending the summer with his grandmother?

I pushed the doorway curtain aside and walked into what would have been a living room in anyone else's house. Books were **scattered** everywhere—on the tables, on the chairs, even on the floor. Three of the walls were **cluttered** with sketches and stuffed fish and charts of the river. Several fishing poles hung from the fourth with a tackle box, a snorkel, and a mask on the floor beneath them. It looked like a river rat's workroom, all right, except that in the middle of everything was a half-finished carving of a bear.

"Been carving that old fellow for years," Grandma called from the kitchen. "The real one hangs out at the dump. Now come get your supper, before I feed it to him."

Dad was right—Grandma found plenty for me to do. In the morning, I stacked firewood, then helped her clean out the rain gutters and change the spark plugs on her truck. The afternoon was almost over when she handed me a cane pole, a bobber, and some red worms.

"Fish fry tonight!" she said, showing me how to bait the hook. "That river's full of fat bluegills. Drop your line near the lily pads and you'll find 'em."

Down at the dock, I looked things over. The lily pads were too close to shore. There couldn't be fish there. I walked to the end of the dock and threw my line out as far as I could. Then I sat down to wait. And wait. And wait. My bobber never moved.

"There's no fish in this stupid river," I said out loud, **disgusted**.

We had hamburgers for supper.

"Give it another try," said Grandma the next evening. "I'll bet you catch something."

Don't count on it, I thought, as I headed back to the dock. I threw my line in the water. Then I stretched out on the dock to wait. I must have fallen asleep, because I was awakened by loud chirping and chattering. I sat up and looked around. A flock of birds was moving toward me along the river, hovering over something floating on the water. It drifted **downstream**, closer and closer, until finally it bumped up against the dock.

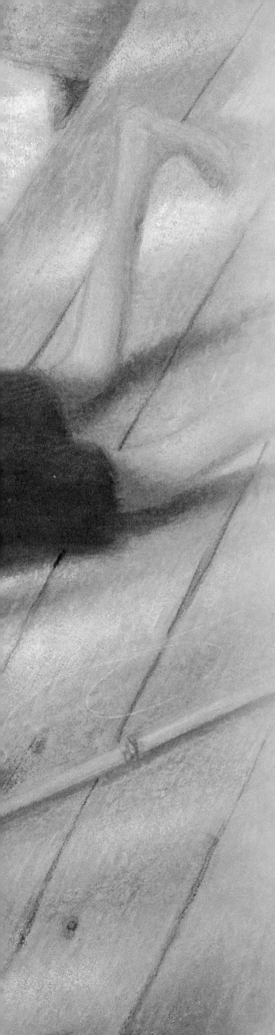

Though it was covered with leaves and branches, now I could tell that it was a **raft**. What was it doing floating down the river all by itself, I wondered. I reached down and pushed some of the leaves aside. Beneath them was a drawing of a rabbit. It looked like those ancient cave paintings I'd seen in books—just outlines, but wild and fast and free.

I cleaned away more leaves and it was like finding presents under the Christmas tree. A bear, a fox, a raccoon—all with the wild look of the rabbit. Who had drawn them, I wondered. Where had the raft come from?

I ran up to the cottage. Grandma was on the porch, reading.

"Do you have some rope I can use?" I asked.

"In the shed, hon," she said. "Help yourself." She didn't ask me what I needed it for, and I decided not to tell her yet.

I pushed the raft into the reeds along the river's edge, then tied it to the dock so it wouldn't drift away. All the while, birds flew over my head, every now and then swooping down to the raft as if it were a friend. A crane waded through the reeds to it. A turtle swam up from the bottom of the river.

The moon had risen yellow over the river by the time I went up to the cottage to go to bed.

I was already down at the dock the next morning when Grandma appeared with a life jacket and a long pole. She didn't seem surprised by the raft at all, or by the animal pictures all over it.

"How did you know . . . ?" I started.

"Let's go," Grandma interrupted, tossing me the life jacket and stepping onto the raft. She pushed the pole hard into the river bottom and we moved smoothly into the current.

"Your turn," she said after a few minutes. She showed me how to hold the pole and push, and I poled us to the middle of the river. Even there, the water wasn't over my head.

We poled the raft up the river, then let it slowly drift back down. The birds kept us company the whole time, soaring, swooping, singing. Some even landed on the raft and rode with us for a while. Hitchhikers, Grandma called them.

After that, I had little time for anything but the raft. I raced through whatever chores there were, then ran down to the dock, wondering what animals I'd see that day.

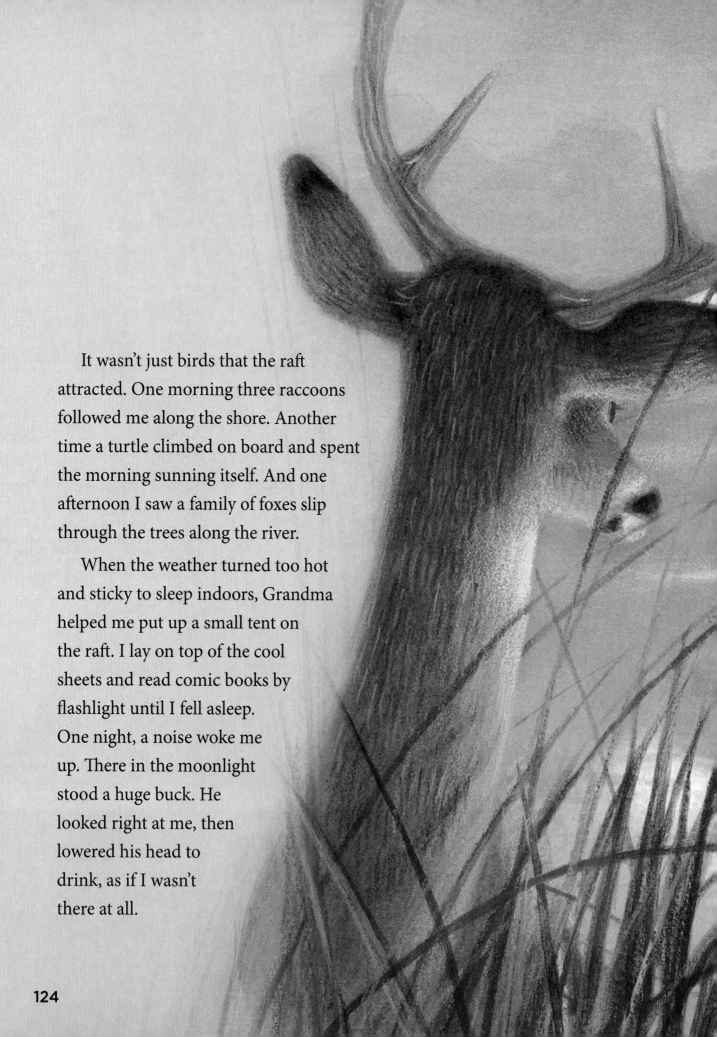

It wasn't just birds that the raft attracted. One morning three raccoons followed me along the shore. Another time a turtle climbed on board and spent the morning sunning itself. And one afternoon I saw a family of foxes slip through the trees along the river.

When the weather turned too hot and sticky to sleep indoors, Grandma helped me put up a small tent on the raft. I lay on top of the cool sheets and read comic books by flashlight until I fell asleep. One night, a noise woke me up. There in the moonlight stood a huge buck. He looked right at me, then lowered his head to drink, as if I wasn't there at all.

I found Grandma the next morning working on her bear carving.

"Do you have some extra paper I could draw on?" I asked her.

She brought out a big sketchpad and a pouch filled with thick pencils and crayons. "I've been saving these just for you," she said. "Better take these, too." She held out the snorkel and mask. "Never know when they might come in handy on a raft."

The sun was hot that afternoon, so I poled into the shade of a willow, then waited to see what animals the raft would bring. It wasn't long before a great blue heron whooshed down with a crayfish in its bill.

I grabbed a pencil and began to sketch. I felt invisible as the bird calmly ate its lunch right in front of me. Then it preened its feathers, looked back up the river, and flew off.

That night I showed my drawing to Grandma.

"Not bad," she said. "Not bad at all!" And she tacked it on the wall on top of one of her own sketches.

Character, Setting

Describe the ways in which Nicky is beginning to enjoy the place where his grandmother lives.

One day I poled upriver farther than I'd ever been. Near a clump of tall cattails, I startled an otter family. They dove underwater, but, as with the other animals, the raft seemed to calm them down. Soon they were playing all around me.

Grandma had been right about the mask and snorkel coming in handy. I slipped them on, then hung my head over the raft and watched the otters play—chasing fish, chasing each other, sometimes just chasing their own tails. I kept very still, but they didn't seem to mind me watching. They played keep away with a small stone, then tug-of-war with a piece of rope. It was like they were showing off for me. They even let me feed them right out of my hand.

Some mornings, Grandma would make a bagful of sandwiches and a thermos of icy lemonade. Then we'd put on our bathing suits, grab some towels, a lawn chair, and an inner tube, and pole upriver to her favorite swimming spot. "I've come swimming here since I was a girl," she told me as we tied the raft to an old dock. "The Marshalls used to live here—all ten of them. What a herd of wild animals we were!"

While Grandma watched from the inner tube, I practiced my flying cannonballs. Then we'd eat our lunch, and she'd tell me stories about growing up on the river. My favorite was of the time she'd found a small black pearl inside a river clam. "I still have it," she said.

Somehow, on the river, it seemed like summer would never end. But of course it did.

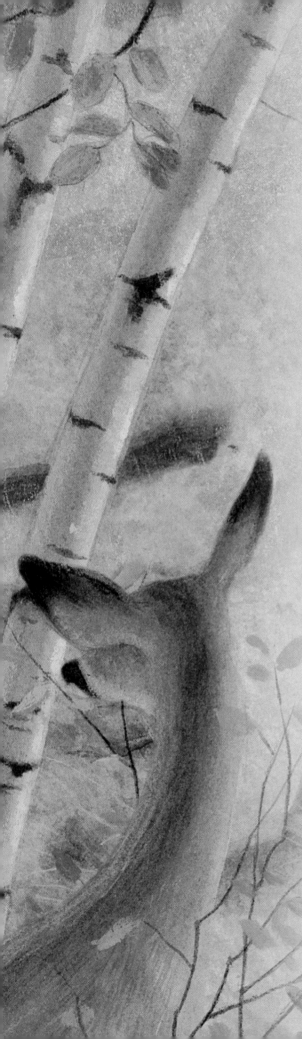

On my last day, I got up extra early and crept down to the dock. The air was cool and a low pearly fog hung over the river. I untied the raft and quietly drifted downstream.

Ahead of me, through the fog, I saw two deer moving across the river, a doe and her fawn. When they reached the shore, the doe leaped easily up the steep bank, then turned to wait for her baby. But the fawn was in trouble. It kept slipping down the muddy bank. The doe returned to the water to help, but the more the fawn struggled, the deeper it got stuck in the mud.

I pushed off the river bottom and drove the raft hard onto the muddy bank, startling the doe. Then I dropped into the water. I was ankle-deep in mud.

"You're okay," I whispered to the fawn, praying that the raft would calm it. "I won't hurt you."

Gradually the fawn stopped struggling, as if it understood that I was there to help. I put my arms around it and pulled. It barely moved. I pulled again, then again. Slowly the fawn eased out of the mud, and finally it was free. Carefully I carried the fawn up the bank to its mother.

Then, quietly, I returned to the raft. From there, I watched the doe **nuzzle** and clean her baby, and I knew what I had to do. I pulled the stub of a crayon from my pocket, and drew the fawn, in all its wildness, onto the old gray boards of the raft. When I had finished, I knew it was just right.

After supper, I showed Grandma my drawing of the fawn and told her my story.

"It's perfect," she said, "but we need to do one more thing." She hurried up to the cottage. When she came back, she had tubes of oil paint and two brushes.

Grandma helped me trace my drawing with the oil paint, which soaked deep into the wood. "That'll keep it," she said. "Now you'll always be part of the river."

"Just like you, Grandma," I told her. "A river rat."

Grandma laughed. "Just like me," she agreed.

A SKETCH OF
JIM LaMARCHE

JIM LaMARCHE is a lot like the boy in this story. Jim spent his summers rafting on a river when he was a child. He grew up near the Milwaukee River in Wisconsin. All year round, the river was a special place to play. Jim also liked drawing and crafting things. Once he made a whole zoo out of clay that he dug up from a field. Even though Jim liked art, he didn't think about becoming an artist when he grew up. Back then, he really wanted to be a magician. Today Jim thinks that creating a book from just a blank piece of paper is not so different from being a magician.

Other books illustrated by Jim LaMarche

BARBARA D. BOOTH
MANDY
ILLUSTRATED BY
JIM LaMARCHE

DONNA JO NAPOLI
ALBERT

LOG ON Find out more about Jim LaMarche at **www.macmillanmh.com**

Author's Purpose
How might Jim LaMarche's own childhood experiences have influenced his purpose for writing *The Raft*? What clues in the story help you to know?

Comprehension Check

Summarize

Use your Setting Flow Chart to help you summarize *The Raft.* Describe the setting of the story.

Setting

Event	→	Character's Reaction

Event	→	Character's Reaction

Event	→	Character's Reaction

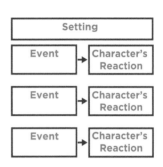

Think and Compare

1. How does the story's setting change Nicky? What could Nicky have done for the summer if the setting had been his own home? **Make Inferences and Analyze: Character, Setting, Plot**

2. Reread page 113 of *The Raft.* What does Nicky expect his vacation with his grandmother to be like? Use story details in your answer. **Analyze**

3. What would it be like if you were able to make use of a **raft** for the summer? **Apply**

4. What information would you use to support the view that the raft was a gift from Nicky's grandmother? **Evaluate**

5. Read "Rafting—Ready or Not" on pages 110-111. How is the narrator's experience on a raft similar to Nicky's? What do the characters discover? Use details from both stories in your answer. **Reading/Writing Across Texts**

Into the Swamp

by Elizabeth Schleichert
Photos by C.C. Lockwood

How would you like to float through twisting canals, **bayous** (streams), and lakes? Some kids from the city of Baton Rouge, Louisiana, did just that! They went canoeing in the huge Atchafalaya (uh-CHAFF-uh-LIE-uh) **Swamp**. Baton Rouge is only 20 miles (32 km) from the swamp, but most of the kids had never been there before. Now they were able to explore its winding waterways up close!

The kids met up at the boat dock before sunrise. They couldn't wait to push off and start their adventure! They were especially excited about camping out that night. Before getting in their canoes, they crowded around a map of the Atchafalaya.

"Here's where we are now," said Anthony, pointing to the map. He, Adam, and Edward were trying to figure out where they would be heading. But in fact, they didn't really have to worry about a thing. Their **guide** for the trip, photographer C.C. Lockwood, knew every bend and bayou in the Atchafalaya. There was no way he was going to get them lost! C.C. gave the group some canoeing pointers, and then they paddled into the morning mist.

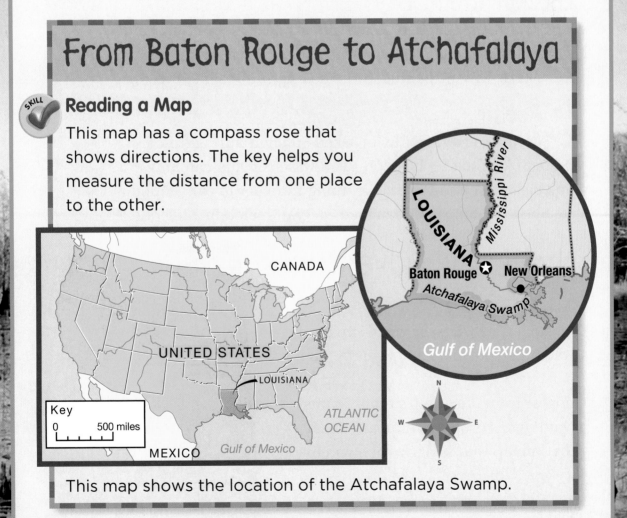

From Baton Rouge to Atchafalaya

SKILL ✓ Reading a Map

This map has a compass rose that shows directions. The key helps you measure the distance from one place to the other.

This map shows the location of the Atchafalaya Swamp.

Shhh . . . Swamp Creatures!

Yikes!

As the canoes followed C.C.'s, someone yelled "Alligator!" The kids paddled over to check it out. The 'gator swam around the canoes. One of the kids said, "It was so close, we could almost touch it!"

Nearby, the kids spied a super-sized female golden silk spider. It was waiting to snag a buggy meal in its golden web.

Checkin' It Out

Edward and Stephen poked around near an **ancient** bald cypress stump. Long ago, loggers had chopped down lots of trees here, leaving behind eerie-looking stumps like this one.

I'm Reelin'

"Wanna go fishing?" Ryan asked Stephen during lunch. "Sure," came the reply. Soon Ryan was excitedly catching one bass after another and grinning from ear to ear. Stephen steadied the canoe and laughed as Ryan reeled in a big one.

Nighttime Adventures

Whooo's There?

No telling who—or what—might be watching you on a dark swampy night! A barred owl was perched quietly in a tree not far from the group's tents. It was waiting to swoop down on any meal that might walk, wriggle, or swim by.

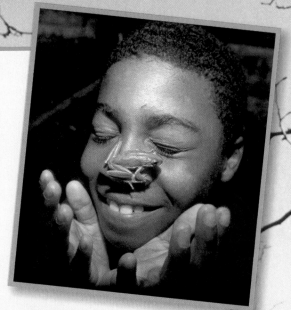

Noisy Frogs

Anthony giggled when C.C. put a green tree frog on his nose. "It kind of tickled," he said. The boys couldn't believe how noisy these frogs were, filling the nighttime swamp with their loud "quonks." Frog calls were just some of the sounds that kept the kids awake that night. Scary campfire ghost stories didn't help them go to sleep either.

So Long, Swamp!

Before leaving the swamp, the kids hung out at the water's edge. They'd had to put up with some heavy rain and tons of mosquitoes, but Anthony said, "I'll never forget the fun I had on this camping trip." And the other kids nodded, *You got that right!*

Connect and Compare

1. Look at the map on page 139. In what direction would you travel to get from Baton Rouge to the Atchafalaya Swamp? **Reading a Map**

2. How important is it to have a guide when exploring the Atchafalaya Swamp? Why do you think so? **Evaluate**

3. Think about this article and *The Raft.* How is Grandma's river like the Atchafalaya Swamp? How is it different? **Reading/Writing Across Texts**

Social Studies Activity

Research another body of water. Draw a map to show its location. Then write about the wildlife you might find there.

 Find out more wildlife facts at **www.macmillanmh.com**

Write a Journal Entry

Writer's Craft

Details

Adding important details helps to make your writing more informative. Delete unimportant details that do not support the topic.

My journal entry has details about nature and wildlife.

I included fun details that support my topic.

October 25

Today Dad and I went on a fantastic hike in the foothills. After about ten minutes I saw some hoof prints in the soft dirt of the trail. Then I looked up, and I saw a doe and her tiny spotted fawn. Dad and I stood there very quietly. Then they turned and walked into some thick brush.

Wow! I had never been so close to a wild animal. Dad patted me on the shoulder and told me there's a first time for everything.

Your Turn

Spend some time being a nature watcher. Safely observe birds, insects, or other animals that live in your area. Write a journal entry about your experience. Choose details that express your feelings about the experience. Use the Writer's Checklist to check your writing.

Writer's Checklist

☑ **Ideas and Content:** Did I include important details and delete unimportant details about my experience?

✓ **Organization:** Did I tell the events in the order that they happened?

✓ **Voice:** Does my writing show how I feel?

✓ **Word Choice:** Did I use strong, colorful words to tell what happened?

✓ **Sentence Fluency:** Did I vary the length of my sentences?

✓ **Conventions:** Did I fix any run-on sentences by dividing them into separate sentences? Did I fix any sentence fragments by making them into complete sentences? Did I check my spelling?

A Walk on the Beach

by Doreen Beauregard

> **CHARACTERS:**
>
> | | |
> |---|---|
> | **JENNY** | **DEREK** |
> | **JENNY'S DAD** | **JENNY'S MOM** |

Setting: The kitchen of Jenny's house

JENNY: You've never been to the beach? You've never seen the ocean? Are you kidding me, Derek?

DEREK: No, I've never seen it.

JENNY'S DAD: Derek lives in New Mexico, Jen. Look it up on the map. It's nowhere near the ocean. That's one of the reasons your cousin's visiting. Right, Derek? You came to see the Pacific?

DEREK: Right. Hey, when was the last time you saw a desert?

JENNY: I've never seen a desert.

DEREK: (*Imitating Jenny*) What? You've never seen a desert? Are you kidding me?

Go On ▶

JENNY'S DAD: *(Smiling)* Okay, you two. Finish your juice, then put your sneakers on. Mom's taking you on a beach walk.

(On the beach, near the dunes)

DEREK: Wow! The ocean really is huge! The waves are amazing!

JENNY'S MOM: Beautiful, isn't it?

JENNY: Check out the dunes. They're beautiful, too.

DEREK: How can all those plants grow in the sand?

JENNY'S MOM: They have their ways. Some have leaves with a waxy coating or little hairs to keep the water inside.

DEREK: Desert plants do that, too!

JENNY: Hey, it's low tide. We can look in the tide pools. There's lots of fun stuff living in the tide pools. C'mon.

JENNY'S MOM: Tide pools are fragile. Walk carefully so you don't harm anything.

green sea anemone

DEREK: What's that weird plant near the rock?

JENNY: That's not a plant. It's an anemone.

DEREK: An enemy?

JENNY: An A-NEM-A-NEE. It's an animal.

(Suddenly, a loud barking noise is heard. Derek, Jenny, and Jenny's mom look out toward some rocks offshore.)

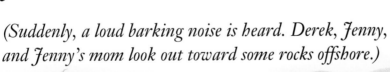

Go On   145

DEREK: Wow! Those are seals out there! They're pretty loud.

JENNY'S MOM: Those are sea lions actually.

DEREK: Hey, what's that thing on the sand? Is that seaweed?

JENNY: Yep. It's kelp. These round things are called gas bladders.

JENNY'S MOM: There's a big kelp forest out there.

DEREK: Are these the roots?

JENNY'S MOM: Not roots, exactly—that's the kelp's holdfast.

DEREK: (*Laughing and waving the kelp around*) Not any more! So what other fun stuff is out there?

JENNY: Ummm . . . there are white shrimp that look like ghosts. There are shovelnose guitarfish—

DEREK: Cool! What songs do they play?

JENNY'S MOM: (*Laughing*) We'll go to the aquarium on Saturday to see all these things. Now let's go back and get some lunch.

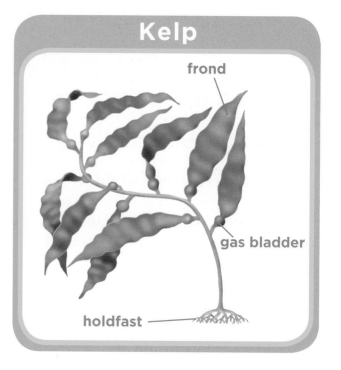

Kelp

frond

gas bladder

holdfast

Directions: Answer the questions.

Tip

Keep reading. The answer may be in more than one place.

1. What are tide pools?

A pools of water surrounded by plants
B pools of water filled with delicate living things
C pools of deep water
D waves caused by high tides

2. Based on the play and the diagram of the kelp, what is the purpose of the holdfast?

A to keep the plant green
B to help the plant breathe
C to anchor the plant to the ocean floor
D to keep sand away from the water

3. Which of these statements BEST describes Derek's character?

A He dislikes the beach and ocean.
B He is curious and excited about new things.
C He is afraid of new places.
D He does not like to ask questions.

4. Describe the plot of the play.

5. What is Derek's problem in this play? What does he do to help solve his problem?

Writing Prompt

Think of a place you love to visit. Why is it special? Write a letter home, about three paragraphs long, describing this place.

STOP 147

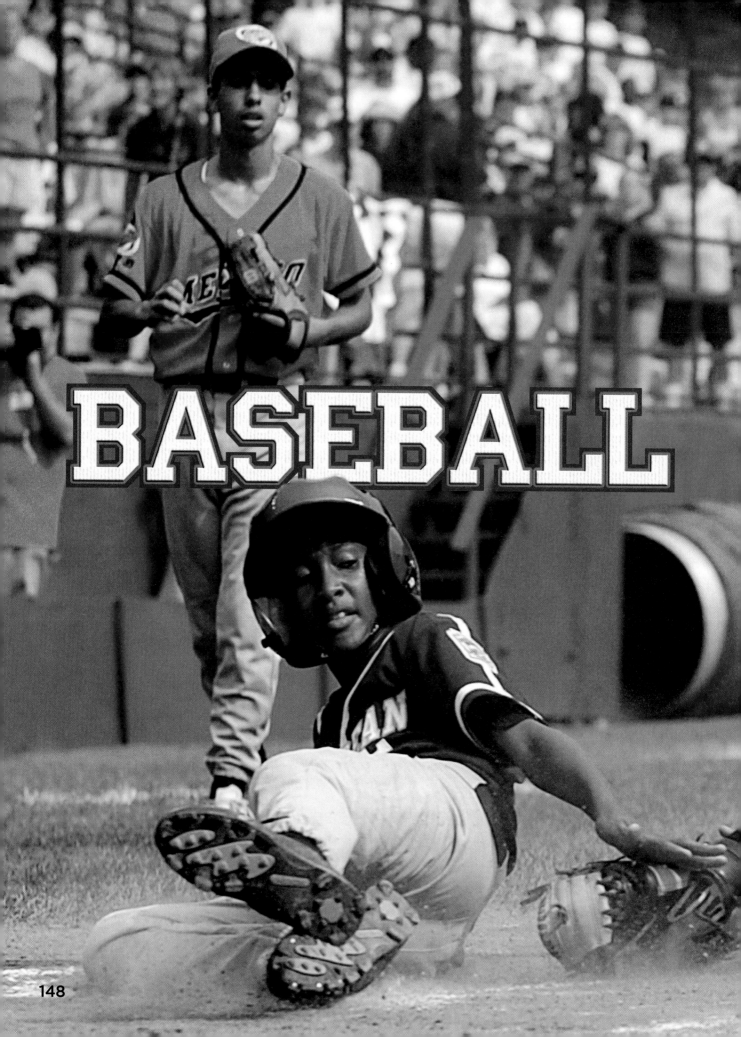

BASEBALL

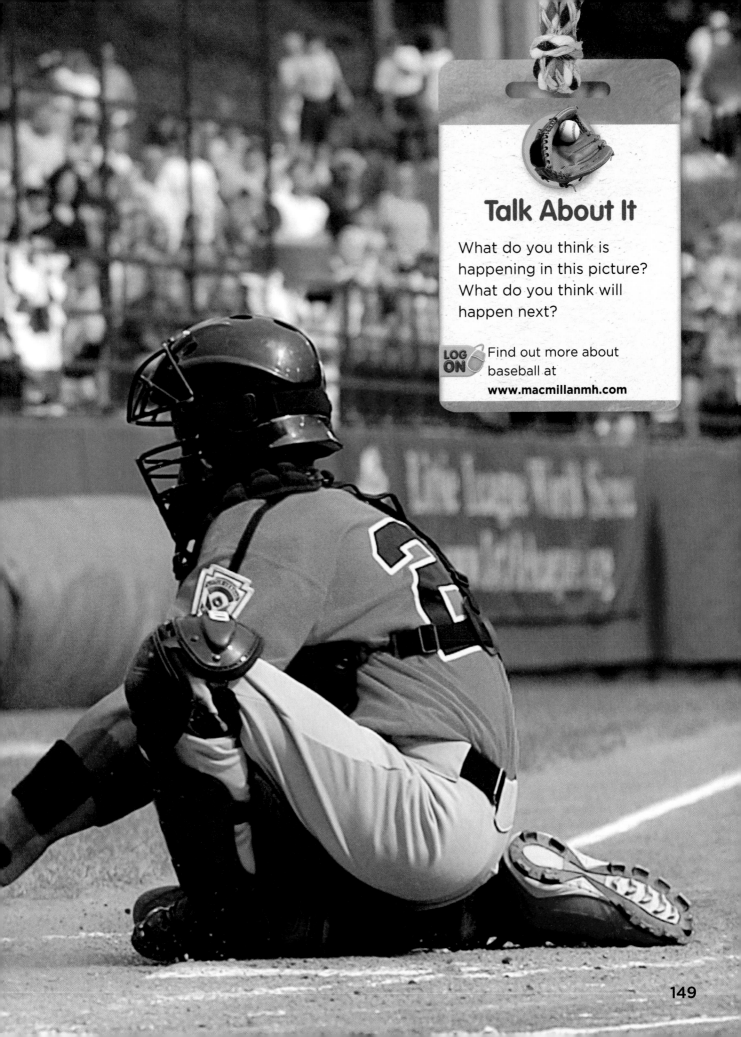

Talk About It

What do you think is happening in this picture? What do you think will happen next?

LOG ON Find out more about baseball at **www.macmillanmh.com**

Vocabulary

legendary   insult
muttered   fluke
gaped   flinched
snickering

Context Clues

Descriptions in the text can help you figure out what a word means. Figure out the meaning of *snickering*.

WOMEN PICK UP THE BALL

by Jenny Hull

Lucy's class was at Cooperstown—site of the **legendary** Baseball Hall of Fame. Lucy wasn't thrilled to be there. "Who cares about the All-American Girls Professional Baseball League?" Lucy **muttered** quietly to herself.

The League's Beginning

The guide explained that in 1942, most young men were being drafted to fight World War II. Some feared that major league baseball parks would close. But Philip Wrigley, the owner of the Chicago Cubs, decided to start a girls' league. Some may have **gaped** at the idea, but it soon caught on.

Lucy wondered what it was like for those girls. If people laughed in a mean way, did they notice the baseball fans **snickering**?

Woman baseball player makes a leaping catch.

150

The League Succeeds

Girls as young as 15 tried out for the league. The $45 to $85 a week salaries were a big draw. That might seem like an **insult** today, but back then it was a lot of money.

Players had to follow strict rules of behavior and take classes. They were taught how to dress, act, and take care of themselves.

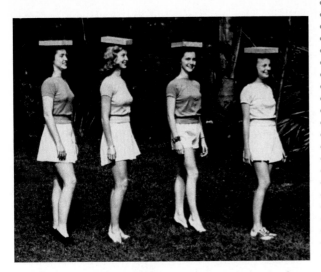

Walking with blocks on their heads for balance and posture

The success of the league was no **fluke**. During the war, many women worked in factories. This changed the image of what women could do.

The League Ends

After the war ended, interest lessened and the league fell apart. One reason was that many people got TVs in the early 1950s. They could watch major league games without buying a ticket or leaving the house!

Time to Leave

Lucy **flinched** when her teacher called the class together. She wasn't ready to leave. She wanted to learn more. But Lucy would have to wait until her next visit to learn more about this interesting time in baseball history.

Reread for **Comprehension**

Make Inferences and Analyze

Author's Purpose An author's purpose is the reason he or she wrote a selection. To learn an author's purpose, you usually must make inferences and analyze information.

An Author's Purpose Map can help you decide if the author's purpose is to inform, to persuade, or to entertain. Reread the selection to find clues to the author's purpose.

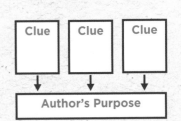

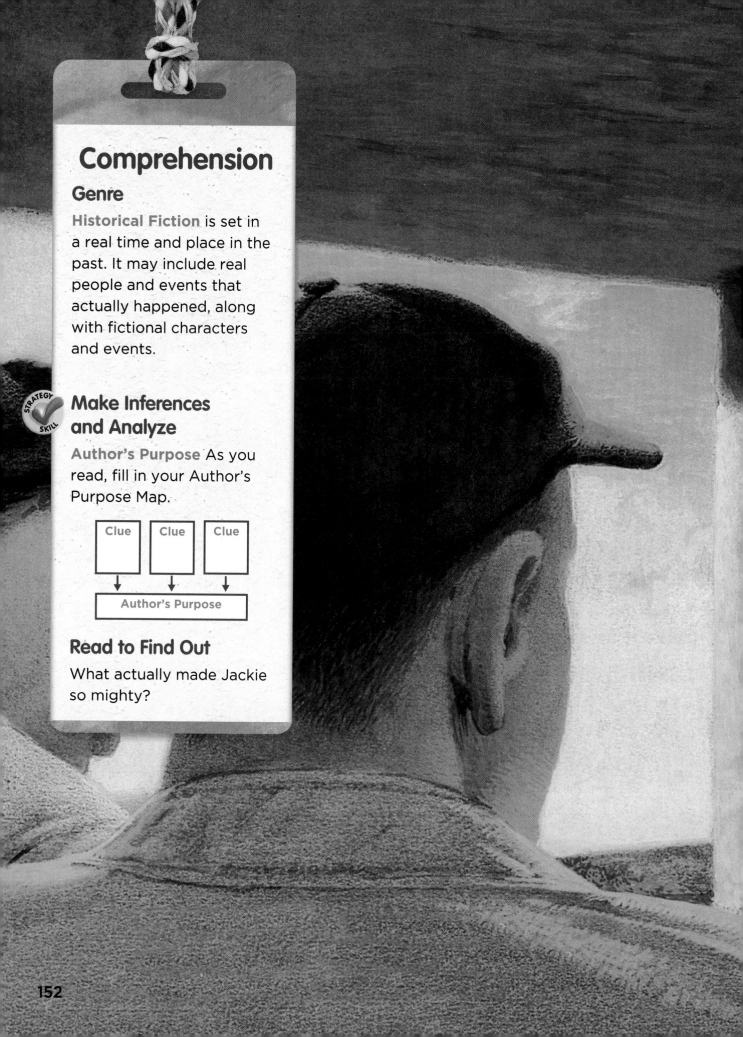

Comprehension

Genre

Historical Fiction is set in a real time and place in the past. It may include real people and events that actually happened, along with fictional characters and events.

Make Inferences and Analyze

Author's Purpose As you read, fill in your Author's Purpose Map.

Clue	Clue	Clue
↓	↓	↓

Author's Purpose

Read to Find Out

What actually made Jackie so mighty?

MIGHTY JACKIE
The Strike-out Queen

by Marissa Moss • Illustrated by C.F. Payne

Award Winning Illustrator

It was April 2, 1931, and something amazing was about to happen. In Chattanooga, Tennessee, two teams were about to play an exhibition game of baseball.

One was the New York Yankees, a **legendary** team with famous players—Babe Ruth, Lou Gehrig, and Tony Lazzeri.

153

The other was the Chattanooga Lookouts, a small team, a nothing team, except for the pitcher, Jackie Mitchell.

Jackie was young, only seventeen years old, but that's not what made people sit up and take notice. Jackie was a girl, and everyone knew that girls didn't play major-league baseball.

The *New York Daily News* sneered that she would swing "a mean lipstick" instead of a bat. A reporter wrote that you might as well have "a trained seal behind the plate" as have a woman standing there. But Jackie was no trained seal. She was a pitcher, a mighty good one. The question was, was she good enough to play against the New York Yankees?

As long as she could remember, Jackie had played ball with her father. She knew girls weren't supposed to. All the kids at school, all the boys in her neighborhood told her that. When one boy yelled at another one, "You throw like a girl!" it was an **insult**—everyone knew girls couldn't throw. Or that's what they thought.

Day after day, in the neighborhood sandlot, Jackie's father told her differently. He said she could throw balls, and she did. She ran bases, she swung the bat. By the time she was eight years old, Dazzy Vance, the star pitcher for the Brooklyn Dodgers, had taught her how to pitch. A real pitcher talking to a little girl was all Jackie needed to start dreaming of playing in the World Series. Her father saw her talent and so did Dazzy. He told her she could be good at whatever she wanted, as long as she worked at it. And Jackie worked at baseball. She worked hard.

She practiced pitching till it was too cold and dark to stay outside. She threw balls until her shoulder ached and her fingers were callused. She pitched until her eyes blurred over and she couldn't see where she was throwing. But it didn't matter, her arm knew.

Author's Purpose
Why do you think the author is providing so much information about Jackie's childhood?

And now she was finally going to have her chance to play on a *real* baseball team, to pitch to *real* players. The stands were packed. A crowd of four thousand had come to see the strange sight of a woman on the pitcher's mound.

She stood tall on the field and looked back at the crowd in the bleachers. They were waiting for her to make a mistake, and she knew it. They were waiting for her to prove that baseball was a man's game, not *her* game.

"It *is* my game," she **muttered** to herself and bit her lip. The Yankees were up, top of the first, and the batter was walking up to the plate. Jackie was ready for him, the ball tight in her left hand.

Except the batter was Babe Ruth—Babe Ruth, the "Home Run King," a big mountain of a man—and Babe didn't like the idea of a woman pitcher at all. He thought women were "too delicate" for baseball. "They'll never make good," he said. "It would kill them to play ball every day." He walked to the plate and tipped his cap at Jackie. But if she thought he was going to go easy on her, she could forget it! He gripped the bat and got ready to slam the ball out of the ballpark.

Jackie held that ball like it was part of her arm, and when she threw it, she knew exactly where it would go. Right over the plate, right where the Babe wasn't expecting it, right where he watched it speed by and *thwunk* into the catcher's mitt.

"STRRRRIKE ONE!"

Babe Ruth **gaped**—he couldn't believe it! The crowd roared. Jackie tried to block them out, to see only the ball, to feel only the ball. But Babe Ruth was facing her down now, determined not to let a girl make a fool out of him. She **flinched** right before the next pitch, and the umpire called a ball.

"Hmmmph," the Babe snorted.

"You can do it!" Jackie told herself. "Girls can throw—show them!"

But the next pitch was another ball.

Now the crowd was hooting and jeering. The Babe was **snickering** with them.

Jackie closed her eyes. She felt her fingers tingling around the ball, she felt its heft in her palm, she felt the force of her shoulder muscles as she wound up for the pitch. She remembered what her father had told her: "Go out there and pitch just like you pitch to anybody else."

"STRRRRIKE TWO!"

Now the Babe was mad.

This was serious. The Babe was striking out, and the pitcher was a girl!

Jackie wasn't mad, but she wasn't scared either. She was pitching, really pitching, and it felt like something was happening the way it had always been meant to. She knew the batter would expect the same pitch, close and high, even if the batter was Babe Ruth. So this time she threw the ball straight down the middle with all the speed she could put on it.

"STRRRRIKE THREE!"

Babe Ruth glared at the umpire and threw the bat down in disgust. He told reporters that that would be the last time he'd bat against a woman! The crowd was stunned. A girl had struck out the "Sultan of Swat"! It couldn't be! It was a mistake, a **fluke**! What would the papers say tomorrow? But wait, here came Lou Gehrig, the "Iron Horse," up to the plate. He'd show her. She couldn't strike him out too.

Lou Gehrig swung with a mighty grunt, but his bat hit nothing but air.

"STRRRRIKE ONE!"

He looked stunned, then dug in his heels and glared at Jackie.

"STRRRRIKE TWO!"

Jackie grinned. She was doing what she'd worked so hard and long to do, and nothing could stop her.

She pitched the ball the way she knew best, a lefty pitch with a low dip in it. No one could touch a ball like that when it was thrown right.

"STRRRRIKE THREE!"

The crowd, so ready to boo her before, rose with a roar, clapping and cheering like crazy. Back to back, Jackie had struck out two of baseball's best batters, Babe Ruth and Lou Gehrig. She'd proven herself and now the fans loved her for it.

But Jackie didn't hear them. She was too proud and too happy. She'd done what she'd always known she could do. She'd shown the world how a girl could throw—as hard and as fast and as far as she wanted.

 Author's Purpose
What was Marissa Moss's purpose in writing this story?

The Winning Team:
Marissa and C. F.

Marissa Moss likes to write about real women like Jackie who have done unusual things. She has also written about a female train engineer and the first woman to fly across the English Channel. Marissa hopes that when kids read her books they will discover things about the past that remind them of their own lives.

Other books by Marissa Moss and C. F. Payne

C. F. Payne has stepped up to the plate to illustrate other baseball stories. C. F. often does caricatures, a kind of art that exaggerates the way people look or act, making them seem larger than life.

LOG ON Find out more about Marissa Moss and C. F. Payne at **www.macmillanmh.com**

Author's Purpose

Marissa Moss based this story on the life of Jackie Mitchell. Does the fact that the main character was a real woman have an effect on the author's purpose? How do you know?

Comprehension Check

STRATEGY SKILL

Summarize

Summarize *Mighty Jackie: The Strike-Out Queen.* Be sure to describe the main events, when and where the story is set, and the main character. Use information from your Author's Purpose Map to help you summarize.

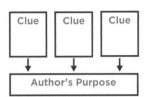

Clue	Clue	Clue

↓ ↓ ↓

Author's Purpose

Think and Compare

STRATEGY SKILL

1. The author stresses the fact that Ruth and Gehrig were **legendary** baseball players. What is the author's purpose in doing that? **Make Inferences and Analyze: Author's Purpose**

2. Read the third paragraph on page 154. What were people's attitudes toward female athletes? Include details. **Analyze**

3. Have you ever reached a goal that you or other people may have thought was impossible to achieve? Explain. **Apply**

4. Why was proving her pitching talent so important to Jackie? Explain your opinion. **Analyze**

5. Read "Women Pick Up the Ball" on pages 150–151. How did women's role in professional baseball change from the 1930s to the 1940s? What caused this change? Use details from both selections in your answer. **Reading/Writing Across Texts**

Social Studies

Genre

Almanacs have brief information, facts, and figures about many different subjects.

Text Feature

A **Table** presents a large amount of information, such as names and numbers, in a compact way.

Content Vocabulary

career accomplishments

orphanage disease

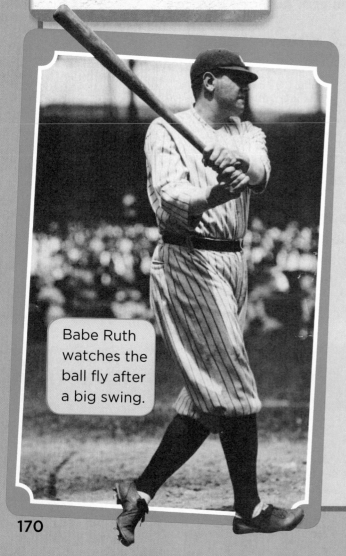

Babe Ruth watches the ball fly after a big swing.

Baseball Greats

by Liz Ray

Babe Ruth

Babe Ruth is one of the most famous baseball players of all time. People called him "The Sultan of Swat" and "The Home Run King" because he hit a record 714 home runs in his **career**. That record has since been broken, but Babe Ruth is still the only baseball player who has hit three home runs in a World Series game twice.

Babe Ruth learned to play baseball in the **orphanage** and reform school where he spent his childhood. He grew up to pitch and play outfield for the Boston Red Sox, and was an outfielder for the New York Yankees. Ruth was one of the first five players elected to the Baseball Hall of Fame.

Facts and Statistics

Full Name: George Herman Ruth, Jr.

Born:	February 5, 1895, in Baltimore, Maryland
Died:	August 16, 1948, in New York, New York
Teams:	Baltimore Orioles 1913 · Boston Red Sox 1914–1919 · New York Yankees 1920–1934 · Boston Braves 1935
Batted and Threw:	Left
Games Played:	2,503
Runs Scored:	2,174
Runs Batted In:	2,213
Home Runs:	714
Batting Average:	0.342

Elected to the Baseball Hall of Fame in 1936

The Top 10 Home Run Hitters

Reading a Table

Almanacs often have tables as well as charts, lists of facts, and other information.

Name	Home Runs	Rank
Hank Aaron	755	1
Babe Ruth	714	2
Barry Bonds	703	3
Willie Mays	660	4
Frank Robinson	586	5
Mark McGwire	583	6
Sammy Sosa	574	7
Harmon Killebrew	573	8
Reggie Jackson	563	9
Mike Schmidt	548	10

Current through 2004 season

Lou Gehrig

Lou Gehrig's batting **accomplishments** earned him a place in the Baseball Hall of Fame. Fans loved him because he was so dedicated.

Lou Gehrig played first base for the New York Yankees from 1923 until 1939. Gehrig set a record by playing in 2,130 straight games, even when he was sick or hurt. His record wasn't broken until 1995. He also set records for the number of runs batted in and grand slam home runs.

When Gehrig quit baseball because of a rare **disease**, thousands of fans came to honor him. He thanked them, saying he was "the luckiest man on the face of the earth."

Lou Gehrig gets in position to field a grounder.

Facts and Statistics

Full Name:	Henry Louis Gehrig
Born:	June 19, 1903, in New York, New York
Died:	June 2, 1941, in Riverdale, New York
Team:	New York Yankees, 1923–1939
Batted and Threw:	Left
Games Played:	2,164
Runs Scored:	1,888
Runs Batted In:	1,995
Batting Average:	0.340

Elected to the Baseball Hall of Fame in 1939

Connect and Compare

1. Look at the table of Top 10 Home Run Hitters from the almanac. Which baseball player hit more home runs than Babe Ruth? How many home runs did he hit? **Reading a Table**

2. What are some words you would use to describe Lou Gehrig? Explain your answer. **Evaluate**

3. How was Jackie Mitchell from *Mighty Jackie* like Babe Ruth and Lou Gehrig? How was she different from them? **Reading/Writing Across Texts**

 Social Studies Activity

Research another baseball player. Write a short paragraph about his or her life, and create a list or table of facts and statistics.

 Find more baseball facts at **www.macmillanmh.com**

701 S. Washington Street
Beeville, TX 78102
May 28, 2008

Dear Jorge,

I narrowed my topic to persuade my friend to come with me to baseball camp.

   I really hope you will come to baseball camp. It's going to be at Wilson Field in June. Professional ballplayers will teach us how to play every position, and we can improve our batting averages. You can work on pitching. So let's go! Call me!!!

I gave good reasons to support my topic.

Your pal,
David

Your Turn

Write a letter to convince a friend or family member to do something. Narrow the focus of your topic. Be sure to include good reasons. Use the Writer's Checklist to check your writing.

Writer's Checklist

☑ **Ideas and Content:** Did I narrow the focus of my **topic**? Did I present good reasons?

✓ **Organization:** Did I save my strongest reason for last?

✓ **Voice:** Does it sound as if I really care?

✓ **Word Choice:** Did I use strong words that will help convince my reader to do something?

✓ **Sentence Fluency:** Did my writing sound smooth when I read it out loud?

✓ **Conventions:** Did I capitalize proper nouns? Did I check my spelling?

New Places, New Faces

Talk About It

Where do you think this is? Would you like your face to appear on this flag? Explain why.

LOG ON Find out more about immigration at **www.macmillanmh.com**

Comprehension

Genre

Realistic Fiction is a made-up story that could have happened in real life.

Generate Questions

Make Inferences As you read, fill in your Inferences Word Web.

```
  Clue    Clue
      \  /
   Inference
      /  \
  Clue    Clue
```

Read to Find Out

What benefits does Amada get from keeping a diary?

180

My Diary
from Here to There

By Amada Irma Pérez

Illustrated by Maya Christina Gonzalez

Award
Winning
Selection

Dear Diary, I know I should be asleep already, but I just can't sleep. If I don't write this all down, I'll burst! Tonight after my brothers—Mario, Víctor, Héctor, Raúl, and Sergio—and I all climbed into bed, I **overheard** Mamá and Papá whispering. They were talking about leaving our little house in Juárez, Mexico, where we've lived our whole lives, and moving to Los Angeles in the United States. But why? How can I sleep knowing we might leave Mexico forever? I'll have to get to the bottom of this tomorrow.

Today at breakfast, Mamá explained everything. She said, "Papá lost his job. There's no work here, no jobs at all. We know moving will be hard, but we want the best for all of you. Try to understand." I thought the boys would be upset, but instead they got really excited about moving to the States.

"The big stores in El Paso sell all kinds of toys!"

"And they have escalators to ride!"

"And the air smells like popcorn, yum!"

Am I the only one who is scared of leaving our home, our beautiful country, and all the people we might never see again?

My best friend Michi and I walked to the park today. We passed Don Nacho's corner store and the women at the tortilla shop, their hands blurring like hummingbird wings as they worked the dough over the griddle.

At the park we braided each other's hair and promised never to forget each other. We each picked out a smooth, heart-shaped stone to remind us always of our friendship, of the little park, of Don Nacho and the tortilla shop. I've known Michi since we were little, and I don't think I'll ever find a friend like her in California.

"You're lucky your family will be together over there," Michi said. Her sisters and father work in the U.S. I can't imagine leaving anyone in our family behind.

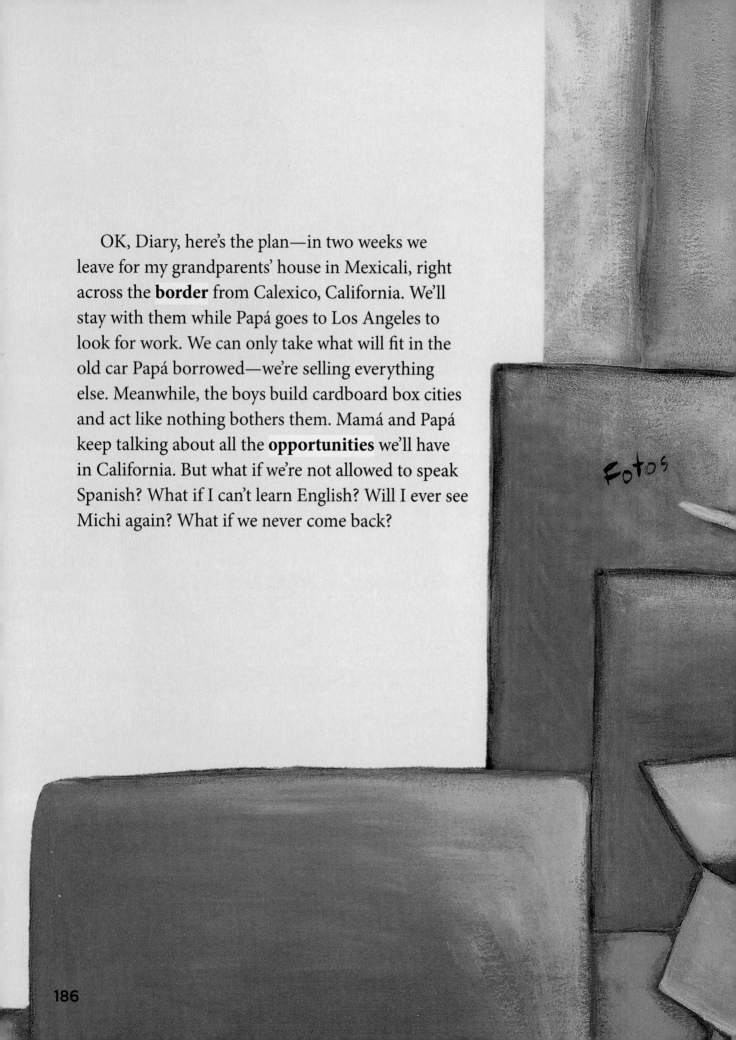

OK, Diary, here's the plan—in two weeks we leave for my grandparents' house in Mexicali, right across the **border** from Calexico, California. We'll stay with them while Papá goes to Los Angeles to look for work. We can only take what will fit in the old car Papá borrowed—we're selling everything else. Meanwhile, the boys build cardboard box cities and act like nothing bothers them. Mamá and Papá keep talking about all the **opportunities** we'll have in California. But what if we're not allowed to speak Spanish? What if I can't learn English? Will I ever see Michi again? What if we never come back?

Today while we were packing, Papá pulled me aside. He said, "Amada, *m'ija*, I can see how worried you've been. Don't be scared. Everything will be all right."

"But how do you know? What will happen to us?" I said.

He smiled. "*M'ija*, I was born in Arizona, in the States. When I was six—not a big kid like you—my Papá and Mamá moved our family back to Mexico. It was a big change, but we got through it. I know you can, too. You are stronger than you think." I hope he's right. I still need to pack my special rock (and you, Diary!). We leave tomorrow!

Make Inferences
Based on Amada's journal entries, what do you think she is feeling about the move? How can you tell?

Our trip was long and hard. At night the desert was so cold we had to huddle together to keep warm. We drove right along the border, across from New Mexico and Arizona. Mexico and the U.S. are two different countries, but they look exactly the same on both sides of the border, with giant saguaros pointing up at the pink-orange sky and enormous clouds. I made a wish on the first star I saw. Soon there were too many stars in the sky to count. Our little house in Juárez already seems so far away.

We arrived in Mexicali late at night and my grandparents Nana and Tata, and all our aunts, uncles and cousins (there must be fifty of them!) welcomed us with a feast of *tamales*, beans, *pan dulce*, and hot chocolate with cinnamon sticks. It's so good to see them all! Everyone gathered around us and told stories late into the night. We played so much that the boys fell asleep before the last blanket was rolled out onto the floor. But, Diary, I can't sleep. I keep thinking about Papá leaving tomorrow.

Papá left for Los Angeles this morning. Nana comforted Mamá, saying that Papá is a U.S. **citizen**, so he won't have a problem getting our "green cards" from the U.S. government. Papá told us that we each need a green card to live in the States, because we weren't born there.

I can't believe Papá's gone. Tío Tito keeps trying to make us laugh instead of cry. Tío Raúl let me wear his special *medalla*. And Tío Chato even pulled a silver coin out of my ear. The boys try to copy his tricks but coins just end up flying everywhere. They drive me nuts sometimes, but today it feels good to laugh.

We got a letter from Papá today! I'm pasting it into your pages, Diary.

My dear family,

*I have been picking grapes and strawberries in the fields of Delano, 140 miles north of Los Angeles, saving money and always thinking of you. It is hard, tiring work. There is a man here in the fields named César Chávez, who speaks of **unions**, **strikes**, and **boycotts**. These new words hold the hope of better conditions for us farmworkers.*

So far, getting your green cards has been difficult, for we are not the only family trying to start a new life here. Please be patient. It won't be long before we are all together again.

Hugs and kisses, Papá

Make Inferences
What does Papá have to take into consideration as he plans his family's move to California?

I miss Papá so much—it feels like he left ages ago. It's been tough to stay hopeful. So far we've had to live in three different houses with some of Mamá's sisters. First, the boys broke Tía Tuca's jewelry box and were so noisy she kicked us out. Then, at Nana's house, they kept trying on Tía Nena's high heels and purses. Even Nana herself got mad when they used her pots and pans to make "music." And they keep trying to read what I've written here, and to hide my special rock. Tía Lupe finally took us in, but where will we go if she decides she's had enough of us?

FINALLY! Papá sent our green cards—we're going to cross the border at last! He can't come for us but will meet us in Los Angeles.

The whole family is making a big farewell dinner for us tonight. Even after all the trouble the boys have caused, I think everyone is sad to see us go. Nana even gave me a new journal to write in for when I finish this one. She said, "Never forget who you are and where you are from. Keep your language and culture alive in your diary and in your heart."

We leave this weekend. I'm so excited I can hardly write!

My first time writing in the U.S.A.! We're in San Ysidro, California, waiting for the bus to Los Angeles. Crossing the border in Tijuana was crazy. Everyone was pushing and shoving. There were babies crying, and people fighting to be first in line. We held hands the whole way. When we finally got across, Mario had only one shoe on and his hat had fallen off. I counted everyone and I still had five brothers. Whew!

Papá is meeting us at the bus station in Los Angeles. It's been so long—I hope he recognizes us!

What a long ride! One woman and her children got kicked off the bus when the immigration patrol boarded to check everyone's papers. Mamá held Mario and our green cards close to her heart.

Papá was waiting at the station, just like he promised. We all jumped into his arms and laughed, and Mamá even cried a little. Papá's hugs felt so much better than when he left us in Mexicali!

I wrote to Michi today:

Dear Michi,

I have stories for you! Papá found a job in a factory, and we're living in a creaky old house in El Monte, east of Los Angeles. It's not at all like Juárez. Yesterday everything started shaking and a huge roar was all around us—airplanes, right overhead! Sometimes freight trains rumble past our house like little earthquakes.

Every day I hold my special rock and I think about home— Mexico—and our walks to the park. Papá says we might go back for the holidays in a year or two. Until then, write me!

Missing you,

Amada Irma

Well, Diary, I finally found a place where I can sit and think and write. It may not be the little park in Juárez, but it's pretty. You know, just because I'm far away from Juárez and Michi and my family in Mexicali, it doesn't mean they're not here with me. They're inside my little rock; they're here in your pages and in the language that I speak; and they're in my memories and my heart. Papá was right. I AM stronger than I think—in Mexico, in the States, anywhere.

P.S. I've almost filled this whole journal and can't wait to start my new one. Maybe someday I'll even write a book about our journey!

From the Diaries of . . .

Amada Irma Pérez used memories of her own journey from Mexico to the United States to write this story. Just like the girl in the story, she was both excited and scared about moving. Today Amada still writes in a journal. She believes that diaries help keep our memories alive.

Another book by Amada Irma Pérez

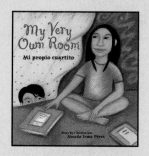

Maya Christina Gonzalez has always loved to draw. When she was a child, she could not find any pictures of Mexican American children like herself in books. Maya would draw her own picture on a blank page in each book she read. Today Maya's books show lots of people of color so readers can feel proud of who they are.

LOG ON Find out more about Amada Irma Pérez and Maya Christina Gonzalez at **www.macmillanmh.com**

Author's Purpose
Do you think using her own memories affected Amada Irma Pérez's purpose for writing? What clues tell you whether the story mainly informs, explains, or entertains?

200

Comprehension Check

Summarize

Summarize *My Diary from Here to There.* State the most important events, where the story takes place, and how the main character thinks and acts as the story progresses.

Think and Compare

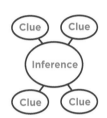

1. What clues from your Inferences Word Web help you figure out what Amada is like? **Generate Questions: Make Inferences**

2. Reread page 184. What conclusions can you draw about employment **opportunities** in Mexico at the time of this story? Use details from the story to support your answer. **Analyze**

3. Suppose Amada writes another story about her experiences in the U.S. What would you like her to write about? **Synthesize**

4. Compare Amada's feelings with those of her brothers. Are some of their feelings the same? Use details from the story. **Analyze**

5. Read "Mexico: My New Home" on pages 178–179. How is Paul's situation similar to Amada's? How is it different? Use details from both selections in your answer. **Reading/Writing Across Texts**

Immigrants in the Northeast

The Big Picture

Between 1890 and 1914, what had been a steady stream of **immigrants** turned into a flood. More than 12 million people arrived on America's shores. That's about as many people as live in the state of Pennsylvania today! Many of these immigrants came from countries in Europe such as Poland, Russia, Italy, and Greece. Others came from China, Japan, and Mexico.

◄ **Immigrants gaze at the Statue of Liberty, symbol of the United States' opportunities.**

Most immigrants traveled by boat and arrived on the Pacific or Atlantic coasts. They settled all across our country, but millions stayed where they had landed, such as in New York City. The arrival of these immigrants transformed the Northeast into an exciting **region** made up of many different **ethnic** groups.

The Ellis Island Museum

Pretend that your class is visiting the Ellis Island Immigration Museum. Before going inside, you learn from your guide that it usually took a ship about three weeks to cross the Atlantic Ocean. Few immigrants enjoyed the voyage because it was long and **overcrowded**. No wonder passengers rejoiced when they saw the city in the distance.

The immigrants' first stop, however, was Ellis Island, which stood a mile off the coast. Beginning in 1892, this island welcomed 17 million people to the United States. After closing in 1954, Ellis Island reopened as a museum in 1990.

Primary Sources (SKILL)

Oral History

This primary source is an oral history. Someone describes her experiences at a certain time and place. Primary sources are written in the witness's own words.

"When I was about 10 years old I said, 'I have to go to America.' Because my uncles were here already, and it kind of got me that I want to go to America, too.... I was dreaming about it. I was writing to my uncles, I said 'I wish one day I'll be in America.' I was dreaming to come to America.... And I was dreaming, and my dream came true. When I came here, I was in a different world. It was so peaceful. It was quiet. You were not afraid to go out in the middle of the night.... I'm free. I'm just like a bird. You can fly and land on any tree and you're free."

Helen Cohen, Poland

Arrived in 1920 • Age 20

Arriving at Ellis Island

"This was where the boats docked," your guide explains. "Sometimes 5,000 people a day walked through these doors. Guards tied numbered tags to their coats. Then they were shown to the Registry Room."

Immigrants had to wait in long lines to be examined by doctors to make sure they were healthy enough to work. Some people were sent back home, but most continued on to an immigration officer who asked them questions. After answering the questions, most immigrants walked down a hallway to a door that said: PUSH TO NEW YORK. Beyond that door were a ferry, New York City, the United States, and hope for a new life.

Ellis Island as it looked in 1905 ▼

"I never saw such a big building [Ellis Island]—the size of it. I think the size of it got me. According to the houses I left in my town, this was like a whole city in one, in one building. It was an enormous thing to see, I tell you. I almost felt smaller than I am to see that beautiful [building], it looked beautiful.

"My basket, my little basket, that's all I had with me. There was hardly any things. My mother gave me the <u>sorrah</u> [a kind of sandwich], and I had one change of clothes. That's what I brought from Europe."

Celia Adler

Russia

Arrived in 1914 • Age 12

Connect and Compare

1. Look back at the oral histories on this page and page 203. What kind of information do they give that you don't find in the rest of the textbook excerpt? **Reading Primary Sources**

2. After reading the primary source on this page, how do you think Celia Adler must have felt to have brought only a change of clothes with her from Europe? **Evaluate**

3. What does Amada in *My Diary from Here to There* have in common with those whose oral histories you read? How are their stories different? **Reading/Writing Across Texts**

 Social Studies Activity

Research what it is like for immigrants to come to a new country. Try to find a primary source. Present your research as if you were the immigrant.

 Find out more about Ellis Island at **www.macmillanmh.com**

Writer's Craft

Transitions

Good writing has a logical flow. Using **transition words** between paragraphs helps a writer connect the ideas in his or her writing.

I wrote this radio ad about a great local place to visit.

The word <u>while</u> connects ideas in my ad.

Sleep on a Tall Ship

by Kenji C.

Would you like to sleep on a tall ship? You and your class can stay overnight on the *Elissa* at the Texas Seaport Museum. Learn about sails, masts, and ropes. Help set a sail and watch over the harbor. Write in the ship's log. Experience what it is like to be a sailor!

While you are at the museum, visit the immigration exhibits to see photographs of people who came to the United States through the port of Galveston.

Your Turn

What kinds of radio ads make you pay close attention? Write a radio ad to advertise a great place to visit. It may be about a place you have visited or a place you would like to visit. Use precise nouns as well as transition words. Use the Writer's Checklist to check your writing.

Writer's Checklist

✓ **Ideas and Content:** Did I include details that will persuade the reader to visit this place?

✓ **Organization:** Does the order in which I present information build excitement for my listeners?

✓ **Voice:** Does the ad show excitement?

✓ **Word Choice:** Did I use **transition words** between paragraphs?

✓ **Sentence Fluency:** Did I use different kinds of sentences to make my ad interesting?

✓ **Conventions:** Did I use commas after items in a series? Did I check my spelling?

Talk About It

How would you describe the country and people of China?

LOG ON Find out more about the people of China at **www.macmillanmh.com**

中华人民共和国万岁

Focus on China

Vocabulary

temples
dynasties
heritage
preserve
overjoyed

WELCOME TO CHINA

China's Great Wall once kept out invaders. Many tourists visit it now.

China is an enormous country. It has the largest population of any nation. In fact, one out of every five people on Earth is Chinese! China has barren deserts, lush valleys, and towering mountains. It also has busy cities where ancient **temples** stand beside gleaming skyscrapers.

For thousands of years China was ruled by powerful families called **dynasties**. These families were like royalty, treated like kings and queens by the Chinese people. Just over fifty years ago, China became a communist country. Under communism, a harsh central government controls all business and property.

Records of Chinese history and culture go back more than 2,000 years. Today this rich **heritage** can be seen in China's food, art, and traditions. The Chinese invented paper, ink, the compass, and silk.

Today, China is one of the world's most powerful countries. However, it faces some of the toughest challenges of any nation. China's citizens live with many strict rules. The government fails to provide enough jobs for its growing population. As a result, millions of people are poor. China's rich heritage is a source of strength, but it must continue to change.

210

ANCIENT WARRIORS

Scientists in China are racing against the clock . . . and nature! They are working to **preserve** hundreds of ancient clay warriors, horses, and chariots. The statues were discovered in a tomb near the city of Beijing, the capital. They have been buried for 2,000 years. If the painted decorations on the statues are exposed to the air for too long, they will fade.

Villagers planting trees in the area were **overjoyed**

Some of the foot-tall soldiers are on horseback.

when they found these foot-tall soldiers. The discovery gives researchers new information about the Han dynasty. This powerful family ruled China from 206 B.C. to 220 A.D.

The clay soldiers are buried in order of their rank. David Sensabaugh is an Asian art expert at the Yale University Art Gallery. He thinks the figures are a display of power. How powerful is this army? It's too soon to tell, but it may be thousands strong!

China's Great Inventions

Many things were invented in China throughout history. Here are some Chinese inventions and what they were used for in the past. Which ones do we still use today?

Invention	When	Use
Silk	4,000 years ago	clothing for wealthy Chinese
Kite	3,000 years ago	to send messages during battles
Paper	2,000 years ago	to record events; make books
Paper money	1,000 years ago	for buying and selling
Gunpowder	1,000 years ago	to make firecrackers; send signals
Compass	1,000 years ago	to help sailors find their way

LOG ON Find out more about Ancient China at **www.macmillanmh.com**

Comprehension

Genre

A **Nonfiction Article** in a newspaper or magazine tells a true story.

Make Inferences and Analyze

Fact and Opinion

A fact is something that can be proved to be true. An opinion is a belief that does not have to be supported by facts.

This Buddha was nearly smuggled out of Cambodia by a tourist.

STEALING BEAUTY

To whom do a country's valuable objects from past civilizations belong?

During the day, the people of Xiaoli (ZHOW•LEE), China, sit outside their mud-brick shacks. Xiaoli is a poor village. Most people in town are farmers. It has become difficult to make a good living from farming, however. So the farmers wait for darkness to fall. That's when Xiaoli comes alive. At night, tomb raiders get to work.

Nearly 5,000 years of Chinese history lie underground in Xiaoli. Fields contain tombs of royalty of many **dynasties**. Valuable works of art are buried in the tombs. Stealing these treasures, called looting, can bring the poor farmers of Xiaoli lots of money.

Little Su, a doctor in Xiaoli, paid for medical school by selling stolen art. He was also able to buy a big-screen TV. Over the past few years, thieves have broken into at least 220,000 tombs in China, according to China's National Cultural Relics Bureau.

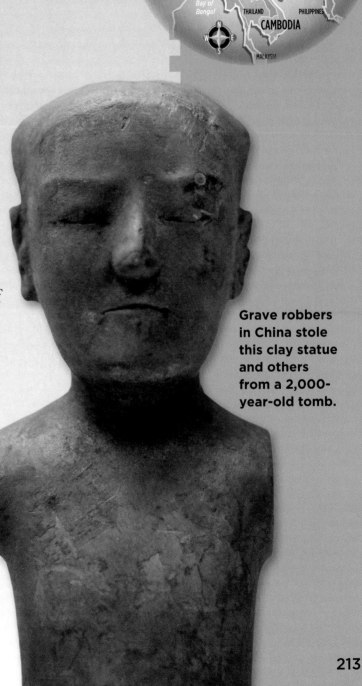

"If the looting continues at this pace, we'll soon have nothing left to remind us of our glorious past," says He Shuzhong (HUH SHOO•JOONG). He's the head of Cultural Heritage Watch in Beijing.

Worldwide Problem

Stealing ancient treasures has become a major problem for other countries, too. Police in India recently stopped criminals who had stolen hundreds of sculptures from **temples** and monuments. In Cambodia, thieves ripped out carved faces of gods from an eleventh-century site. Cambodian police recently found truckloads of ancient sculptures that were taken from archaeological sites.

What happens to these ancient treasures? Many art pieces are sent to collectors in the United States and Europe. Wealthy art collectors pay large amounts of money for ancient statues, sculptures, and vases.

Money can't replace ancient history, though. Many people believe that stealing artwork is like stealing a country's history and culture.

Grave robbers in China stole this clay statue and others from a 2,000-year-old tomb.

213

"Why are we as a people, as a government, as a country, allowing our **heritage** to slip through our fingers?" asks Michel Tranet. He has the job of protecting Cambodia's treasures and heritage.

Interpol is an international police agency, with more than 180 member countries. It maintains a database of stolen cultural properties. The database can help local and national law enforcement officials identify property that has been looted. It also helps individuals and museums avoid buying stolen objects.

Coming Home

Some people in these countries, however, see looting as a way to get rich. Ancient royal statues can sell for $80,000 each or more at auction! A few years ago, small ceramic statues were stolen from the 2,000-year-old tomb of Empress Dou in the city of Xi'an (SHEE•AHN), China. Six of the small statues ended up for sale at an auction in New York City. Luckily, the sale was stopped in time to **preserve** some of China's history.

This Buddha figurine sold for $295,000 at an auction in Hong Kong.

214

Today, those six small figures, valued at $6,000 to $8,000 each, have been returned to Xi'an. They are on display in a small museum. Li Ku, the vice director of the museum, believes the statues are an essential part of the city's history and culture. He is **overjoyed** at their return. "Looking at these figures, I feel like my family has come home at last," he says.

FINDERS KEEPERS?

Most thefts of ancient art are never reported. One reason is that it's hard to say who owns some of the treasures. Many Asian countries were once colonies of European countries. Settlers took thousands of pieces of art, monuments, and sculptures. Treasures stolen centuries ago by invaders are often thought to be the property of whoever has them now. But some people don't agree. They say the art should be returned to the country in which it originally belonged. What do you think?

Think and Compare

1. According to this article, what countries are having a problem with the theft of ancient treasures?

2. Why are farmers in China stealing treasures from tombs?

3. Many people say stealing ancient treasures is stealing a nation's past. Is this a fact or their opinion? Explain.

4. What theme do the articles "Ancient Warriors" and "Stealing Beauty" have in common?

215

So Far From Home

 Test Strategy

Author and Me
The answer is not directly stated. Think about what you have read to figure it out.

Early one morning, eight-year-old Sonam Dolker was shaken awake by her father. He whispered to her that she and her six-year-old sister would have to escape secretly from their home in Tibet to a new life in India. Sonam's parents had planned the trip for weeks. They hadn't told the girls because they were afraid the Chinese police would find out. That would mean prison for the entire family. "My escape was so secret that I couldn't even say goodbye to my best friend," says Sonam.

For the next two months, the girls and their guide stumbled over the snow and ice of the jagged Himalaya mountains. Their guide punished them when they slowed down. Finally, they arrived safely at Dharamsala (dar•am•SAHL•a), India.

Thousands of Tibetans, including more than a thousand children, have made the illegal crossing. They risk frostbite, arrest, and their very lives. They are willing to brave these dangers to escape the harsh rule in China, which governs Tibet. The ones who survive the trip will have more freedom in India. But they will face new troubles in their new home.

Tibetan children at their new school in India. The mountains they crossed are in the background.

Go On ▶

Directions: Answer the questions.

1. This article is MOSTLY about

    A   the beauty of Tibet.

    B   Tibet's form of government.

    C   leaving Tibet to find freedom.

    D   differences between China and India.

2. Tibetans living in India probably DO NOT feel

    A   angry that they were forced to leave Tibet.

    B   lonely for their families in Tibet.

    C   happy about the Chinese ruling Tibet.

    D   sad to have left their homeland and families.

3. Which statement would the author MOST LIKELY agree with?

    A   Many Tibetans are now returning to their country.

    B   Police in India send people back to Chinese prisons.

    C   Anything is better than living under Chinese rule.

    D   Life in India is calm and carefree.

4. What information in the article describes the difficult journey from Tibet to India?

5. Why do you think people are willing to make such dangerous trips? Use details from the article to support your answer.

> **Tip**
>
> You have to think about the entire passage to choose the best answer.

Write to a Prompt

In the selection "Stealing Beauty" you read about how a country's culture and heritage are lost when ancient objects are stolen. Write a one-page journal entry about a time when something that belonged to you was stolen or lost. Tell the story in sequence.

I organized my story and wrote a strong ending.

Dear Diary:

I'm so upset! At practice yesterday, I took off my necklace and put it next to my backpack. When practice was over, I grabbed my bag and headed home. But I forgot my necklace!

I didn't notice it was missing until this morning. So after school today, I rushed back to the field. My friends and I searched high and low, but no luck. Jake said a dog could have chewed it up. Lisa said someone might have swiped it.

I got the necklace at the beach last summer during our family vacation. Whenever I looked at it, I remembered the great time we had. I still have the memories, but it's not the same.

As always,
Me

Writing Prompt

Think about a time when you lost something that had a special meaning for you. What was lost? Where were you when you lost it? How did it make you feel? What did you do to try to find it? Write a one-page story about the experience. Be sure to organize your story according to how things happened.

Writer's Checklist

☑ Ask yourself, who is my audience?

☑ Think about your purpose for writing.

☑ Plan your story before you begin writing.

☑ Use details to support your story.

☑ Make sure your ideas are organized.

☑ Be sure your story has a beginning, a middle, and an ending.

☑ Use your best spelling, grammar, and punctuation.

Talk About It

What's happening here?
Would *you* put your hand
on that shiny ball? Why?

 Find out more about
electricity at
www.macmillanmh.com

Bright
Ideas

He Made the World Brighter

by Susan Dickson

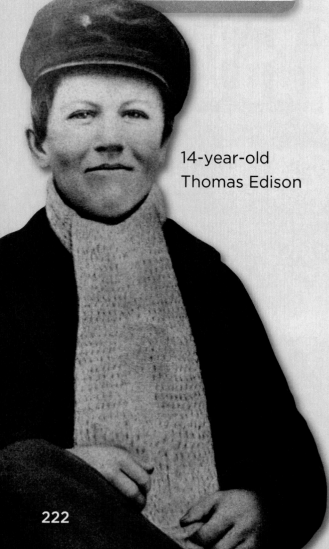

14-year-old Thomas Edison

Thomas Edison was a poor student. **Hilarious**? It *is* funny when you know how he turned out. Even if his grades didn't show it, the mother of this future inventor was **convinced** he was smart. After a few disappointing months in school, she decided to teach Thomas herself at home.

Thomas's Childhood

Thomas Alva Edison was born in 1847 in Ohio. Always curious and prone to **mischief**, Thomas read whenever he could.

Thomas's first job, at thirteen, was selling newspapers. Back then, that's when most boys started working. At sixteen he became a telegrapher. This gave Thomas **independence** and an opportunity to travel. Shortly after this, Edison decided to be an inventor.

222

The Young Inventor

Not everything Thomas invented was a success. In fact, his first invention, an electric vote recorder, failed. Edison thought it would **come in handy** for counting votes. No one else found it useful, but that didn't stop Edison.

Edison's Greatest Challenge

Back then, gas was the best lighting source, but burning it was dirty and unhealthy. Gas could also be very dangerous. The idea of using electricity for lighting had been around for over 50 years. But nobody had developed anything practical or safe.

Edison set out to solve this problem. He improved upon what others had learned about electricity. He tested thousands of ideas in a **whirlwind** of activity. Several men helped Edison with his experiments.

By 1880, they had burned a light bulb for more than 1,500 hours. They must have felt **dizzy** with excitement!

This was just the beginning. Edison's success led to the invention of an entire electric lighting system. **Nowadays**, many appliances and lights run on electricity. It is hard to imagine life without it. So, next time you turn on your computer, think of Thomas Edison—and say "Thanks."

Edison with lamps he created

Reread for **Comprehension**

Generate Questions

Problem and Solution Problems and solutions are important parts of most stories. Asking yourself questions as you read can help you understand problem and solution.

Reread the selection to find a problem and solution. Use a Problem and Solution Chart to help you.

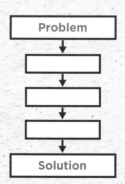

Comprehension

Genre

A **Biography** is a story about the life of a real person written by someone else.

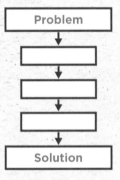

General Questions

Problem and Solution

As you read, fill in your Problem and Solution Chart.

```
┌─────────────────┐
│    Problem      │
└─────────────────┘
         ↓
┌─────────────────┐
│                 │
└─────────────────┘
         ↓
┌─────────────────┐
│                 │
└─────────────────┘
         ↓
┌─────────────────┐
│                 │
└─────────────────┘
         ↓
┌─────────────────┐
│    Solution     │
└─────────────────┘
```

Read to Find Out

What was it like to be Ben Franklin?

224

Award Winning
Author
and
Illustrator

How
BEN FRANKLIN
STOLE THE
LIGHTNING

ROSALYN SCHANZER

 t's true!

The great Benjamin Franklin really did steal lightning right out of the sky! And then he set out to tame the beast. It goes to figure, though, because he was a man who could do just about anything.

Why, Ben Franklin could swim faster, argue better, and write funnier stories than practically anyone in colonial America. He was a musician, a printer, a cartoonist, and a world traveler! What's more, he was a newspaper owner, a shopkeeper, a soldier, and a politician. He even helped to write the Declaration of **Independence** and the Constitution of the United States!

Ben was always coming up with newfangled ways to help folks out, too. He was the guy who started the first lending library in America. His post office was the first to deliver mail straight to people's houses.

He also wrote almanacs that gave **hilarious** advice about life and told people when to plant crops, whether there might be an eclipse, and when the tides would be high or low.

And he helped to start a hospital!

A free academy!

A fire department!

In colonial days, fire could break out at any time. And it was lightning that caused some of the worst fires. Whenever thunderstorms were brewing, they would ring the church bells for all they were worth, but it didn't do anybody a lick of good.

Of course, after Ben stole the lightning, there weren't nearly as many fires for firefighters to put out. "Now, why was that?" I hear you ask. "And how did he steal any lightning in the first place?" Well, it's a long story, but before we get to the answer, here's a hint. One of the things Benjamin Franklin liked to do best was to make inventions.

Problem and Solution
Name a common problem in colonial times.

Why, Ben was a born inventor. He loved to swim fast, but he wanted to go even faster. So one day when he was a mere lad of eleven, he got some wood and invented swim paddles for his hands and swim fins for his feet. Ben could go faster, all right, but the wood was pretty heavy, and his wrists got plumb worn out.

That's why his second invention was a better way to go fast. He lay on his back, held on to a kite string, and let his kite pull him lickety-split across a big pond. (You might want to remember later on that Ben always did like kites.)

Ben kept right on inventing better ways to do things for the rest of his life.

Take books, for example. Ben read so many books that some of them sat on shelves way up high near the ceiling. So he invented the library chair. If he pulled up the seat, out popped some stairs to help him reach any books on high shelves. And in case climbing stairs made him **dizzy**, he invented a long wooden arm that could grab his books, too.

He also invented an odometer that told how far he had ridden to deliver the mail. And the first clock with a second hand. And he even thought up daylight saving time. Then he invented bifocals so older folks could see up close and far away without changing glasses.

Everybody and his brother and sister just had to find better ways to heat their houses in wintertime. So Ben came up with a Franklin stove that could warm up cold rooms faster and use a lot less wood than old-fashioned stoves and fireplaces.

People all over Europe and America loved Ben's glass armonica. This instrument could spin wet glass bowls to make music that sounded like it came straight from heaven. Mozart and Beethoven wrote music for it, and it was even played at a royal Italian wedding.

But as popular as warmer stoves and glass armonicas were, they aren't anywhere near as celebrated **nowadays** as the invention Ben made after he stole the lightning.

Another hint about Ben's most famous invention is that it helped make life easier for everyone. His scientific ideas were helpful, too, and were often way ahead of their time. For example, he had a lot of ideas about health. He said that exercise and weight lifting help keep folks fit, but they have to work hard enough to sweat if they want to do any good.

He wrote that breathing fresh air and drinking lots of water are good for you. He was the guy who said "an apple a day keeps the doctor away."

And before anyone ever heard of vitamin C, he wrote that oranges, limes, and grapefruit give people healthy gums and skin. Sailors soon got wind of this idea. They began eating so many limes to stop getting sick from scurvy at sea that they became known as limeys.

Didn't the man ever stop to rest? Even when he was outside, Ben kept right on experimenting.

For instance, he often sailed to England and France to do business for America. As he crossed the Atlantic Ocean, he charted the Gulf Stream by taking its temperature. Once sailors knew the route of this fast, warm "river" in the cold ocean, they could travel between America and Europe in a shorter time than ever before.

He was probably the first person to write weather forecasts, too. Once he chased a roaring **whirlwind** by riding over the hills and forests of Maryland just to find out how it worked.

Ben had an old scientific trick that he liked to show people every chance he got. He used to store some oil inside a bamboo walking stick, and whenever he poured a few drops onto angry waves in a pond or lake, the water became smooth as glass!

Meanwhile, over in Europe, people called "electricians" had started doing some tricks of their own. One trick was to raise a boy up near the ceiling with a bunch of silk cords, rub his feet with a glass "electric tube," and make sparks shoot out of his hands and face.

Another mean trick made the king of France laugh so hard he could hardly stop. His court electrician had run an electric charge through 180 soldiers of the guard, and they jerked to attention faster than they ever had in their entire lives.

But although people were doing lots of tricks with electricity, nobody had a clue about why or how it worked. So Benjamin Franklin decided to find out. He asked a British friend to send him an electric tube so that he could do some experiments.

In one experiment, he made a cork "electric spider" with thread for legs. It kept leaping back and forth between a wire and an electric tube just like it was alive.

Another time he asked a lady and gentleman to stand on some wax. One held an electric tube, the other held a wire, and when they tried to kiss, they got shocked by all the sparks shooting between their lips.

Ben even figured out how to light up a picture of a king in a golden frame. Anyone trying to remove the king's gold paper crown was in for a shock!

Doing all these tricks gave Ben his idea for stealing
lightning out of the sky. He believed that lightning was
nothing more nor less than pure electricity. Now he set
out to prove it.

First he made a silk kite with a wire on top to attract
some lightning. Next he added a kite string, tied a key
to the bottom, and knotted a silk ribbon below the key.
Ben and his son William stood out of the rain inside the
doorway of a shed on the side of a field. To keep from
getting shocked, Ben held on to the dry silk ribbon.
Then he flew his kite straight up toward a big rain cloud.

For the longest time, nothing happened.

Just as Ben and William were about to give up, the hair on that wet kite string began to rise up and stand at attention. Ben put his knuckle near the key, and YIKES!!!! Out jumped a bright spark of genuine electricity!

Real lightning had traveled all the way down that kite string! Ben had stolen electric fire out of the heavens and proven that he was right.

(Of course, now we know that if the storm had been any stronger, the great inventor would have been toast.)

Finally! Here's the part of the story where Ben's practice from thinking up all those inventions **came in so handy**. Way back then, you remember, lightning was always setting fire to ships, houses, and church spires. Even the best fire departments couldn't keep entire towns from going up in smoke. So Ben decided to make his most famous invention of all—the lightning rod!

The whole idea was to pull lightning safely out of the
sky before it could do any **mischief**. Ben showed people
how to put a pointed iron rod on the tip-top of a roof or
ship's mast and connect it to a wire leading all the way
down under the ground or into water. Now the lightning
could follow a safe path without burning up a thing.

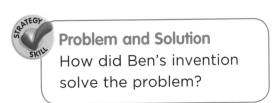

Problem and Solution
How did Ben's invention
solve the problem?

239

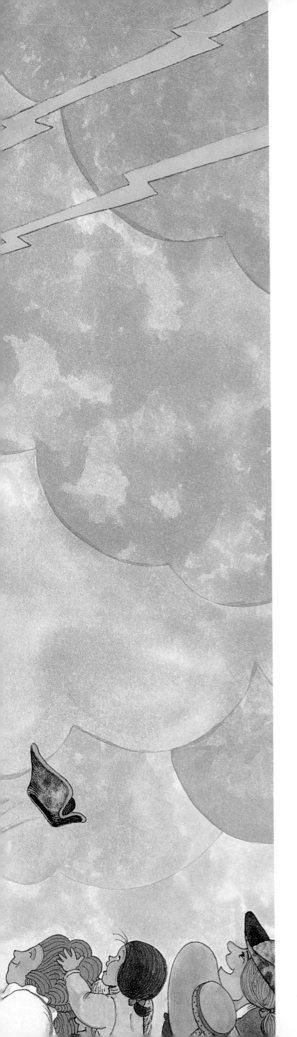

This simple but brilliant invention worked beautifully. It saved more lives than anyone can count and made Ben Franklin a great hero.

Scientists from around the world lined up to give Ben medals and awards. But during his long life, he became much more than the master of lightning. Why, when America fought against Great Britain for the right to become a free nation, Ben **convinced** France to come help win the war, and when it was over, he helped convince Great Britain to sign the peace. He had helped in so many ways that the people of France honored him with a beautiful medallion. It says "He snatched the lightning from heaven and the scepter from tyrants."

And he did.

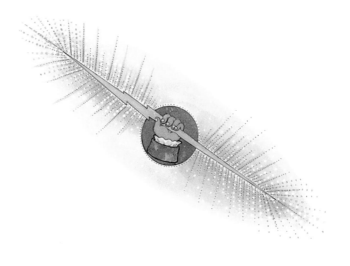

MEET THE INVENTOR

*R*OSALYN *S*CHANZER spent a lot of time in Philadelphia to write this piece. She visited the places where Ben Franklin lived and worked to make sure that her words and pictures would be accurate. Rosalyn probably would have gotten along really well with Ben. She is a great swimmer, just like he was. Once she even swam past sharks on a trip to Belize! Rosalyn also shares Ben's curiosity about the world. She's explored a jungle, visited an ancient city, and sailed a boat more than 800 miles.

Other books by Rosalyn Schanzer

 Find out more about Rosalyn Schanzer at **www.macmillanmh.com**

Author's Purpose

What was the author's purpose for writing *How Ben Franklin Stole the Lightning*? What clues helped you decide if Rosalyn Schanzer was trying to inform, explain, or persuade?

# Comprehension Check

Summarize

Summarize *How Ben Franklin Stole the Lightning.* Include some of the problems Ben Franklin saw and how he solved them. Use your Problem and Solution Chart to help you.

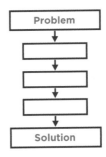

Problem
↓
↓
↓
↓
Solution

Think and Compare

1. What was Ben Franklin's most famous invention, and what problem did it solve? Use story details to support your answer. **Generate Questions: Problem and Solution**

2. Reread pages 235–236. Why was Ben Franklin so **convinced** that lightning was a form of electricity? **Analyze**

3. If you could improve on any of the inventions mentioned in the story, what new invention would you create? **Apply**

4. Based on what you know, do you think Ben Franklin was ever bored? Give reasons for your opinion. **Evaluate**

5. Read "He Made the World Brighter" on pages 222–223. How was Thomas Alva Edison like Ben Franklin? Use details from both selections in your answer. **Reading/Writing Across Texts**

Poetry

A **Concrete Poem** has words arranged in the shape of the thing it describes.

 ### Literary Elements

Figurative Language uses words to evoke mental images.

Alliteration is the repetition of the same consonant sound in a series of words.

Light Bulb

Thomas Edison didn't hesitate to let ideas incubate, and try again, if they weren't right. One day to his intense delight, he **squeezed** his thoughts into a bulb and then turned on the light light light !!!

Edison didn't really squeeze his thoughts into a bulb. This figurative language helps the reader picture how hard Edison was thinking.

— *Joan Bransfield Graham*

Lightning Bolt

NEWS FLASH!

BEN FRANKLIN USES KITE & KEY TO UNLOCK ELECTRICITY!

This use of "kite" and "key" is an example of alliteration.

— *Joan Bransfield Graham*

Connect and Compare

1. Which words in "Lightning Bolt" show figurative language? **Figurative Language**

2. What do the shapes of these poems have to do with their topics? **Analyze**

3. How is the information presented in "Lightning Bolt" similar to the information in *How Ben Franklin Stole the Lightning*? In what ways is it different? **Reading/Writing Across Texts**

LOG ON Find out more about concrete poems at **www.macmillanmh.com**

Writer's Craft

A Strong Opening

Good writers start with a **strong opening**. They may lead with an interesting question, quotation, or description.

I started with a strong opening question.

I wanted to recommend a book I liked, so I answered the question.

Kids' Bright Ideas

by Katie G.

Do you dream of being a great inventor? Then read <u>Invented by Kids</u> by Cynthia Mills. You'll find out about some great ideas by kids. The Auto-Off Candle goes out after a set time. A natural poison wards off mosquitoes while being safe to use in an animal's drinking water.

If you like experimenting with new ideas, I recommend this book. These inventors inspired me. You'll be inspired, too!

Your Turn

Think about a book you have read recently. Would you recommend it to others? Write a book review. Briefly summarize the book. Tell why a reader will or won't enjoy it. Begin with a strong opening. Use the Writer's Checklist to check your writing.

Writer's Checklist

☑ **Ideas and Content:** Will my **strong opening** grab my readers' attention?

✓ **Organization:** Did I summarize the book and include details about it?

✓ **Voice:** Did I make my feelings clear?

✓ **Word Choice:** Did I choose precise words?

✓ **Sentence Fluency:** Did I avoid choppy writing by including both short and long sentences?

✓ **Conventions:** Did I capitalize the main words in the book title? Did I underline the title? Did I check my spelling?

Talk About It

How does this snake make you feel? Explain why you feel that way.

LOG ON Find out more about snakes at **www.macmillanmh.com**

Snakes

NAME THAT REPTILE

by Catherine Lutz

Narrator: Mark and Jean have been studying together **weekdays** after school for a big test on Friday. Jean takes a card from a **cardboard** box. The card has the name of a reptile on it. Now Mark will ask questions and try to name the reptile. Can you guess the answer before Mark?

Mark: Is it furry?

Jean: No. Remember, reptiles don't have fur.

Mark: That's right. Where does it live?

Jean: Mostly in the southwestern United States.

Mark: What does it eat?

Jean: It eats small birds, rabbits, mice, and squirrels.

Mark: Is it a crocodile?

Jean: No. Crocodiles live near streams, and this reptile lives where it's dry.

Mark: How big is it?

Jean: Some can be 7 feet long. Others are only 2 feet long.

Mark: It's probably not a turtle or a lizard. Is it a snake?

Jean: Yes!

Is it a crocodile?

Mark: Remember when my pet snake got loose and **slithered** across my mother's foot? I had to return it to the pet store.

Jean: What did the store say?

Mark: I think they were **genuine** when they offered to speak with my mom. I knew that wouldn't help, though.

Jean: Did you **apologize** to your mom and say you were sorry?

Mark: Of course, but she didn't change her mind.

Jean: Okay, back to studying.

Mark: Does the snake crush its prey?

Jean: No.

Mark: So it's not a python. Is it **harmless**?

Jean: No. It's dangerous. Its bite can be fatal. If you get bitten, you'd need an **ambulance**!

Mark: Yikes. Does it give a warning before it attacks?

Jean: Its tail shakes and makes a noise. Each time the snake sheds, its tail gets a new segment in it.

Mark: I've got it! It's a rattlesnake!

Narrator: Did you guess the reptile before Mark did?

It's a rattlesnake!

Reread for **Comprehension**

Generate Questions

Make Inferences Generating questions as you read can help you make inferences. For example, ask yourself, "Why did the character just say that?" or "What are some clues to what might happen next?"

Reread the selection and make inferences. Write the clues in the Inferences Word Web.

Clue   Clue
Inference
Clue   Clue

251

Comprehension

Genre

Humorous Fiction is a made-up story written to make the reader laugh.

Generate Questions

Make Inferences As you read, fill in your Inferences Word Web.

Read to Find Out

What do you learn when you read between the lines?

Dear Mr. Winston

by Ken Roberts
Illustrated by Nicole E. Wong

Dear Mr. Winston,

My parents said that I have to write and **apologize**. Dad says he is going to read this letter before it's sent and that I'd better make sure my apology sounds truly **genuine**. So, I am truly, genuinely sorry for bringing that snake into the library yesterday.

My parents say that what I did was wrong, even though the **cardboard** box was shut, most of the time, and there was no way that snake could have escaped if you hadn't opened the box and dropped it on the floor.

My parents say it's my fault for having brought that snake into the library and I truly, genuinely apologize but I still don't know how I was supposed to find out what kind of snake I had inside that box without bringing the snake right into the library so I could look at snake pictures and then look at the snake and try to find a picture that matched the snake.

I told my parents something that I didn't get a chance to remind you about before the **ambulance** took you away. I did come into the library without the snake, first. I left the box outside, hidden under a bush and tried to borrow a thick green book with lots of snake pictures. You told me that the big green book was a reference book which meant that it had to stay inside the library and I couldn't take it out, even for ten minutes.

My parents say I still shouldn't have brought that snake into the library and that I have to be truly, genuinely sorry if I ever hope to watch Galactic Patrol on television again. My parents picked Galactic Patrol because it's my favorite show, although I'm not sure what not watching a television program has to do with bringing a snake into the library.

The people at the library say you hate snakes so much that you won't even touch a book with a picture of snakes on the cover and that is why you won't be back at the library for a few more weeks. If you want, you could watch Galactic Patrol. It's on at 4:00 P.M. **weekdays**, on channel 7. There are no snakes on the show because it takes place in space.

Did the flowers arrive? Dad picked them out but I have to pay for them with my allowance for the next two months. The flowers are proof that I am truly, genuinely sorry for having brought that snake into the library. I hope the people who work at the library find that snake soon! Did they look under all the chairs?

That snake isn't dangerous. It is a local snake, and there are no poisonous snakes in Manitoba. The people at the library say you know that too because that was one of the reasons you decided to move here. I bought that snake from a friend. I paid one month's allowance for it, which means that snake has cost me a total of three months' allowance and I only owned it for one hour!

Mom says I don't have to tell who sold me that snake so I won't tell you either because Dad says he is going to read this letter. Besides, I don't want you to be mad at anyone else when I am the one who brought that snake into the library yesterday. I am truly, genuinely sorry.

Make Inferences

Do you think the girl is truly, genuinely sorry for bringing the snake into the library? Why or why not?

257

I want you to know that I didn't plan to show you that snake. I didn't mean to scare you at all. I knew where the big green snake book was kept. I put the box on a table close to the book and tried to find the right picture. I looked at a picture, then at the snake, at another picture, and then the snake. I did that five times and can tell you that the snake inside the library is not a python, a rattlesnake, an anaconda, an asp, or a cobra.

Anyway, I was surprised when you wanted to see what was inside the box because I didn't ask for any help and there were plenty of people in the library who did need help.

Dad says that the fact that I said, "Nothing," instead of "A snake," is proof that I knew I was doing something wrong when I brought that snake into the library. I am truly, genuinely sorry even though my friend Jake Lambert promised me that the snake I bought from him is perfectly **harmless**.

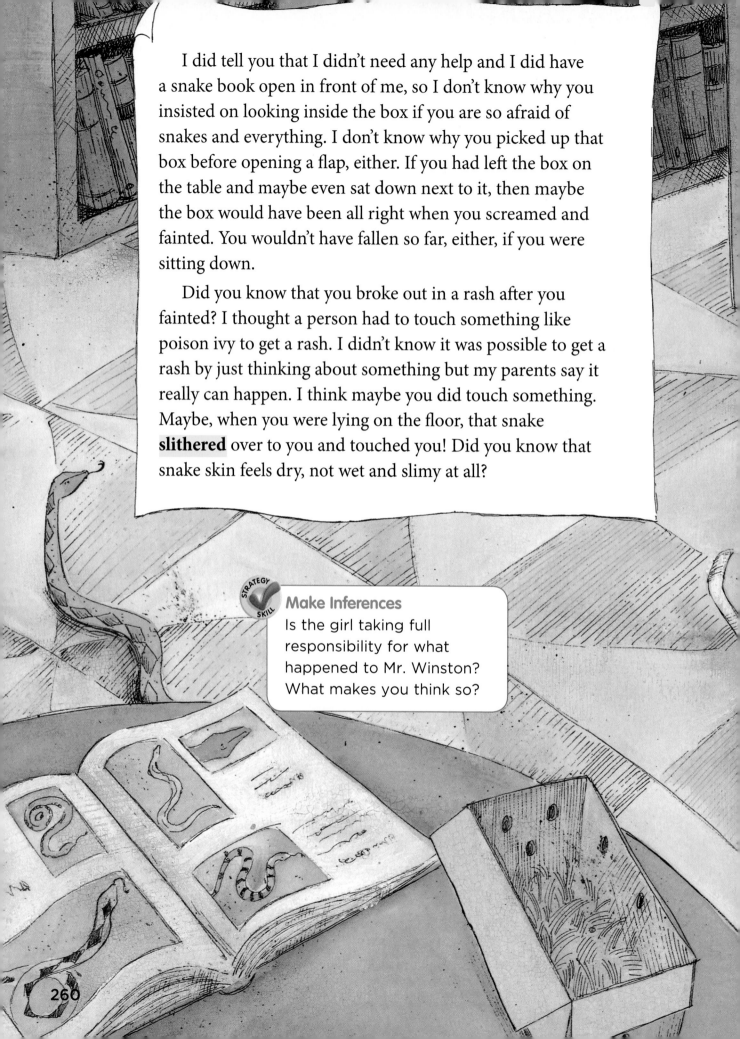

I did tell you that I didn't need any help and I did have a snake book open in front of me, so I don't know why you insisted on looking inside the box if you are so afraid of snakes and everything. I don't know why you picked up that box before opening a flap, either. If you had left the box on the table and maybe even sat down next to it, then maybe the box would have been all right when you screamed and fainted. You wouldn't have fallen so far, either, if you were sitting down.

Did you know that you broke out in a rash after you fainted? I thought a person had to touch something like poison ivy to get a rash. I didn't know it was possible to get a rash by just thinking about something but my parents say it really can happen. I think maybe you did touch something. Maybe, when you were lying on the floor, that snake **slithered** over to you and touched you! Did you know that snake skin feels dry, not wet and slimy at all?

Make Inferences
Is the girl taking full responsibility for what happened to Mr. Winston? What makes you think so?

260

I just thought of something. Maybe everyone's looking in the library for that snake but it's not in the library. Maybe it crawled into one of your pockets or up your sleeve and rode with you to the hospital! Wouldn't that be funny? Why don't you get one of the nurses to check? If it's not in your clothes, it might have crawled out and might be hiding inside the hospital someplace. I think people should be looking there, too.

I am sure you will be talking to the people in the library, to make sure they find that snake before you go back to work. I hope they do find it, even though my parents say that I can't keep it. If that snake is found, could you ask the people at the library to give me a call? I would be interested in knowing that it is all right. And if they do find that snake and do decide to give me a call, could you ask them if they could compare that snake with the snake pictures in that big green reference book before they call me? I would still like to know what kind of snake I owned for an hour.

I am truly, genuinely sorry.
Your friend,

Cara

Identify the
Author and Illustrator

Ken Roberts is actually a librarian. He often writes funny stories with unusual characters, like the girl in this piece. Ken has many talents. He is a storyteller, puppeteer, juggler, and magician. He was once a champion runner, too.

Nicole E. Wong has been interested in art all her life and even went to college to study it. She has been very fortunate to have turned her passion and training into her career in illustration. Nicole's artwork has appeared in several books, including Jan Wahl's *Candy Shop*, and various magazines. Nicole lives in Massachusetts with her husband, Dan, and their dog, Sable.

Another book illustrated by Nicole E. Wong

LOG ON Find out more about Ken Roberts and Nicole E. Wong at **www.macmillanmh.com**

Author's Purpose

Why did Ken Roberts write *Dear Mr. Winston*? Did the fact that he is a librarian affect his purpose? What clues helped you decide if he wrote to entertain or inform?

Comprehension Check

Summarize

Summarize *Dear Mr. Winston*. Include the main characters and tell the most important events in the correct order.

Think and Compare

1. Was Cara's apology to Mr. Winston truly **genuine**? Use your Inferences Word Web to help you decide. Tell what clues helped you make this inference. **Generate Questions: Make Inferences**

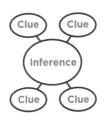

2. Reread the second paragraph of the story. Who does Cara seem to say was responsible for the snake's escape? Use story details in your answer. **Analyze**

3. How would you have avoided Cara's mistake? **Synthesize**

4. Do you think that Mr. Winston will ever be able to see the humor in this event? Explain your answer. **Evaluate**

5. Read "Name That Reptile" on pages 250–251. How is the problem that Mark is trying to solve similar to Cara's problem? How is it different? Use details from both selections in your answer. **Reading/Writing Across Texts**

Science

Genre

Electronic Encyclopedias include articles, diagrams, and photographs on many topics.

Text Feature

Toolbars help you find more information or move to a different area in an electronic encyclopedia.

Content Vocabulary

reptiles
camouflage
hibernate
digested

▼　article outline

Snakes

Physical Characteristics

Snakes are **reptiles**. They have flexible skeletons and no legs. Their bodies are covered with scales. Clear scales even cover their eyes. Most snakes are colored to **camouflage** them. For example, the emerald tree boa is green. This helps it hide among tree leaves. Other snakes, like coral snakes, are brightly colored to warn enemies that they are poisonous. Snakes range greatly in size. The dwarf blind snake is 10 cm (around 4 in.) long. The anaconda and reticulated python can be as long as 10 m (about 33 ft.).

Behavior

Like all reptiles, snakes are cold-blooded. They cannot make their own body heat. Snakes need the sun or warm surroundings to keep them warm. In cool weather, many snakes gather underground or in other sheltered places. There, they **hibernate**, meaning they stay at rest during the winter.

Timber rattlesnakes (*crotalus horridus*), northeastern United States

Printers

Features Tools Options Favorites Help

Contents Page Multimedia Related Articles

Anaconda

Coral Snake

Emerald Tree Boa

Skeleton

Using a Toolbar

SKILL ✓ Click on the Related Articles menu and select the subject about which you want to learn more.

Coral Snake a kind of poisonous snake found in North and South America. There are about 30 species. Coral snakes all have bright bands of color on their bodies and are two to three feet in length. They hunt lizards and other snakes.

Anaconda a member of the boa family living in swamps and rivers in South America. The anaconda, like other boas, wraps itself around its prey to suffocate it. It is one of the longest and thickest snakes and bears live young.

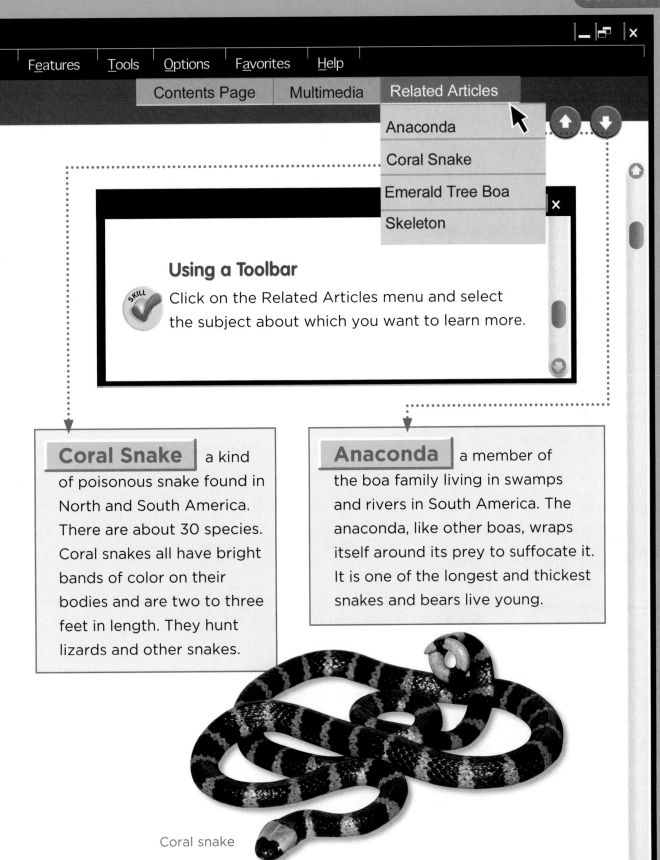

Coral snake

Hunting and Eating

Egg-Eater Snake
(*Dasyreptis scabra*),
Savannah, South Africa

Snakes are meat eaters but do not chew their prey. They swallow animals whole. Snakes can stretch their jaws far apart. This lets them eat animals that are bigger than their own heads.

Constrictors, such as boa constrictors, wrap themselves around their prey. These snakes suffocate their prey and then swallow it. Some snakes are venomous and kill their prey with poison. Venomous snakes, such as rattlesnakes, inject the poison through their fangs. Some poisons kill the animal. Others break down the animal's flesh so that it is partly **digested** by the time the snake eats it.

Raising Young

Cobra hatching

Most female snakes lay eggs that have soft leathery shells. Some females stay close to guard the eggs. Others, such as pythons, coil around the eggs to keep them warm. Some snakes give birth to live babies. Garter snakes can have more than 40 baby snakes at once. Snakes do not usually take care of their young.

Boa Constrictor

Garter Snake

Python

Rattlesnake

Garter Snake a common and harmless type of snake in North America. They are fairly small (about two feet long) and usually have dark colors, with stripes running along their bodies. They live in moist areas and feed on toads, frogs, earthworms, and similar animals.

Connect and Compare

1. Look at the Related Articles menu on this page. What would you click on to find out how constrictors kill their prey? **Using a Toolbar**

2. Constrictors often hunt animals that have sharp teeth, claws, or hooves. Why do you think they need to kill their prey before swallowing it? **Analyze**

3. Think about this article and *Dear Mr. Winston*. Which of the snakes you have read about would not make a good pet for Cara? Explain your answer. **Reading/Writing Across Texts**

Science Activity

Research a snake. If possible, use an electronic encyclopedia. Write a paragraph or two about the snake, and draw a picture of it.

 Find out about kinds of snakes at **www.macmillanmh.com**

Test Strategy

Think and Search
The answer is in more than one place. Keep reading to find the answer.

Protect
Our Valuable Oceans

by Deepak Mallavarpu

We live in a watery world. It has five oceans: the Pacific, the Atlantic, the Indian, the Arctic, and the Antarctic. Water makes up more than 70% of the surface of our planet. No wonder astronauts see Earth as a beautiful blue world!

Oceans do more for us than just make the world look pretty from space. They give us fish, seaweed, and shellfish. Tons of food are taken from the oceans each year. Some of our salt, fertilizers, and minerals come from the sea. A great deal of the world's oil is drilled offshore. That means it comes from beneath the ocean floor. We get some of our natural gas this way too.

Oceans provide us with transportation. Freight and fuel travel by boat. Oceans are also used for recreation. They allow us to explore, swim, snorkel, study wildlife, and ride waves.

The oceans help make our weather. They play a huge role in spreading the sun's warmth all over our planet. Oceans fuel storm systems, too. And storms bring fresh water to land.

Even though our oceans do so much for us, we have not been taking care of them. They are getting more and more polluted. Some kinds of fish are dying out. Coral reefs are being damaged by water that is too warm.

Go On ▶

Pollution may be the biggest problem. Some pollution results from things people dump into the oceans. For example, cruise ships dump waste into the ocean every day. Other pollution comes from industries dumping their waste into rivers. The rivers carry it to the sea.

Often, we harm the oceans without knowing it. For example, nitrogen gets into the oceans from fertilizers. Nitrogen is carried to the oceans as runoff. As water "runs off" the ground, it flows into our streams and rivers. The rivers and streams carry it out to sea. Other pollutants go into the air. Later, they reach the water. For example, most of the mercury found in the ocean comes from power plants that use coal.

When pollutants reach the oceans, problems occur. For example, nitrogen reduces the amount of oxygen in the ocean. Less oxygen can kill some sea animals or cause diseases. Sometimes pollution upsets the balance of nature. Too much nitrogen can make algae, tiny plants, grow so much that they hurt other plants and animals.

Luckily, there are things we can do to protect the oceans. A good start is by learning about the oceans. Another thing that we can all do is get rid of waste properly. You should always use water wisely. And finally, we can ask our government to get involved. The oceans do a lot for us, but they won't last if we don't take care of them.

What You Can Do to Protect Our Oceans

Conserve water.
Don't be wasteful when washing your car or watering your lawn.

Reduce household pollutants.
Properly dispose of chemicals and cleaning products.

Reduce waste.
Dispose of trash properly, and don't leave fishing lines, nets, or plastic items in or near the water.

Reduce automobile pollution.
Use fuel efficient vehicles, carpool, recycle motor oil, and repair oil and air conditioning leaks.

Protect ocean wildlife.
Be considerate of sea-life habitats. Don't feed sea birds, mammals and turtles, or disturb their nesting grounds.

Get involved.
Take part in a beach cleanup or other ocean-oriented activities.

Go On ▶

Directions: Answer the questions.

1. **Which of the following solutions would NOT help protect our oceans?**

   A conserving salt

   B conserving water and reducing waste

   C informing people about environmental problems

   D reducing nitrogen "runoff"

2. **What is the BEST reason for learning about oceans?**

   A There is more water than land on Earth.

   B We need to keep the water clean and blue.

   C People enjoy water sports and boating.

   D We depend on oceans for food and our climate.

3. **What can you do to protect our oceans?**

   A Reduce automobile pollution and protect ocean wildlife.

   B Ask people not to fish or catch seafood.

   C Dump chemicals and waste products into the water.

   D Kill algae and eat seaweed.

4. **Read the poster. How is the information it presents the same as or different from the information in the article?**

5. **What can you do to protect the oceans? Include information from the article in your response.**

Writing Prompt

Write an essay to your principal about an issue at school you care about, such as a safer playground or a better cafeteria. State your opinion and support it with reasons. Write three paragraphs.

STOP 275

Friend or Foe?

Talk About It

Is this crocodile a friend or a foe of this frog? Why?

LOG ON Find out more about friends and foes at **www.macmillanmh.com**

277

ROADRUNNERS: SURPRISING BIRDS

by Adam Savage

"Today we will hear from Pam," said Mr. Sanders.

Pam stood in front of the class. "I'm going to talk about roadrunners," she said, smiling.

Someone snickered, but Pam didn't let a little noise **interfere** with her presentation. She knew that her topic was interesting.

Pam was prepared, so she didn't feel **awkward**, or uncomfortable. Holding up her photo album, Pam began her report. "This is a roadrunner." She looked around the room. No one seemed interested. Pam knew she had to do something to get everyone's attention.

Holding up the next photo, Pam **proclaimed** with confidence, "This amazing bird is so fast and **agile** it can catch a rattlesnake!"

"Whoa, that's cool!" called Peter from the back row. "What else can it do?"

Now every eye was on Pam. "Roadrunners can run up to 15 miles per hour!" she continued.

"Do they fly?" someone asked.

"They can fly when they sense danger. But not very far."

Pam held up the next photo. It showed the roadrunner's black-and-white spotted feathers and the crest on its head.

"Where did you get the photos?" asked Mr. Sanders.

"I took these while I was visiting my grandmother in Arizona," explained Pam.

"I see," said Mr. Sanders. "Is there anything else you'd like to tell us?"

"I learned that a roadrunner is a very clever **guardian** of its young. Let's say an enemy comes near a roadrunner's nest. The roadrunner pretends to have a broken leg, and leads the enemy away. I watched a roadrunner as it **tottered** along. It was so brave!"

Someone asked another question, but Mr. Sanders said to save it for next time. When the class groaned, "Awww," Pam knew her report was a winner.

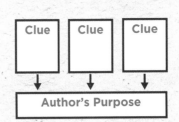

Reread for **Comprehension**

Evaluate

Author's Purpose When evaluating an author's purpose, look for exaggeration, humor, or dialogue. These can help you decide if the purpose is to inform or entertain.

An Author's Purpose Map can help you understand the author's purpose. Reread the selection to confirm your conclusion about why the author wrote.

Clue	Clue	Clue

↓ ↓ ↓

Author's Purpose

Comprehension

Genre

A **Folk tale** is a story based on the traditions of a people or region, told by parents to children and then by the children to their children.

Evaluate

Author's Purpose As you read, fill in your Author's Purpose Map.

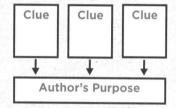

Clue	Clue	Clue

↓ ↓ ↓

Author's Purpose

Read to Find Out

What does this folk tale teach you about life?

ROADRUNNER'S DANCE

By Rudolfo Anaya • Illustrated by David Diaz

Award Winning
Author
and
Illustrator

"*Ssss,*" hissed Snake as he slithered out of his hole by the side of the road. He bared his fangs and frightened a family walking home from the cornfield.

The mother threw her basketful of corn in the air. The children froze with fright.

"Father!" the children called, and the father came running.

"*Ssss,*" Snake threatened.

"Come away," the father said, and the family took another path home.

"I am king of the road," Snake boasted. "No one may use the road without my permission."

That evening the people of the village gathered together and spoke to the elders.

"We are afraid of being bitten by Snake," they protested. "He acts as if the road belongs only to him."

The elders agreed that something should be done, and so the following morning they went to Sacred Mountain, where Desert Woman lived. She had created the desert animals, so surely she could help.

"Please do something about Snake," the elders said. "He makes visiting our neighbors and going to our fields impossible. He frightens the children."

Desert Woman thought for a long time. She did not like to **interfere** in the lives of the people and animals, but she knew that something must be done.

"I have a solution," she finally said.

Dressed in a flowing gown, she traveled on a summer cloud across the desert to where Snake slept under the shade of a rocky ledge.

"You will let people know when you are about to strike," Desert Woman said sternly. And so she placed a rattle on the tip of Snake's tail.

"Now you are Rattlesnake. When anyone approaches, you will rattle a warning. This way they will know you are nearby."

Convinced she had done the right thing, Desert Woman walked on the Rainbow back to her home in Sacred Mountain.

However, instead of inhibiting Rattlesnake, the rattle only made him more threatening. He coiled around, shaking his tail and baring his fangs.

"Look at me," Rattlesnake said to the animals. "I rattle and hiss, and my bite is deadly. I am king of the road, and no one may use it without my permission!"

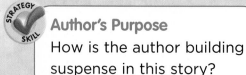

Author's Purpose

How is the author building suspense in this story?

284

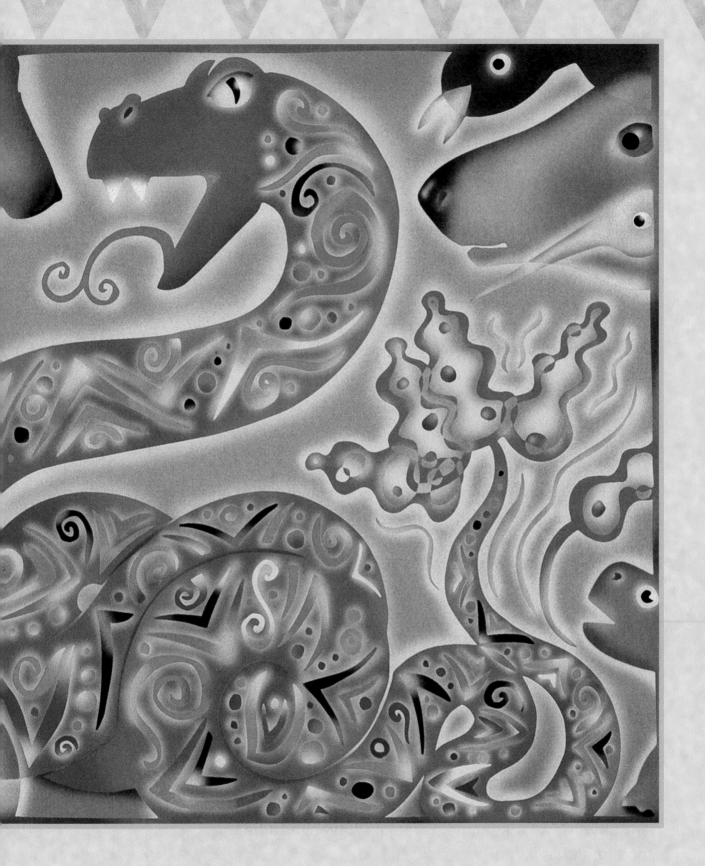

Now the animals went to Desert Woman to complain.

"Who, who," Owl said, greeting Desert Woman with respect. "Since you gave Rattlesnake his rattle, he is even more of a bully. He will not let anyone use the road. Please take away his fangs and rattle!"

"What I give I cannot take away," Desert Woman said. "When Rattlesnake comes hissing and threatening, one of you must make him behave."

She looked at all the animals assembled. The animals looked at one another. They looked up, they looked down, but not one looked at Desert Woman.

"I am too timid to stand up to Rattlesnake," Quail whispered.

"He would gobble me up," Lizard cried and darted away.

"We are all afraid of him," Owl admitted.

Desert Woman smiled. "Perhaps we need a new animal to make Rattlesnake behave," she suggested.

"Yip, yip," Coyote barked. "Yes, yes."

"If you help me, together we can make a **guardian** of the road," Desert Woman said. "I will form the body, and each of you will bring a gift for our new friend."

She gathered clay from the Sacred Mountain and wet it with water from a desert spring. Working quickly but with great care, she molded the body.

"He needs slender legs to run fast," said Deer. He took two slender branches from a mesquite bush and handed them to Desert Woman.

She pushed the sticks into the clay.

"And a long tail to balance himself," said Blue Jay.

"Caw, Caw! Like mine," croaked Raven, and he took long, black feathers from his tail.

"He must be strong," cried the mighty Eagle, and he plucked dark feathers from his wings.

"And have a long beak to peck at Rattlesnake," said Heron, offering a long, thin reed from the marsh.

"He needs sharp eyes," said Coyote, offering two shiny stones from the riverbed.

As Desert Woman added each new gift to the clay body, a strange new bird took shape.

"What is your gift?" Owl asked Desert Woman.

"I will give him the gift of dance. He will be **agile** and fast," she answered. "I will call him Roadrunner."

Then she breathed life into the clay.

Roadrunner opened his eyes. He blinked and looked around.

"What a strange bird," the animals said.

Roadrunner took his first steps. He **tottered** forward, then backward, then forward, and fell flat on his face.

The animals sighed and shook their heads. This bird was not agile, and he was not fast. He could never stand up to Rattlesnake. He was too **awkward**. Disappointed, the animals made their way home.

Desert Woman helped Roadrunner stand, and she told him what he must do. "You will dance around Rattlesnake and peck at his tail. He must learn he is not the king of the road."

"Me? Can I really do it?" Roadrunner asked, balancing himself with his long tail.

"You need only to practice," Desert Woman said.

Roadrunner again tried his legs. He took a few steps forward and bumped into a tall cactus.

"Practice," he said. He tried again and leaped over a sleeping horned toad.

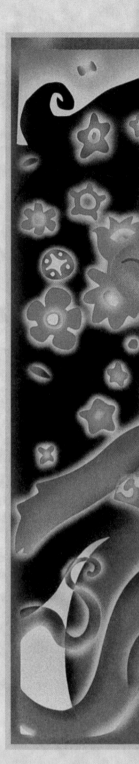

289

He tried jumping over a desert tortoise, but landed right on her back. The surprised turtle lumbered away, and Roadrunner crashed to the ground.

"I'll never get it right," he moaned.

"Yes, you will," Desert Woman said, again helping him to his feet. "You need only to practice."

So Roadrunner practiced. He ran back and forth, learning to use his skinny legs, learning to balance with his tail feathers.

"Practice," he said again. "Practice."

With time, he was swirling and twirling like a twister. The once awkward bird was now a graceful dancer.

"I've got it!" he cried, zipping down the road, his legs carrying him swiftly across the sand. "Thank you, Desert Woman."

"Use your gift to help others," Desert Woman said, and she returned to her abode on Sacred Mountain.

"I will," Roadrunner called.

He went racing down the road until his sharp eyes spied Rattlesnake hiding under a tall yucca plant.

"*Sssss*, I am king of the road," Rattlesnake hissed and shook his tail furiously. "No one may use *my* road without *my* permission."

"The road is for everyone to use," Roadrunner said sternly.

"Who are you?"

"I am Roadrunner."

"Get off my road before I bite you!" Rattlesnake glared.

"I'm not afraid of you," Roadrunner replied.

The people and the animals heard the ruckus and drew close to watch. Had they heard correctly? Roadrunner was challenging Rattlesnake!

"I'll show you I *am* king of the road!" Rattlesnake shouted, hissing so loud the desert mice trembled with fear. He shook his rattle until it sounded like a thunderstorm.

He struck at Roadrunner, but Roadrunner hopped out of the way.

"Stand still!" Rattlesnake cried and lunged again.

But Roadrunner danced gracefully out of reach.

Rattlesnake coiled for one more attempt. He struck like lightning, but fell flat on his face. Roadrunner had jumped to safety.

Now it was Roadrunner's turn. He ruffled his feathers and danced in circles around Rattlesnake. Again and again he pecked at the bully's tail. Like a whirlwind, he spun around Rattlesnake until the serpent grew dizzy. His eyes grew crossed and his tongue hung limply out of his mouth.

"You win! You win!" Rattlesnake cried.

"You are not king of the road, and you must not frighten those who use it," Roadrunner said sternly.

"I promise, I promise," the beaten Rattlesnake said and quietly slunk down his hole.

The people cheered and praised the bird.

"Now we can visit our neighbors in peace and go to our cornfields without fear!" the elders **proclaimed.** "And the children will no longer be frightened."

"Thank you, Roadrunner!" the children called, waving as they followed their parents to the fields.

Then the animals gathered around Roadrunner.

"Yes, thank you for teaching Rattlesnake a lesson," Owl said. "Now you are king of the road."

"No, now there is no king of the road," replied Roadrunner. "Everyone is free to come and go as they please. And the likes of Rattlesnake had better watch out, because I'll make sure the roads stay safe."

Author's Purpose
What purpose do you think the author had for writing this story?

Dancing with Rudolfo and David

Rudolfo Anaya did not have to do any research on roadrunners to write this story. The birds run free all around his home in the southwestern United States. When Rudolfo was a boy in New Mexico, he heard lots of Mexican American folk tales called *cuentos*. Now he writes his own tales to share his Mexican/Native American heritage.

Other books by Rudolfo Anaya and David Diaz

David Diaz likes to experiment when he illustrates a book. He always tries different art techniques for a story before deciding on one. David has even tried using a computer to do some of his illustrations. He believes that using different techniques makes his art more interesting.

 Find out more about Rudolfo Anaya and David Diaz at **www.macmillanmh.com**

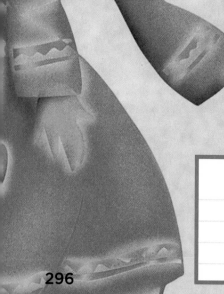

Author's Purpose

What details from *Roadrunner's Dance* do you find entertaining? Do you think the author's Mexican/Native American heritage affected his purpose for writing? Explain.

Comprehension Check

Summarize

Summarize *Roadrunner's Dance.* Tell about the plot of the story, where it happens, and who the main characters are.

Think and Compare

1. What lesson is the author trying to teach? Use your Author's Purpose Map to organize clues and discover the lesson. **Evaluate: Author's Purpose**

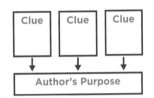

2. Look at the last page of the story. Why do you think Roadrunner turned down the offer to be king of the road? Use story details in your answer. **Analyze**

3. How would you have dealt with a bully like Snake? **Apply**

4. Why was it better that Desert Woman did not **interfere** by taking away Snake's new rattle? **Evaluate**

5. Read "Roadrunners: Surprising Birds" on pages 278–279. What information did you learn about roadrunners from this selection that was not provided in *Roadrunner's Dance?* Use details in your answer. **Reading/Writing Across Texts**

FLYCATCHER AND COYOTE

by Gillian Reed

Many years ago, Flycatcher visited a lake whose water was a spectacular shade of blue. At that time, Flycatcher's feathers were dull, gray, and ugly, and so the bird loved to look at the beautiful blue water. Coyote hid nearby to watch Flycatcher.

Flycatcher loved the blue of the lake so much that she swooped down from the tree to bathe in the lake. She did this four times every morning for four days in a row. Each time the bird bathed in the water, she sang this song:

> *Lovely lake,*
> *So pure and blue,*
> *Let me dip myself,*
> *So I'll be blue, too.*

Coyote appears near the start of the story. This foreshadows the important role that Coyote has in the story.

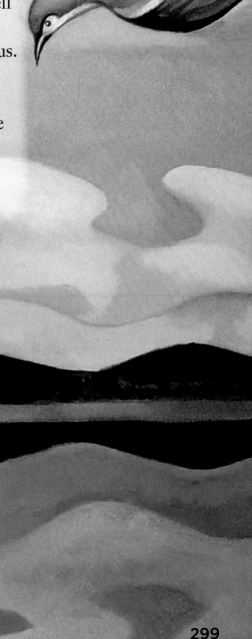

On the fifth morning that Flycatcher went bathing, something amazing happened. When she flew out of the water, her feathers had become a dazzling blue. Flycatcher was now the same color as the lake.

This whole time, Coyote had been watching the bird. Coyote didn't admire the bird or want to learn more about her. No, Coyote was trying to think of a way to trick the bird and eat her. But Coyote was afraid of the water and could never get close enough to Flycatcher.

On the day that Flycatcher turned blue, Coyote was so impressed that he forgot all about catching it. He called up to Flycatcher, who was perched safely in a tree, "How did your ugly gray feathers turn that wonderful blue? Tell me how you did it, so that I can be blue, too."

Flycatcher was so happy that she was feeling generous. She remained safely on her branch, but she told Coyote, "This is what you must do. Jump in the lake four times every morning for four mornings. Then jump in the lake on the fifth morning, and you will turn blue. You might try singing my song, too." Flycatcher taught Coyote her song and then flew merrily on her way.

Well, Coyote really wanted to be blue. So even though he hated the water, he jumped into the lake four times the next morning.

He sang the bird's song, and he shivered as he sang. He did this for four days. On the fifth morning, Coyote emerged from his lake bath with lovely blue fur. Coyote whistled to himself. "I'm blue and beautiful."

Coyote couldn't wait to show off his new color. He thought his fine blue fur would make him the envy of all the desert creatures. He strolled along, looking left and right for someone to admire him. Coyote walked for hours, but he didn't find any admirers. He grew impatient. Then Coyote remembered a canyon where many animals and people lived. They would notice him, but he would have to hurry to reach the canyon before sundown.

As Coyote ran, he noticed the late afternoon shadows around him. He wondered if his shadow was as blue as he was. He twisted his blue head around to take a look. Coyote got a good look at his shadow, which was not blue. But he failed to see the big boulder directly ahead of him. Coyote ran smack into the boulder and fell to the ground.

He rolled over and over in the dirt, his blue legs flying. When he finally stopped and stood up, Coyote was the color of the dusty desert earth. Coyote shook himself, but the dusty color stayed on him. To this day, all coyotes are the color of the dusty desert. And to this day, because her intentions were pure, the flycatcher is the color of the beautiful blue lake.

Coyote decided not to go to the canyon after all. No one would be impressed by his color now. He headed for home, stopping only to give the boulder a good, swift kick.

The dull, dusty color of his fur is a symbol of his hurt pride.

Connect and Compare

1. What event is foreshadowed by the flycatcher's song? **Foreshadowing**

2. What do you learn about Coyote's personality in this trickster tale? **Analyze**

3. Compare what happens to Coyote to what happens to Rattlesnake in *Roadrunner's Dance*. Use information from the stories to support your answers. **Reading/Writing Across Texts**

 Find out more about trickster tales at **www.macmillanmh.com**

Write Dialogue

Writer's Craft

Transition Words

Use **transition words** in sentences to show cause and effect. Words such as "because" and "as a result" can make your writing clearer.

I included the word "since" to explain why Hare thought he should have won.

I used the word "because" to explain why Hare thought he lost.

Hare and Tortoise Again

by Keisha F.

Hare met Tortoise in the park one day.

"Since I am faster, I should have won that race!" shouted Hare sternly.

Tortoise laughed, "You are not a good loser, Hare."

"Because I was tired that day, I lost," said Hare. "Let's race again!"

"Why don't we invite others to race, too?" suggested Tortoise.

Hare thought for a minute. "We'll challenge Coyote, too. He's new in town."

"I'll see you there!" answered Tortoise.

Your Turn

Choose characters from your favorite folk
tale and write a page of dialogue for them.
Include quotation marks, commas, and
correct sentence punctuation
in the dialogue. Also use transition words.
Then read your dialogue aloud. Does it
sound like something those characters
would say? Use the Writer's Checklist to
check your writing.

Writer's Checklist

☑ **Ideas and Content:** Did my dialogue show what
my characters think and feel?

☑ **Organization:** Are my sentences in correct order?

☑ **Voice:** Do the characters' words match their
personalities?

☐ **Word Choice:** Do **transition words** help show cause
and effect?

☑ **Sentence Fluency:** Did my dialogue sound like a
real conversation when I read it out loud?

☑ **Conventions:** Did I use quotation marks and
punctuation in the right places? Did I check
my spelling?

PEOPLE WHO MADE A DIFFERENCE

Talk About It

Why would someone paint such a large picture?

LOG ON Find out more about people who made a difference at **www.macmillanmh.com**

305

IT TOOK COURAGE

by Lily Tuttle

CIVIL RIGHTS are equal opportunities to all citizens regardless of race, religion, or gender. At one time, **unfair** laws gave some people more opportunities than others. Several brave people took a stand and made a difference.

Thurgood Marshall

Thurgood Marshall's family had come a long way from the time when their **ancestors** were slaves. But when he wanted to attend the University of Maryland Law School, the school rejected him because he was black. Marshall had to go to a different law school.

Later, in one of his first court cases, Marshall helped a young African American student sue the University of Maryland. The school had denied him admission, too.

Marshall worked hard to win **numerous** cases. One of his best-known trials was *Brown v. Board of Education* in 1954. In this case, the Supreme Court decided to end **segregation** in schools. The Court made it illegal for black students and white students to be sent to separate locations.

Ruby Bridges

In 1960, six-year-old Ruby Bridges was the first black child to go to an all-white school in the South. Ruby was young and **unsuspecting**. She didn't realize how brave she was to do this. The white parents decided to take their children out of school. For a whole year, Ruby and her teacher were the only people there. Eventually, some white children returned. The following year, more black children came. Ruby Bridges made a difference.

Dr. Martin Luther King, Jr.

Dr. Martin Luther King, Jr., was a leader in the 1950s and 1960s. He **avoided** violence and asked others to fight in peaceful ways to end **injustice**.

King organized a march on Washington, D.C. There, he and thousands of others demanded equal rights for all people. He gave a famous speech that day. He said, "I have a dream." King's dream was that all people would be treated fairly and equally.

Reread for **Comprehension**

Evaluate

Author's Purpose Does the author use facts or humor to get her point across? Facts suggest an author wants to inform the reader. Humor suggests an author is writing to entertain.

An Author's Purpose Map can help you evaluate what you read. Reread the selection to find the author's purpose.

Clue	Clue	Clue
↓	↓	↓

Author's Purpose

Comprehension

Genre

A **Biography** is a story about the life of a real person written by someone else.

Evaluate

Author's Purpose As you read, fill in your Author's Purpose Map.

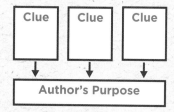

Read to Find Out

What does Dr. Martin Luther King's sister want you to know about him?

my brother
MARTIN

Award Winning Illustrator

A SISTER REMEMBERS
GROWING UP WITH THE REV. DR. MARTIN LUTHER KING JR.

BY CHRISTINE KING FARRIS
ILLUSTRATED BY CHRIS SOENTPIET

We were born in the same room, my brother Martin and I.
I was an early baby, born sooner than expected. Mother
Dear and Daddy placed me in the chifforobe drawer that
stood in the corner of their upstairs bedroom. I got a crib a
few days afterward. A year and a half later, Martin spent his
first night in that hand-me-down crib in the very
same room.

The house where we were born belonged to Mother
Dear's parents, our grandparents, the Reverend and

Mrs. A. D. Williams. We lived there with them and our
Aunt Ida, our grandmother's sister.

And not long after my brother Martin—who
we called M. L. because he and Daddy had the
same name—our baby brother was born. His name
was Alfred Daniel, but we called him A. D., after
our grandfather.

They called me Christine, and like three peas in one pod, we grew together. Our days and rooms were filled with adventure stories and Tinkertoys, with dolls and Monopoly and Chinese checkers.

And although Daddy, who was an important minister, and Mother Dear, who was known far and wide as a musician, often had work that took them away from home, our grandmother was always there to take care of us. I remember days sitting at her feet, as she and Aunt Ida filled us with grand memories of their childhood and read to us about all the wonderful places in the world.

And of course, my brothers and I had each other. We three stuck together like the pages in a brand-new book. And being normal young children, we were almost *always* up to something.

Our best prank involved a fur piece that belonged to our grandmother. It looked almost alive, with its tiny feet and little head and gleaming glass eyes. So, every once in a while, in the waning light of evening, we'd tie that fur piece to a stick, and, hiding behind the hedge in front of our house, we would dangle it in front of **unsuspecting** passersby. Boy! You could hear the screams of fright all across the neighborhood!

Then there was the time Mother Dear decided that her children should all learn to play piano. I didn't mind too much, but M. L. and A. D. preferred being outside to being stuck inside with our piano teacher, Mr. Mann, who would rap your knuckles with a ruler just for playing the wrong notes. Well, one morning, M. L. and A. D. decided to loosen the legs on the piano bench so we wouldn't have to practice. We didn't tell Mr. Mann, and when he sat . . . *CRASH!* down he went.

But mostly we were good, obedient children, and M. L.
did learn to play a few songs on the piano. He even went off
to sing with our mother a time or two. Given his love for
singing and music, I'm sure he could have become as good
a musician as our mother had his life not called him down a
different path.

But that's just what his life did.

Author's Purpose
Why does the author choose to tell
so much about Martin's childhood?

My brothers and I grew up a long time ago. Back in a time when certain places in our country had **unfair** laws that said it was right to keep black people separate because our skin was darker and our **ancestors** had been captured in far-off Africa and brought to America as slaves.

Atlanta, Georgia, the city in which we were growing up, had those laws. Because of those laws, my family rarely went to the picture shows or visited Grant Park with its famous Cyclorama. In fact, to this very day I don't recall ever seeing my father on a streetcar. Because of those laws, and the indignity that went with them, Daddy preferred keeping M. L., A. D., and me close to home, where we'd be protected.

We lived in a neighborhood in Atlanta that's now called Sweet Auburn. It was named for Auburn Avenue, the street that ran in front of our house. On our side of the street stood two-story frame houses similar to the one we lived in. Across it crouched a line of one-story row houses and a store owned by a white family.

When we were young all the children along Auburn Avenue played together, even the two boys whose parents owned the store.

And since our house was a favorite gathering place, those boys played with us in our backyard and ran with M. L. and A. D. to the firehouse on the corner where they watched the engines and the firemen.

The thought of *not* playing with those kids because they were different, because they were white and we were black, never entered our minds.

Well, one day, M. L. and A. D. went to get their playmates from across the street just as they had done a hundred times before. But they came home alone. The boys had told my brothers that they couldn't play together anymore because A. D. and M. L. were Negroes.

And that was it. Shortly afterward the family sold the store and moved away. We never saw or heard from them again.

Looking back, I realize that it was only a matter of time before the generations of cruelty and **injustice** that Daddy and Mother Dear and Mama and Aunt Ida had been shielding us from finally broke through. But back then it was a crushing blow that seemed to come out of nowhere.

"Why do white people treat colored people so mean?" M. L. asked Mother Dear afterward. And with me and M. L. and A. D. standing in front of her trying our best to understand, Mother Dear gave the reason behind it all.

Her words explained the streetcars our family **avoided** and the WHITES ONLY sign that kept us off the elevator at City Hall. Her words told why there were parks and museums that black people could not visit and why some restaurants refused to serve us and why hotels wouldn't give us rooms and why theaters would only allow us to watch their picture shows from the balcony.

But her words also gave us hope.

She answered simply: "Because they just don't understand that everyone is the same, but someday, it will be better."

And my brother M. L. looked up into our mother's face and said the words I remember to this day.

He said, "Mother Dear, one day I'm going to turn this world upside down."

In the coming years there would be other reminders of the cruel system called **segregation** that sought to keep black people down. But it was Daddy who showed M. L. and A. D. and me how to speak out against hatred and bigotry and stand up for what's right.

Daddy was the minister at Ebenezer Baptist Church. And after losing our playmates, when M. L., A. D., and I heard our father speak from his pulpit, his words held new meaning.

And Daddy practiced what he preached. He always stood up for himself when confronted with hatred and bigotry, and each day he shared his encounters at the dinner table.

When a shoe salesman told Daddy and M. L. that he'd only serve them in the back of the store because they were black, Daddy took M. L. somewhere else to buy new shoes.

Another time, a police officer pulled Daddy over
and called him "boy." Daddy pointed to M. L. sitting
next to him in the car and said, "This is a boy. I am
a man, and until you call me one, I will not listen
to you."

These stories were as nourishing as the food that
was set before us.

Years would pass, and many new lessons would be learned. There would be **numerous** speeches and marches and prizes. But my brother never forgot the example of our father, or the promise he had made to our mother on the day his friends turned him away.

And when he was much older, my brother
M. L. dreamed a dream . . . that turned the
world upside down.

 Author's Purpose
Why does the author echo Martin's words,
"I'm going to turn this world upside down"?

The Stories of **Christine and Chris**

Christine King Farris wrote this story to show boys and girls that her famous brother was once a kid just like them. She saw firsthand how young Martin laughed, played, and sometimes got into trouble. Christine wants readers to see that ordinary people can grow up to do great things.

Chris Soentpiet does a lot of research when he illustrates historical stories like this one. He goes to the library to study what clothes people wore and how they lived. Sometimes he even visits the actual places where story events took place. That is why it often takes Chris up to a year to illustrate a book.

Other books illustrated by Chris Soentpiet

 LOG ON Find out more about Christine King Farris and Chris Soentpiet at **www.macmillanmh.com**

Author's Purpose
Did Christine King Farris write *My Brother Martin* to explain, inform, or persuade? How do you think the author's relationship with her brother influenced her purpose for writing? Give details.

Comprehension Check

Summarize

Summarize *My Brother Martin.* State who is telling the story. Explain who Martin is and include the most important events of his childhood.

Think and Compare

1. Why do you think the author wrote about the childhood experiences of her brother? Use your Author's Purpose Map to answer. **Evaluate: Author's Purpose**

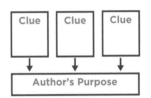

2. Reread the last two pages of *My Brother Martin.* What does the author mean when she says her brother's dream "turned the world upside down"? **Analyze**

3. Suppose you had met Rev. Dr. Martin Luther King, Jr. when he was a child. What character traits would you both have in common? Use story details in your answer. **Synthesize**

4. Why is it important to correct **injustice**? Use story details and your own experience to support your answer. **Evaluate**

5. Read "It Took Courage" on pages 306-307. Compare the experiences of Thurgood Marshall and Rev. Dr. Martin Luther King, Jr. How did segregation affect both men? What did they both accomplish? Use details from both selections in your answer. **Reading/Writing Across Texts**

Dear Mrs. Parks

by Rosa Parks with Gregory J. Reed

Introduction

In 1955, civil rights **activist** Rosa Parks was arrested for refusing to give up her seat on a bus to a white person. Her action helped bring about a bus boycott in Montgomery, Alabama. For over a year, thousands of African Americans refused to ride buses in that city. The boycott ended when the U.S. Supreme Court said that separate seating for whites and blacks on the city's buses was **unconstitutional**.

The following letters are from a collection of letters between children and Rosa Parks.

Dear Mrs. Parks,

I live in the New England area, and I always wondered about the South. When you were growing up in Alabama, did you think that things would ever get better for African Americans?

Kelli
Hartford, Connecticut

We knew that they had to get better! The South had suffered under the unjust laws of segregation far too long. It was time for something to happen to turn things around.

During my childhood years, I had been bothered by the fact that white children had privileges that I did not. I was deeply hurt by the hate that some white people, even children, felt toward me and my people because of our skin. But my mother and grandmother taught me to continue to respect myself and stay focused on making myself ready for opportunity. They felt that a better day had to come, and they wanted me to be a part of it. But it was up to us to make it better.

As an adult, I would go home thirsty on a hot summer day rather than take a drink from the "colored only" fountain. I would not be a part of an unjust system that was designed to make me feel inferior.

I knew that this type of system was wrong and could not last. I did not know when, but I felt that the people would rise up and demand justice. I did not plan for that point of change to begin with my actions on the bus that evening in 1955. But I was ready to take a stand.

Dear Mrs. Parks,

What is hope? I have read that you hope for this world to be a better place to live in, and you haven't given up. I'm still figuring out what is "hope," and then maybe I can help "hope" out to make this a better world and be like you.

Elizabeth
Grosse Point, Michigan

Elizabeth, many times we as adults seek to teach students like you without giving you examples of what the true meanings of words are so that you can learn from them.

Hope is wanting something that means a lot to you. It is like wanting something that you do not have. Hope is something we feel with our hearts. When we hope for something with our hearts, it becomes an expectation.

Hope is also something we believe in. Many people I have known believed in ending racial segregation in this country, and their hope that it could happen influenced their actions and brought about change. A friend of mine, the Reverend Jesse Jackson, says, "We must keep hope alive." I agree. You can help keep hope alive by believing in yourself. Your hope for yourself and for the future can make this world a better place to live.

Dear Mrs. Parks,

I always like hearing Dr. Martin Luther King, Jr.'s speeches. He was a great man. I wish he was still living. I believe he can straighten out this mess this country is in. Were you ever afraid of him dying and leaving you here?

Wilbar
Kerhonkson, New York

I, too, wish Dr. King was still with us. It has always been very difficult and very painful to think about Dr. King's death. He was a very dear friend of mine. He spoke with authority and conviction. His faith, his words, and his commitment to **nonviolence** inspired us all in the Civil Rights movement.

You are right in saying that our country has many problems. We have a long way to go. But we can work together, young and old, to achieve Dr. King's dream of equality and justice. I hope that you will keep that dream in your heart and make it your own.

Connect and Compare

1. Look at the form of the letters to Mrs. Parks. What parts do all the letters have in common? **Reading Letters**

2. What would you do if there were an empty seat on the bus and someone told you that you couldn't sit in it? **Evaluate**

3. Think about this week's main selection, *My Brother Martin*. What might Martin's sister say in a letter to Rosa Parks? **Reading/Writing Across Texts**

 Social Studies Activity

Write a letter to a famous person about something they did which you would like to know more about.

 Find more about writing letters at **www.macmillanmh.com**

Writer's Craft

Formal and Informal Language

Good writers often use both **formal and informal language** to show their feelings. In a poem, make every word count.

I wrote about my hero using both formal and informal language.

To show how I feel, I included this thought about my subject.

My Hero

by Joseph M.

Rosa Parks worked hard.

Her feet ached.

She wanted that seat.

The driver said he'd call the police.

"You may go on and do so,"

Said Rosa Parks,

My hero, Rosa Parks.

She took a stand

By sitting down.

"You may go on and do so,"

Said Rosa Parks.

Your Turn

Write a poem about a person who inspires you. It can be a family member, a friend, or someone famous. Explain why this person has made a difference. Choose language that clearly shows your enthusiasm. Use the Writer's Checklist to check your writing.

Writer's Checklist

✓ **Ideas and Content:** Have I made clear why this person is important to me?

✓ **Organization:** Did I express my ideas in order?

❑ **Voice:** Have I clearly shown my feelings through my use of **formal and informal language**?

✓ **Word Choice:** Have I chosen colorful words?

✓ **Sentence Fluency:** Do the sentences read smoothly when I read my poem aloud?

✓ **Conventions:** Did I use the right tense for each verb? Did I check my spelling?

Talk About It

What can kids do to achieve their own goals and also help others?

LOG ON Find out more about kids getting it done at **www.macmillanmh.com**

KIDS GET IT DONE

331

Vocabulary

identified

enterprising

persistence

venture

Gidget Schultz

Their Way All the Way!

Gidget Schultz couldn't bear to see kids living on the streets near her Encinitas, California, home. So Gidget, now 14, started her own charity.

Gidget's Way gives backpacks, jackets, and school supplies to homeless kids. Gidget also gives teddy bears to local police to keep in their cars. Officers give the bears to kids who are scared, sad, or hurt. "Running Gidget's Way is a full-time job," says Gidget.

Jhordan Logan of New Castle, Indiana, **identified** a different need. She discovered there were hardly any good books for kids to read at Riley Hospital for Children in Indianapolis. Jhordan organized a Read It Again drive that collected over 5,000 books. Another program she started matches elementary school students with nursing home residents.

Gidget and Jhordan share an **enterprising**, high-energy attitude. "No matter what age you are, you can always volunteer," says Jhordan.

Tips for Planning a Service Project

Kids around the world use their skills and time to help make our world a better place. A service project can be as big as building a home for a family or as simple as collecting coins for charity. Choose something that will inspire you—something that you really care about and makes you want to work hard. Here are some helpful tips.

1. Identify a problem that exists in your community.
2. Learn more about the problem; think about ways to solve it.
3. Set a goal for the project.
4. Decide what supplies and help you'll need.
5. Get others involved.
6. Stick with it! Your **persistence** and hard work will keep the project on track.
7. Have fun! Knowing that you are helping your community should make you feel good.

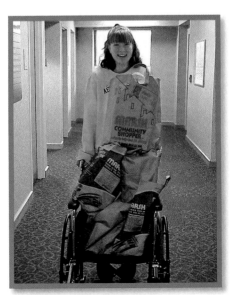

Jhordan Logan, 13, delivers books to kids in the hospital.

Kids' Jobs

Do you think about getting a job when you're older? Maybe you'll want to earn spending money or save for college. These are the types of businesses that employ the most teenagers. Don't forget, though, you can also start your own **venture**—business or project—and be your own boss!

Male	Percent of All Youths Who Work
Restaurants	31.3%
Grocery Stores	13.6
Entertainment and Recreation Services	4.5
Agriculture	3.6
Construction	3.6
Department Stores	3.1
Female	Percent of All Youths Who Work
Restaurants	32.6%
Grocery Stores	9.9
Private Households (babysitting, etc.)	5.7
Department Stores	4.4
Entertainment and Recreation Services	4.0

Source: U.S. Department of Labor

LOG ON Find out more about kids' jobs at **www.macmillanmh.com**

STORY: **Kid Scientist Starts Kids' Charity**

Martin, who lives in New York, is a computer buff, plays the piano, and wants to be an airline pilot when he grows up. When he got the assignment to interview Andrew Hsu, he expected to be talking about science. After all, Andrew had just become the youngest winner of the Washington State Science and Engineering Fair. The 11-year-old scientist won the grand prize for identifying a particular gene that plays an important role in keeping the human body healthy.

Martin soon discovered that being a science whiz is just one of Andrew's accomplishments. He's also an athlete who competes in swimming. But the main thing Andrew wanted to tell Martin about was the World Children Organization (WCO). Andrew founded this organization along with his brother Patrick. The brothers started this **venture** in order to help improve the lives of children. In that way its mission is similar to that of the U.N. Special Session on Children. The U.N. special session **identified** three high-priority issues. In contrast, WCO focuses on a single issue for now.

Andrew and Patrick believe that improving education is the best way they can make a positive difference for children. They know that, unlike the United States, there are places where a free education isn't available to all kids.

Andrew Hsu, 11, receives the grand prize award at the 2003 Washington State Science and Engineering Fair.

To help meet that need, Andrew and Patrick had the idea of producing videos about science, math, and languages for children in countries where there aren't enough qualified teachers. "Without education," Andrew said, "the problems of poverty, hunger, child labor, and other abuses of children's rights will never end."

At age 11, Andrew was already a "working" scientist.

STORY: Different Reporters, Different Stories, a Common Theme

Terrence and Martin both wrote about kids and organizations involved in helping children. In Terrence's story, the organization—the United Nations—is a large one that was founded by the nations of the world. The kids involved came from many different countries. The size and political power of the U.N. enables it to work on several high-priority issues at once. In Martin's story, the organization is a small one—the World Children Organization—founded by two kids. For now, the WCO focuses on education as its single issue.

Clearly, all of these kids—at the U.N. Special Session, Andrew and Patrick at WCO, and reporters Terrence and Martin—share a commitment to making the world a better place for everyone, especially children.

Think and Compare

1. What skills do Terrence and Martin need to be good reporters?

2. If you were a kid reporter, what topic would you like to investigate?

3. If you could choose one way to improve the lives of the children of the world, what would it be?

4. What do Gidget Schultz, Jhordan Logan, the attendees at the U.N. Special Session, and Andrew and Patrick Hsu have in common? How are their projects different?

Test Strategy
Think and Search
Read on to find the answer. Look for information in more than one place.

Child Labor in the U.S.A.

Throughout its history, the United States has counted on kids to lend a hand on farms and in factories. In the 1800s, children as young as 7 worked in textile mills for 12 hours a day. By the end of the nineteenth century, almost 2 million kids performed hazardous jobs in mills, mines, and factories.

Many concerned citizens worked to change this. Photographer Lewis Hine, who took these pictures of young cotton mill workers, was one of them. In 1938, a U.S. law was passed that limits work hours for kids. The law also requires safe conditions. The law still exists, but some people break it. An estimated 800,000 children work illegally in the U.S. today. Most of them work on farms and jobs related to farming. Some work with heavy machinery, poisonous chemicals, or under other conditions that could harm them.

These photos of young boys working in U.S. cotton mills were taken by Lewis Hine around 1911.

Go On ▶

Directions: Answer the questions.

1. What happened before the 1938 child labor law was passed?

A   Children were not allowed to work in factories.

B   Children were not required to go to school.

C   Children worked long hours at unsafe jobs.

D   Children were prevented from working on farms.

2. This selection is MOSTLY about

A   farming jobs.

B   protecting children who work.

C   photographer Lewis Hine.

D   finding the right job.

> **Tip**
> Look for information in more than one place.

3. What has NOT changed since the 1800s?

A   Kids still work in mines and factories.

B   Kids still work in cotton mills.

C   Lewis Hine is still photographing children.

D   Kids still work at dangerous jobs.

4. Why are some jobs harmful to children?

5. Laws in the United States require children to attend school. Do you think the United States still needs those laws? Explain your answer.

Write to a Prompt

Gidget Schultz, Jhordan Logan, and Andrew and Patrick Hsu started their own charitable organizations. As reporters, Terrence Cheromcka and Martin Jacobs conducted interviews. Imagine you are starting your own magazine and you're trying to interview a famous person. Persuade that person that he or she should agree to be interviewed for your magazine.

I started my writing by stating facts that describe the topic.

January 17, 2008

Dear Mr. President,

    I'm starting a new magazine for kids. It's called <u>Kids Today</u>. The magazine talks about everything that happens in a kid's life: school, friends, sports, music, and more.

    In each issue, we talk to a famous person about what it was like for him or her as a kid. Every kid knows what you do, but we don't know what your childhood was like. I know you're very busy, but this would be a good thing for you to do.

                  Sincerely,
                  Rebecca H.

Writing Prompt

In "Tips for Planning a Service Project" you read about things you can do to get a project started. One tip is "Get others involved." Imagine you are starting your own service project. Choose one person whose help would be very important to you in getting your project started. Write a letter to persuade that person to help you. Provide reasons why he or she should get involved. State your opinion and support it with convincing reasons.

Writer's Checklist

☑ Ask yourself, who is my audience?

☑ Think about your purpose for writing.

☑ Choose the correct form for your writing.

☑ Use reasons to support your opinion.

☑ Be sure your ideas are logical and organized.

☑ Use your best spelling, grammar, and punctuation.

GREAT PLAINS INDIANS

Talk About It

What are these people doing? How do you think they dress every day?

LOG ON Find out more about Great Plains Indians at **www.macmillanmh.com**

HISTORY
AT YOUR FEET

by André Melillo

Vocabulary

sores	midst
loosened	responsibility
mysterious	patchwork
amazement	

Dictionary

Homophones sound the same but have different spellings and meanings.

Sores and *soars* are homophones.

"Do I have to go?" Sam asked. "Look, I've got **sores** on my feet from walking so much."

Sam, his sister Kim, and their family were on their way to the Pawnee Indian Village Museum.

Mom gave Sam some bandage strips and said, "You'll enjoy learning about the people of the Pawnee nation."

Letting out a big sigh, Sam **loosened** his sandal straps and trudged out to the car.

Who Were the Pawnee?

The origins of the Pawnee tribe are **mysterious**. In the early 1800s, there were 10,000–30,000 Pawnee living in four separate bands.

"This museum is located where one band of Pawnee settled back in 1820," explained Mom.

Anikarus Rushing of the Pawnee tribe

"We're standing exactly where the Pawnee lived!" exclaimed Kim in **amazement**.

"That's right," said Dad. "Here's part of the original floor," he said, pointing. "You can see some burned timbers from the fire that destroyed the village."

What Was Life Like?

Sam had to admit that being in the **midst** of all that history was exciting. "What was it like to live back then?" he wondered aloud.

A museum guide spoke up. "It happens to be my **responsibility** to tell you just that. The Pawnee hunted mostly buffalo and used every part of the animals they killed for food or clothing. They let nothing go to waste."

"Clothing?" said Kim. "Buffalo aren't shaped like any clothing I've ever seen."

Everyone chuckled. "They'd sew a **patchwork** of pieces into warm winter robes and pants," explained the guide.

A battle between the Pawnees and the Konzas painted on a bison hide

Reread for Comprehension

Summarize

Sequence When you summarize a story, include the most important events in sequence. Sequence is the order in which events in a story take place.

A Sequence Chart can help you summarize a selection. Reread the selection to find the sequence of events. Then write a summary.

Event
↓
↓
↓

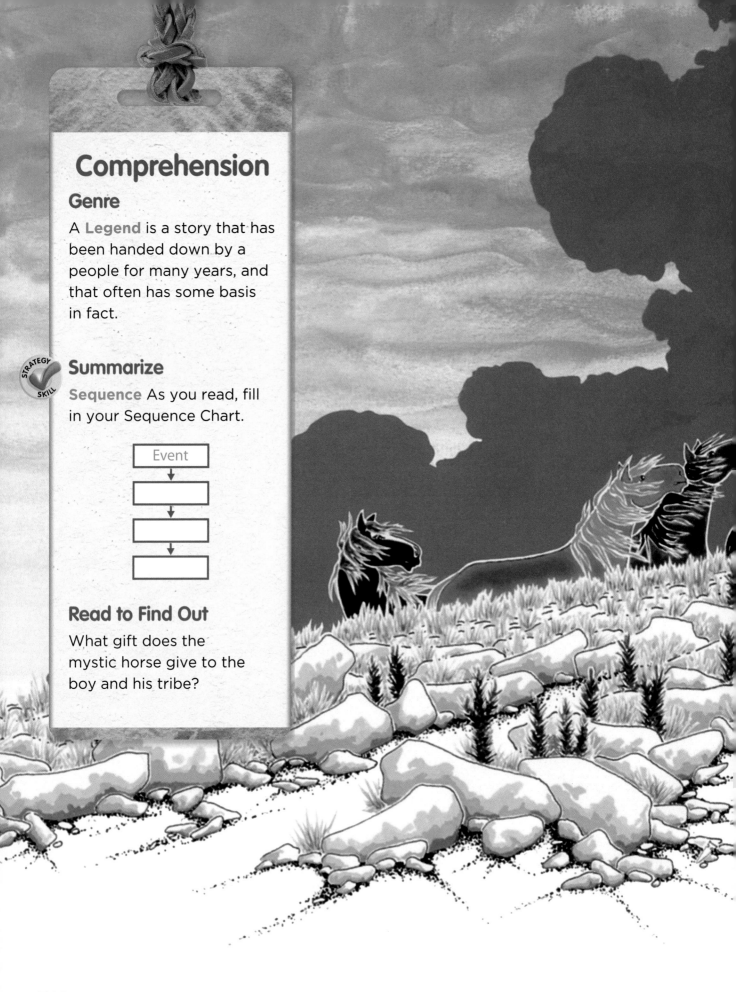

Comprehension

Genre

A **Legend** is a story that has been handed down by a people for many years, and that often has some basis in fact.

Summarize

Sequence As you read, fill in your Sequence Chart.

Event

↓

↓

↓

Read to Find Out

What gift does the mystic horse give to the boy and his tribe?

Award Winning Author

Mystic Horse
written and illustrated by PAUL GOBLE

IN THOSE LONG AGO DAYS, when the Pawnee people had harvested their crops of corn and squash, they would leave their earth-lodge villages and travel out on the Great Plains to hunt buffalo. They had horses to ride and to carry their tipis and belongings when they went great distances in search of the wandering herds.

When they were not traveling, and the tipis were pitched, it was the **responsibility** of the older boys, the young men, to look after the herds of horses, and to guard the village. They would stay with the horses at pasture throughout the day, often far away from the camp. All the while they would keep a good lookout for enemies.

Traveling with the people were an old woman and her grandson. They were poor, living alone without any relatives at the edge of the village. Their only shelter was made of sticks and a **patchwork** of pieces of old tipi covers which people had thrown away. Nobody took much notice of them.

When the people moved from one camping place to another, the old woman and her grandson would stay behind to look for scraps of food, and to pick up discarded clothes. They had no horse. They walked, and what their dogs could not carry, they packed on their own backs. Their life was hard, but they were happy.

One day, as they followed far behind the village, they came upon a sad and sickly worn-out horse standing in the trail. He was terribly thin, with **sores** on his back.

"Grandmother," the boy said, "nobody wants this poor old horse. If we are kind and look after him, he will get well again. He will help us carry our packs! Then I will be able to join the buffalo hunt, and we will have meat, and fresh skins as well!"

And so they led the old horse, limping along behind
them. People laughed: "You've got yourself a great
warhorse, boy! How will we keep up with you now?"
But the boy loved his horse, and looked after him well.

Sequence
What is the first thing the boy
does when he finds the horse?

After some days had passed, the boys who were out on the hills looking after the horses spotted enemies approaching on horseback. They quickly drove the herds back to the safety of the camp. The men grabbed their weapons, mounted their fastest horses, and rode out to meet the enemy.

The boy, riding the poor old horse, followed shyly at a distance. But the men pointed at the horse and laughed: "Look! Here's the one who'll leave us all behind! Boy, that's an old good-for-nothing half-starved horse. You'll be killed. Go back home!"

The boy was ashamed, and rode off to one side where he could not hear their unkind remarks. The horse turned his head and spoke to the boy: "Listen to me! Take me down to the river and cover me with mud." The boy was alarmed to hear him speak, but without hesitation he rode to the river and daubed mud all over his horse.

Then the horse spoke again: "Don't take your bow and arrows. Cut a long willow stick instead. Then ride me, as hard as you can, right into the enemy's **midst** and strike their leader with the stick, and ride back again. Do it four times, and the enemy will be afraid; but do not do it more than four times!"

While the horse was speaking, he was tossing his head, stamping and prancing this way and that, until the boy could hardly hold him back. He **loosened** the reins, and the horse galloped toward the enemy. He was no longer an old sickly worn-out horse! He flew like a hawk, right to where the enemy riders were formed up in line of battle. The boy struck their leader with his willow stick, turned, and rode back to his people with arrows flying past him like angry wasps.

He turned again without stopping, and the horse carried him back to strike another enemy rider. By then his people were cheering loudly. Four times the boy charged back and forth, and each time he hit one of the enemy, just as his horse had told him.

STRATEGY SKILL

Sequence
Retell the horse's instructions, using sequence words.

The men watched the boy with **amazement.** Now they, too, felt brave enough to follow his example, and they drove the enemy in full retreat from the village. It was like chasing buffalo.

The boy was eager to join the chase. He said to himself: "I have struck four times, and I have not been hurt. I will do it once more." And so, again, he rode after the retreating enemy riders. He whipped another with his stick, but at that very instant his horse was pierced by an arrow, and fell. The horse tried to stand, but he could not.

When the enemy had fled, the men returned and gathered round the boy. His horse was dead. They wanted to touch the horse, for they knew he had been no ordinary one, but a horse with mystic powers.

The leader spoke: "Today this boy has shown that he is braver than all of us. From now on we will call him Piraski Resaru, Boy Chief."

But the boy cried. He was sad for his horse, and angry with himself that he had not done what the **mysterious** horse had told him. He untied the lariat, pulled out the arrow, and carefully wiped away the blood.

He climbed to the top of a nearby hill to mourn. He sat on a rock and pulled his blanket over his head. While he sat there crying, fearsome dark clouds closed across the sky, and it grew dark as if night was falling. Lightning flashed! Thunder shook the hilltop, and it rained with a terrific downpour.

Looking through the downpour, he imagined he saw the dead horse move his legs a little, and that he even tried to lift his head. He wondered if something strange and wonderful was happening. And then he knew it was true: the horse slowly stretched out his front legs, and then stood up!

The boy was a little afraid, but he ran down from the hilltop and clasped his arms round the horse's neck, crying with joy that he was alive again.

The horse spoke softly to him: "Tirawahat, Our Father Above, is good! He has forgiven you. He has let me come back to you."

The storm passed; the rain stopped. All was still and fresh, and the sun shone brilliantly on his beautiful living horse. "Now take me up into the hills, far away from people," the horse told him. "Leave me there for four days, and then come for me."

When the four days had passed, Boy Chief left the village and climbed into the pine tree hills.

A horse neighed, and the mysterious horse appeared, followed by a herd of spirited horses. They surrounded Boy Chief, snorting and stamping excitedly, horses of every color—beautiful bays, chestnuts, shiny blacks, whites, grays, and paints.

Mounted on his mysterious horse, Boy Chief drove the horses round and round the village. He stopped in front of his grandmother's shelter.

"Grandmother," he said, "now you will always have horses! You need never walk again! Choose the ones you want, and give the rest to those who need them most." And so it was done.

After that, the boy and his grandmother rode whenever they moved camp. They lived in a tipi and were not poor any longer. And, just as his grandmother had looked after him when he was young, so he, too, always took good care of her for all her years.

Meet Paul Goble

Paul Goble first became interested in Native Americans when he was a boy growing up in England. He thought their beliefs, art, and tales were wonderful. When Paul grew up, he moved to the western United States to live and learn among the Native Americans. Paul began to write and illustrate books that retold traditional tales. Before writing each book, he carefully researches Native American customs and clothing. He also likes his books to show how people and nature are connected.

Other books by Paul Goble

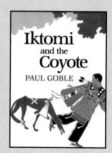

LOG ON Find out more about Paul Goble at **www.macmillanmh.com**

Author's Purpose

Legends often have some basis in fact. Why did Paul Goble write *Mystic Horse*? Was it mainly to explain, inform, entertain, or persuade?

366

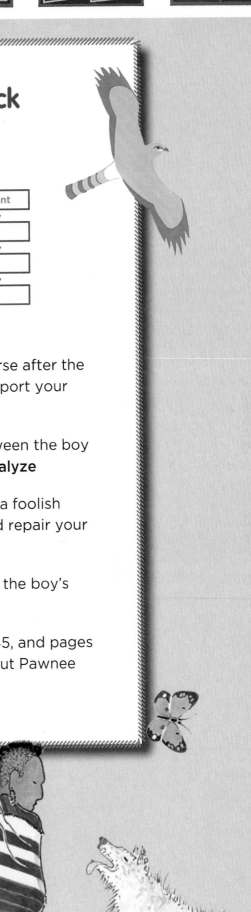

Comprehension Check

Summarize

STRATEGY SKILL

Use your Sequence Chart to help you as you summarize *Mystic Horse.* Tell the events of the story in the order in which they happened.

Event
↓
↓
↓

Think and Compare

STRATEGY SKILL

1. What **mysterious** change happened to the old horse after the boy covered it with mud? Use story details to support your answer. **Summarize: Sequence**

2. Use story details to examine the relationship between the boy and the horse. Why did they trust each other? **Analyze**

3. Suppose you lost a friendship because you made a foolish mistake. How would you correct your mistake and repair your friendship? **Apply**

4. Based on what you know, how would you explain the boy's actions in battle? **Evaluate**

5. Read "Who Were the Pawnee?" on pages 344–345, and pages 349–350 of *Mystic Horse.* What did you learn about Pawnee life? **Reading/Writing Across Texts**

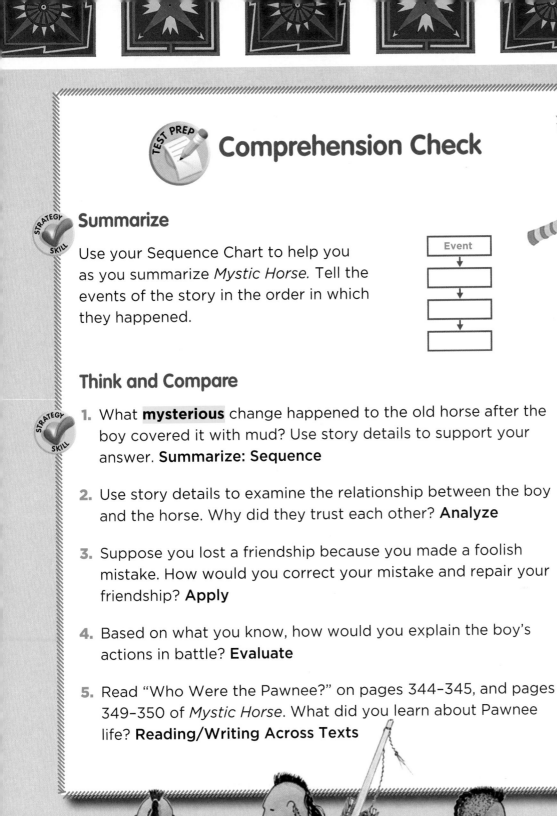

powwow | Search

Social Studies

Genre

Online Articles provide information and links to a topic.

Text Feature

Links, also called hyperlinks, connect one web page to another.

Content Vocabulary

powwow
traditions
sacred

PRINT THIS ARTICLE

E-MAIL THIS ARTICLE TO A FRIEND

WATCH A VIDEO

LISTEN TO POWWOW MUSIC

THE BLACK HILLS POWWOW

by Peter Lightfoot

Have you ever been to a **powwow**? A powwow is a huge celebration of Native American **traditions** where friends and families gather. Outsiders also come to learn about native ways.

The Black Hills Powwow is an annual, or yearly, event. It is held in the Black Hills, the **sacred** land of the Lakota, Dakota, and Nakota people. Hundreds of dancers and drummers come. Many are from the northern plains.

Many things happen at a powwow. People dance and play music. They play hand games from the past. They buy and sell handmade crafts. On Youth Day, rap music, face painting, and other activities are all part of the fun.

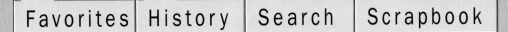

Favorites | History | Search | Scrapbook

 Using Links

Use links to move from one online article to another. If a word or phrase is blue and underlined, that usually means you can click it for more information. When you click, another page will appear. By clicking on a link, you can learn more about your subject or a related subject.

Address: www.example.com/powwows.htm

Search

What Is a Powwow?

POWWOWS are large gatherings. They help keep <u>Native American culture</u> alive. Often, people from many tribes plan a powwow. Some powwows take place every year. They can go on for days. <u>Dancing</u> is the central activity. Often, the dances are contests, and prize money is awarded to the winners. Powwows also feature drumming. Sometimes, people tell stories. Handcrafted clothing, animal carvings, and dreamcatchers are displayed and sold. Some powwows are held in large, open fields. Others take place in schools and gyms.

Search

Powwow Dancing

Dancing is a big part of today's powwows. Some dances are social, such as the round dance. Other dances are competitions. Judges rate the dancers on both their dancing and their outfit. Each dance competition features several different kinds of dances, such as men's traditional dance, women's traditional dance, men's grass dance, women's fancy shawl dance, and others. Little kids also get a chance to take part, and to join the dance tradition, in the "Tiny Tots" dance.

PRINT THIS ARTICLE

E-MAIL THIS ARTICLE TO A FRIEND

WATCH A VIDEO

LISTEN TO POWWOW MUSIC

Connect and Compare

1. Reread the Using Links box on page 369. When should you click on a link and when should you not? **Using Links**

2. If you want to see dancing at a powwow, how would you find out where to go? **Apply**

3. Compare this article and *Mystic Horse*. What are some things that the native people of the Plains still value? **Reading/Writing Across Texts**

 Social Studies Activity

Use the Internet to find a schedule for a powwow. Print it out and circle or highlight the different activities.

 Find out more about powwows at **www.macmillanmh.com**

Writer's Craft

Dialogue

Good, well-chosen **dialogue** makes characters sound natural and believable. Forced word choice can make characters sound unbelievable.

I took a *scene* from a folk tale about Coyote and began with this sentence of dialogue.

Here in the *scene* I present Coyote's idea. Then I end with a statement from the Old Man. The dialogue expresses their feelings.

Coyote Offers to Help

by Kaya N.

Setting: A Native American village. Two men sit in the sun.

Young Man:	Feel how Sun warms us.
Old Man:	(sadly) I wish we had a small piece for winter.
Young Man:	Yes, then we would be warm!
Coyote:	(feeling sorry) I will go to the Fire Beings on the mountain.
Young Man:	You! How can you help us?
Coyote:	Oh, I have a plan. I will bring you a piece of fire.
Old Man:	Let him try. Perhaps he can succeed.

Your Turn

Choose a scene from a favorite folk tale and turn it into a one-page scene from a play. Bring the characters to life by adding stage directions that describe the characters' feelings and actions. Put the stage directions in parentheses before each character's dialogue. Use the Writer's Checklist to check your writing.

Writer's Checklist

 Ideas and Content: Is it clear what is happening in the play scene? Should I add any stage directions?

 Organization: Does the action happen with a beginning, middle, and end that make sense?

✓ **Voice:** Do the characters have clear personalities?

☐ **Word Choice:** Did I choose precise words for the **dialogue** to express the characters' feelings?

✓ **Sentence Fluency:** Does my dialogue sound natural?

✓ **Conventions:** Did I use the verbs *is, are, was,* and *were* correctly? Did I check my spelling?

Talk About It

What do you think has happened in this photograph?

LOG ON Find out more about precipitation at **www.macmillanmh.com**

PRECIPITATION

Let It Snow

by Cynthia Robey

Do you have a **technique** for catching snowflakes? Some people run in circles trying to catch them. Others stand perfectly still with their tongue sticking out. It might look like **foolishness**, but it's fun!

Crystals to Flakes

A snowflake's shape is formed long before it lands on Earth. First, an ice crystal forms around a tiny piece of dirt in a cloud. Now it's a snow crystal. The crystal's shape depends on the temperature of the cloud.

Finally, as the crystals fall from the clouds, they stick together to form snowflakes. Each snowflake is made up of 2 to 200 separate snow crystals.

Studying Snowflakes

Snow crystals form into one of seven shapes. You probably know the stellar crystal best. These star-shaped crystals are not the most common, but they're the kind that **inspire** the work of most artists.

How can you study snowflakes before they **evaporate** and disappear? First, go outside when it's not windy and about 25° F. Second, bring a piece of dark cloth with you. This will make it easier to see the crystals. Finally, you will need to use a **microscope** to **magnify** the crystal to get a good look at it.

Wilson "Snowflake" Bentley learned how to make the crystals show up in photographs. He cut away the dark parts of the **negatives**.

Dangerous Snowflakes

If conditions are just right, beautiful snowflakes can turn into a dangerous storm called a **blizzard**. In blizzards, strong winds can blow the snow around. This causes "whiteout" conditions, making it very difficult to see where you're going.

Always pay attention to the weather. That way you can safely catch and study all the snowflakes you want.

Reread for **Comprehension**

Evaluate

Summarize When you summarize what you read, include only the important details. To decide which details are important, think about the main idea of the selection. Then ask yourself, "Do these details support the main idea?"

A Main Idea Web can help you decide which details are important. Reread the selection and summarize the main idea and the important details that support it.

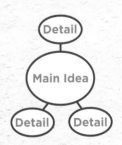

Comprehension

Genre

A **Biography** is a story about the life of a real person written by someone else.

Evaluate

Summarize

As you read, fill in your Main Idea Web.

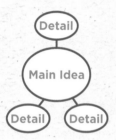

Read to Find Out

What did the world give to Snowflake Bentley, and what did he give to the world?

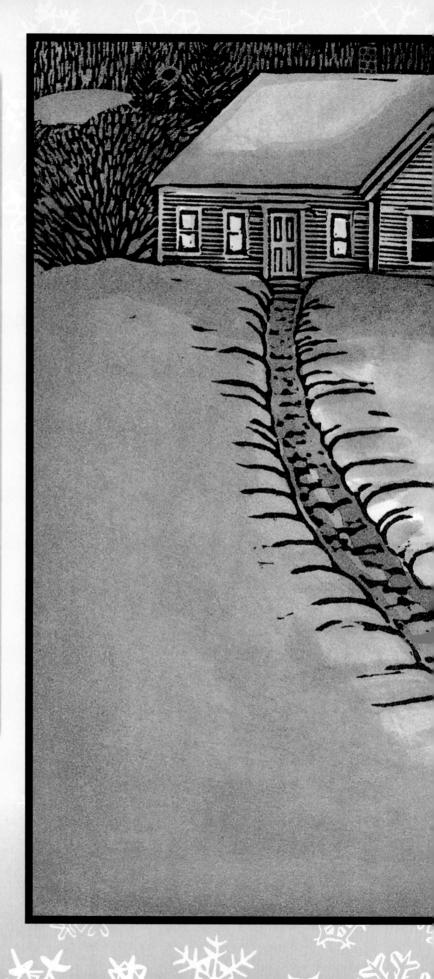

SNOWFLAKE BENTLEY

By Jacqueline Briggs Martin
Illustrated by Mary Azarian

Wilson Bentley was born February 9, 1865, on a farm in Jericho, Vermont, between Lake Champlain and Mount Mansfield, in the heart of the "snowbelt," where the annual snowfall is about 120 inches.

In the days when farmers worked with ox and sled and cut the dark with lantern light, there lived a boy who loved snow more than anything else in the world.

Willie Bentley's happiest days were snowstorm days. He watched snowflakes fall on his mittens, on the dried grass of Vermont farm fields, on the dark metal handle of the barn door. He said snow was as beautiful as butterflies, or apple blossoms.

Willie's mother was his teacher until he was fourteen years old. He attended school for only a few years. "She had a set of encyclopedias," Willie said. "I read them all."

He could net butterflies and show them to his older brother, Charlie. He could pick apple blossoms and take them to his mother. But he could not share snowflakes because he could not save them.

From his boyhood on he studied all forms of moisture. He kept a record of the weather and did many experiments with raindrops.

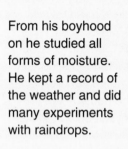

When his mother gave him an old **microscope**, he used it to look at flowers, raindrops, and blades of grass. Best of all, he used it to look at snow.

While other children built forts and pelted snowballs at roosting crows, Willie was catching single snowflakes. Day after stormy day he studied the icy crystals.

He learned that most crystals had six branches (though a few had three). For each snowflake the six branches were alike. "I found that snowflakes were masterpieces of design," he said. "No one design was ever repeated. When a snowflake melted . . . just that much beauty was gone, without leaving any record behind."

Starting at age fifteen he drew a hundred snow crystals each winter for three winters.

Their intricate patterns were even more beautiful than he had imagined. He expected to find whole flakes that were the same, that were copies of each other. But he never did.

Willie decided he must find a way to save snowflakes so others could see their wonderful designs. For three winters he tried drawing snow crystals. They always melted before he could finish.

The camera made images on large glass **negatives**. Its microscope could **magnify** a tiny crystal from sixty-four to 3,600 times its actual size.

When he was sixteen, Willie read of a camera with its own microscope. "If I had that camera I could photograph snowflakes," he told his mother.

Willie's mother knew he would not be happy until he could share what he had seen.

"Fussing with snow is just **foolishness**," his father said. Still, he loved his son.

When Willie was seventeen his parents spent their savings and bought the camera.

It was taller than a newborn calf, and cost as much as his father's herd of ten cows. Willie was sure it was the best of all cameras.

Even so his first pictures were failures—no better than shadows. Yet he would not quit. Mistake by mistake, snowflake by snowflake, Willie worked through every storm.

Winter ended, the snow melted, and he had no good pictures.

Willie's experiment: He used a very small lens opening, which let only a little light reach the negative, but he kept the lens open for several seconds—up to a minute and a half.

He learned, too, that he could make the snow crystals show up more clearly by using a sharp knife to cut away all the dark parts of the negative around the crystals. This etching meant extra hours of work for each photograph, but Willie didn't mind.

He waited for another season of snow. One day, in the second winter, he tried a new experiment. And it worked!

Willie had figured out how to photograph snowflakes! "Now everyone can see the great beauty in a tiny crystal," he said.

The best snowstorm of his life occurred on Valentine's Day in 1928. He made over a hundred photographs during the two-day storm. He called the storm a gift from King Winter.

But in those days no one cared. Neighbors laughed at the idea of photographing snow.

"Snow in Vermont is as common as dirt," they said. "We don't need pictures."

Willie said the photographs would be his gift to the world.

    While other farmers sat by the fire or rode to town
with horse and sleigh, Willie studied snowstorms.
He stood at the shed door and held out a black tray to
catch the flakes.

    When he found only jumbled, broken crystals, he
brushed the tray clean with a turkey feather and
held it out again.

He learned that each snowflake begins as a speck, much too tiny to be seen. Little bits—molecules—of water attach to the speck to form its branches. As the crystal grows, the branches come together and trap small quantities of air.

He waited hours for just the right crystal and didn't notice the cold.

If the shed were warm the snow would melt. If he breathed on the black tray the snow would melt. If he twitched a muscle as he held the snow crystal on the long wooden pick the snowflake would break. He had to work fast or the snowflake would **evaporate** before he could slide it into place and take its picture. Some winters he was able to make only a few dozen good pictures.

Some winters he made hundreds.

STRATEGY SKILL

Summarize
Summarize how Willie would capture and photograph snow crystals. Include only important information.

Many things affect the way these crystal branches grow. A little more cold, a bit less wind, or a bit more moisture will mean different-shaped branches. Willie said that was why, in all his pictures, he never found two snowflakes alike.

Willie's nieces and nephews lived on one side of the farmhouse that Willie shared with his brother Charlie. Willie often played the piano as they sang and shared stories and games with them.

Willie so loved the beauty of nature he took pictures in all seasons.

In the summer his nieces and nephews rubbed coat hangers with sticky pitch from spruce trees. Then Willie could use them to pick up spider webs jeweled with water drops and take their pictures.

On fall nights he would gently tie a grasshopper to a flower so he could find it in the morning and photograph the dew-covered insect.

But his snow crystal pictures were always his
favorites. He gave copies away or sold them for
a few cents. He made special pictures as gifts
for birthdays.

Many colleges and universities bought lantern slide copies of his photographs and added to their collections each year. Artists and designers used the photographs to **inspire** their own work.

He held evening slide shows on the lawns of his friends. Children and adults sat on the grass and watched while Willie projected his slides onto a sheet hung over a clothesline.

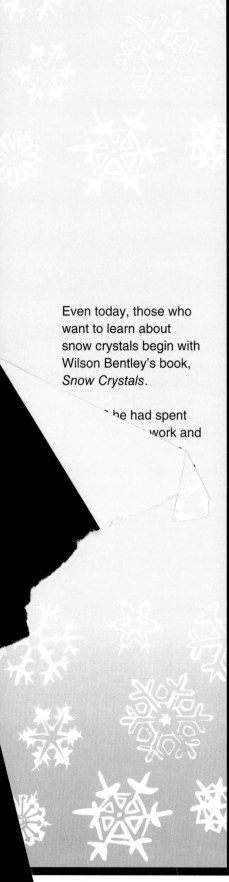

Even today, those who
want to learn about
snow crystals begin with
Wilson Bentley's book,
Snow Crystals.

he had spent
work and

He wrote about snow and published his pictures in magazines. He gave speeches about snow to faraway scholars and neighborhood skywatchers. "You are doing great work," said a professor from Wisconsin.

The little farmer came to be known as the world's expert on snow, "the Snowflake Man." But he never grew rich. He spent every penny on his pictures.

Willie said there were treasures in snow. "I can't afford to miss a single snowstorm," he told a friend. "I never know when I will find some wonderful prize."

Other scientists raised money so Willie could gather his best photographs in a book. When he was sixty-six years old Willie's book—his gift to the world—was published. Still, he was not ready to quit.

Less than a month after turning the first page on his book, Willie walked six miles home in a **blizzard** to make more pictures. He became ill with pneumonia after that walk and died two weeks later.

The plaque on the monument says
"SNOWFLAKE"
BENTLEY
Jericho's world famous snowflake authority

...y years Wilson A.
...simple farmer,
...g
...of o-
...uni...
...shap...
...numb...

...ov...y designs.

A monument was built for Willie in the center of town. The girls and boys who had been his neighbors grew up and told their sons and daughters the story of the man who loved snow. Forty years after Wilson Bentley's death, children in his village worked to set up a museum in honor of the farmer-scientist.

And his book has taken the delicate snow crystals that once blew across Vermont, past mountains, over the earth. Neighbors and strangers have come to know of the icy wonders that land on their own mittens— thanks to Snowflake Bentley.

STRATEGY SKILL

Summarize
Summarize how Snowflake Bentley lived his life.

SNAPSHOTS OF JACQUELINE AND MARY

Jacqueline Briggs Martin began to write this story after she saw a snowflake and thought about an article she had read about a man who loved snow. Jacqueline saw lots of snow when she was growing up. She lived on a farm in Maine, where she enjoyed nature, stories, and history.

Other books illustrated by Mary Azarian

Mary Azarian has also seen a lot of snow. Just like Wilson Bentley, she lives on a farm in Vermont. Mary used her experiences on the farm to create her woodcut illustrations.

LOG ON Find out more about Jacqueline Briggs Martin and Mary Azarian at **www.macmillanmh.com**

Author's Purpose

Why did Jacqueline Briggs Martin write *Snowflake Bentley*? Was her purpose for writing this biographical piece to explain, inform, entertain, or persuade? How do you know?

400

Comprehension Check

Summarize

Use your Main Idea Web to summarize *Snowflake Bentley.* Remember to include only the most important information in your summary.

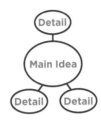

Think and Compare

 STRATEGY SKILL

1. Why did Wilson Bentley choose to make snowflake photography his life's work? **Evaluate: Summarize**

2. Look back at page 384 of *Snowflake Bentley.* Why did Wilson Bentley's father say that his son's hobby was "**foolishness**"? **Analyze**

3. If you could spend your life studying one thing in nature, what would it be? Explain your answer. **Synthesize**

4. Why is it important to study the world—even at the microscopic level? **Evaluate**

5. Compare the information in the main body text with the information in the sidebar text from *Snowflake Bentley.* How is the information different? How is it similar? Use details from both the main body text and the sidebar text in your answer. **Reading/Writing Across Texts**

Poetry

Haiku is poetry that uses three short lines to describe just one moment or scene. The first and third lines often have five syllables each, and the second line may have seven syllables.

Literary Elements

Imagery is the use of words to create a picture in the reader's mind.

Figurative Language goes beyond the usual meaning of words and uses them to describe something in a new way.

Winter solitude—
in a world of one color
the sound of wind.

—*Matsuo Basho*

The words "a world of one color" create a strong image of a snow-covered scene.

Mountains and plains,
all are captured by the snow—
nothing remains.

—*Joso*

The snow is melting
and the village is flooded
with children.

—*Kobayashi Issa*

Children do not really
flood the village. This
figurative language
suggests they are
running through the
streets like water.

No sky at all;
no earth at all—and still
the snowflakes fall....

—*Hashin*

Connect and Compare

1. In the second haiku, by Joso, the word "captured" is figurative language. What has really happened to the mountains and plains? **Figurative Language**

2. Reread "No Sky at All," by Hashin. What moment or scene does it describe? **Analyze**

3. When you read these poems, how do they make you feel about snow? How did you feel about snow when you read *Snowflake Bentley*? Compare the two feelings. **Reading/Writing Across Texts**

 Find out more about haiku at **www.macmillanmh.com**

403

I began with a topic sentence.

In my character sketch, I included both short and long sentences.

My New Character
by Sara K.

May Showers is the meteorologist I made up for my sitcom about a TV news station. Usually a man reports the weather. My meteorologist is a woman on my local TV news. I know you are picturing a heavy, happy weatherman, but May is slim, neatly dressed, and quiet. She doesn't get excited about the weather, except when it rains. Then she smiles, her eyes open wide, and she starts to bounce a little on her feet.

I like it when it rains, so my new character likes rain, too.

Your Turn

Invent a fascinating, original character. Then write one or two paragraphs that describe that character. Include your character's name. Describe his or her appearance. Include details to help your readers see your character's special traits. Begin sentences in different ways to improve fluency. Use the Writer's Checklist to check your writing.

Writer's Checklist

✓ **Ideas and Content:** Does my sketch include important and interesting details?

✓ **Organization:** Did I begin with a topic sentence?

✓ **Voice:** Does my paragraph show that I care about this character?

✓ **Word Choice:** Have I chosen words that help the reader picture this character?

☑ **Sentence Fluency:** Have I used a variety of sentences to make my writing interesting?

✓ **Conventions:** Have I used irregular verbs, such as *do, does,* and *did,* correctly? Did I check my spelling?

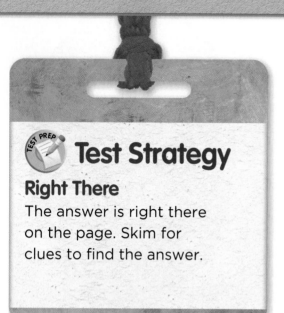

How to Change a Flat Tire on a Bike

by Sarah Tajima

If you ride a road bike, you're going to get flat tires. Sometimes the smallest piece of glass or a tiny stone can stop your ride.

If you do get a flat tire, your ride doesn't have to be over. Just be sure you're carrying a new tube, a pump, and three tire levers. Then follow these steps:

1 Take the bicycle wheel off the frame of the bike. If the tire is not completely flat, release the rest of the air from it.

Go On ▶

2 Pick up a tire lever. Place the thin end of the lever between the tire and the rim of the wheel.

3 Do the same thing with the other two tire levers. Find a spot on the wheel about two spokes over from where you placed the first tire lever.

4 Take the first lever out. Continue working your way around the rim. Stop when the tire is free from the rim. Remove the old tube.

Answer Questions

5 Check the tire for the cause of the flat. Carefully remove any objects. Use your bike pump to put just a little air in your new tube. Put the tube into your old tire. Be sure it doesn't have any twists or kinks.

6 Find the hole in the rim of your wheel for the tire valve. Put the tire valve in the tube through the hole as you pull the tire and tube over the wheel. Use your fingers to ease the tire onto the wheel.

7 Use the bike pump to blow the tire up. The tire should feel firm to the touch. Then put the wheel back on the bicycle frame.

Go On ▶

Tip

Skim for clues.

Directions: Answer the questions.

1. What do you need to do before you can remove the bicycle wheel from the frame?

A   Make sure the tire is completely filled with air.
B   Use the tire levers.
C   Release all the air.
D   Make sure the valve lines up with the hole in the rim.

2. Which word is a synonym for *kink*?

A   rim
B   lever
C   twist
D   tube

3. What should you do when the tire is back on the rim?

A   Check for the cause of the flat.
B   Remove the old tube.
C   Be sure there are no twists or kinks.
D   Use the pump to blow air into the tire.

4. Explain the MAIN steps in changing a flat tire.

5. What do you think is the hardest part of changing a flat tire? Use information from the directions to explain your choice.

Writing Prompt

Write a journal entry of three paragraphs that describes how you once tried to fix something. Describe the problem, what you did to fix it, and what happened as a result.

STOP 409

Talk About It

These dogs are taking a bus ride. Where do you think they are going?

Find out more about dogs at **www.macmillanmh.com**

Man's Best Friend

Puppy Trouble

by Liam Engell

We got back from the grocery store and found the house a mess. I had **neglected** to close the bathroom door again, and our Saint Bernard, Bernie, had left chewed toilet paper all over the house. Bernie was happily jumping up and running in circles. He had no idea that what he had done while we were away was not **appreciated**.

Bernie had already chewed Mom's favorite handbag and my new pair of shoes. Mom was also concerned that Bernie jumped up on people when I took him out for walks. She didn't want to take **risks** with the little kids on the block, and I couldn't blame her.

Mom said that if Bernie didn't start behaving, we couldn't keep him, and I knew Mom wasn't **bluffing**. I could tell she wasn't kidding. Her message was clear, so there was no way it could be **misunderstood**, And now Bernie was in trouble again.

I was **desperate**. If I didn't think of something really fast, I was going to lose my dog!

Then I had a really wonderful idea. It meant I would have to give up watching some of my favorite TV shows to spend more time with Bernie. In the end, though, if I could keep him, it was worth a try.

Just then, Mom finished putting the groceries away. She came into the living room and saw the mess.

"I've had it with this puppy," Mom said in a tired voice. "I'm just about out of patience, Lin."

"I know, Mom," I said, "you've **endured** Bernie's chewing and messes for three months now. But I've never had a pet before. If I'm not training him the right way, then it's not Bernie's fault. Can we try taking him to **obedience** school?" I asked.

And that's just what we did.

Reread for **Comprehension**

Generate Questions

Draw Conclusions Authors don't always tell everything that happens. Readers have to use what they already know and what the author *does* tell to draw conclusions. As you draw conclusions, ask yourself questions, such as, "Are there clues that support my conclusion?"

A Conclusions Chart can help you analyze what you read. Reread the selection to draw conclusions about the ending of the story.

Text Clues	Conclusion

Dear

Comprehension

Genre

A **Fantasy** is a story about characters and settings that could not exist in real life.

Generate Questions

Draw Conclusions As you read, fill in your Conclusions Chart.

Text Clues	Conclusion

Read to Find Out

How close to reality is the picture Ike is painting in his letters to Mrs. LaRue?

414

Mrs. LaRue
Letters from Obedience School

Written and Illustrated by
Mark Teague

Award Winning Selection

The Snort City Register / Gazette

September 30

LOCAL DOG ENTERS OBEDIENCE SCHOOL

"Ike LaRue"

Citing a long list of behavioral problems, Snort City resident Gertrude R. LaRue yesterday enrolled her dog, Ike, in the Igor Brotweiler Canine Academy.

Established in 1953, the Academy has a history of dealing with such issues.

"I'm at my wit's end!" said Mrs. LaRue. "I love Ike, but I'm afraid he's quite spoiled. He steals food right off the kitchen counter, chases the neighbor's cats, howls whenever I'm away, and last week while I was crossing the street he pulled me down and tore my best camel's hair coat! I just don't know what else to do!"

School officials were unavailable for comment . . .

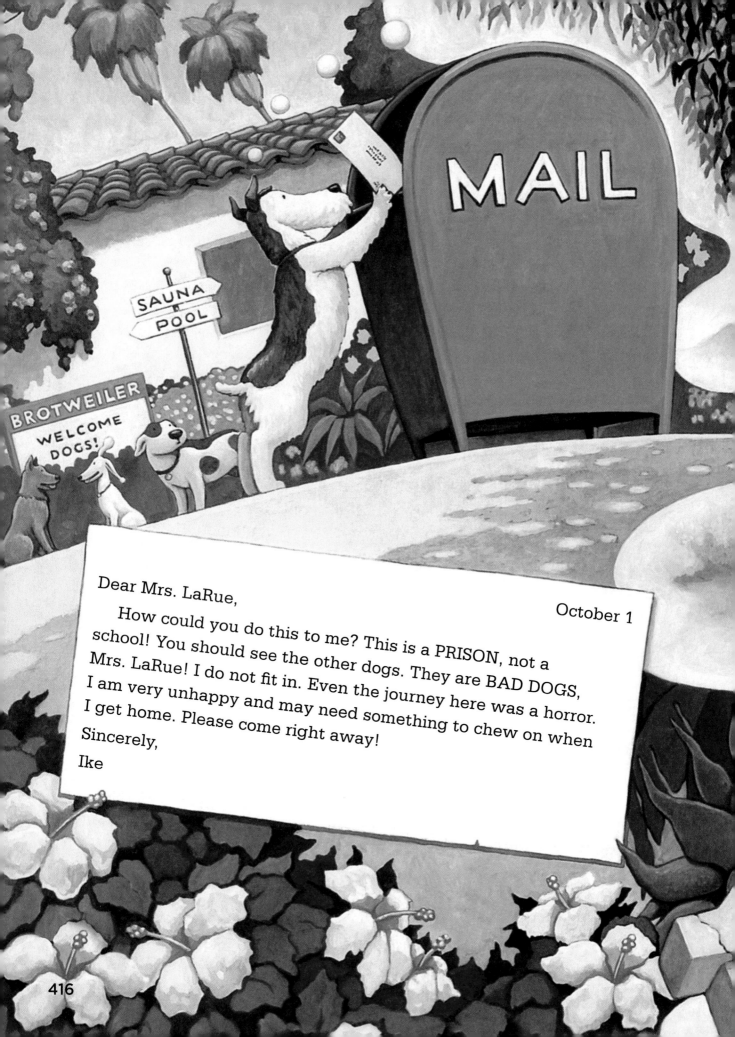

Dear Mrs. LaRue,

October 1

How could you do this to me? This is a PRISON, not a school! You should see the other dogs. They are BAD DOGS, Mrs. LaRue! I do not fit in. Even the journey here was a horror. I am very unhappy and may need something to chew on when I get home. Please come right away!

Sincerely,

Ike

417

October 3

Dear Mrs. LaRue,

    I'd like to clear up some misconceptions about the Hibbins' cats. First, they are hardly the little angels Mrs. Hibbins makes them out to be. Second, how should I know what they were doing out on the fire escape in the middle of January? They were being a bit melodramatic, don't you think, the way they cried and refused to come down? It's hard to believe they were really sick for three whole days, but you know cats.

Your dog,

Ike

October 4

Dear Mrs. LaRue,

You should see what goes on around here. The way my teach — I mean WARDEN, Miss Klondike, barks orders is shocking. Day after day I'm forced to perform the most meaningless tasks. Today it was "sit" and "roll over," all day long. I flatly refused to roll over. It's ridiculous. I won't do it. Of course I was SEVERELY punished.

And another thing: Who will help you cross the street while I'm away? You know you have a bad habit of not looking both ways. Think of all the times I've saved you. Well, there was that one time, anyway. I must say you weren't very grateful, complaining on and on about the tiny rip in your ratty old coat. But the point is, you need me!

Yours,

Ike

Dear Mrs. LaRue,

October 5

The GUARDS here are all caught up in this "good dog, bad dog" thing. I hear it constantly: "Good dog, Ike. Don't be a bad dog, Ike." Is it really so good to sit still like a lummox all day? Nevertheless, I refuse to be broken!

Miss Klondike has taken my typewriter. She claims it disturbs the other dogs. Does anybody care that the other dogs disturb ME?

Yours,

Ike

Dear Mrs. LaRue,

October 6

Were the neighbors really complaining about my howling? It is hard to imagine. First, I didn't howl that much. You were away those nights, so you wouldn't know, but trust me, it was quite moderate. Second, let's recall that these are the same neighbors who are constantly waking ME up in the middle of the afternoon with their loud vacuuming. I say we all have to learn to get along.

My life here continues to be a nightmare. You wouldn't believe what goes on in the cafeteria.

Sincerely,

Ike

P.S. I don't want to alarm you, but the thought of escape has crossed my mind!

October 7

Dear Mrs. LaRue,

I hate to tell you this, but I am terribly ill. It started in my paw, causing me to limp all day. Later I felt queasy, so that I could barely eat dinner (except for the yummy gravy). Then I began to moan and howl. Finally, I had to be taken to the vet. Dr. Wilfrey claims that he can't find anything wrong with me, but I am certain I have an awful disease. I must come home at once.

Honestly yours,

Ike

Draw Conclusions
What conclusion can you draw about Ike's illness?

October 8

Dear Mrs. LaRue,

Thank you for the lovely get well card. Still, I'm a little surprised that you didn't come get me. I know what Dr. Wilfrey says, but is it really wise to take **risks** with one's health? I could have a relapse, you know.

With fall here, I think about all the fine times we used to have in the park. Remember how sometimes you would bring along a tennis ball? You would throw it and I would retrieve it EVERY TIME, except for once when it landed in something nasty and I brought you back a stick instead. Ah, how I miss those days.

Yours truly,

Ike

P.S. Imagine how awful it is for me to be stuck inside my tiny cell!

P.P.S. I still feel pretty sick.

427

October 9

Dear Mrs. LaRue,

By the time you read this I will be gone. I have decided to attempt a daring escape! I'm sorry it has come to this, since I am really a very good dog, but frankly you left me no choice. How sad it is not to be **appreciated!** From now on I'll wander from town to town without a home — or even any dog food, most likely. Such is the life of a **desperate** outlaw. I will try to write to you from time to time as I carry on with my life of hardship and danger.

Your lonely fugitive,

Ike

October 10

LARUE ESCAPES DOGGY DETENTION

Former Snort City resident Ike LaRue escaped last night from the dormitory at the Igor Brotweiler Canine Academy. The dog is described as "toothy" by local police. His current whereabouts are unknown.

"To be honest, I thought he was **bluffing** when he told me he was planning to escape," said a visibly upset Gertrude R. LaRue, the dog's owner. "Ike tends to be a bit melodramatic, you know. Now I can only pray that he'll come back." Asked if she would return Ike to Brotweiler Academy, Mrs. LaRue said that she would have to wait and see. "He's a good dog basically, but he can be difficult. . . ."

Dear Mrs. LaRue,

October 11 — Somewhere in America

I continue to suffer horribly as I roam this barren wasteland. Who knows where my wanderings will take me now? Hopefully to someplace with yummy food! Remember the special treats you used to make for me? I miss them. I miss our nice, comfy apartment. But mostly, I miss you!

Your sad dog,

Ike

P.S. I even miss the Hibbins' cats, in a way.

October 12 — Still Somewhere

Dear Mrs. LaRue,
 The world is a hard and cruel place for a "stray" dog. You would scarcely believe the misery I've **endured**. So I have decided to return home. You may try to lock me up again, but that is a risk I must take. And frankly, even more than myself, I worry about you. You may not know it, Mrs. LaRue, but you need a dog!
 Your **misunderstood** friend,

 Ike

431

October 13

HERO DOG SAVES OWNER!

Ike LaRue, until recently a student at the Igor Brotweiler Canine Academy, returned to Snort City yesterday in dramatic fashion. In fact he arrived just in time to rescue his owner, Gertrude R. LaRue of Second Avenue, from an oncoming truck. Mrs. LaRue had made the trip downtown to purchase a new camel's hair coat. Apparently she **neglected** to look both ways before stepping out into traffic.

The daring rescue was witnessed by several onlookers, including patrolman Newton Smitzer. "He rolled right across two lanes of traffic to get at her," said Smitzer. "It was really something. I haven't seen rolling like that since I left the police academy."

433

Mrs. LaRue was unhurt in the incident, though her coat was badly torn. "I don't care about that," she said. "I'm just happy to have my Ike back home where he belongs!"

LaRue said she plans to throw a big party for the dog. "All the neighbors will be there, and I'm going to serve Ike's favorite dishes. . . ."

Write Home About
Mark Teague

Mark Teague says that this story is one of his favorites. He had lots of fun pretending he was Ike and writing from a dog's point of view. Mark based Ike on two dogs he and his brother had. One dog loved to eat, the other dog liked to play tricks. Now Mark has cats. He put them in this story, too. Mark gets ideas for many of his books from things he did as a boy. Then he adds a twist or two to make his stories really funny.

Other books by Mark Teague

LOG ON Find out more about Mark Teague at **www.macmillanmh.com**

MAIL

Author's Purpose

What clues can you use to determine Mark Teague's purpose for writing *Dear Mrs. LaRue*? Did the author want to explain, entertain, or persuade?

436

Comprehension Check

Summarize

Summarize *Dear Mrs. LaRue*. Include the most important events. Be sure to tell who is writing the letters and why.

Think and Compare

Text Clues	Conclusion

1. Do you think Mrs. LaRue **misunderstood** Ike? Why or why not? Review your Conclusions Chart to organize clues and answer the question. **Generate Questions: Draw Conclusions**

2. Look again at pages 420–421 of *Dear Mrs. LaRue.* Why do you think the cats were on the fire escape in January? Use story details in your answer. **Analyze**

3. If you were Mrs. LaRue, would you believe what Ike said in his letters? Why or why not? **Apply**

4. Sometimes people exaggerate a lot, the way Ike does. Why do you think people do this? **Analyze**

5. Read "Puppy Trouble" on pages 412–413. Compare it with *Dear Mrs. LaRue.* Which story is a fantasy, and which is realistic? How can you tell? Use details from both selections in your answer. **Reading/Writing Across Texts**

DOG AMAZES SCIENTISTS!

Rico the border collie has a knack for learning words.

by Kim Christopher

GERMANY – A border collie named Rico is amazing scientists with his knowledge of human language. Rico recognizes at least 200 words and quickly learns and remembers even more.

Rico began his training when he was ten months old. His owner, Susanne Baus, put toys in different places and had Rico fetch them by name. She rewarded Rico with food or by playing with him. Rico continued to learn more and more new words. Scientists first noticed Rico when he showed off his talent on a popular German game show.

Border collies are **intelligent** medium-sized dogs that have a lot of energy and are easily trained. They like to stay busy, and they like to please their owners.

Even though nine-year-old Rico knows 200 words, he doesn't know as many words as even the average two-year-old person does. Human nine-year-olds know thousands and thousands of words, and they learn about ten new words a day. Still, Rico's ability to find objects by name is so **impressive** that scientists wanted to study him.

Number of Words a Child Understands

 Reading a Line Graph

This graph shows how many words a child understands at different ages.

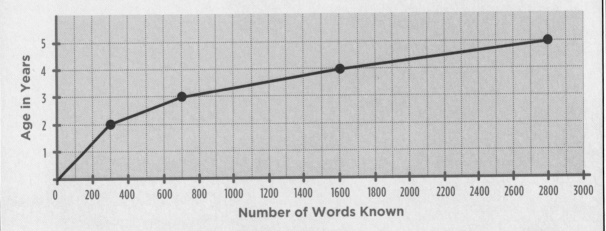

Number of Words Known

Humans have the ability to learn words far faster than even the smartest dog.

Scientists learned a lot about Rico as they watched him fetch familiar toys by name. Then Rico **demonstrated** something amazing. He showed scientists that he could pick out toys he had never seen before by name! Scientists put some familiar toys in a room. They added a new toy. Rico's owner asked him to fetch the new toy. Most of the time in these tests, Rico picked out the right toy.

Scientists think that Rico connects new words to new things. Since Rico already knows the names of old toys, he knows he should pick out a new toy when he hears a new word.

Rico can also remember the name of a new toy after just one **exposure**, or experience, with that toy. This shows scientists that even though animals are unable to talk, they can understand words. Rico's vocabulary seems to be as large as that of animals that have been trained in language. Those animals include apes, sea lions, dolphins, and parrots.

Most dog owners will tell you that their pets are very smart. But just how smart is Rico? Is he an outstanding dog in a breed known to be very intelligent? Or is Rico a "dog genius"?

Scientists are now studying Rico to learn more. They want to know if Rico can understand **phrases** such as "put the toy in the box." Rico's owner thinks that he can. The answers to questions about Rico's intelligence are still to come. The outcome of the study will be interesting to both scientists and dog owners all over the world.

Connect and Compare

1. Look at the line graph on page 439. About how many words does a 4-year-old understand? **Reading a Line Graph**

2. If you were a scientist, what other animals would you test for language skills? How would you do that? **Synthesize**

3. Think about this article and *Dear Mrs. LaRue*. What do you think Rico would say if he wrote a letter to his owner? **Reading/Writing Across Texts**

Science Activity

Research border collies. Report to the class where this breed originated and what it does best.

 Find out more about border collies at **www.macmillanmh.com**

I started with a topic sentence.

I explained how I solved my problem. I arranged my sentences in sequence order.

Write About Solving a Problem

Keep That Collar On

by Tammy G.

Our dog, Daisy, always used to slip out of her collar and run away. When she started to do this, we would chase her down and scold her.

My family discussed how to solve the problem. We listed different ideas we had. We crossed out the ideas that wouldn't work, like my brother's idea that we should stop taking Daisy for walks. Then we chose the best one. We got a stretchy collar, so it would stay on Daisy better. The problem was solved!

442

Your Turn

Write one or two paragraphs to explain how you solved a problem. Begin by stating the problem. Then list the steps you took to solve it. Be sure to rearrange ideas if necessary. Use the Writer's Checklist to check your writing.

Writer's Checklist

 Ideas and Content: Did I clearly describe the problem and how I solved it?

 Organization: Did I begin with a topic sentence and then rearrange ideas, if neccessary, to improve the order?

Voice: Can the reader tell that I care about this topic?

Word Choice: Did I choose words that are precise?

 Sentence Fluency: Does my writing sound choppy when I read it aloud? Can I join some sentences to improve the flow of my writing?

 Conventions: Do pronouns and their antecedents agree? Did I check my spelling?

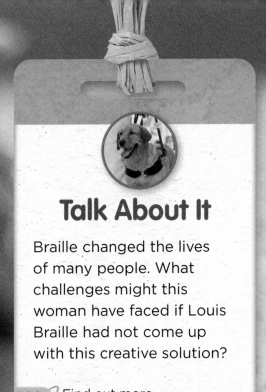

Talk About It

Braille changed the lives of many people. What challenges might this woman have faced if Louis Braille had not come up with this creative solution?

LOG ON Find out more about Braille at **www.macmillanmh.com**

CREATIVE SOLUTIONS

Through Elizabeth's Eyes

by Theresa Wisniewski

Elizabeth got out of bed, stretched, and dressed. She ate her favorite breakfast of scrambled eggs, toast, and juice. Her mother gave her a kiss before opening the front door and wishing her daughter a good day.

Elizabeth, **cautiously** tapping along, made her way down the sidewalk to her best friend Katrina's front door. Elizabeth used to attend a special school for the blind. Today she was joining Katrina at Washington Carver Elementary.

"Here comes my brother," Elizabeth remarked.

Katrina looked around but saw no one. Then, suddenly, Joshua came around the next corner on his skateboard. "How did you know Joshua was coming?" Katrina asked.

"From the rattle of the loose wheel on his board," replied Elizabeth. "I'd know it anywhere."

Katrina listened again until she heard that one **faint** sound **disguised** amongst all the much louder noises on the street. "You're amazing, Elizabeth," she exclaimed.

Joshua **crisscrossed** the sidewalk, coasting from one side to the other and back again, until he came to a stop in front of Elizabeth and Katrina. "Hey Sis," he said. "Good luck today!"

"Thanks, Josh," said Elizabeth. "Any words of **wisdom** for me?"

"Yeah," her brother replied, smirking. "Stay away from the sloppy joes in the cafeteria."

Katrina wondered if Elizabeth remembered being four or five, before her vision began to **fade**.

Katrina wondered how often her friend felt a twinge of **jealousy** toward the people around her who could see. She decided to ask.

"I used to think I couldn't do everything," explained Elizabeth. "But now I know that I can do most things. I just need a little more learning time."

Katrina gave her friend's hand a squeeze. "You really are amazing, Elizabeth," she said.

Reread for **Comprehension**

Generate Questions

Draw Conclusions Authors don't always spell out every detail. Readers often must apply what they know to the information the author *does* provide. As you draw conclusions, generate questions. For example, ask yourself, "Does this conclusion make sense?"

A Conclusions Chart can help you analyze what you read. Reread the selection to draw conclusions about Elizabeth.

Text Clues	Conclusion

Comprehension

Genre

Realistic Fiction is a made-up story that could have happened in real life.

Generate Questions

Draw Conclusions As you read, fill in your Conclusions chart.

Text Clues	Conclusion

Read to Find Out

What can a blind man and a young hunter learn from each other?

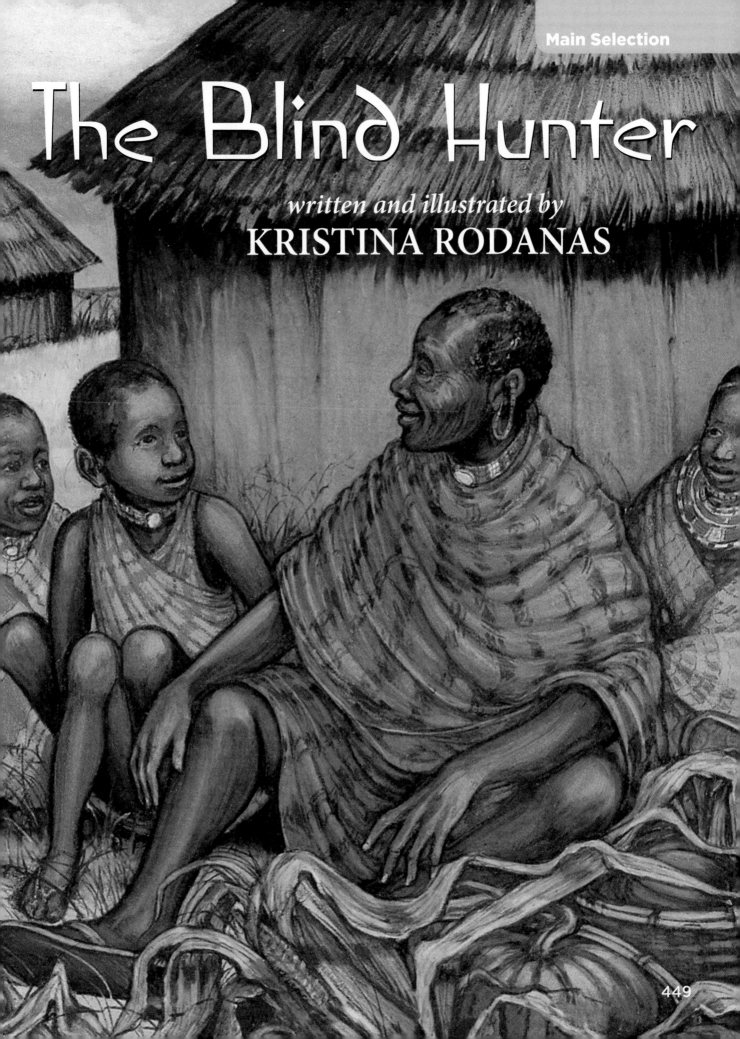

The Blind Hunter

written and illustrated by
KRISTINA RODANAS

In Africa, not so many years ago, a man named
Chirobo lived all by himself in a village of round huts. Each
day he went to work in his garden, carefully tending rows of
sunflowers, pumpkins, and corn. As he worked he sang sweet
songs, and birds of many colors flew out of the trees just to
hear him sing.

Chirobo was known to be wise and very kind. People often
came to him with questions, for it was said that his answers
were never wrong. When children came to visit, he always
stopped what he was doing so he could laugh with them and
listen to their stories.

Everyone in the village liked this gentle man with the warm smile. Hardly anyone ever seemed to notice that he was blind.

Early one evening, as Chirobo sat stirring a pot of stew, a stranger paused nearby to admire his garden. "Your crops are as beautiful as they are bountiful!" he exclaimed.

Chirobo beamed with pride and asked the young man if he had traveled far. The stranger explained that he was on a hunting trip. He was called Muteye and had come from a village a half day's walk from the west.

"When I return to my home, I will have a sack full of fat birds on my back," he boasted. "Then I will be welcomed as a great hunter!"

"Before my eyes began to **fade** I, too, was a hunter," said Chirobo. "Come sit with me and eat some of this fine stew. We will have much to talk about."

Muteye gladly accepted Chirobo's offer and joined him beside the cooking fire. He stayed for many hours sharing tales, laughing, and singing.

When the moon had climbed high above the distant trees, the young man got to his feet.

"Thank you, my friend, for your kindness," he said. "Is there anything I can do for you in return?"

Chirobo was silent for a few moments. "It would make me very happy if I could go hunting with you," he replied.

The young man laughed and said, "I will not hunt with a man who cannot see."

"I will be no trouble," Chirobo assured him. "I know how to see in other ways."

"Very well, then," said the young man. "Tomorrow, when the sun rises, we will go hunting. You may use one of my traps. Whatever you catch will be yours to keep."

 Draw Conclusions
What conclusion can you draw about Muteye's expectations for his hunting trip with Chirobo?

At the first light of dawn, the two men went out into the bush. The young man led the way, holding the end of a long, straight walking stick. Behind him the blind man followed, clutching the other end. They walked along a narrow path that wound through groves of crooked trees.

All of a sudden, Chirobo pulled back on the walking stick. He stood stone still, his hands cupped behind his ears. "We must be careful," he whispered. "There is a leopard nearby."

The young man gazed all around but could not see the
leopard. Then he glanced upward, where a strange pattern
caught his eye.

Above the path, draped along an acacia limb, a large cat
lay sleeping.

When they had safely passed the sleeping beast, Muteye
asked, "How does a man who lives in darkness know when a
leopard is near?"

Chirobo answered simply, "I know how to see with my ears."

The two men walked on without speaking, into a dense forest where the cool air echoed with the sound of a rushing stream. Again Chirobo tugged at the walking stick, stopping in his tracks. He tilted his head and breathed deeply.

"We must be careful," he warned. "There are warthogs around."

The young man looked in all directions but could not see them.

He hurried to the crest of a nearby hill and peered down through the brush. To his surprise, a herd of warthogs trotted into view, their sharp tusks flashing in the midday sun.

After the two hunters had safely passed the wild pigs, Muteye asked, "How does a man who lives in darkness know when there are warthogs about?"

The blind man smiled and said, "I know how to see with my nose."

They continued on into a wide valley that was thick with thorn bushes and the sweet scent of flowers. Once again, Chirobo gave the walking stick a tug and paused, his feet spread wide beneath him. He fell to his knees and placed his hands upon the ground.

"We must be careful," he murmured. "There are rhinos coming this way."

Muteye glanced about the thicket but could not see the rhinos.

Cautiously, he pushed aside the dense bushes and scanned the surrounding landscape. All of a sudden, a pair of rhinos appeared, stomping through the tall grass.

When the hunters had safely passed the two creatures, the young man turned and faced his friend. He asked, "How does a man who lives in darkness know when there are rhinos approaching?"

Quietly, Chirobo gave his answer, "I know how to see with my skin."

Together the men made their way deeper into the valley until they reached a shallow pond. Countless tracks of birds **crisscrossed** the soft, muddy bank.

"Birds come here for water," observed Muteye. "It is a good place to set our traps."

Following his friend's instructions, Chirobo placed his trap near the edge of the pond while the other man set his trap a short distance away. After he had **disguised** both traps, the young man said, "We will camp nearby and return tomorrow. Then we will see what we have caught."

That night they talked about many things. Muteye grew to admire the blind man's **wisdom** and asked him questions about which he had wondered for a long time.

Early the next morning, they returned to their hunting place. Chirobo knew right away that they had been successful. Excited, he cried, "There are birds in our traps. I can hear them!"

The young man checked his own trap first and discovered that he had caught a small, thin quail. Although he was disappointed, he carefully removed it and put it into a goatskin sack. Then he went to check the other trap.

As he kneeled down to look inside, his heart filled with **jealousy**. The blind man's trap contained a large duck, fat enough to feed a hungry jackal.

For a few moments Muteye hesitated as he considered the two birds and wondered, "How would a man who lives in darkness ever know which bird belonged to him?"

His mind made up, he quickly switched the thin bird for the plump one.

"Your bird is the larger of the two," he said as he handed the quail over to his companion. "It will make a fine meal."

Chirobo stroked the bird's scraggly wings and thoughtfully passed his fingers along its bony back and breast. Without speaking, he put it into his own sack.

Then the men gathered their traps and began the journey back to the village.

In silence they walked and walked, until they stopped to rest beneath an old baobab tree. Muteye was eager to continue the conversation of the night before, so he took the opportunity to ask his friend a question that had worried him since he was a small boy.

"Why do people fight each other?" he inquired.

Chirobo thought about his answer for a long time. When at last he began to speak, his voice was full of sadness.

He said slowly, "People fight because they take from each other what does not belong to them—as you have just done to me."

The young man was stunned by Chirobo's response. He tried to speak, but the words caught in his throat. Deeply ashamed, he reached for his sack and took out the large duck. He gently placed it into the blind man's hands.

In a **faint** voice, Muteye asked, "How does a man who has been unkind earn the forgiveness of his friend?"

Chirobo's blind eyes seemed to look deep into the young hunter's soul. He said, "By learning to see with his heart—as you have just done with me."

Draw Conclusions
What was the most important lesson the hunters learned?

Kristina Rodanas decided to write this story after she read a similar story in a collection of African folk tales. Kristina thought the tale had a special message worth sharing with readers all over the world.

Other books by Kristina Rodanas

DRAGONFLY'S TALE
Kristina Rodanas

THE STORY OF BLUE ELK
Retold by Gerald Hausman
Illustrated by Kristina Rodanas

LOG ON Find out more about Kristina Rodanas at **www.macmillanmh.com**

Author's Purpose

What was the author's purpose for writing *The Blind Hunter*? Do you think Kristina Rodanas wanted mainly to explain, persuade, entertain, or inform? How do you know? Point to clues in the story that support your answer.

Comprehension Check

Summarize

Summarize *The Blind Hunter*. Describe the story events in the order in which they happen. Include the main characters and the setting.

Think and Compare

1. Draw conclusions about Chirobo's character. What kind of person is he? What clues helped you draw that conclusion? Use your Conclusions Chart to organize your clues. **Generate Questions: Draw Conclusions**

Text Clues	Conclusion

2. Reread page 460 of *The Blind Hunter.* Why do you think Chirobo said nothing when he realized that Muteye had taken his bird? **Analyze**

3. If you could meet Chirobo, what would you ask him? **Apply**

4. What would happen if more people solved their problems with **wisdom** the way Chirobo does? **Apply**

5. Read "Through Elizabeth's Eyes" on pages 446–447. How are Elizabeth and Chirobo alike? Use details from both stories in your answer. **Reading/Writing Across Texts**

Social Studies

Genre

Magazine Articles give facts and information about interesting topics.

Text Feature

A **Glossary** defines selected words used in a text.

Content Vocabulary

devices   microphone
limited   accessories
refreshes

Make Life Easier for Everybody

by Adam Alexander

Our world changes every day. New inventions make life easier, better, and a lot more fun. People with disabilities benefit from new technology too. There are now many tools and **devices** that help them do what they want to do. Here are just a few.

At Home

At one time, people with disabilities were **limited** in what they could do at home. Many simple activities were difficult or impossible. With today's technology, they can do more. From faucet grippers to automated doors, handy devices now make working and relaxing at home a *lot* easier.

Using a Glossary

A **glossary** is an alphabetized list of definitions for difficult words or technical terms found within a text. A glossary usually appears at the back of a book and gives the same kind of information as a dictionary.

de·vice (di vīs´) *n.* something made for a particular purpose. The *device* permitted people to use the telephone without having to hold the handset. *syn.* invention, mechanism.

de·vise (di vīz´) *v.* to think out; invent.

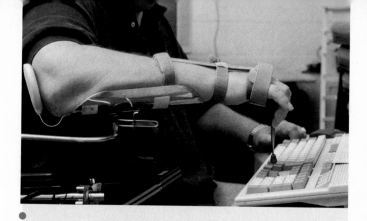

At Play

Do you enjoy skiing, biking, or playing sports? So do people with disabilities. Today they can find cleverly designed pieces of equipment for almost *any* activity.

Winter sports lovers can fly down ski slopes on sit skis. The skis lift up so skiers can get onto the chairlift. For water skiers, there are specially designed boards. And two-wheel hand bikes make bike riding exciting and fun. There are even short golf clubs for use with wheelchairs!

At the Computer

Computers play an important part in our lives today. Thanks to new technology, people with disabilities can use the computer for fun, learning, and communicating with others.

For people who find it hard to type, keyboards have been designed with special keys or spacing. There are even on-screen keyboards. These work using touch, a pointer, or a mouse.

People with limited or no sight can link a Braille display to their computer. Information from the computer is sent to the display. The display forms raised Braille characters that are read by touch. After each line is read, the display **refreshes**. The old line drops down and a new line of characters lifts up.

Computer programs for people with disabilities are being designed all the time. Some programs read aloud what is on a computer screen. Other programs write text as a person speaks into a **microphone**.

Getting Around

Many people with limited mobility use wheelchairs to get around. There are many kinds of wheelchairs, and many wheelchair **accessories**, or "add-ons." Accessories include special wheels and support arms for things like cameras and fishing poles. There are even wheelchairs designed for basketball, tennis, or the beach!

Connect and Compare

1. Look at the glossary entries on page 465. What does *devise* mean? **Using a Glossary**

2. What device would you design to help someone with a disability? How would the device make her or his life better? **Synthesize**

3. Think about *The Blind Hunter.* What might Chirobo say about the new devices for people with disabilities? Give reasons for your answer. **Reading/Writing Across Texts**

Social Studies Activity

Research a sport played by people with disabilities. Write about it. Include a title, drawing, and caption.

LOG ON Find out more about creative solutions at **www.macmillanmh.com**

Writer's Craft

Time-Order Words

Writers use **time-order words** such as *first, next,* and *then* when they write directions. These words help readers know exactly what to do and when to do it.

My directions begin with a time-order word.

I used other time-order words to tell the sequence of the steps.

Vegetable Barley Soup
by Harry H.

Yesterday Dad decided to show me how to make soup. He said some of the best chefs were men. He also said making soup kept him alive in college. This is how we easily made soup.

First, you fill a big pot 3/4 full with water and place it over a burner. Next, you see what vegetables you have. Dad sliced carrots and celery. I added a jar of tomato sauce and barley. Later, you have to skim off the junk that floats on top. The soup starts getting thicker as the water boils away. Then, you add some olive oil and spices, and you have soup!

Your Turn

Think about something you know how to do or how to make. Try to pick something that other people might want to learn how to do. Then write one or two paragraphs explaining how to do it. State your topic clearly in your opening sentence. List any materials that are needed. Then explain each step in order, using sequence words. Use the Writer's Checklist to check your writing.

Writer's Checklist

 Ideas and Content: Does my writing show knowledge of my subject? Did I leave out any important steps?

 Organization: Are my steps listed in sequence order?

 Voice: Will my readers sense my interest in this topic and want to try out my directions?

 Word Choice: Did I use time-order words such as *first, next,* and *then*?

 Sentence Fluency: Are my sentences easy to read and understand?

 Conventions: Did I use subject and object pronouns correctly? Did I check my spelling?

Talk About It

Does it matter what kind of energy we use and where we get it? Why or why not?

LOG ON Find out more about kinds and sources of energy at **www.macmillanmh.com**

Energy:
Power Source

Vocabulary

electrical
globe
fuels
decayed

A windmill farm in California uses clean technology to turn wind energy into electricity.

Clean as a Breeze

High wind speeds in the San Gorgonio Pass make conditions just right for delivering clean electricity to homes. Since 1998, Californians have been able to choose the source of their electricity. I am proud to say that my parents switched to a clean source of **electrical** power.

Though it costs a bit more to generate electricity from wind than from fossil fuels, my parents decided to help the environment. They knew that burning fossil fuels always releases pollutants into the air.

"Choosing wind or solar power is the key to making sure that Earth's future is bright," says Nancy Hazard. Part of an organization that promotes the use of non-polluting energy sources, Ms. Hazard also says, "Creating that vision and really going for it—that's how we'll get energized!"

Around the **globe**, more people than ever are willing to pay extra for clean sources of energy. If you live in a place where power might be generated with a clean technology, get things rolling by talking to your parents and teachers. Remember: "Clean Energy for a Bright, Pollution-Free Future!"

Tiayana Banks, Palm Springs, CA

LOG ON Find out more about renewable energy sources at **www.macmillanmh.com**

U.S. Energy Sources

Nuclear power plants generate some of the energy we use, but most of our energy comes from **fuels** such as oil, natural gas, and coal. These fuels are called fossil fuels. Over millions of years, heat and pressure from deep within Earth have reacted with the remains of plants and animals that have **decayed** to form fuel. Once these natural resources are used up, they are gone forever.

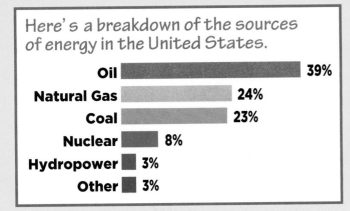

Nuclear power plant

Here's a breakdown of the sources of energy in the United States.

Oil	39%
Natural Gas	24%
Coal	23%
Nuclear	8%
Hydropower	3%
Other	3%

Renewable energy sources can be reused, and they create much less pollution than fossil fuels.

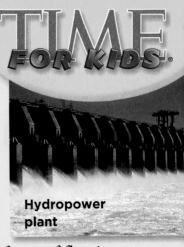

Hydropower plant

- Hydropower uses the force of flowing water to create electricity.
- Solar energy comes from the sun.
- Wind turbines are machines that look like giant windmills. They use the force of the wind to create electricity.
- Geothermal energy comes from heat in Earth's core that is used to create electricity.
- Biomass includes natural products such as wood and corn. These materials are burned and used for heat.

Top 5 Oil Users

= 1 million barrels

Worldwide, people use more than 80 million barrels of oil per day. A barrel contains 42 gallons. These countries are the biggest oil guzzlers. China's oil consumption is growing faster than that of any other country.

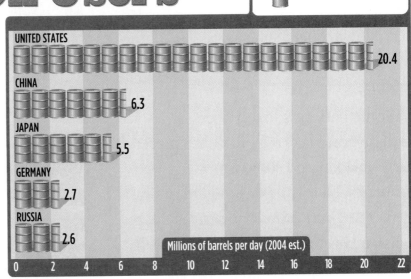

UNITED STATES 20.4
CHINA 6.3
JAPAN 5.5
GERMANY 2.7
RUSSIA 2.6

Millions of barrels per day (2004 est.)

0 2 4 6 8 10 12 14 16 18 20 22

THE POWER OF OIL

WHAT MAKES OIL SO VALUABLE AND ALSO SO CHALLENGING?

What can you find deep beneath Earth's surface? Here's a hint: it's shiny, sticky, slick, and very powerful. It's oil.

Oil began forming hundreds of millions of years ago as plant and animal remains were covered with layers of rock. Over the ages, those remains **decayed**. They turned into a mighty black brew that we use to make **fuels**. Fuels, such as gasoline, are energy sources that are usually burned to produce power.

Some nations sit atop huge underground lakes of oil. Other places, such as Japan and some European countries, have little or no oil of their own. The United States produces oil, but it also buys about 59% of what it needs.

Oil field worker

Oil is a very important fuel because it helps power cars, trucks, trains, planes, factories, and **electrical** plants. Oil is also an ingredient in some products such as tires, crayons, and other things.

Oil is also a messy fossil fuel. When fossil fuels burn, they release carbon dioxide and other polluting gases. The gases are bad for our health and our planet. They can trap heat near Earth's surface, contributing to the worldwide rise in temperatures known as global warming. Ships carrying oil also have spilled millions of gallons, polluting oceans and shorelines and killing sea life.

HOOKED ON OIL

The United States uses more oil than any other country on the **globe**. Most is pumped into our 200 million cars in the form of gasoline. On average, an American burns through 25 barrels of oil each year. Compare this with 15 barrels for a citizen of Japan or 12 for a person living in France.

Some of the 200 million cars on American roads

WHERE DOES ALL THE OIL GO?

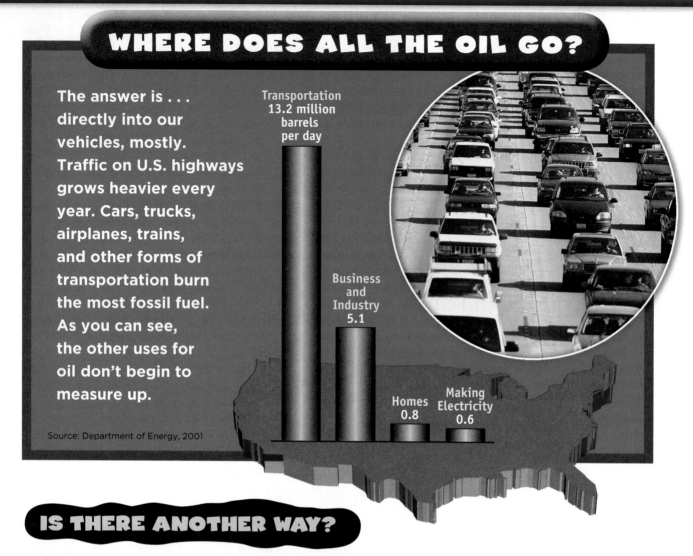

The answer is . . . directly into our vehicles, mostly. Traffic on U.S. highways grows heavier every year. Cars, trucks, airplanes, trains, and other forms of transportation burn the most fossil fuel. As you can see, the other uses for oil don't begin to measure up.

Source: Department of Energy, 2001

Transportation
13.2 million
barrels
per day

Business
and
Industry
5.1

Homes
0.8

Making
Electricity
0.6

IS THERE ANOTHER WAY?

If oil causes so many problems, why do we depend on it? For starters, nearly all of our cars and factories are designed to use oil and gas. Changing them to use other fuels would be very costly.

Still, it's possible to use less. In 1973, a few oil-producing nations got angry at the U.S. The price of oil tripled in just a few months. Gasoline was in short supply and there were long lines at gas stations. That forced auto companies to build cars that use less gas. In 1975, the average car could go just 12 miles on one gallon of gas. By 1990, some cars could travel 30 miles on just one gallon.

In recent years, oil prices dropped and Americans went back to buying big gas-guzzlers. About one of every four cars now sold is a sport utility vehicle (SUV), which get as little as 10 or 11 miles per gallon. But that's starting to change, too.

WHAT ARE YOU WAITING FOR?

Hybrid car

The Facts Are In

Research says roughly 88,000 hybrids were sold in the United States in 2004. That total will climb to 535,000 hybrids per year by 2011. Hybrids use electric motors and battery packs to improve fuel efficiency. A hybrid engine gets better gas mileage than one that runs on gasoline. Hybrid owners save money at the pumps, and through 2006 they are also getting a $2,000 tax break. Best of all, hybrid drivers are cutting their annual emission levels by a whopping 90%!

What Hybrid Drivers Are Saying

- Bill says, "I'd have to throw an anchor out of my window to get mileage less than 40 mpg."
- Dennis says, "I have 60,000 miles on my hybrid. Love it! My lifetime mileage is 53 mpg!"

Celebrities Are Joining the Bandwagon

Many actors and professional athletes are driving hybrids. They are raving about the performance of their cars and feeling good about making the responsible choice.

Come See for Yourself!

In celebration of Earth Day, alternative energy groups across the nation will be hosting at least one presentation of hybrid vehicles in every state. Find the location of the one near you by logging on to www.earthdayevents.example.com. See for yourself! "The Hybrid—It's the Future Now."

Think and Compare

1. What is oil made from?

2. How did the oil supply affect the design of American cars?

3. If you wanted to persuade someone to buy a hybrid vehicle, what persuasive argument would you make? Which techniques of persuasion would you use?

4. Based on what you have read in "Clean as a Breeze" and "What Are You Waiting For?" how would you explain the relationship between clean energy choices and emission levels?

Mackenzie Burkhart

Test Strategy
Author and Me
The answer is not always directly stated. Think about everything you have read to figure out the best answer.

Windmills on the Prairies

"Prairies are beautiful places," says Mackenzie Burkhart. "The long, flowing grass looks just like the ocean."

This sixth-grader from Park Ridge, Illinois, worries that nuclear reactors threaten the prairies in his state. A dozen reactors produce nearly three-quarters of all the electricity for the state. Mackenzie believes nuclear reactors have the potential to be extremely dangerous. In an accident at a nuclear power plant, nuclear waste could leak out. That could have devastating effects on the plants and animals of the prairies.

Burkhart's proposed solution: Provide energy from a more environmentally safe source—windmills!

Big, colorful windmills caught Mackenzie's eye while he was on vacation in Denmark with his family. "Windmills were everywhere, and they provided power for much of the country," he says.

Not only would windmills be environmentally safer, but, as Mackenzie points out, they are also a renewable source of power. Unlike fossil fuels or even nuclear fuels, he says, "wind is endless."

Go On

Directions: Answer the questions.

1. **Why are nuclear reactors used as a power source?**

   A   to replace nonrenewable sources like fossil fuels
   B   because they are the only safe source of power
   C   they can never endanger the environment
   D   they are the cheapest form of energy

2. **Some countries use windmills for power.
   What is the problem with using windmills?**

   A   They create pollution.
   B   They can hurt animals and wildlife.
   C   They only work when there is enough wind.
   D   They only work in the summer.

> **Tip**
> You have to think about the entire passage to choose the best answer.

3. **Why is it important to create alternatives to nonrenewable energy sources?**

   A   Winters are getting colder in many parts of the world.
   B   Global warming increases our need for energy.
   C   People want to choose where their power comes from.
   D   Our limited supply of natural resources won't last forever.

4. **What reasons would you give for switching from nuclear power to windmill power in your town?**

5. **What is another alternative energy source to replace fossil fuels and nuclear reactors? Describe this source and tell why you think it would work. Use details from the article to support your response.**

Write to a Prompt

In the selection "The Power of Oil" you read about the importance and challenges of oil. Imagine you own a hybrid car and are taking a road trip with friends. Suddenly you spot something in the road. In one or more paragraphs, write about what you see. Make sure your story has a beginning, a middle, and an ending.

I made sure my ending included the solution to the problem.

On the Road

Jake, Krista, Alex, and I were cruising down the road in my hybrid. I slammed on the brakes. A large, unfamiliar object sat in the middle of the road.

We saw that several people were standing in front of the object. They all looked upset, but a kid about 10 seemed most upset of all. "What happened?" I asked.

"We ran out of gas," the kid told me. "I'll never make soccer practice!" He slumped against the huge hulk. Suddenly I realized what it was: a gas guzzler, a kind of car lots of people had years ago.

My friends and I didn't know people still drove gas-powered cars. Luckily, Alex had an idea. "You can hop in with us," he said. "Leave your car here."

"Good idea," I said. "We'll make some calls. We can probably find someone who knows how to get some gas."

Writing Prompt

In the selection "The Power of Oil" you read about some of the problems of oil. Imagine you are the inventor of a car that uses solar or wind energy. You are out driving in your new car when the unexpected happens. Write a story about what happens. Make sure your story has a beginning, a middle, and a strong ending.

Writer's Checklist

- ☑ Ask yourself, who will read my story?
- ☑ Think about your purpose for writing.
- ☑ Plan your writing before beginning.
- ☑ Use details to support your story.
- ☑ Be sure your story has a beginning, a middle, and an ending.
- ☑ Use your best spelling, grammar, and punctuation.

Talk About It

Have you seen a whale in a movie or on TV? At the aquarium or in the sea? What were some of the things you thought or felt?

 Find out more about whales at **www.macmillanmh.com**

WHALES

Vocabulary

rumbling	massive
snoring	tangles
unique	politicians
dove	

Dictionary

Homographs are words that are spelled the same but have different meanings and may have different pronunciations.

dove = past tense of *dive*

dove = a type of bird

A Whale
of a Trip!
by Kristin Gold

"**L**adies and gentlemen," shouted Matty, our guide. He had to yell over the **rumbling** sounds of the boat's engines. "I don't want to hear any **snoring**," he teased. "You're in for a **unique** and exciting trip."

Matty continued, "I want to give you a little information about whales." First he explained that whales are mammals, not fish. He also informed us that a group of whales is called a pod.

The first thing we saw were birds flying alongside our boat. One **dove** sharply toward the water, and then flew up again! "That's a dovekie," explained Matty. "Whales may be nearby."

"There are two major groups of whales," Matty continued, "baleen whales and toothed whales. Instead of teeth, baleen whales have plates that act like a big sieve and collect food. These birds hang around to eat the tiny fish that slip out of the whales' mouths!"

When a whale suddenly surfaced, I couldn't believe how big it was. It was **massive**!

Soon we saw another whale slap its tail on the water.

"Is it angry?" I asked Matty.

"Probably not," said Matty. "That's called lobtailing. Some scientists think it's a warning to other whales. Others think they're just playing or cleaning their tails."

Matty explained that it's against the law to hunt humpback whales, but whales get killed anyway. The huge nets fishermen use to catch tuna often trap whales, too. Matty said these **tangles** can be prevented by using other kinds of nets. Some concerned people want the **politicians** to help by passing more laws to protect whales.

When we reached the dock, we realized that Matty was right. The whale watching trip had been exciting and one-of-a-kind.

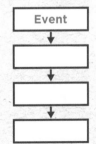

Reread for **Comprehension**

Analyze Text Structure

Sequence Sometimes authors use signal words to help readers know the order in which events occur. Words like *first, next,* and *last* are signal words.

A Sequence Chart can help you analyze text structure, or understand how a selection is organized. Reread to find the sequence of events on the field trip.

Event

Comprehension

Genre

A **Photo Essay** is an article or book composed mostly of photographs to express a theme or topic.

Analyze Text Structure

Sequence As you read, fill in your Sequence Chart.

Event
↓
↓
↓

Read to Find Out

How have the yearly visits of the whales affected Adelina's life?

Adelina's WHALES

Text and photographs by
RICHARD SOBOL

487

La Laguna is the name of a quiet, dusty fishing village on the sandy shore of Laguna San Ignacio, in Baja California, Mexico. A few dozen homesites are scattered along the water's edge. These little houses are simple one- or two-room boxes patched together with plywood and sheet metal. Drinking water is stored outside in fifty-gallon plastic barrels, and electricity is turned on for only a few hours each day.

Adelina Mayoral has lived her whole life in La Laguna. She is a bright ten-year-old girl. She loves the ocean and the feeling of the ever-present wind that blows her long, dark hair into wild **tangles**. She knows what time of day it is by looking at the way the light reflects off the water. Adelina can tell what month it is by watching the kind of birds that nest in the mangroves behind her home. She can even recognize when it is low tide. Simply by taking a deep breath through her nose, she can smell the clams and seaweed that bake in the hot sun on the shoreline as the water level goes down.

In late January, every afternoon after school, Adelina walks to the beach to see if her friends—the gray whales—have returned. At this same time every year the whales come, traveling from as far away as Alaska and Russia. They slowly and steadily swim south, covering more than five thousand miles along the Pacific Coast during November, December, and January.

One night Adelina is awakened by a loud, low, **rumbling** noise. It is the sound of a forty-ton gray whale exhaling a room-size blast of hot wet air. As she has always known they would, the gray whales have come again to visit. Adelina smiles and returns to her sleep, comforted by the sounds of whales breathing and **snoring** outside her window. At daybreak she runs to the lagoon and sees two clouds of mist out over the water, the milky trails of breath left by a mother gray whale and her newborn calf.

The waters of the protected lagoon are warm and shallow. The scientists who have come to visit and study the whales have explained that Laguna San Ignacio is the perfect place for the mother whales to have their babies and then teach them how to swim. But Adelina knows why they really come—to visit her!

Adelina's family lives far away from big cities with highways and shopping malls. Her little village does not have any movie theaters or traffic lights, but she knows that her hometown is a special place. This is the only place on earth where these giant gray whales—totally wild animals—choose to seek out the touch of a human hand. Only here in Laguna San Ignacio do whales ever stop swimming and say hello to their human neighbors. Raising their **massive** heads up out of the water, they come face-to-face with people. Some mother whales even lift their newborns up on their backs to help them get a better view of those who have come to see them. Or maybe they are just showing off, sharing their new baby the way any proud parent would.

491

The whales have been coming to this lagoon for hundreds of years, and Adelina is proud that her grandfather, Pachico, was the first person to tell of a "friendly" visit with one. She loves to hear him tell the story of that whale and that day. She listens closely as he talks about being frightened, since he didn't know then that the whale was only being friendly. He thought he was in big trouble.

Adelina looks first at the tight, leathery skin of her grandfather, browned from his many years of fishing in the bright tropical sun. From his face she glances down to the small plastic model of a gray whale that he keeps close by. As he begins to tell the story of his first friendly whale encounter, there is a twinkle in his eye and a large smile on his face. Adelina and her father, Runolfo, smile too, listening again to the story that they have heard so many times before.

In a whisper, her grandfather begins to draw them in.
Adelina closes her eyes to imagine the calm and quiet on that
first afternoon when his small boat was gently nudged by a
huge gray whale. As the boat rocked, her grandfather and
his fishing partner's hearts pounded. They held tight and
waited, preparing themselves to be thrown into the water by
the giant animal. The whale **dove** below them and surfaced
again on the opposite side of their boat, scraping her head
along the smooth sides. Instead of being tossed from the
boat, they were surprised to find themselves still upright
and floating.

For the next hour the whale glided alongside them,
bumping and bobbing gently—as gently as possible for an
animal that is as long as a school bus and as wide as a soccer
goal. As the sun started to set behind them, the whale gave
out a great blast of wet, snotty saltwater that soaked their
clothes and stuck to their skin. The whale then rose up
inches away from their boat and dove into the sea. Her first
visit was over.

As her grandfather finishes the story, he looks to Adelina, who joins him in speaking the last line of the story: "Well, my friend, no fish today!" they say before breaking into laughter.

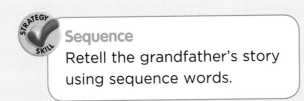

Sequence

Retell the grandfather's story using sequence words.

After this first friendly visit with the whales, word quickly spread of the **unique** encounter between a wild fifty-foot whale and a tiny fishing boat. Scientists and whale watchers started to come to Laguna San Ignacio to see the whales themselves. Perhaps word spread among the whales, too, because now dozens of whales began to approach the small boats. With brains as large as a car's engine, gray whales might even have their own language. They "talk" in low rumbles and loud clicks, making noises that sound like the tappings of a steel drum or the ticking that a playing card makes as it slaps against the spokes of a turning bicycle wheel. Maybe they told each other that it was safe to visit here.

Adelina's favorite time of the day is the late afternoon, when her father and grandfather return from their trips on the water, guiding visitors to see the whales. They sit together as the sun goes down behind them, and she listens to stories of the whales. She asks them lots and lots of questions.

Adelina has learned a lot about the gray whales. She knows that when a whale leaps out of the water and makes a giant splash falling back in, it's called breaching. When a whale pops its head straight up out of the water, as if it is looking around to see what is going on, it is called spyhopping. Adelina also learned how the whale's wide, flat tail is called a fluke, and when it raises its tail up in the air as it goes into a deep dive, that is called fluking.

Although her home is a simple one on a sandy bluff hugging the edge of the Pacific Ocean, Adelina has many new friends who come to share her world. She has met people who come from beyond the end of the winding, bumpy road that rings the lagoon. Some are famous actors. Some are **politicians**. Some speak Spanish. Some speak English. Those that weigh forty tons speak to her in their own magical style. The whales have taught her that the world is a big place.

Adelina knows that she has many choices in her future. Sometimes she giggles with delight at the idea of being the first girl to captain a *panga* (a small open fishing boat) and teach people about the whales in the lagoon. Or sometimes she thinks she may become a biologist who studies the ocean and can one day help to unlock some of the mysteries of the whales in her own backyard. Or maybe she will take pictures like the photographer whom she watches juggling his three cameras as he stumbles aboard the whale-watching boat. But no matter what she chooses, the whales will always be a part of her life.

For these three months Adelina knows how lucky she is to live in Laguna San Ignacio, the little corner of Mexico that the gray whales choose for their winter home. This is the place where two worlds join together. She wouldn't trade it for anything.

Sequence
What events drew whale watchers to Laguna San Ignacio? Be sure to name the events in the order in which they occurred.

In the early spring the lagoon grows quiet. One by one the whales swim off, heading north for a summer of feeding. On their heads and backs they carry the fingerprints of those they met, the memories of their encounters in Mexico. Maybe, as the whales sleep, they dream of the colorful sunsets of Laguna San Ignacio.

Every afternoon Adelina continues to gaze across the water. Sometimes now, when she closes her eyes, she can still see the whales swimming by. And if she listens *really* closely, she can even hear their breathing.

Limericks

A Whale of a Meal

There once was a whale named Alene
Who strained all her meals through baleen.
But she dreamed of a lunch
With a food that goes "crunch"
Like a truckload of just-picked string beans.
—Doreen Beauregard

Whale Watch

The meter in these three lines is created by emphasizing the third, sixth, and ninth syllables.

Near our boat is a mammal named Luke
Who's exceedingly proud of his fluke.
Just don't call it a tail
Or this dignified whale
Will respond with a splashy rebuke.
—Doreen Beauregard

The Podless Whale

There once was a whale near Cape Cod
Who just could not locate his pod.
So he joined with a mass
Of bewildered sea bass
Who found this behavior quite odd.
—Doreen Beauregard

The last line of a limerick always rhymes with the first two lines. The second and third lines have a different rhyme.

Connect and Compare

1. What is the rhyme scheme of "Whale Watch"? What if the last line rhymed with the third and fourth lines? **Rhyme Scheme**

2. Why were the sea bass in "The Podless Whale" bewildered? **Apply**

3. How are the whales in these poems similar to the ones in *Adelina's Whales?* How are they different? **Reading/Writing Across Texts**

 Find out more about limericks at **www.macmillanmh.com**

Writer's Craft

Voice

Writers want their readers to understand their point of view. They use appropriate words to show **voice** and to share their opinions.

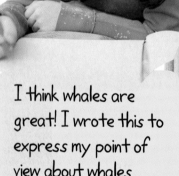

I think whales are great! I wrote this to express my point of view about whales.

I tried to show why I feel that whales are important.

Why We Need Whales

by Maggie W.

We learned in class today that some kinds of whales are in danger of becoming extinct. I think we should try to save them. We need whales.

Why do we need whales? We don't need them for food. They don't do any work for us. But they are fascinating to watch. They seem to play and talk together. The world would be less interesting if there were no whales.

I want the world to be an interesting place, so I hope there will always be whales making their wonderful noises.

Your Turn

Write an article of one or two paragraphs to explain your point of view about the importance of animals. You may write about animals in general or one kind of animal in particular. State your opinion and give strong reasons for it. Save your strongest reason for last. Back up your reasons with examples. End by restating your opinion. Use the Writer's Checklist to check your writing.

Writer's Checklist

 Ideas and Content: Did I explain my point of view clearly?

 Organization: Did I state my opinion first and then give reasons to explain it? Did I save the strongest reason for last?

 Voice: Is my voice clear as I write about the topic?

 Word Choice: Did I choose words carefully?

 Sentence Fluency: Did I vary the length of my sentences?

 Conventions: Did I spell possessive pronouns correctly?

The SEA

Talk About It

If you could explore under the sea, where would you like to go? What would you want to see?

LOG ON Find out more about the sea at **www.macmillanmh.com**

Coral Reefs

by Mindy Smith

Vocabulary

coral   eventually

reef   brittle

partnership   suburbs

current

Context Clues

Descriptions in the surrounding text can give clues to the meaning of an unfamiliar word.

Use context clues to find the meaning of *suburbs*.

Coral comes in a variety of shapes, colors, and sizes. It can be the size of the head of a pin or a foot in diameter. Although corals are often mistaken for rocks or plants, they are actually very small animals. When thousands of these animals are grouped together to form a mound or a tree shape, it is called a coral colony. Thousands of these colonies make up a **reef**.

There are more than 700 kinds of coral but only two main types. Each kind of coral is either a soft coral or a hard coral.

The easiest way to identify a hard coral is by its appearance. A colony of hard corals can resemble a vase, a plate, a little tree, a boulder, a brain, or the antlers of an elk. Hard corals have groups of six, smooth tentacles around their mouths. They get their name from the hard cup-like skeletons of limestone that they produce out of seawater.

Soft corals always have eight feathery tentacles around their mouths. They have names like sea fan, sea whip, or sea fingers and are as soft and bendable as plants or tree branches. Soft corals do not have hard skeletons. They have woody cores that support them instead. Soft corals often live on coral reefs along with hard corals, but soft corals can also live in cool, dark regions where hard corals would die.

Hard corals cannot live as far from the surface as soft corals because hard corals have plants, called algae, living inside of them. Through this **partnership**, the algae provide most of the coral polyp's food and the polyp gives the algae protection from the predators that eat them. The algae, though, require sunlight in order to live.

Hard corals begin their lives as fertilized eggs. These develop into soft larvae which drift with the **current** of the waves until they attach themselves to a part of the existing reef. **Eventually** the coral polyps die and other living larvae attach themselves to their skeletons.

Scientists believe that the existing coral reefs began to grow over 50 million years ago. When seaweed, sponges, giant clams, oysters, starfish, and **brittle** stars die, they serve as the foundations upon which another generation of hard coral polyps will attach and grow. In this way, the hard corals are the architects of the community—from the downtown area out to the **suburbs**.

The sprawling structures of the coral reefs support a quarter of all known sea animals. This includes over 4,000 different kinds of fish, along with mollusks, octopus and squid, sponges, algae, seaweed, shrimp, sea turtles, and sharks.

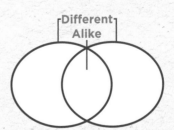

Reread for **Comprehension**

Analyze Text Structure

Compare and Contrast Authors sometimes organize a selection by comparing and contrasting two or more things. Comparing is telling how things or people are alike. Contrasting is telling how they are different.

A Venn Diagram can help you analyze text structure. Reread the selection and diagram how soft and hard corals are alike and different.

Different
Alike

Comprehension

Genre

Narrative Nonfiction is a true story or account about actual persons, living things, situations, or events.

Analyze Text Structure

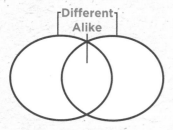

Compare and Contrast
As you read, fill in your Venn Diagram.

Different
Alike

Read to Find Out

How does a coral reef change and grow?

AT HOME IN THE
Coral Reef

by Katy Muzik • Illustrated by Katherine Brown-Wing

513

Down, down, down in the tropical clear blue sea lives a beautiful **coral** reef. The coral **reef** is a wonderful home for hundreds of kinds of fish and thousands of other kinds of creatures. The reef itself is made of zillions of tiny animals called coral polyps.

Each tiny coral polyp catches food with its little arms, called tentacles. The polyps share their food and live so close together that their skeletons are connected.

Some kinds of coral polyps make soft skeletons that sway gently back and forth in the water. These polyps have 8 tentacles. Other coral polyps make skeletons that are as hard as rock. Their hard skeletons form the coral reef. A hard coral polyp has 12, or 24, or 48, or more tentacles! Together, over 50 kinds of hard coral form this reef in the Caribbean Sea.

tentacles

coral polyp

planula

blue headed
wrasses

adult

coral egg

baby

What are these pink things? Coral eggs! Once a year, coral polyps have babies. Eggs and sperm pop out of the polyps and float up and up to the top of the blue sea. There each fertilized egg becomes a baby coral called a planula. Now it is ready to search for a new home.

The planula is completely covered with little hairs. It swims by waving them through the water, but it cannot swim very fast. Watch out for those hungry wrasses!

Just in time, a big wave carries the planula away to the crest, or top, of the coral reef. Here the water is very shallow. Because it is so shallow, the waves break and crash into the reef.

Splash! Crash! The breaking waves make the water very rough. It's so rough that only a few animals can live here. A fireworm holds on tight. A school of blue tangs darts in and out, hunting for food.

Crash! Splash! Will this be home for the planula? No, it's too rough. The planula is swept along, riding a wave over the crest to the lagoon.

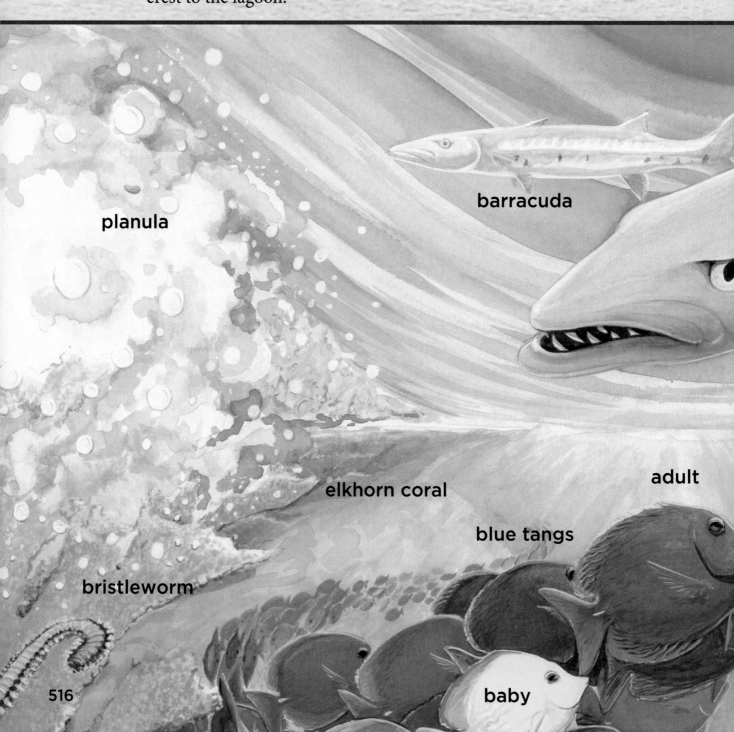

planula

barracuda

adult

elkhorn coral

blue tangs

bristleworm

baby

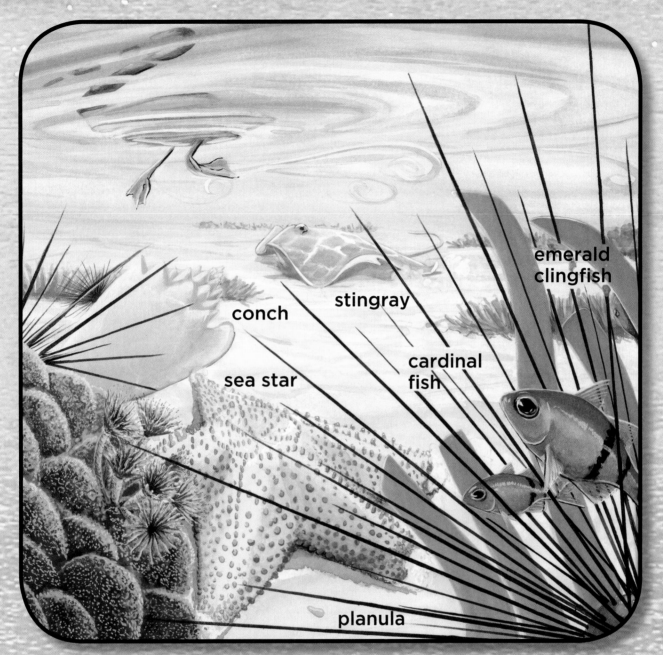

emerald
clingfish

stingray

conch

cardinal
fish

sea star

planula

The water in the lagoon is calm. Although the lagoon seems peaceful, it is really a busy place, from top to bottom. At the top, a pelican gulps a pouchful of fish. At the bottom, a stingray slurps up shrimp.

Many animals looking for food in the lagoon are hard to see. An emerald clingfish hides on a blade of turtle grass. Clams and crabs hide in the sand.

Compare and Contrast
How are the crest at the coral reef and the lagoon alike and different?

517

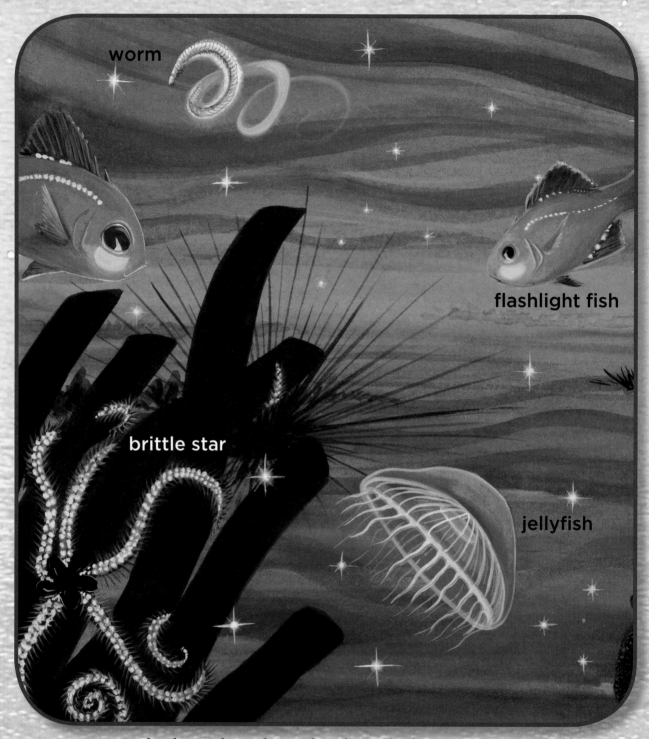

worm

flashlight fish

brittle star

jellyfish

Such a busy place, day and night in the lagoon.

Flash! Glow! Blink! What could these lights be? They twinkle like stars in the sky, but they are all under water.

These lights are made by animals. Animals almost too small to see are twinkling. **Brittle** stars flash to scare away lobsters and crabs. Worms glow to show other worms where they are. Flashlight fish attract their food by blinking.

Can the planula live here? No, it is too sandy.

The planula needs a rocky place. It floats along to the red mangrove trees near the shore of the lagoon. Red mangroves can grow in salty water. Their roots grow out and hang down right into the ocean. Sponges and seaweeds grow on the roots.

Millions of baby fish and baby shrimp start life in the water around mangrove roots. There's lots of food for them there. Will this be a home for the planula, too?

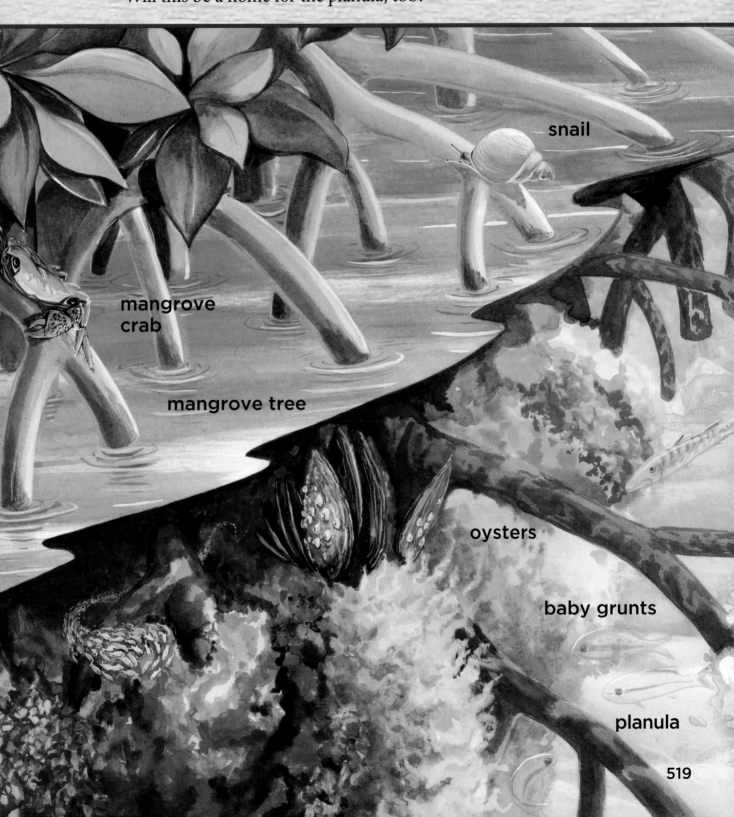

snail

mangrove crab

mangrove tree

oysters

baby grunts

planula

mangrove tree

palm trees

beach

planula

No, the water here is too shady for the planula. It turns away and swims to the shallow water near the beach of the lagoon.

The sunshine heats the sandy beach. The sand was made by the ocean waves. Over thousands of years, the waves have pounded the skeletons of reef animals and plants into smaller and smaller bits. **Eventually**, the bits formed so many grains of sand that they covered the bottom of the lagoon and washed up on shore to make a beach.

Will this be home for the planula? No, it is too shallow and too hot here.

The planula catches a **current** to deeper water. Oh, no, the water is dirty! The water is so dirty, the coral is dying. The dirt smothers the coral polyps and blocks the sunlight they need.

Chemicals washed down the rivers from factories and farms poison the coral. In the dirty water harmful bacteria grow over the coral and kill it. Careless divers hurt the coral too. They step on it and break it with their boat anchors.

Without living coral, the fish and other animals will leave. The planula cannot live here either.

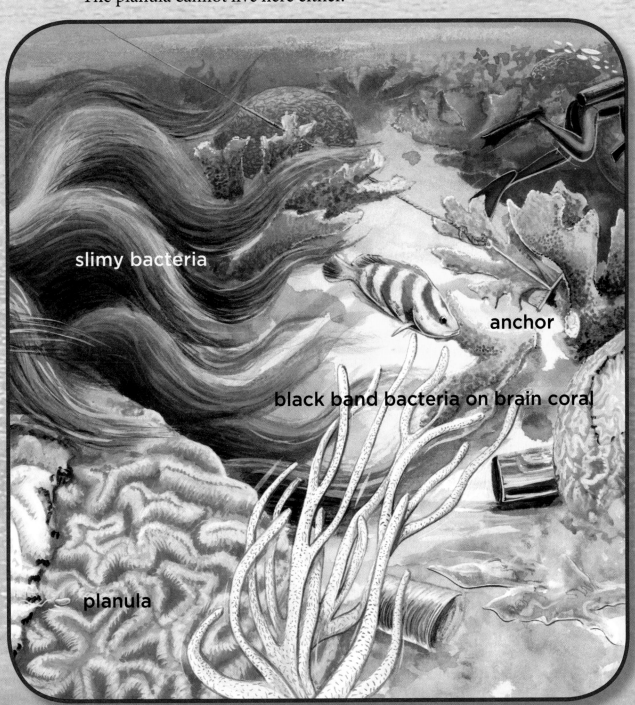

slimy bacteria

anchor

black band bacteria on brain coral

planula

Luckily, a current carries it out of the lagoon, over the top of the reef, and down the other side of the reef deeper and deeper and deeper to a healthy part of the reef.

At last! A safe spot for the planula to settle down. The spot is hard and rocky. It is sunny but not too hot. Gentle currents bring clean water, and plenty of food. It will be a perfect home.

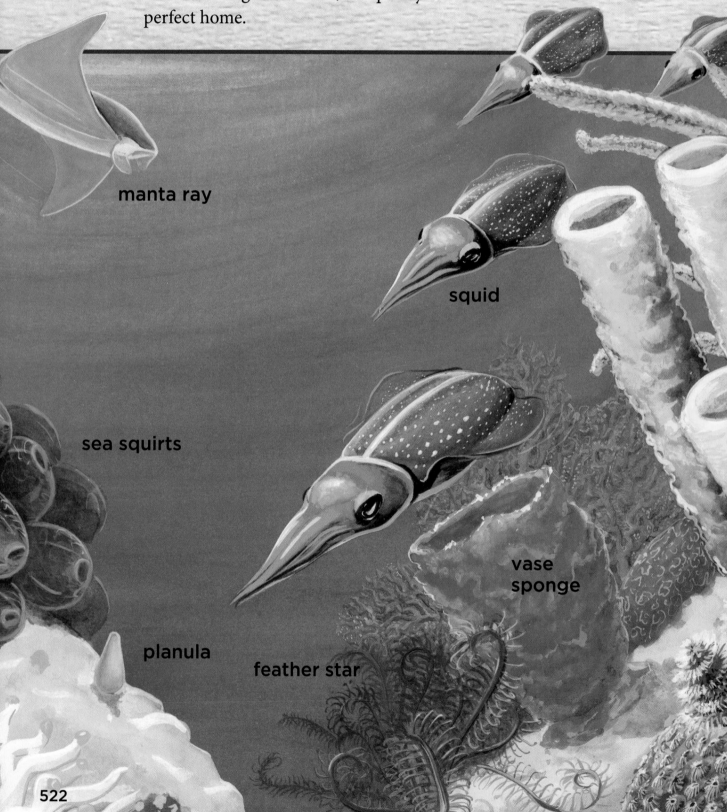

manta ray

squid

sea squirts

vase sponge

planula

feather star

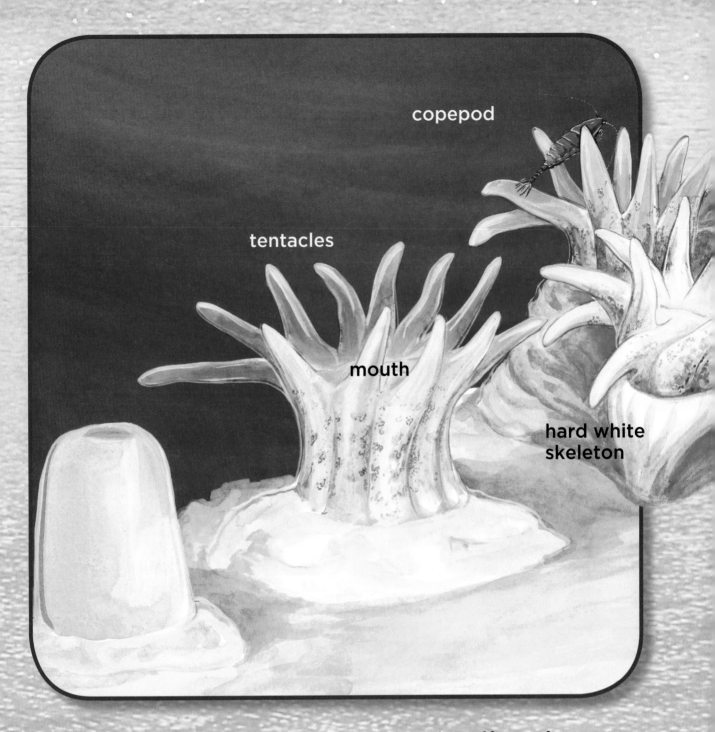

copepod

tentacles

mouth

hard white
skeleton

The planula begins to change. First, it sticks itself to a safe
spot. Then, around its mouth it grows twelve little tentacles.
Now it is a polyp. It looks like a flower, but it really is an animal.

Under its soft body, the polyp starts to grow a hard white
skeleton. In a few weeks it makes another tiny polyp exactly
like itself. The polyps are connected to each other. Together,
the two polyps have twenty-four tentacles for catching food.

The planula is growing up to be a staghorn coral. More
polyps grow, and more and more.

butterfly fish

2-year-old staghorn coral

Here comes a reef butterfly fish. It eats coral. The coral polyps warn each other of danger. Quick as a wink, they hug their tentacles in. They hide their soft bodies down inside their hard white skeleton. When the danger is past, the coral polyps slowly come out and open up their tentacles again.

Many creatures in the reef are partners that help each other hide or find food. A crab hides in the coral to escape from a hungry octopus. A shrimp lives safely inside a vase sponge.

At a cleaning station, gobies eat what they clean from the teeth of a big grouper. The grouper holds its mouth wide open for the gobies. Away from the station, the grouper would eat gobies!

Even the tiny polyps have partners. The polyps get special food from little golden plants living just inside their skin. In return, the plants get a home. This **partnership** helps the coral grow big enough to form reefs.

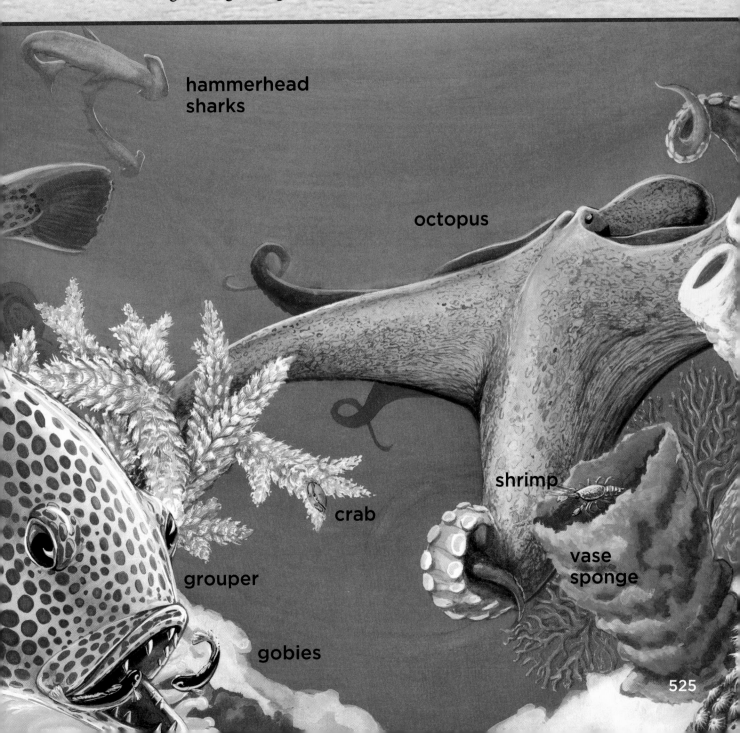

hammerhead sharks

octopus

shrimp

crab

vase sponge

grouper

gobies

Down, down, down in the tropical clear blue sea, this coral reef is alive and well. The place where it lives is clean. Zillions of coral animals have been adding their skeletons to the reef for over 8,000 years.

It takes thousands of years for a reef to grow but only a few years for one to be destroyed! This reef and other coral reefs all around the world are in danger because the oceans are becoming dirty. Coral reefs need our help.

Compare and Contrast
How was the safe spot the planula chose different from the other places? How were they all alike?

pork fish

queen angelfish

15-year-old staghorn coral

squirrel fish

dolphins

sea
turtle

octopus

What can we do to help a little baby planula grow up to become part of a big coral reef? The first step is to discover how what we do on land affects life in the sea.

All living creatures—including corals and people—need clean water. We all use water on our farms, in our **suburbs**, and in our cities. We throw many things into it that make it dirty. This dirty water flows into rivers, lakes, and underground streams, and eventually ends up in the sea. There it hurts the coral reef and all the creatures that make it their home.

But we can make a difference. We can make our rivers and lakes and oceans clean again. We can learn about life on the coral reef and share what we learn. We can help people everywhere to care about the amazing reefs and the tiny coral animals that build them.

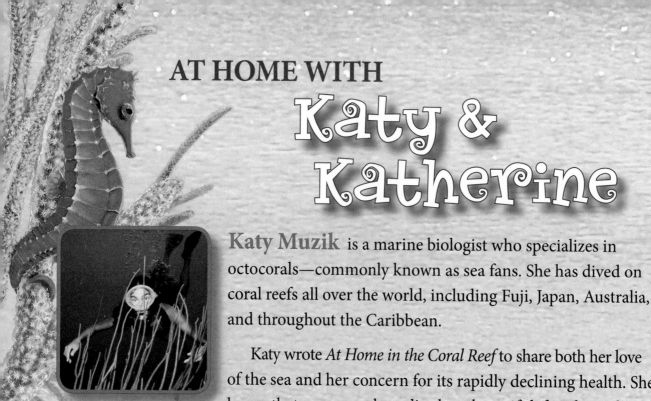

AT HOME WITH
Katy & Katherine

Katy Muzik is a marine biologist who specializes in octocorals—commonly known as sea fans. She has dived on coral reefs all over the world, including Fuji, Japan, Australia, and throughout the Caribbean.

Katy wrote *At Home in the Coral Reef* to share both her love of the sea and her concern for its rapidly declining health. She hopes that once people realize how beautiful, fragile, and important corals are, they will change their behavior to help preserve coral reefs. Katy lives near the ocean in Isabela, Puerto Rico.

Katherine Brown-Wing studied at the Art Institute of Boston. She works as a biological illustrator, and her pictures have been published in numerous scientific journals. Katherine lives in North Kingstown, Rhode Island, with her husband.

 LOG ON Find out more about Katy Muzik at **www.macmillanmh.com**

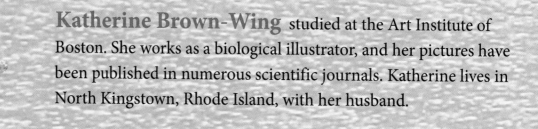

Author's Purpose

How do you think the author's job affected her purpose for writing *At Home in the Coral Reef*? What clues tell whether she wanted to inform, explain, entertain, or persuade?

528

Comprehension Check

Summarize

Summarize what you learned from *At Home in the Coral Reef*. Include only the most important information in your summary.

Think and Compare

1. Use your Venn Diagram to show how the sandy beach and the coral reef are alike and how they are different. Use story details and illustrations to support your answers. **Analyze Text Structure: Compare and Contrast**

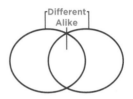

2. Reread pages 519–520 of *At Home in the Coral Reef.* Why do you think baby fish and baby shrimp live among the mangrove roots instead of in the **coral reef**? Use story details in your answer. **Analyze**

3. What changes in your life could you make to avoid adding pollution to ocean waters? Explain. **Synthesize**

4. Suppose there was a large increase in butterfly fish. How would this change the coral reef community? **Evaluate**

5. Read "Coral Reefs" on pages 510–511 and page 514 of *At Home in the Coral Reef.* What did you learn about hard and soft coral from each selection? Explain. **Reading/Writing Across Texts**

Poseidon *and the* Kingdom *of* Atlantis

retold by Gillian Reed

At the beginning of time, the immortal Greek gods of Mount Olympus divided the world among themselves. Zeus, the king of the gods, ruled over the sky and the thunderbolt. Poseidon, his brother, was the god of the sea, the lake, and the earthquake. Poseidon's power and bad temper earned him the name "Earth Shaker." He could stir up the oceans with his trident, a three-pronged fishing spear. He could also calm the sea, riding over the waves in his golden chariot.

In this paragraph we learn about Poseidon. We see that he will be the protagonist of this story.

Along with the seas, Poseidon ruled over an island in the middle of the Atlantic Ocean called Atlantis. The people of the island grew wheat, fruit, and vegetables in its fertile soil. Gold and other metals lay beneath the soil. Herds of magnificent elephants and other animals lived in the forests. Poseidon created hot and cold springs, so the people always had fresh water to drink, and warm water in which to bathe.

On the island of Atlantis lived a beautiful woman named Cleito. Poseidon was so taken by Cleito's beauty that he married this mortal woman. He built a palace for Cleito on a graceful hill in the middle of the island. To protect Cleito, Poseidon surrounded the hill with circular belts of water and land. A canal from the ocean to the hill cut across these belts. Cleito and Poseidon became the parents of five sets of twins, all of them boys. The boys grew up to rule over their father's territory, with the oldest, Atlas, ruling as king.

Atlantis was the greatest island kingdom ever known. The power of its rulers extended beyond the island to Europe and Africa. For many generations, Atlantis was a rich and happy land. The walls of the city were lined with brass and tin. Gold covered the temple of Poseidon. The people of Atlantis were noble and virtuous and lived by a set of laws that Poseidon had created. But, over time, the kings and the people became petty and greedy. They ignored Poseidon's laws and began to war against other nations.

Zeus saw what was happening to this great race of people and was angry. He called the gods to Mount Olympus. Pointing his finger at Poseidon, he blamed him for allowing Atlantis to become spoiled.

Using his powers, Poseidon took his trident and furiously whipped up the seas. A gigantic wave washed over the kingdom of Atlantis and flooded the island. Atlantis instantly sank into the sea.

> Saying that Atlantis "instantly" sank into the sea is an exaggeration and an example of hyperbole.

There are some who believe that the great island kingdom of Atlantis really existed. The Greek philosopher Plato described such a place in his writings. Many people have searched for the sunken island, but no one has ever found it.

Connect and Compare

1. Pretend that you are writing your own version of this myth. Use hyperbole to describe Poseidon, Atlantis, or the island's destruction. **Hyperbole**

2. In this myth, the god Poseidon is blamed for sinking Atlantis. Can you think of a natural cause for such an event? **Analyze**

3. If Atlantis did exist, it might now be covered by coral reefs. Think about what you learned from *At Home in the Coral Reef*. In what kind of waters would Atlantis have to lie to be a home to coral reefs? **Reading/Writing Across Texts**

 Find out more about myths at **www.macmillanmh.com**

Write About a Community Project

"Sparkles like diamonds" creates a strong mental picture.

My last sentence describes a trash pile.

Keeping It Clean

by Kyle M.

Do you want a clean beach that sparkles like diamonds? If so, then here's what you can do. You can organize a community beach cleanup. You can advertise it with posters at school, in the library, and in supermarkets.

On cleanup day, gather at the beach. Then, everyone should put on gloves and pick up litter. Be careful not to touch broken glass. Look for plastic bags and bottles along the edge of the water. Put everything in big trash bags. Finally, have a clean-beach party. Just be sure to pick up your mountain of trash!

Your Turn

Write one or two paragraphs explaining how to join or start a community project. Identify your topic and tell why it is important. Then explain the steps for getting it done. When you're done, read your work. Can you change or add words to improve your writing? Use the Writer's Checklist to check your writing.

Writer's Checklist

- **Ideas and Content:** Did I experiment with figurative language to present a familiar topic in a fresh way?

- ✓ **Organization:** Did I make my directions clear?

- ✓ **Voice:** Did I share my feelings in a way that will get others interested in the topic?

- ✓ **Word Choice:** Did my choice of precise words show that I know about my topic?

- ✓ **Sentence Fluency:** Did I try changing or adding words to make my sentences sound better?

- ✓ **Conventions:** Did I use contractions and possessives correctly? Did I check my spelling?

Go On ▶

Test Strategy

Author and Me

The answer is not directly stated. Connect the clues to figure it out.

Silent Spring No Longer:
Rachel Carson

Rachel Carson was an author and a scientist who loved nature—especially the sea. Rachel began writing at a very young age. She published her first piece of writing in a magazine for children in 1918, when she was just 11 years old. She kept writing throughout her entire life.

Rachel Carson was born on a farm in Springdale, Pennsylvania, in 1907. There she learned to adore nature. She often said that it was her mother who first showed her the wonders of nature. When Carson went to college, she planned to become a writer, but her love of nature took over. She changed her major from English to marine biology. Marine biology is the study of life in the sea. After college, Carson taught for five years before joining the U.S. Bureau of Fisheries. The bureau later became the U.S. Fish and Wildlife Service.

Carson's new job allowed her to share her love of the sea with other people. She wrote a radio show, called "Romance Under the Waters," that explored life in the seas. Carson's writing made the sea come alive for listeners. She wrote three books about the sea: *Under the Sea Wind, The Sea Around Us,* and *The Edge of the Sea.* These books all became bestsellers and won many awards. Carson soon left her job so she could write all the time.

In the late 1940s and 1950s, people used chemicals called pesticides to kill unwanted insects. One of these pesticides was DDT. Scientists began to learn that pesticides were harmful to other living things. DDT did kill harmful insects, but it also killed birds. Birds took the chemical into their bodies when they ate insects infected with DDT. The chemicals made the birds' eggs very frail. The delicate eggs broke easily, and many baby birds did not hatch. Birds such as peregrine falcons began to die and were likely to become extinct.

Rachel Carson became concerned about this problem. Because she was an excellent scientist, she spent a lot of time gathering the facts. When she was ready, she began to write her book, *Silent Spring*. She wanted to make people aware that birds were dying and that if things didn't change, people would no longer hear birds' songs in the springtime.

The companies that made the chemicals tried to stop Carson's book by saying that she was mistaken. Other people believed she was right, though. President John F. Kennedy called for testing of the chemicals. Tests showed that Carson had not been misled, and that her ideas were correct. Pesticides were harming the environment and causing birds to die.

Rachel Carson published *Silent Spring* in 1962. Because she died in 1964, Rachel Carson did not get to see her work change history. The use of DDT in the United States was banned in 1972. Since then, birds that were in danger of disappearing have returned. Now, each spring, you can hear birds singing in the trees. Thanks to Rachel Carson, spring has not become silent.

pair of blue jays with young

Go On ▶

Directions: Answer the questions.

Tip

Connect the clues or ideas from the passage to choose the best answer.

1. Why did it take ten years for the government to ban DDT after *Silent Spring* was published?

A People did not care that birds were dying.
B Chemical companies tried to argue that she was wrong.
C Rachel Carson's ideas had been proven wrong.
D Tests showed that DDT did more good than harm.

2. Why did birds return after DDT was banned?

A There is no connection between birds and DDT.
B There were fewer insects for the birds to eat.
C Birds did not like the smell of DDT.
D More baby birds hatched from healthy eggs.

3. Chemical companies claimed that Rachel Carson was mistaken. What does *mistaken* mean?

A confused
B wrong
C unhappy
D right

4. If you could interview Rachel Carson about her life and work, what question would you like to ask her?

5. What impact does Rachel Carson's work have on people's lives today? Include examples from the selection in your answer.

Writing Prompt

Write a set of directions on how to do an interview. Explain how to prepare and what kinds of questions you should ask. Write at least six steps that are clear and easy to follow.

STOP 539

Going to the Library

Talk About It

Libraries have more than books. In what other ways can you learn at the library?

LOG ON Find out more about the library at **www.macmillanmh.com**

A Library Card for Emilio

by Susan Pinter

Vocabulary

peculiar   selecting

snuffled   consisted

positive   advanced

Dictionary

Connotation/Denotation

Connotation is the feeling associated with a word. Denotation is the dictionary meaning. What are the connotation and denotation of *peculiar*?

"Hurry or we'll miss the bus to the library, Emilio!" called Mrs. Mendoza. The Mendoza family had moved to Boston, from San Juan, Puerto Rico last month, and Emilio was going to get his library card today.

On the bus, Emilio's grandmother noticed something **peculiar**. Emilio was very quiet and looked rather sad. "Is something wrong, honey?" she asked.

Emilio **snuffled** and took out a tissue to blow his nose. "My speaking of English is not very good. What if the library lady is not able to understand what I am saying?" he said.

"Your English gets better and better every day. I'm one hundred percent **positive** that the librarian will understand you," Mrs. Mendoza said confidently. "I am sure that you will be able to take some books home today."

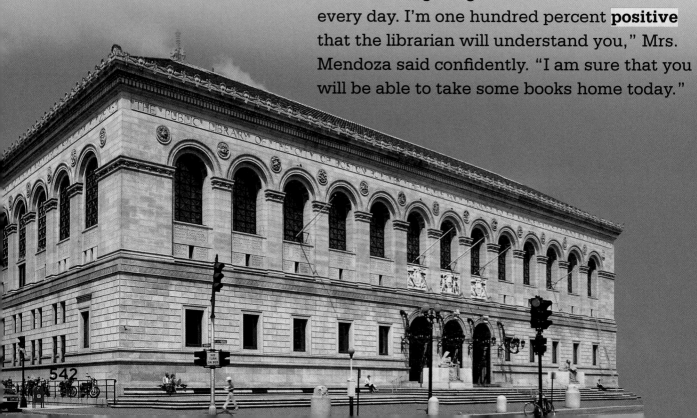

542

Inside the library, there were lots of people. Some were reading magazines and newspapers. Others were **selecting** books that they wanted to borrow from the shelves.

"May I help you with anything?" asked the librarian. She was smiling and seemed friendly.

Emilio stuttered a little as he began to explain. "I... I am here for my card for library books."

"That's just terrific!" said the librarian. She asked him to complete a form that **consisted** of questions about Emilio and where he and his family lived.

Mrs. Mendoza smiled. She noticed that her grandson had no trouble understanding the form. He filled it in quickly and returned it to the librarian.

"It will take me a few minutes to process your card, Emilio," said the librarian."Why don't you select a few books to borrow today? If you're an **advanced** reader, you might want to look over there."

"Thank you," said Emilio.

"*Abuela*," Emilio whispered to Mrs. Mendoza, "My English must be better than I thought!"

Reread for Comprehension

Evaluate

Summarize When you summarize, include only the important parts of a story. Although details make a story clearer or more interesting, they do not belong in a summary.

A Summarizing Chart can help you evaluate which events are important and keep track of them. Reread the selection and list each important event in a separate box. Summarize the story by discussing the information on your chart.

Event
↓
↓
↓

Comprehension

Genre

Realistic Fiction is a made-up story that could have happened in real life.

Evaluate

Summarize

As you read, fill in your Summarizing Chart.

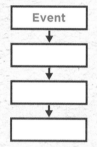

Event
↓
↓
↓

Read to Find Out

What happened that day at the library?

Because of Winn-Dixie

by Kate DiCamillo

I spent a lot of time that summer at the Herman W. Block Memorial Library. The Herman W. Block Memorial Library sounds like it would be a big fancy place, but it's not. It's just a little old house full of books, and Miss Franny Block is in charge of them all. She is a very small, very old woman with short gray hair, and she was the first friend I made in Naomi.

It all started with Winn-Dixie not liking it when I went into the library, because he couldn't go inside, too. But I showed him how he could stand up on his hind legs and look in the window and see me in there, **selecting** my books; and he was okay, as long as he could see me. But the thing was, the first time Miss Franny Block saw Winn-Dixie standing up on his hind legs like that, looking in the window, she didn't think he was a dog. She thought he was a bear.

This is what happened: I was picking out my books and kind of humming to myself, and all of a sudden, there was this loud and scary scream. I went running up to the front of the library, and there was Miss Franny Block, sitting on the floor behind her desk.

"Miss Franny?" I said. "Are you all right?"

"A bear," she said.

"A bear?" I asked.

"He has come back," she said.

"He has?" I asked. "Where is he?"

"Out there," she said and raised a finger and pointed at Winn-Dixie standing up on his hind legs, looking in the window for me.

"Miss Franny Block," I said, "that's not a bear. That's a dog. That's my dog. Winn-Dixie."

"Are you **positive**?" she asked.

"Yes ma'am," I told her. "I'm positive. He's my dog. I would know him anywhere."

Miss Franny sat there trembling and shaking.

"Come on," I said. "Let me help you up. It's okay." I stuck out my hand and Miss Franny took hold of it, and I pulled her up off the floor. She didn't weigh hardly anything at all. Once she was standing on her feet, she started acting all embarrassed, saying how I must think she was a silly old lady, mistaking a dog for a bear, but that she had a bad experience with a bear coming into the Herman W. Block Memorial Library a long time ago and she never had quite gotten over it.

"When did that happen?" I asked her.

"Well," said Miss Franny, "it is a very long story."

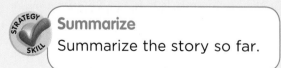

Summarize

Summarize the story so far.

548

"That's okay," I told her. "I am like my mama in that I like to be told stories. But before you start telling it, can Winn-Dixie come in and listen, too? He gets lonely without me."

"Well, I don't know," said Miss Franny. "Dogs are not allowed in the Herman W. Block Memorial Library."

"He'll be good," I told her. "He's a dog who goes to church." And before she could say yes or no, I went outside and got Winn-Dixie, and he came in and lay down with a "huummmppff" and a sigh, right at Miss Franny's feet.

She looked down at him and said, "He most certainly is a large dog."

"Yes ma'am," I told her. "He has a large heart, too."

"Well," Miss Franny said. She bent over and gave Winn-Dixie a pat on the head, and Winn-Dixie wagged his tail back and forth and **snuffled** his nose on her little old-lady feet. "Let me get a chair and sit down so I can tell this story properly."

B ack when Florida was wild, when it **consisted** of nothing but palmetto trees and mosquitoes so big they could fly away with you," Miss Franny Block started in, "and I was just a little girl no bigger than you, my father, Herman W. Block, told me that I could have anything I wanted for my birthday. Anything at all."

Miss Franny looked around the library. She leaned in close to me. "I don't want to appear prideful," she said, "but my daddy was a very rich man. A very rich man." She nodded and then leaned back and said, "And I was a little girl who loved to read. So I told him, I said, 'Daddy, I would most certainly love to have a library for my birthday, a small little library would be wonderful.' "

"You asked for a whole library?"

"A small one," Miss Franny nodded. "I wanted a little house full of nothing but books and I wanted to share them, too. And I got my wish. My father built me this house, the very one we are sitting in now. And at a very young age, I became a librarian. Yes ma'am."

"What about the bear?" I said.

"Did I mention that Florida was wild in those days?" Miss Franny Block said.

"Uh-huh, you did."

"It was wild. There were wild men and wild women and wild animals."

"Like bears!"

"Yes ma'am. That's right. Now, I have to tell you, I was a little-miss-know-it-all. I was a miss-smarty-pants with my library full of books. Oh, yes ma'am, I thought I knew the answers to everything. Well, one hot Thursday, I was sitting in my library with all the doors and windows open and my nose stuck in a book, when a shadow crossed the desk. And without looking up, yes ma'am, without even looking up, I said, 'Is there a book I can help you find?'

"Well, there was no answer. And I thought it might have been a wild man or a wild woman, scared of all these books and afraid to speak up. But then I became aware of a very **peculiar** smell, a very strong smell. I raised my eyes slowly. And standing right in front of me was a bear. Yes ma'am. A very large bear."

"How big?" I asked.

"Oh, well," said Miss Franny, "perhaps three times the size of your dog."

"Then what happened?" I asked her.

"Well," said Miss Franny, "I looked at him and he looked at me. He put his big nose up in the air and sniffed and sniffed as if he was trying to decide if a little-miss-know-it-all librarian was what he was in the mood to eat. And I sat there. And then I thought, 'Well, if this bear intends to eat me, I am not going to let it happen without a fight. No ma'am.' So very slowly and very carefully, I raised up the book I was reading."

"What book was that?" I asked.

"Why, it was *War and Peace*, a very large book. I raised it up slowly and then I aimed it carefully and I threw it right at that bear and screamed, 'Be gone!' And do you know what?"

"No ma'am," I said.

"He went. But this is what I will never forget. He took the book with him."

"Nuh-uh," I said.

"Yes ma'am," said Miss Franny. "He snatched it up and ran."

"Did he come back?" I asked.

"No, I never saw him again. Well, the men in town used to tease me about it. They used to say, 'Miss Franny, we saw that bear of yours out in the woods today. He was reading that book and he said it sure was good and would it be all right if he kept it for just another week.' Yes ma'am. They did tease me about it." She sighed. "I imagine I'm the only one left from those days. I imagine I'm the only one that even recalls that bear. All my friends, everyone I knew when I was young, they are all dead and gone."

She sighed again. She looked sad and old and wrinkled. It was the same way I felt sometimes, being friendless in a new town and not having a mama to comfort me. I sighed, too.

Winn-Dixie raised his head off his paws and looked back and forth between me and Miss Franny. He sat up then and showed Miss Franny his teeth.

"Well now, look at that," she said. "That dog is smiling at me."

"It's a talent of his," I told her.

"It is a fine talent," Miss Franny said. "A very fine talent." And she smiled back at Winn-Dixie.

"We could be friends," I said to Miss Franny. "I mean you and me and Winn-Dixie, we could all be friends."

Miss Franny smiled even bigger. "Why, that would be grand," she said, "just grand."

Summarize
How did they become friends? Leave the details out of your summary.

And right at that minute, right when the three of us had decided to be friends, who should come marching into the Herman W. Block Memorial Library but old pinch-faced Amanda Wilkinson. She walked right up to Miss Franny's desk and said, "I finished *Johnny Tremain* and I enjoyed it very much. I would like something even more difficult to read now, because I am an **advanced** reader."

"Yes dear, I know," said Miss Franny. She got up out of her chair.

Amanda pretended like I wasn't there. She stared right past me. "Are dogs allowed in the library?" she asked Miss Franny as they walked away.

"Certain ones," said Miss Franny, "a select few." And then she turned around and winked at me. I smiled back. I had just made my first friend in Naomi, and nobody was going to mess that up for me, not even old pinch-faced Amanda Wilkinson.

Because of **Kate**

Kate DiCamillo wrote this story while she was shivering in Minnesota one winter. Kate had moved there from Florida and was very homesick. She also felt sad because she was not allowed to have a dog in her apartment. When Kate went to sleep, she dreamed she heard a girl say she had a dog named Winn-Dixie. Kate started writing the story as soon as she woke up.

Because of Winn-Dixie became the first book that Kate published. It won a Newbery Honor, which is one of the most respected awards a children's book can receive. She is also the author of *The Tiger Rising* and of *The Tale of Despereaux: Being the Story of a Mouse, a Princess, Some Soup, and a Spool of Thread,* which received the Newbery Medal in 2004.

When Kate wrote *Because of Winn-Dixie,* she would get up early every day to write two pages before leaving for her job at a bookstore. She no longer works at the bookstore, but she still writes two pages every morning.

Other books
by Kate DiCamillo

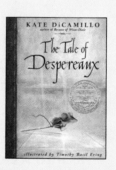 

LOG ON Find out more about Kate DiCamillo at **www.macmillanmh.com**

Author's Purpose
This selection is realistic fiction—a made-up story that has true-to-life details. What was the author's purpose for writing? Why do you think so?

Summarize

Use your Summarizing Chart to help you summarize *Because of Winn-Dixie*. Include the most important plot events.

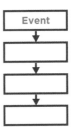

Think and Compare

1. Summarize the **peculiar** story that Miss Franny Block tells Opal. Focus on the main events of her story. **Evaluate: Summarize**

2. Reread pages 548–552 of *Because of Winn-Dixie*. What does Miss Franny mean when she says she never had quite gotten over it? **Analyze**

3. What funny story would you share with a new friend? **Apply**

4. Why are Miss Franny Block and Opal a good match for each other? **Evaluate**

5. Read "A Library Card for Emilio" on pages 542–543. How is Emilio like Opal in *Because of Winn-Dixie?* How are they different? Use details from both selections in your answer. **Reading/Writing Across Texts**

I Love the Look of Words

Poetry

Free Verse Poems do not have to follow rhyme schemes but often contain rhythmic patterns and other poetic elements.

Literary Elements

Onomatopoeia is the use of a word that imitates the sound that it stands for, such as *hiss*.

A **Simile** compares two different things, usually by using the words *like* or *as*.

The word *popping* sounds like the thing it describes. This is an example of onomatopoeia.

Popcorn leaps, popping from the floor
of a hot black skillet
and into my mouth.
Black words leap,
snapping from the white
page. Rushing into my eyes. Sliding
into my brain which gobbles them
the way my tongue and teeth
chomp the buttered popcorn.

When I have stopped reading,
ideas from the words stay stuck
in my mind, like the sweet
smell of butter perfuming my
fingers long after the popcorn
is finished.

> This simile compares ideas
> sticking in the poet's mind to
> the smell of butter sticking
> to her fingers.

I love the book and the look of words
the weight of ideas that popped into my mind
I love the tracks
of new thinking in my mind.
> — Maya Angelou

Connect and Compare

1. Although it doesn't rhyme, this free verse poem contains
   elements of poetry, such as onomatopoeia. Besides the word
   popped, what other examples of onomatopoeia can you find?
   Onomatopoeia

2. The poet uses a simile to compare her brain to something.
   What is it? **Analyze**

3. Compare the narrator in this poem with the narrator in
   Because of Winn-Dixie. How are they alike? How are they
   different? **Reading/Writing Across Texts**

 Find out more about free verse poems at **www.macmillanmh.com**

Writer's Craft

Multiple Paragraphs

Writers arrange **multiple paragraphs** in a logical order when they compare and contrast. You can use Venn diagrams to sort out similarities and differences before you write.

Write a Comparison

I arranged my paragraphs in a logical order.

First I told how the characters are different. Then I told how they are alike.

Ike and Cara

by Ramona C.

I am writing to compare two characters from the books we read this year. One is Ike from <u>Dear Mrs. LaRue</u>, and the other is Cara from <u>Dear Mr. Winston</u>.

Right away, you can tell that Ike's character could never be real—dogs cannot talk or write letters to their owners. Cara's character could be real. She looks and writes like a real person. Ike uses a typewriter. Cara types her letter on a computer.

The two characters are alike in that they are both clever, they get in trouble, and they were invented to make readers like me laugh.

Your Turn

Choose two characters you know from books. Then write a description that compares and contrasts the characters. Start your writing by introducing your subjects. Tell how they are alike in one paragraph and how they are different in another paragraph. Use the Writer's Checklist to help you evaluate your writing.

Writer's Checklist

 Ideas and Content: Did I choose clear similarities and differences?

 Organization: Are my multiple paragraphs in a logical order? Did I tell how my characters are alike in one paragraph and different in another?

Voice: Is it clear how I feel about the characters?

Word Choice: Did I use adjectives that paint vivid pictures of the characters?

 Sentence Fluency: Did I use a variety of sentence lengths and types?

 Conventions: Did I use correct punctuation throughout? Did I capitalize proper nouns?

PUTTING ON A PLAY

Talk About It

Make up a story about the play these kids are performing. What is it called? What happens?

LOG ON Find out more about plays at **www.macmillanmh.com**

5

The Frog Prince

by Marcia Stevens

Vocabulary

selfish   exasperated

bumbling   specialty

cranky   famished

commotion

Thesaurus

Antonyms are words that have opposite meanings.

Cranky and *cheerful* are antonyms.

Narrator: There once was a beautiful princess whose favorite amusement was a golden ball. One day the princess tossed the ball too high, and it landed in the well. As the princess cried over her lost treasure, she heard someone ask a question.

Frog: Why are you so miserable, beautiful princess?

Narrator: The princess looked around and saw only a frog.

Princess: My favorite golden ball fell into the well.

Frog: I can retrieve it for you, but first, you must agree to one condition. You must promise to take me home and be my friend.

Narrator: The princess had no intention of being friends with a frog, but she promised anyway. When the frog brought her the ball, the princess snatched it from him and scampered home.

Frog: What a **selfish** princess. I'm certain that she has forgotten her promise. I'll just hop over to the castle to remind her.

Narrator: The frog hop-hop-hopped through the meadow and knocked on the heavy door of the castle.

Princess: What are you doing here, you **bumbling** frog?

Frog: My, aren't *we* **cranky**? And as for bumbling, *I* wasn't the one who dropped the ball in the well. I am here to remind you of the promise you made.

Narrator: The princess slammed the door in the frog's face with a big BANG.

King: I heard a door slam. What's all the **commotion**? If you made a promise you must honor it.

Narrator: The princess was **exasperated** but obeyed her father. So, the king, the princess, and the frog enjoyed dinner together. It was mutton stew, the cook's **specialty**.

Frog: I was **famished**, but now I'm full. Thank you for dinner. Kindly show me to my bed now.

Narrator: The princess did as she was asked, but the frog looked sad.

Frog: You have welcomed me into your home, but I can tell that you don't want to be my friend.

Narrator: The princess blushed, for what the frog said was true. She bent down to kiss the frog, but ended up kissing a prince.

Frog: I am a prince who was turned into a frog, and your kiss turned me back. Thank you, dear friend!

Narrator: The prince and princess were wonderful friends from that day on and lived happily ever after.

Reread for **Comprehension**

Evaluate

Make Judgments Readers learn about the characters in a story by evaluating what they say and do. These actions, plus what you know from your own experiences, can help you make judgments about characters.

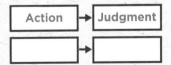

A Make Judgments Flow Chart can help you understand the characters you read about. Reread the selection for the actions of the characters and add them to the chart. Then use their actions, along with your own experiences, to make judgments about the characters.

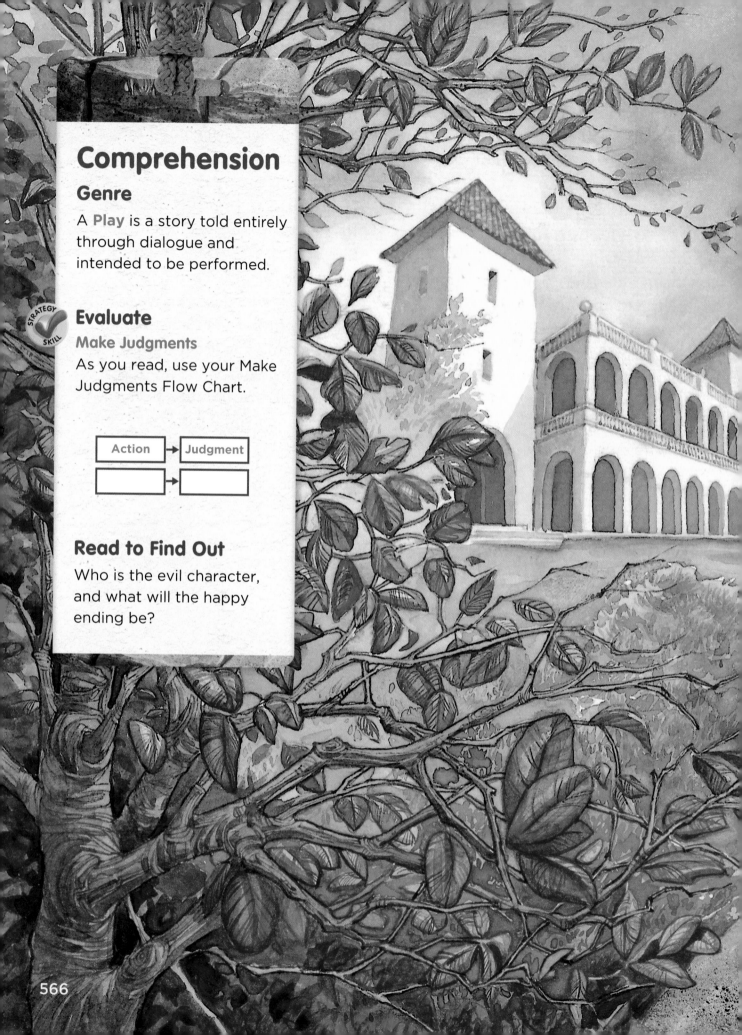

Comprehension

Genre
A **Play** is a story told entirely through dialogue and intended to be performed.

Evaluate
Make Judgments
As you read, use your Make Judgments Flow Chart.

Action	→	Judgment
	→	

Read to Find Out
Who is the evil character, and what will the happy ending be?

Ranita

The Frog Princess

by Carmen Agra Deedy

illustrated by Renato Alarcão

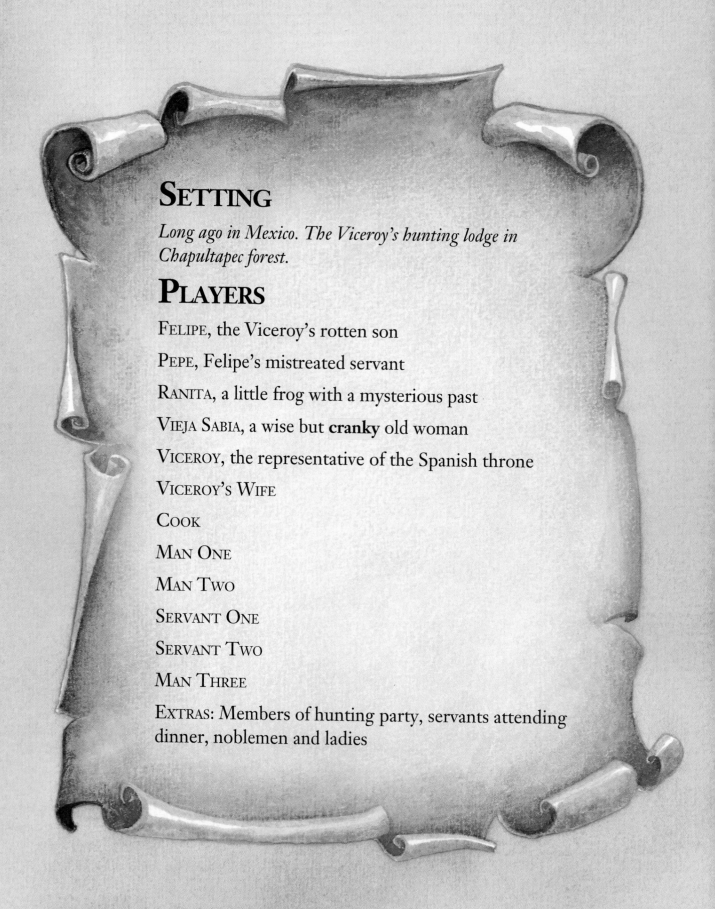

SETTING

Long ago in Mexico. The Viceroy's hunting lodge in Chapultapec forest.

PLAYERS

FELIPE, the Viceroy's rotten son

PEPE, Felipe's mistreated servant

RANITA, a little frog with a mysterious past

VIEJA SABIA, a wise but **cranky** old woman

VICEROY, the representative of the Spanish throne

VICEROY'S WIFE

COOK

MAN ONE

MAN TWO

SERVANT ONE

SERVANT TWO

MAN THREE

EXTRAS: Members of hunting party, servants attending dinner, noblemen and ladies

Scene 1

In a forest clearing, men are frantically searching the ground. From a nearby stone well, Ranita watches but remains unnoticed.

Man One: *(Frustrated)* Keep looking! If we don't find that golden arrow—

Man Two: —we'll be on *tortillas* and water for the next month!

(Men, grumbling, all agree.)

(Enter Felipe.)

Felipe: *(Loud and demanding)* Well? Have you found my golden arrow yet?

Man Three: Not yet, Señor!

Felipe: *(Sweetly, hand over heart)* It was a gift from my dear mother. *(Turning suddenly and hissing)* Find it or I will feed you to the jaguars—starting with my **bumbling** servant, Pepe. It's his fault I missed my mark. Now, out of my sight, all of you!

(Men exit hurriedly.)

Felipe: *(Stomping foot and whining)* I want my golden arrow back!

Ranita: *(Sitting on top of well, holding the golden arrow)* You mean, *this* golden arrow?

Felipe: *(Joyously)* My golden arrow! You found it! You—*(Stops cold)*—you're a frog.

Ranita: You were expecting a Mayan princess, perhaps?

Felipe: *(Rolls eyes)* Well, I wasn't expecting a talking frog!

Ranita: *(Sighs)* I'm under a spell. I don't like to talk about it.

Felipe: *(Pauses to think)* Not my problem. Hand over the arrow.

Ranita: *(Plink! Drops it back down the well)* Hmm, looks like it's your problem now.

Felipe: N-n-noooo! *(Threateningly)* What have you done, you foolish frog?

Ranita: If I am so foolish, how come I am the one with the arrow while you are the one standing there talking to a *rana*, a frog?

Felipe: I would squish you right now—*(Sniffs)*—but you are only a frog.

Ranita: *(Warningly)* You want that golden arrow?

Felipe: *(Suspicious)* In exchange for what?

Ranita: A promise.

Felipe: *(Relieved)* Oh, is that all?

Ranita: A promise is a very serious thing.

Felipe: *(Coughing)* Yes, yes, of course—go on.

Make Judgments
What judgment can you make about Felipe's character? Does he take promises seriously?

Ranita: IF I rescue your golden arrow, you must promise to let me eat from your *plato*, sleep in your *cama*, and give me a *beso* when the sun comes up.

Felipe: *(Just stares)* Eat from my plate? Sleep in my bed? KISS you? *That* is disgusting!

Ranita: No promise, no golden arrow.

Felipe: *(Crossing his fingers behind his back)* I promise.

(Ranita fetches the arrow. Felipe bows and runs off.)

Ranita: *Espera!* Wait! I can't hop that fast! *(Hangs her head and begins to cry)* He's gone. Now I'll never break this evil spell.

(Enter wise woman, leaning on two canes.)

Vieja Sabia: It doesn't feel very good, does it?

Ranita: *(Blows nose)* Please, no lectures today, old woman.

Vieja Sabia: My name is Vieja *Sabia*.

Ranita: Sorry, *Wise* Old Woman. *(Sadly)* You've already turned me into a frog. Isn't that enough?

Vieja Sabia: You wouldn't be a frog if you hadn't refused to give me a drink from this well, so long ago.

Ranita: I was a **selfish** child then. I have paid for that, haven't I? I have learned what it is like to be alone and forgotten.

Vieja Sabia: Perhaps you have . . .

Ranita: *(Brightening)* Then, you will turn me into a girl again?

Vieja Sabia: No. But I will take you as far as the Viceroy's hunting lodge. You must make the leap from there.

(Exit Vieja Sabia and Ranita.)

573

Scene 2

Hunting lodge with Viceroy, his wife, noblemen and women, all seated at long banquet table. Servants scurry in and out with bowls of food.

Servant One: *(Placing bowl of soup before Viceroy)* Sopa, Señor?

Viceroy: *(Exasperated)* Sí, sí. Where is Felipe?

Viceroy's Wife: *(Wistfully)* Dear boy. He is probably feeding the birds.

Servant Two: *(Aside)* To the cat.

Servant One: *(Muffles laugh)*

(Enter Felipe.)

Felipe: I am **famished**. What a day I've had today. First, I lost my golden arrow—

(Shouting from the kitchen can be heard.)

Felipe: *(Louder)*—then I met this ridiculous, demanding—

(Enter Ranita, running from the kitchen chased by cook and servants.)

Felipe: *(Slack-jawed)*—frog.

Cook: You hop back here! *(To servant)* Stop her, right now!

Servant One: *(Tries to catch frog)* Aaaaayyyy! She's a slippery one!

Servant Two: Ooooooeeeee! She bit me!

Cook: Get her, Pepe. *(Pepe catches Ranita under the table, smiles, and lets her go. A* **commotion** *follows as the cook and servants chase Ranita.)*

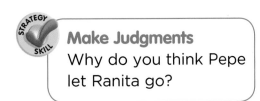

Make Judgments
Why do you think Pepe let Ranita go?

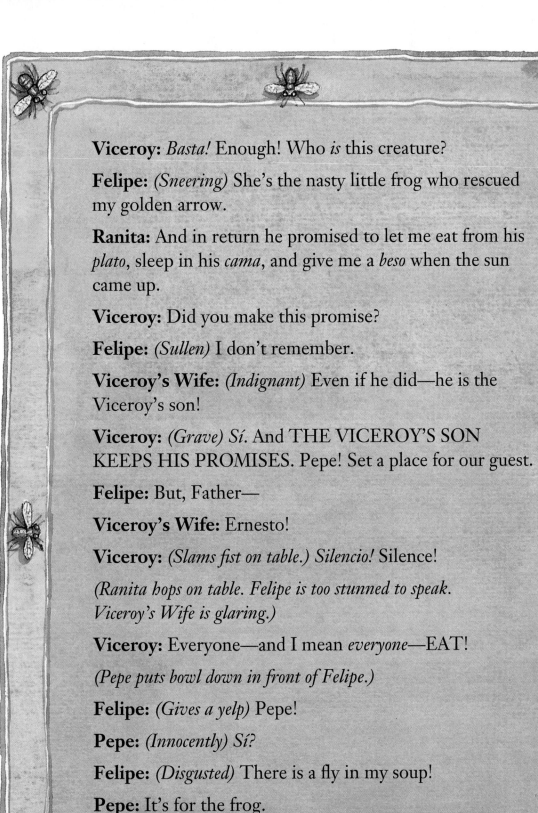

Viceroy: *Basta!* Enough! Who *is* this creature?

Felipe: *(Sneering)* She's the nasty little frog who rescued my golden arrow.

Ranita: And in return he promised to let me eat from his *plato*, sleep in his *cama*, and give me a *beso* when the sun came up.

Viceroy: Did you make this promise?

Felipe: *(Sullen)* I don't remember.

Viceroy's Wife: *(Indignant)* Even if he did—he is the Viceroy's son!

Viceroy: *(Grave) Sí.* And THE VICEROY'S SON KEEPS HIS PROMISES. Pepe! Set a place for our guest.

Felipe: But, Father—

Viceroy's Wife: Ernesto!

Viceroy: *(Slams fist on table.) Silencio!* Silence!

(Ranita hops on table. Felipe is too stunned to speak. Viceroy's Wife is glaring.)

Viceroy: Everyone—and I mean *everyone*—EAT!

(Pepe puts bowl down in front of Felipe.)

Felipe: *(Gives a yelp)* Pepe!

Pepe: *(Innocently) Sí?*

Felipe: *(Disgusted)* There is a fly in my soup!

Pepe: It's for the frog.

Viceroy: Excellent. Eat up, Felipe.

Viceroy's Wife: *(Revolted)* Arggh.

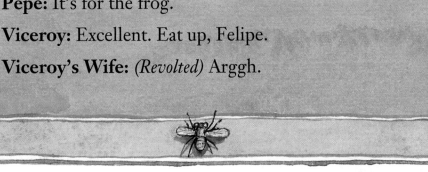

Scene 3

(Felipe's bedroom)

Felipe: *(On bed)* I refuse to sleep next to a FROG. Pepe!!!!!!!!

Pepe: *(Enters immediately)* Sí, Señor?

Felipe: *(Snappish)* What took you so long? Hurry—tell my father I can't do this. *(Desperate)* Tell him I'll get warts.

(Enter Viceroy.)

Viceroy: *(Annoyed)* With any luck, you will get one on your oath-breaking tongue, boy.

Felipe: *(Whining)* Father—

Viceroy: You made a promise, Felipe. *(To Pepe)* Help him keep his word, eh, Pepe?

(Exit Viceroy.)

578

Felipe: *(Throws pillow at Pepe. Falls on bed and begins to wail.)* AAAAAAAYYYYYYYY!

Pepe: *(Blows out candle and sits in chair.)* Hasta mañana . . . until tomorrow. Sweet dreams, Felipe.

Felipe: *(Growls)* I will dream of roasted frog legs.

Ranita: I'm telling.

Felipe: Bug breath!

Ranita: Big baby!

Pepe: *(Sighs)* It's going to be a long night.

(Next morning)

Ranita: *(Cheerful)* Despierta, wake up! It's "beso time!"

[Felipe rubs eyes, sees Ranita, and shrieks.]

Felipe: *(Whimpers, clutching his blanket)* It wasn't a bad dream, after all. Forget it, frog! I am not kissing you!

Ranita: *(Stubbornly)* You promised.

Felipe: Well, *(Smiles slowly)* I've just had a better idea. *(Kicks chair to wake his servant)* Pepe!

Pepe: *(Groggy)* Señor!

Felipe: You are sworn to obey me in all things, sí?

Pepe: *(Confused)* Sí, Señor.

Felipe: (*Smug*) KISS . . . THE . . . FROG.

[Pepe shrugs and kisses Ranita's cheek.]

(*No longer a frog, Ranita is now a beautiful Mayan Princess.*)

Felipe: (*Dazzled*) I—but who? (*Bowing*) Allow me to introduce myself, I am—

Ranita: —the Spanish Viceroy's Rotten Son. And I am . . . the Mayan Emperor's Lucky Daughter.

(*Felipe and Pepe fall on their knees.*)

Ranita: I have been enchanted for 200 years.

Felipe: (*Looks up*) You've been a frog for 200 years? What's so LUCKY about that?

Ranita: I'll tell you. As a princess, I could have ended up the wife of a spoiled brat like you. Instead, I found myself a prince . . . (*Takes Pepe's hand*) a prince of a husband, that is.

(*Pepe kisses the Princess's hand, while Felipe has a screaming tantrum.*)

Epilogue

The same clearing in the forest as in Scene 1

Felipe: *(Kicks a stone)* If they think I'm going to their ridiculous wedding . . . ha! May they have a dozen ugly tadpole children!

(Enter Vieja Sabia.)

Vieja Sabia: *Agua!* Water from the well, my son, before I die of thirst.

Felipe: *(Snarling)* I'm no water boy. I'm the Viceroy's son! Get your own water, you old *cucaracha!*

Vieja Sabia: *(With gentle concern)* Cockroach? It's very rude to speak to your elders that way. Has no one taught you manners?

Felipe: *(Puzzled)* No.

Vieja Sabia: *(Smiling wickedly)* Well *(pointing finger at Felipe)*, that is my **specialty**.

(**POOF** Felipe the Frog hops onto the top of the well.)

Vieja Sabia: *(to audience)* And now you know how the Frog Prince ended up in that well.

Once Upon a Time . . .

Carmen Agra Deedy came to the United States from Cuba in 1960, after a revolution made it dangerous for her family to live there. Hoping for a more peaceful life, Carmen and her family settled in Georgia. Carmen has not forgotten her Cuban heritage. She combines it with the heritage of the southern United States when writing her stories.

Other books by Carmen Agra Deedy

Renato Alarcão was born, raised, and currently lives in Rio de Janeiro, Brazil. Among his many art projects was the creation of 13 murals around Paterson and Passaic, New Jersey, all done with a team of artists and local teens.

Author's Purpose

Why did Carmen Agra Deedy write the play *Ranita, the Frog Princess*? Was her purpose to explain, inform, entertain, or persuade? How do you know?

LOG ON Find out more about Carmen Agra Deedy at **www.macmillanmh.com**

584

Comprehension Check

Summarize

Summarize *Ranita, the Frog Princess*. Tell what Ranita's problem was and how it was solved.

Think and Compare

1. What kind of person is the Viceroy? Look for clues about his character and put them in your Make Judgments Flow Chart. Use the clues to make a judgment about the Viceroy's character. **Evaluate: Make Judgments**

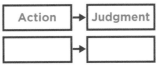

Action	→	Judgment
	→	

2. Reread Scene 2 of *Ranita, the Frog Princess* on pages 574–575. How does the Viceroy's wife feel about Felipe? How do the servants feel? **Analyze**

3. How would you respond to the deal that Ranita offered Felipe? **Apply**

4. Did Felipe deserve the punishment he received for being **selfish**? Give reasons for your answer. **Evaluate**

5. Read "The Frog Prince" on pages 564–565. How is this story like *Ranita, the Frog Princess*? How are the stories different? Use details from both selections in your answer. **Reading/Writing Across Texts**

PRESENTING THE PUDDLEJUMP PLAYERS

by Liz Ray

Have you and your friends ever put on a play? A group of children in Massachusetts did more than that. First, they found a **director**. Then they began performing classic and new plays. The group called itself the Puddlejump Players.

Children have been performing with the Puddlejump Players for more than ten years. The actors are 3 to 17 years of age. The director and many other staff members are adults.

Perry Kroll, one of the oldest child actors in the group, answered some questions about the Puddlejump Players.

Q: Do children have to try out for **roles** in the Puddlejump Players?

A: The children do **audition** for the roles that interest them. They often give the director a list of parts they'd like, and then try out for one or two of them.

During the auditions, stand-ins are sometimes required. These are actors who read the lines for the other characters in the scenes that have been selected. It's not uncommon for a stand-in to do so well that they end up with that part!

Q: Who makes the **casting** decisions?

A: A few older members can have a little influence, but it is really the director's decision. I am always surprised by the way she can predict someone's skill at a role they didn't audition for.

Reading an Interview

SKILL

An interview is made up of questions and answers. The letter Q stands for the question, and the letter A stands for the answer. Each Q paragraph may have a question mark at the end, but it also may not.

Q: How many plays are performed a year?

A: One play per year, in the spring.

Q: How long does the company **rehearse** before performing a play?

A: Rehearsals usually start in January. The auditions begin in November or December. The show is in May.

Q: Do children do any behind-the-scenes work, such as making sets?

A: Absolutely! There is a core group who helps Sheila [the director]. Sheila usually designs the sets herself—though during the last show a few members of the cast painted some pieces. Then she stays up nearly around the clock putting them up with help from the older members.

Q: Who makes the costumes and props?

A: In general, cast members find or create their own costumes, make-up, and props. Sheila makes some of the more complicated ones herself.

Q: Do children play music for the performances?

A: The music is usually played live by a few parents with musical experience. In the past a few excellent musicians from the cast have helped as well.

When the curtain rises and the actors step on stage, all the hard work pays off. Once again, the children get to put on a play and an audience experiences a wonderful performance.

Connect and Compare

1. In this interview, how can you tell when a question is being asked? How do you know when you are reading an answer? **Reading an Interview**

2. Do you think that adults should help in a children's theater company like the Puddlejump Players? Explain your answer. **Evaluate**

3. If the Puddlejump Players were putting on *Ranita, the Frog Princess*, what might the actor playing Ranita use for a costume and make-up? What about the actor playing Vieja Sabia? **Reading/Writing Across Texts**

Performing Arts Activity

Research a play that a children's theater group could put on. Act out a scene from the play with some friends.

 Find out more about the performing arts at **www.macmillanmh.com**

Write a Descriptive Poster

School Spring Funfest!

I wanted to vary my word choices on my poster.

I used colorful adjectives.

School Spring Funfest!

by Jenny G.

Enjoy yourself at the Annual All-School Spring Funfest on April 10 from 12–6 p.m.

The Spring Funfest is a festival for everyone. Kids can have their faces painted like birds or lions or bears. You can eat spicy tamales, crunchy eggrolls, and hot dogs that are a foot long. Grades 3 and 4 will put on a play called <u>The Frog Princess</u> in the gym, and all the teachers will dress up in elegant, old-fashioned costumes.

For sports fans, there will be an exciting soccer game outside between parents and 6th graders.

Everyone will have a great time. Mark your calendars!

590

Your Turn

Make a poster that announces a school event. It may be a real event at your school or an imaginary one. Begin with a catchy title. Explain what the event is and then describe it in a paragraph. Use precise adjectives that will get your readers' attention and make them want to attend. Include details about the date, time, and place of the event. Use the Writer's Checklist to check your writing.

Writer's Checklist

✓ **Ideas and Content:** Did I clearly state the purpose of the event? Did I explain what will happen?

✓ **Organization:** Did I start with a catchy title? Did I include the date, time, and place of the event?

✓ **Voice:** Will my readers feel my enthusiasm?

☑ **Word Choice:** Did I strengthen my word choices? Did I use precise adjectives?

✓ **Sentence Fluency:** Does my writing flow smoothly?

✓ **Conventions:** Did I use the articles *a* and *an* correctly? Did I check my spelling?

Talk About It

What is the definition of an explorer? What do you think motivates a person to explore?

LOG ON Find out more about explorers at
www.macmillanmh.com

592

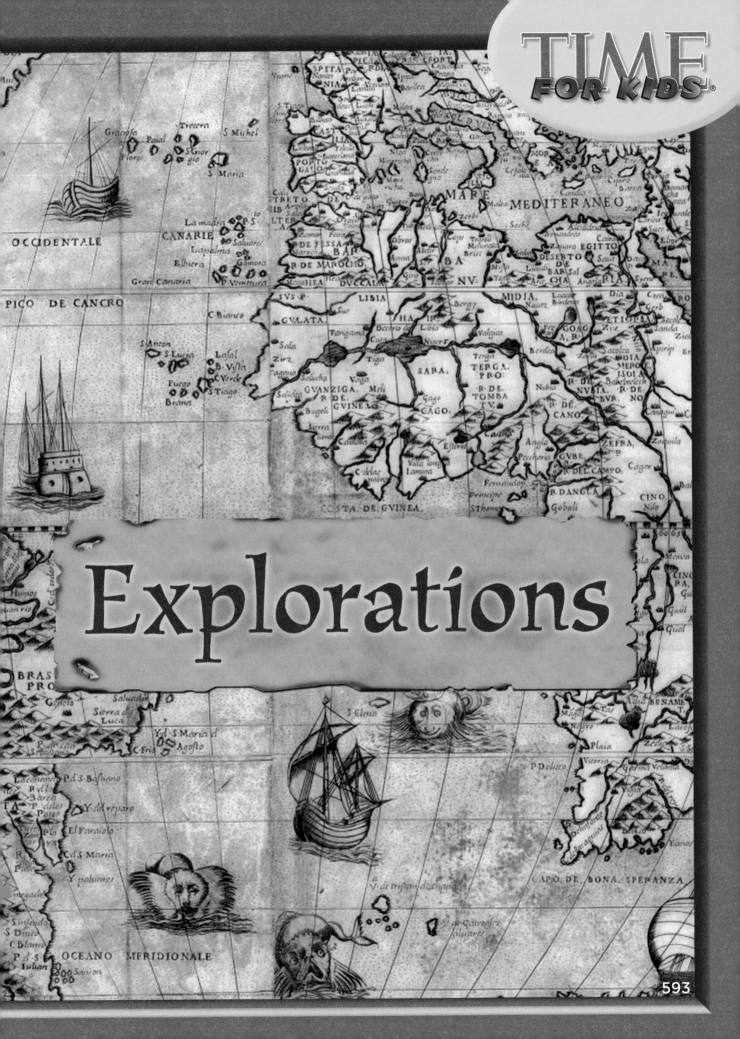

Explorations

BACK IN TIME WITH SPANISH EXPLORERS

Vocabulary

- **period**
- **vessels**
- **valuable**
- **documenting**
- **estimated**

The sixteenth century was a **period** of great exploration by European countries. Facing known and unknown dangers, explorers set sail in the best sea-going **vessels** of their day. Many of those explorers who set sail for North America were from Spain.

1492-1500: Christopher Columbus, sailing under the Spanish flag, explores the area around the Caribbean Sea.

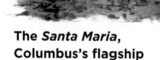

The *Santa Maria*, Columbus's flagship

1508: Juan Ponce de León travels to Puerto Rico.

1510: Diego Velázquez de Cuellar and 300 men conquer Cuba.

1513: Ponce de León is the first European to land in Florida.

1513: Vasco Núñez de Balboa is the first European to see the Pacific Ocean.

1518: Hernán Cortés leaves Cuba to explore Mexico.

1519: Alonso Álvarez de Pineda claims Texas for Spain.

1520: Álvarez de Pineda proves Florida is not an island but part of a gigantic continent instead.

1542: Alvar Núñez Cabeza de Vaca publishes a book about his travels in what is now Arizona, Texas, and New Mexico.

1539 to 1542: Hernando de Soto is the first European to see the Mississippi River.

1592: Juan de Fuca sails up the west coast of North America from Mexico to Vancouver Island.

1602: Sebastián Vizcaíno finds Monterey Bay and sets the scene for the settlement of what we now call California.

Tales of the Taino

Deep in a forest of the Dominican Republic is an unusual well. It contained more than 240 objects—chairs, jars, baskets, and bowls—that are at least 500 years old. Far from being worthless, these old everyday objects are extremely **valuable**. They are giving scientists new information about the Taino (tie•EE•no).

The Taino were people who lived throughout the Caribbean, including the countries now called Cuba, Puerto Rico, Haiti, and the Dominican Republic. When European explorers started arriving in the Caribbean in 1492, the lives of the Taino were changed forever. Explorers took their land. Many of the Taino were killed. By the 1520s very little was left of the Taino civilization except some artifacts and a few words. *Hurricane*, *barbecue*, and *canoe* are Taino words we still use today.

Scientists and historians are **documenting**—making a record of—and studying the items from the well. After 500 years of silence, it seems that the story of the Taino will finally be told.

This carved figure represents a Taino idol or god.

THE COMMONWEALTH OF PUERTO RICO

Puerto Rico is a territory of the United States. That means it belongs to the U.S. but is not one of the 50 states. Puerto Rico is located in the Caribbean Sea, southeast of Miami, Florida. It consists of the island of Puerto Rico and the smaller islands of Vieques, Culebra, and Mona.

Capital: San Juan
Land area: 3,459 square miles
Estimated population: 3,886,000
Languages: Spanish and English

LOG ON Find out more about Puerto Rico at www.macmillanmh.com

Exploring the Undersea Territory

Why are scientists devoting their lives to learning about the least explored territory on Earth—the ocean?

Off the coast of Hawaii in 2000, Sylvia Earle pilots a one-person submarine designed by a company she helped found.

Fifteenth- and sixteenth-century European explorers arrived in North America after dangerous ocean voyages. Today we are in another **period** of ocean-based exploration. Now the focus is on exploring the worlds found under the water. Explorers of the past and the present have a lot in common. However, modern explorers have **vessels** equipped with technologies that sea captains of the past could never have imagined.

SYLVIA EARLE: "HER DEEPNESS"

Many things set Sylvia Earle apart from the great explorers of the past and the present. In 1979 she set the record for the deepest ocean dive—1,250 feet—ever made by a human alone and untethered—not connected in any way to a vessel or other object. That feat earned her the title "Her Deepness." In 1985 she set another record for diving solo. This time she dove to 3,000 feet in a submersible—a "compact" version of a submarine—she helped design.

Over the course of Earle's career of more than fifty years, she spent more than 6,000 hours under water. She held the positions of Explorer-in-Residence at the National Geographic Society and Chief Scientist at the National Oceanic and Atmospheric Administration (NOAA)—the first woman ever to hold that post. She co-founded and served as chief executive of a company that designs diving equipment. Add to this list the titles of mother and grandmother.

According to Earle, "This is the Lewis and Clark era for oceans." She was referring to the historic 1805 expedition to explore the huge and largely unknown area of the U.S. known as the Louisiana Purchase. Lewis and Clark mapped and documented the new territory.

Sylvia Earle at Woods Hole, Massachusetts, in 1995

"The ocean is the cornerstone of all life," Earle pointed out. "It produces most of the oxygen in the atmosphere. It shapes climate and weather. If the sea is sick, we will feel it. If it dies, we die." She based her work on her belief that ignorance is the greatest threat of all to this resource that is so **valuable** to life on Earth. "We know more about Mars than we know about the oceans," she has said. This scientist who is also an explorer, a businesswoman, and a grandmother has dedicated her life to both exploring and protecting the oceans of the world.

ROBERT BALLARD: EXPLORING "SHIPWRECK ALLEY"

Robert Ballard is best known as the explorer who located the wreck of the luxury steamship *Titanic*. Like Sylvia Earle, he is a National Geographic Society Explorer-in-Residence. As Director of the Institute for Exploration (IFE), Ballard continues to dedicate his work to revealing the mysteries of the world's oceans. He and his team locate and study ancient shipwrecks in an effort to understand early human history.

Ballard's team is studying wrecks like this one (left) in Lake Huron. It is the freighter *Montana*, shown below in 1872.

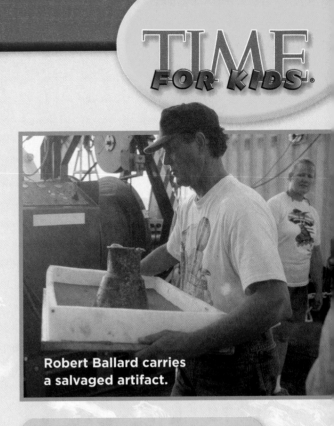

Ballard and his team don't always have to travel to distant oceans to find interesting old shipwrecks. In fact they don't have to go any further than Lake Huron, one of the Great Lakes. There, within the Thunder Bay National Marine Sanctuary and Underwater Preserve, is an area known as "Shipwreck Alley." It is **estimated** that more than 100 shipwrecks dating back to the 1800s sit on the bottom of the lake. Ballard believes that finding and **documenting** them will tell an important story about trade and shipbuilding in North America.

Using a submersible called *Little Hercules*, the IFE team has identified a number of well-preserved wrecks. One is the *Cornelia B. Windiate*, which sank on November 28, 1875. It went down with all crew members and 332 tons of wheat. Cameras have photographed the ship's three wooden masts, still standing tall; its anchors, deck, and rigging; and its name, carved into the hull.

As their work in "Shipwreck Alley" continues, Ballard and his team expect to increase awareness of one aspect of U.S. history.

Robert Ballard carries a salvaged artifact.

A sonogram—a picture made with sound waves— shows the *Cornelia B. Windiate* on the floor of Lake Huron.

Think and Compare

1. How did Sylvia Earle earn the nickname "Her Deepness"?

2. Why does Robert Ballard want to investigate the shipwrecks in Lake Huron?

3. What facts does Sylvia Earle use to support her opinion that it is important to understand and protect the world's oceans?

4. Based on these selections, what generalization can you make about explorers both past and present?

Test Strategy

On My Own

The answer is not in the selection. Form an opinion about what you read for questions 4 and 5.

LORDS OF THE SEAS

Viking ship from 850-900 A.D. on display in the Viking Ship Museum, Oslo, Norway

Nearly 500 years before Christopher Columbus, bold Viking sailors crossed the Atlantic Ocean. Vikings were the first Europeans to reach North America. They lived in a part of Northern Europe called Scandinavia. Most Vikings were peaceful farmers, traders, and gifted craftsmen. But they were also excellent shipbuilders.

Viking ships were brilliantly designed. They were tough enough to sail hundreds of miles on the open sea. They were light enough to be carried over land. When there was no wind, the crews could row the ships with oars.

Vikings traveled far in search of goods such as silk, glass, and silver. Some Vikings sailed west and settled the islands of Iceland and Greenland. Between 997 and 1003 A.D., a Viking named Leif Eriksson landed in what is now Canada. The Vikings probably stayed for less than ten years, though they traded with Native Americans for much longer. A bit of their culture can still be found on our calendar. Tuesday, Wednesday, Thursday, and Friday are named for Viking gods!

A tenth-century Viking helmet

Go On ▶

Directions: Answer the questions.

1. Where did the Vikings originally live?

   A   Canada

   B   Scandinavia

   C   Iceland and Greenland

   D   the Atlantic coast

2. According to the selection, which of these was a feature of Viking ships?

   A   They were large enough to hold many people.

   B   They were light enough to be carried over land.

   C   They had very colorful sails.

   D   They were made from rare and expensive wood.

3. Which of these answers shows the cultural influence of the Vikings?

   A   Some days of the week have Viking names.

   B   Vikings left ships in North America.

   C   Vikings were gifted craftsmen.

   D   Americans adopted Viking ship designs.

4. Vikings were superb shipbuilders. What made their ships so good? Use the picture and the text to support your response.

5. People have explored new lands and the oceans. Should we continue to explore space and the skies beyond Earth? Why or why not?

Tip
Form an opinion.

Write to a Prompt

In the selection "Exploring the Undersea Territory" you read about two modern-day explorers. How did their personal qualities, interests, and skills help them become undersea explorers? Write your response in three or more paragraphs, and use details from the article.

Being a Deep-Sea Explorer

People who do what Sylvia Earle and Robert Ballard do have to like danger, like to travel, and like to study. It's hard to think of a more dangerous job than getting into a little submarine alone and diving to the bottom of the ocean. Any kind of problem could mean death.

Earle and Ballard are both scientists. They went to college and studied hard in order to be able to do the work they do. Earle is actually a botanist—a scientist who studies plants. But the plants she studies grow underwater. Ballard is a marine geologist and geophysicist. That is a scientist who studies the structure of oceans. To be any kind of scientist takes a person who can focus on details.

Explorers like Earle and Ballard use science to help others. That's the quality I admire most.

I used details to explain my ideas.

602

Writing Prompt

Sylvia Earle and Robert Ballard are both explorers. Explain how their interest in the sea has made a difference in their lives and in ours. Write three paragraphs, and use details from the article in your answer.

Writer's Checklist

☑ Ask yourself, who is my audience?

☑ What is the purpose for writing?

☑ Plan your writing before beginning.

☑ Use details to support your main idea.

☑ Be sure your ideas are clear and organized.

☑ Use your best spelling, grammar, and punctuation.

Artists at
Work

605

SECONDHAND ART

by David Walcott

Danny and Emma decided to enter the school art contest. Today they are working together on their project. The problem is, they can't decide what to make.

"Danny, maybe we should make models of modern **skyscrapers**. Mr. Buckle said, 'The sky's the limit.'" Danny and Emma laughed.

"Seriously," said Danny, "how about making a **collage** out of pictures we cut from magazines?"

"We could," said Emma, "but I'll bet a lot of kids will make collages. Let's try to do something different."

Danny's mom walked into the kitchen. She reminded Danny to put the recycling bin in her car. Danny's eyes lit up.

"I've got it!" he said. "Mr. Buckle is always talking about taking care of the Earth. Let's make our project out of that stuff!"

"Great idea," agreed Emma.

They got right to work. There were tons of aluminum cans from last week's outdoor hamburger and hot dog **barbecue**.

They used empty plastic bottles and jars, and cardboard. They cut up strips of newspaper to make papier-mâché. Finally, Danny and Emma were ready to paint.

"Let's use bright yellow," Emma suggested. "It's such a **glorious** color, isn't it?"

Danny giggled. "You're so dramatic, Emma."

He started **strutting** around the room. "Yellow is such a *glorious* color," he said, teasing Emma. Emma **flicked** her paintbrush at Danny.

The next day, Danny and Emma presented their art project. Everyone loved it, especially Mr. Buckle. Danny and Emma won first prize. **Swarms** of people came up to congratulate them.

"Who knew recycling could be so much fun?" said Emma.

"The best part was that I didn't have to haul everything into Mom's car," said Danny with a grin.

Reread for **Comprehension**

Monitor Comprehension

Character To monitor your comprehension of characters, think about their traits, or the long-lasting parts of their personalities. Thinking about a character's traits will help you understand why a character does or says things and what he or she might do next.

A Character Web will help you gather information about a character's traits. Reread the story to find examples of Emma's traits.

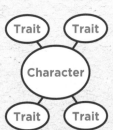

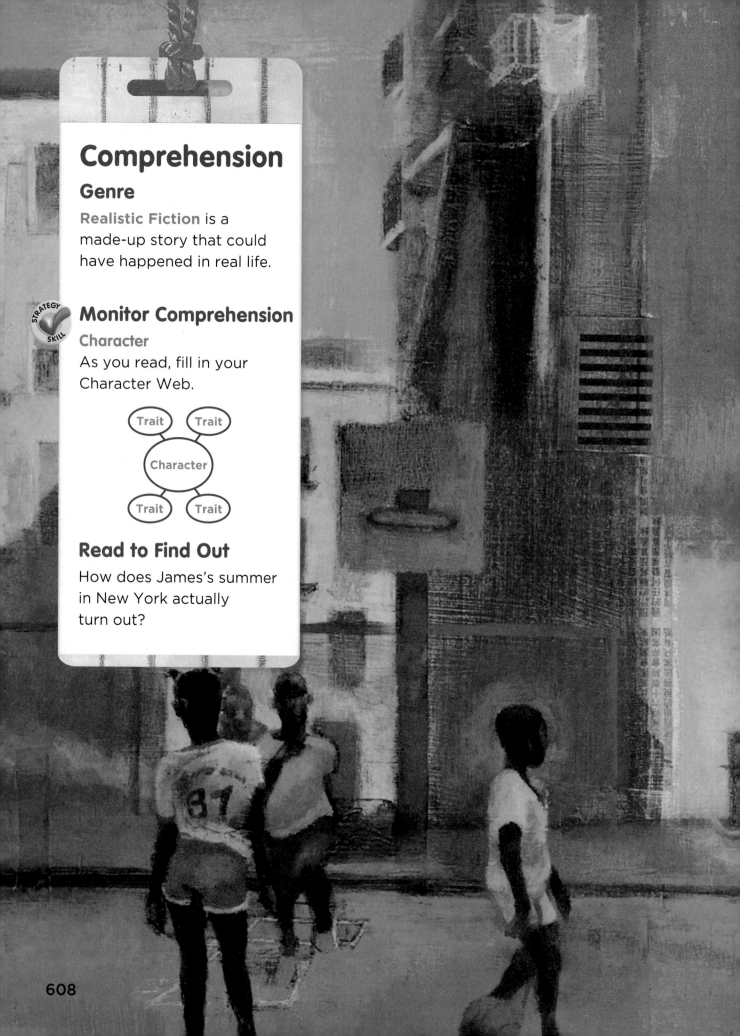

Comprehension

Genre

Realistic Fiction is a made-up story that could have happened in real life.

Monitor Comprehension

Character

As you read, fill in your Character Web.

Trait   Trait

Character

Trait   Trait

Read to Find Out

How does James's summer in New York actually turn out?

ME and UNCLE ROMIE

Award Winning Illustrator

by CLAIRE HARTFIELD
pictures by
JEROME LAGARRIGUE

It was the summer Mama had the twins that I first met my uncle Romie. The doctor had told Mama she had to stay off her feet till the babies got born. Daddy thought it was a good time for me to visit Uncle Romie and his wife, Aunt Nanette, up north in New York City. But I wasn't so sure. Mama had told me that Uncle Romie was some kind of artist, and he didn't have any kids. I'd seen his picture too. He looked scary—a bald-headed, fierce-eyed giant. No, I wasn't sure about this visit at all.

The day before I left home was a regular North Carolina summer day. "A good train-watching day," my friend B.J. said.

We waited quietly in the grass beside the tracks. B.J. heard it first. "It's a'coming," he said. Then I heard it too—a low rumbling, building to a roar. *WHOOO—OOO!*

"The *Piedmont!*" we shouted as the train blasted past.

"I'm the greatest train-watcher ever," B.J. boasted.

"Yeah," I answered, "but tomorrow I'll be *riding* a train.
I'm the lucky one."

Lucky, I thought as we headed home. *Maybe*.

That evening I packed my suitcase. Voices drifted up
from the porch below.

"Romie's got that big art show coming up," Mama said
quietly. "I hope he's not too busy for James, especially on
his birthday."

"Romie's a good man," Daddy replied. "And Nanette'll
be there too."

Character

Who is the narrator of this
story? How would you
describe this character?

The light faded. Mama called me into her bedroom. "Where's my good-night kiss?" she said.

I curled up next to her. "I'll miss the way you make my birthday special, Mama. Your lemon cake and the baseball game."

"Well," Mama sighed, "it won't be those things. But Uncle Romie and Aunt Nanette are family, and they love you too. It'll still be a good birthday, honey."

Mama pulled me close. Her voice sang soft and low. Later, in my own bed, I listened as crickets began their song and continued into the night.

The next morning I hugged Mama good-bye, and Daddy and I headed for the train. He got me seated, then stood waving at me from the outside. I held tight to the jar of pepper jelly Mama had given me for Uncle Romie.

"ALL A-BOARD!" The conductor's voice crackled over the loudspeaker.

The train pulled away. *Chug-a-chug-a-chug-a-chug.* I watched my town move past my window—bright-colored houses, chickens **strutting** across the yards, flowers everywhere.

After a while I felt hungry. Daddy had packed me a lunch and a dinner to eat one at a time. I ate almost everything at once. Then my belly felt tight and I was kind of sleepy. I closed my eyes and dreamed about Mama and Daddy getting ready for those babies. Would they even miss me?

Later, when I woke up, I ate the last bit of my dinner and thought about my birthday. Would they make my lemon cake and take me to a baseball game in New York?

The sky turned from dark blue to black. I was getting sleepy all over again.

"We're almost there, son," the man next to me said.

Then I saw it . . . New York City. Buildings stretching up to the sky. So close together. Not like North Carolina at all.

"Penn Station! Watch your step," the conductor said, helping me down to the platform. I did like Daddy said and found a spot for myself close to the train. **Swarms** of people rushed by. Soon I heard a silvery voice call my name. This had to be Aunt Nanette. I turned and saw her big smile reaching out to welcome me.

She took my hand and guided me through the rushing crowds onto an underground train called the subway. "This will take us right home," she explained.

Home was like nothing I'd ever seen before. No regular houses anywhere. Just big buildings and stores of all kinds—in the windows I saw paints, fabrics, radios, and TVs.

We turned into the corner building and climbed the stairs to the apartment—five whole flights up. *Whew!* I tried to catch my breath while Aunt Nanette **flicked** on the lights.

"Uncle Romie's out talking to some people about his big art show that's coming up. He'll be home soon," Aunt Nanette said. She set some milk and a plate of cookies for me on the table. "Your uncle's working very hard, so we won't see much of him for a while. His workroom—we call it his studio—is in the front of our apartment. That's where he keeps all the things he needs to make his art."

"Doesn't he just paint?" I asked.

"Uncle Romie is a **collage** artist," Aunt Nanette explained. "He uses paints, yes. But also photographs, newspapers, cloth. He cuts and pastes them onto a board to make his paintings."

"That sounds kinda easy," I said.

Aunt Nanette laughed.

"Well, there's a little more to it than that, James. When you see the paintings, you'll understand. Come, let's get you to bed."

Lying in the dark, I heard heavy footsteps in the hall. A giant stared at me from the doorway. "Hello there, James." Uncle Romie's voice was deep and loud, like thunder. "Thanks for the pepper jelly," he boomed. "You have a good sleep, now." Then he disappeared down the hall.

The next morning the door to Uncle Romie's studio was closed. But Aunt Nanette had plans for both of us. "Today we're going to a neighborhood called Harlem," she said. "It's where Uncle Romie lived as a boy."

Harlem was full of people walking, working, shopping, eating. Some were watching the goings-on from fire escapes. Others were sitting out on stoops greeting folks who passed by—just like the people back home calling out hellos from their front porches. Most everybody seemed to know Aunt Nanette. A lot of them asked after Uncle Romie too.

We bought peaches at the market, then stopped to visit awhile. I watched some kids playing stickball. "Go on, get in that game," Aunt Nanette said, gently pushing me over to join them. When I was all hot and sweaty, we cooled off with double chocolate scoops from the ice cream man. Later we shared some **barbecue** on a rooftop way up high. I felt like I was on top of the world.

As the days went by, Aunt Nanette took me all over the city—we rode a ferry boat to the Statue of Liberty . . . zoomed 102 floors up at the Empire State Building . . . window-shopped the fancy stores on Fifth Avenue . . . gobbled hot dogs in Central Park.

But it was Harlem that I liked best. I played stickball with the kids again . . . and on a really hot day a whole bunch of us ran through the icy cold water that sprayed out hard from the fire hydrant. In the evenings Aunt Nanette and I sat outside listening to the street musicians playing their saxophone songs.

On rainy days I wrote postcards and helped out around the apartment. I told Aunt Nanette about the things I liked to do back home—about baseball games, train-watching, my birthday. She told me about the special Caribbean lemon and mango cake she was going to make.

My uncle Romie stayed hidden away in his studio. But I wasn't worried anymore. Aunt Nanette would make my birthday special.

4 ... 3 ... 2 ... 1 ... My birthday was almost here!

And then Aunt Nanette got a phone call.

"An old aunt has died, James. I have to go away for her funeral. But don't you worry. Uncle Romie will spend your birthday with you. It'll be just fine."

That night Aunt Nanette kissed me good-bye. I knew it would not be fine at all. Uncle Romie didn't know about cakes or baseball games or anything except his dumb old paintings. My birthday was ruined.

When the sky turned black, I tucked myself into bed. I missed Mama and Daddy so much. I listened to the birds on the rooftop—their songs continued into the night.

The next morning everything was quiet. I crept out of bed and into the hall. For the first time the door to Uncle Romie's studio stood wide open. What a **glorious** mess! There were paints and scraps all over the floor, and around the edges were huge paintings with all sorts of pieces pasted together.

I saw saxophones, birds, fire escapes, and brown faces. *It's Harlem*, I thought. *The people, the music, the rooftops, and the stoops.* Looking at Uncle Romie's paintings, I could *feel* Harlem—its beat and bounce.

Then there was one that was different. Smaller houses, flowers, and trains. "That's home!" I shouted.

"Yep," Uncle Romie said, smiling, from the doorway. "That's the Carolina I remember."

"Mama says you visited your grandparents there most every summer when you were a kid," I said.

"I sure did, James. *Mmm.* Now that's the place for pepper jelly. Smeared thick on biscuits. And when Grandma wasn't looking. . . I'd sneak some on a spoon."

"Daddy and I do that too!" I told him.

We laughed together, then walked to the kitchen for a breakfast feast—eggs, bacon, grits, and biscuits.

"James, you've got me remembering the pepper jelly lady. People used to line up down the block to buy her preserves."

"Could you put someone like that in one of your paintings?" I asked.

"I guess I could." Uncle Romie nodded. "Yes, that's a memory just right for sharing. What a good idea, James. Now let's get this birthday going!"

He brought out two presents from home. I tore into the packages while he got down the pepper jelly and two huge spoons. Mama and Daddy had picked out just what I wanted—a special case for my baseball cards, and a model train for me to build.

"Pretty cool," said Uncle Romie. "I used to watch the trains down in North Carolina, you know."

How funny to picture big Uncle Romie lying on his belly!

"B.J. and me, we have contests to see who can hear the trains first."

"Hey, I did that too. You know, it's a funny thing, James. People live in all sorts of different places and families. But the things we care about are pretty much the same. Like favorite foods, special songs, games, stories . . . and like birthdays." Uncle Romie held up two tickets to a baseball game!

It turns out Uncle Romie knows all about baseball—he was even a star pitcher in college. We got our mitts and set off for the game.

Way up in the bleachers, we shared a bag of peanuts, cracking the shells with our teeth and keeping our mitts ready in case a home run ball came our way. That didn't happen—but we sure had fun.

Aunt Nanette came home that night. She lit the candles and we all shared my Caribbean birthday cake.

After that, Uncle Romie had to work a lot again. But at the end of each day he let me sit with him in his studio and talk. Daddy was right. Uncle Romie is a good man.

The day of the big art show finally came. I watched the people laughing and talking, walking slowly around the room from painting to painting. I walked around myself, listening to their conversations.

"Remember our first train ride from Chicago to New York?" one lady asked her husband.

"That guitar-playing man reminds me of my uncle Joe," said another.

All these strangers talking to each other about their families and friends and special times, and all because of how my uncle Romie's paintings reminded them of these things.

623

Later that night Daddy called. I had a brand-new brother and sister. Daddy said they were both bald and made a lot of noise. But he sounded happy and said how they all missed me.

This time Aunt Nanette and Uncle Romie took me to the train station.

"Here's a late birthday present for you, James," Uncle Romie said, holding out a package. "Open it on the train, why don't you. It'll help pass the time on the long ride home."

I waved out the window to Uncle Romie and Aunt Nanette until I couldn't see them anymore. Then I ripped off the wrappings!

And there was my summer in New York. Bright sky in one corner, city lights at night in another. Tall buildings. Baseball ticket stubs. The label from the pepper jelly jar. And trains. One going toward the **skyscrapers**. Another going away.

Character

Were the opinions James had of his uncle and his birthday in New York proven correct? How would this story be different if Uncle Romie were the narrator?

Back home, I lay in the soft North Carolina grass. It was the first of September, almost Uncle Romie's birthday. I watched the birds streak across the sky.

Rooftop birds, I thought. *Back home from their summer in New York, just like me.* Watching them, I could still feel the city's beat inside my head.

A feather drifted down from the sky. In the garden tiger lilies bent in the wind. *Uncle Romie's favorite flowers.* I yanked off a few blossoms. And then I was off on a treasure hunt, collecting things that reminded me of Uncle Romie.

I painted and pasted them together on a big piece of cardboard. Right in the middle I put the train schedule. And at the top I wrote:

Visit the Studios of Claire and Jerome

Claire Hartfield based this story on African American artist Romare Bearden. She likes his collages because they seem to tell stories. Claire wrote her story to show how we can use art to share ideas. She's been expressing herself through art since she was young. Claire was a shy child, and she found that dance and art helped her share her feelings.

Jerome Lagarrigue comes from a family of artists. He grew up in France, but came to the United States to study art. Jerome illustrates books and magazines. He also teaches art.

Other books by Jerome Lagarrigue

LOG ON Find out more about Claire Hartfield and Jerome Lagarrigue at **www.macmillanmh.com**

Author's Purpose

Did Claire Hartfield write *Me and Uncle Romie* to entertain, explain, inform, or persuade the reader? How may the author's own love of art have affected her purpose for writing? Explain. Use details from the story.

Comprehension Check

Summarize

Summarize *Me and Uncle Romie.* Tell why James went to New York City to stay with his aunt and uncle and what happened there.

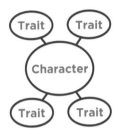

Think and Compare

1. How do Uncle Romie's character traits differ from his physical traits? Use your Character Web to help you. **Monitor Comprehension: Character**

2. Look again at the **collage** on page 625 that James created for his uncle. Why do you think James arranged the pieces of the collage in this way? **Analyze**

3. Have you ever discovered that you were mistaken about someone's character based on the person's appearance? Explain your answer. **Apply**

4. Why is art a good way to express feelings and ideas? **Evaluate**

5. Read "Secondhand Art" on pages 606–607. Compare this story with *Me and Uncle Romie.* How are the stories alike? How are they different? Use details from both selections in your answer. **Reading/Writing Across Texts**

MAKING A COLLAGE

by Claire Hartfield

Choosing a Story or Theme

To begin your project, pick a story or theme for your collage. Do you want to tell about something that really happened? Or would you rather make up a story? Is there a theme that would make a fun collage—things that make you laugh, things you do at bedtime, a list of wishes, favorite songs? To get ideas, think of people, places, or memories that mean a lot to you.

Then think about **images** you can use in your collage to illustrate what you want to say. What do you want in the picture? People? Animals? What are they doing? Where are they? What do they see, hear, smell, taste, and feel?

Materials You Will Need

* A board or thick piece of paper
* Paints, colored markers, or crayons
* Glue or paste
* Anything that can be glued or pasted on your collage

628

Creating Your Collage

Start by deciding whether or not it's important to have the images you'll be using in any particular order. If it is, you can lay them out to get an idea of how they will look together.

Next, paint or color the **background** on your paper or board. Use colors you want to peek through in the finished picture.

Then begin to create your story or theme by cutting and pasting your objects onto the background.

> Words such as *Start, Next,* and *Then* show the steps to follow.

Connect and Compare

1. When making a collage, what do you do before you paint or color the background? What do you do after you paint the background? **Reading Directions**

2. What would happen if you pasted down your materials before you painted the background? **Synthesize**

3. In *Me and Uncle Romie,* James made a collage. What did he do that was similar to the directions in this article? What did he do differently? **Reading/Writing Across Texts**

 Art Activity

Research artists who make collages. Create your own piece of art in the style of one of them.

 Find out more about collages at **www.macmillanmh.com**

Writer's Craft

Mood

Writers often set the **mood** in a speech by expressing their opinions. They use precise words to reinforce the mood.

I admire my older sister, Blanca. I used precise words to introduce her to my class.

I included opinions in my speech to reinforce the mood.

My Sister, the Artist

by Jillian N.

My sister, Blanca, is here today to tell you about drawing. She is the best artist in her high school. She has been painting and drawing since she was only six. Her first picture was of her dog Champ.

She always takes a drawing pad with her when she goes out. When she sees an interesting person, animal, or flower, she quickly sketches it. Then she chooses her favorite sketches and turns them into finished art.

She taught me everything I know about drawing. She is the most incredible teacher, and I hope you can learn a lot!

Your Turn

Think of a person you admire. It could be someone famous, someone you have read about, or someone you know, such as a teacher or relative. Pretend you are going to give a speech that introduces this person to an audience. Include your opinions about this person. Back up your opinions with facts. Then use the Writer's Checklist to check your writing.

Amelia Earhart in her airplane cockpit

Writer's Checklist

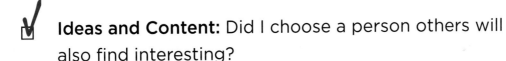

✓ **Ideas and Content:** Did I choose a person others will also find interesting?

✓ **Organization:** Did I start with a strong opening statement? Did I go on to support that statement?

✓ **Voice:** Did I clearly express my opinion of this person?

✓ **Word Choice:** Did I choose precise words to describe this person and reinforce the mood?

✓ **Sentence Fluency:** Did I use a variety of sentence types and sentence lengths?

✓ **Conventions:** Did I use commas to set off people's names? Did I check my spelling?

Talk About It

These wild horses live in a big marsh in southern France. What do you see that tells you they are wild?

LOG ON Find out more about wild horses at **www.macmillanmh.com**

WILD HORSES

The Wild Ponies of Chincoteague

by Gregory Searle

Every year since 1924, a pony swim has taken place between two tiny islands in the Atlantic Ocean. Assateague and Chincoteague Islands are located off the coasts of Maryland and Virginia. Part of Assateague belongs to Maryland and part belongs to Virginia. On a smaller neighboring island, the Chincoteague ponies graze.

These beautiful animals are **descendants** of wild horses. How the ancestors of the ponies ended up on an island, no one knows for sure.

The Pony Swim

The calm, quiet privacy of Assateague provided a **sanctuary** for its residents. However, when several terrible fires broke out on Chincoteague, it was clear that emergency services were needed. The new Volunteer Fire Department needed money to buy equipment. That's how the idea for the annual pony swim started.

Every year thousands of people come to watch the ponies. Many watch from boats out on the **glistening** water. The firemen "round up" the wild ponies on Assateague Island. At first, the ponies feel **threatened** and try to head back into the trees. After some **coaxing**, the ponies swim across the channel to Chincoteague Island.

These ponies are small, but they are not **fragile**. They are very strong and intelligent animals. Many farmers want to buy a Chincoteague pony. Some of the foals are auctioned off to good homes. The rest of the ponies swim back to Assateague Island a few days later. The fire department uses the money that is raised to update their safety equipment.

Protecting the Ponies

The pony swim is important for another reason, too. The number of horses living on Assateague has to be controlled. If too many horses are born, there won't be enough grass for the rest to eat. Keeping the numbers under control protects the **habitat** and its natural resources for future generations.

Reread for Comprehension

Monitor Comprehension

Cause and Effect As you read, remember to monitor your comprehension, or check your understanding, of cause and effect. A cause is why something happens. What happens is the effect. Authors do not always provide a cause and effect. Sometimes readers have to make inferences.

A Cause and Effect Diagram will help you identify what happens in a story or article and why. Reread the selection and identify the causes and effects.

Cause ➔ Effect
➔
➔
➔
➔

Comprehension

Genre

Narrative Nonfiction
is a story or account about
actual persons, living things,
situations, or events.

Monitor Comprehension
Cause and Effect
As you read, fill in your
Cause and Effect Diagram.

Cause ➜ Effect
➜
➜
➜
➜

Read to Find Out

What is it that makes a wild
horse wild?

Wild Horses

by Cris Peterson

photographs by Alvis Upitis

In the deepest, darkest part of night, when the crickets and tree frogs are almost silent, shadowy shapes emerge from the ponderosa pine ridge and tiptoe down to the glassy Cheyenne River below. Their long tangled manes and tails ruffle in the night breeze. Ever alert and watchful for predators, they swiftly drink their fill. Then they turn on their heels and lunge up the rocky hills to safety.

In the misty glow of dawn, one can see these mysterious visitors aren't backyard pasture mares with swishing tails and docile, trusting eyes. These horses are wild—from another century, another era, another world. They are American mustangs, whose freedom, adaptability, and toughness define the western wilderness.

Some of the mares have names. Medicine Hattie is easy to spot. Her dark ears jut out above her ghostly white face and corn-silk mane. Painted Lady's pure white coat is splashed with brown spots; she always seems to know where the sweetest grasses are.

And there are others. Funny Face has a creamy white blaze that slides down the sides of her face like melting ice cream on a hot day. She loves to stand on the highest rock-strewn spot with her face to the wind. Yuskeya, whose name means freedom in the Sioux language, always stands at the edge of the herd, alert for danger and ready to run.

To find these horses, cross Cascade Creek where the South Dakota Black Hills meet the prairie, and turn right onto a pothole-strewn gravel road. This is the land of silver sagebrush and cowboy legends. Scraggly buzzards perch on fence posts near the entry gate to the Black Hills Wild Horse **Sanctuary**, home for more than three hundred wild horses and one determined cowboy-conservationist named Dayton Hyde.

Dayton was a gangly, growing thirteen-year-old boy when he met his first horse. It was a dirt-colored pony he found drinking from a puddle of old soapy dishwater behind his family's summer cabin in northern Michigan. He recalls that for a time he thought all horses blew bubbles out of their noses.

Soon after that encounter, word came from Dayton's cattle rancher uncle in Oregon that his cowboys had just captured a band of wild horses. Dayton hopped a westbound train and arrived on his uncle's doorstep, where he grew up as a cowboy learning to love the western range and its wild horses.

Mustangs are **descendants** of the horses brought to America by Spanish explorers nearly five hundred years ago. By 1900, more than two million smart, fast, surefooted wild horses roamed the West.

When newly invented barbed wire fences began crisscrossing the rangelands, the horses lost access to sources of food and water and became a pesky problem for local residents. Thousands of them were slaughtered for fertilizer or pet food. By 1950, less than seventeen thousand survived.

After a Congressional act prohibited the capture or slaughter of wild horses in 1971, the wild horse population again grew quickly. Many died of thirst and starvation in the harsh western winters. In an attempt to manage the size of the herds, the United States government gathered up the animals and maintained them in fenced feedlots until they could be adopted.

One day in the early 1980s, Dayton Hyde, who by this time owned his uncle's ranch and had a grown family of his own, drove by one of these feedlots. Shocked and dismayed by the sight of dozens of muddy and dejected horses locked in a corral, he felt he had to do something.

Cause and Effect
What caused the mustang population to increase during the 1970s?

After months of searching and many long days spent convincing government officials to accept his plan of creating a special place for wild horses, he acquired eleven thousand acres of rangeland and rimrock near the Black Hills in South Dakota. Here, among yawning canyons and sun-drenched pastures, he hoped wild horses—some too ugly, old, or knobby kneed to be adopted—could run free forever.

Before he could ship his wild horse rejects to their new home, Dayton had to build eight miles of fences to ensure they wouldn't wander into his neighbors' wheat fields. He also fenced in a fifty-acre training field where the horses would spend their first few days on the ranch adjusting to their new surroundings.

On a miserably cold fall day, huge creaking semi-trailers filled with snorting, stomping steeds finally arrived at the ranch. After hours of **coaxing**, Dayton succeeded in getting Magnificent Mary to skitter off the trailer. She was a battle-scarred, mean-eyed mare with a nose about twice as long as it should be. The rest of the herd clattered behind her, eyes bulging with fear.

Dayton's worst fear was that the horses would spook and charge through his carefully constructed six-wire fence, scattering across the prairie like dry leaves in a whirlwind. Aware that wild horses often feel **threatened** by being watched, he sat in the cab of his old pickup truck, peeking at them out of a corner of his eye. Finally, after nearly a week of around-the-clock vigilance, he swung open the gate from the training field to his wild horse sanctuary.

Many years have passed since Dayton held his breath and pushed that corral gate open. Every spring, dozens of his wild horses give birth to tottering colts that learn the ways of the back country from their mothers. They share the vast, quiet land with coyotes, mountain lions, and countless deer. Star lilies, bluebells, and prairie roses nod in the wind along with the prairie short grass that feeds the herd.

Thousands of visitors arrive each summer to get a glimpse of wild horses in their natural **habitat**, a habitat that has been preserved through Dayton's careful planning. Throughout the grazing season, he moves the herd from one area of the ranch to another so the horses don't damage the **fragile** rangeland. In the process, he searches for his marker mares: Painted Lady, Medicine Hattie, Funny Face, Yuskeya, Magnificent Mary, and several others. When he spots them all, he knows the whole herd is accounted for.

Sometimes in the fall while he's checking on the horses, Dayton notices a gaunt, aging mare whose ribs stand out through her ragged coat. He knows this old friend won't survive the winter. As the pale December daylight slips over the rimrock, the old mare lies down and goes to sleep for the last time. After years of running free, the wild mustang returns to the earth and completes the circle of life.

The wild mustangs Dayton Hyde once discovered crowded into a feedlot now gallop across the Cheyenne River free as the prairie wind. They splash through the **glistening** water and bolt up a ravine. Here in this rugged wilderness, one man's vision of a sanctuary for wild horses has become a reality.

Cause and Effect

What were the events that caused the wild horses from the feedlot to be protected in the Sanctuary?

Ride Away with Cris and Alvis

Cris Peterson lives on a big dairy farm in Wisconsin. Tending 500 cows keeps Cris pretty busy, but she still finds time to write. Cris writes a lot about farm life and animals. She often uses her own experiences as inspiration for her books. Cris believes it is very important to give readers a true picture of farms and animals, so she chooses her details carefully.

Alvis Upitis has provided the photographs for many of Cris's books. He is a good partner. When Cris was very busy with farm work and did not think she'd have time to write, Alvis encouraged her to try.

Other books by Cris and Alvis

 Find out more about Cris Peterson and Alvis Upitis at **www.macmillanmh.com**

Author's Purpose

Cris Peterson tried hard to create a true picture of the animals in *Wild Horses*. What does this suggest about her purpose for writing? How well did she succeed at that purpose? Explain.

Comprehension Check

Summarize

Summarize *Wild Horses*. Include only the most important information in your summary. Use your Cause and Effect Diagram to help you.

Cause → Effect
→
→
→
→

Think and Compare

1. What caused the **fragile** wild horse population to almost disappear? **Monitor Comprehension: Cause and Effect**

2. Reread page 638 of *Wild Horses*. What does the author mean by saying these horses are from "another era, another world"? **Analyze**

3. What would you do if you found a horse drinking soapy dishwater? **Apply**

4. Why is it important to care for and protect animals? Explain your opinion. **Evaluate**

5. Read "The Wild Ponies of Chincoteague" on pages 634–635. Compare Assateague Island with the Black Hills Wild Horse Sanctuary. How are the two places alike? How are they different? Use details from both selections in your answer. **Reading/Writing Across Texts**

651

Genre

Tall Tales are stories with events so exaggerated that they are beyond belief. Tall tales are an American form of storytelling.

SKILL

Literary Elements

Hyperbole is the use of exaggeration for emphasis. The author does not expect it to be believed.

A **Figure of Speech** is an expressive use of language that is not meant to be taken literally.

THE Tale OF Pecos Bill

retold by Gillian Reed

Pecos Bill was the best cowboy and toughest man there ever was. He had bounced out of his family's wagon when he was a baby and landed in the Pecos River. He was raised by coyotes, but he didn't talk about that very much.

One day, Bill showed up on the Texas range, wearing a blue bandanna and big Stetson hat. "Hey, partner," Pecos Bill roared at a gold prospector, "I'm lookin' for some real cowhands. Got me a ranch in New Mexico — well, to tell the truth, New Mexico is my ranch. I need some tough guys to work for me. I'm looking for the kind of man who can eat a pot of beans in one gulp and pick his teeth with barbed wire."

Pecos Bill's description of a tough guy is **hyperbole**. It's a humorous exaggeration that the reader is not meant to believe.

652

The prospector said some tough cowhands were camped out 200 miles down the river. Bill and his horse set off in that direction, and before long, a mountain lion leaped from a boulder straight down on Pecos Bill.

Bill's horse didn't wait around to see what happened next. If he had, all he would have seen was a blur of flying fur. He would have heard nothing but hideous snarls and groans. When the fur settled, the big cat was apologizing to Bill.

"How can I make it up to you?" it asked.

"You can't, but I'm putting this saddle on you," said Bill. "You scared off my horse, and I hate walkin'."

So Pecos Bill rode the cat to the tough guys' campsite. Those tough men took one look at Bill on that mountain lion and made him their new boss. Then the whole crew headed out for New Mexico.

THE GOLD RUSH

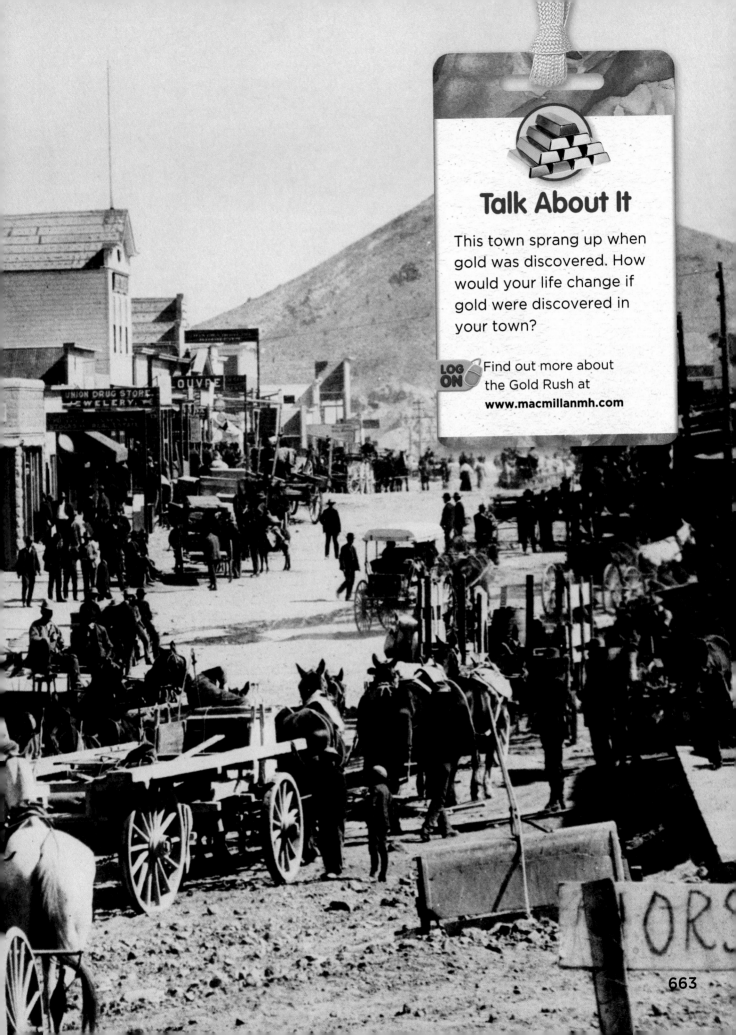

Talk About It

This town sprang up when gold was discovered. How would your life change if gold were discovered in your town?

LOG ON Find out more about the Gold Rush at **www.macmillanmh.com**

In Search of Gold

by Al Ortiz

Mr. Rodriguez's fourth-grade class was on a field trip at the Sutter Gold Mine. Larry couldn't wait to load up on gold. He even brought along some photographs to use as a **reference**. He didn't want to pick up any "fool's gold" by mistake.

Larry's class boarded the Boss Buggy Shuttle that would take them down into the mine. Everyone had to wear a hardhat for safety. On the ride down, their guide Ron gave them some information about the Gold Rush.

"Many **prospectors** came to this area beginning in 1848," explained Ron. "A prospector is someone who searches for valuable metals like gold."

Margaret commented, "Everyone must have gotten rich!"

"Actually," said Ron, "not everyone was successful. Many left the mines filled with **disappointment**. People often turned to farming or ranching to make a living instead."

"If I don't find any gold today, I'll be really **annoyed**," Larry thought to himself.

The underground tour lasted about an hour. Then it was time to go to the mining flumes and pan for gold. Ron handed out pans and demonstrated how to swirl them in a **circular** motion.

"It's okay to let some of the water splash out," said Ron. "If there's any gold in your pan, it will sink to the bottom."

Larry found an open place at one of the flumes. With his arm **outstretched**, he dipped his pan below the surface of the water. Then he swished around the water. "Nothing," he said with a sigh.

Larry repeated the process several times. Then he noticed something at the bottom of his pan. Larry angled the pan so he could get a better look. Whatever it was, it **glinted** in the sunlight. Larry pulled out the photos and compared them with what was in his pan. Then he went to show Ron.

"You've found gold!" Ron exclaimed with surprise.

Everyone gathered around to see. It was just a small piece, but Larry felt like he had hit the jackpot.

Reread for **Comprehension**

STRATEGY SKILL

Analyze Story Structure

Cause and Effect In many stories, cause and effect is an important part of the story structure. A cause is why something happens. What happens is the effect. An author doesn't always write about the cause before the effect. The reader must read the text carefully.

A Cause and Effect Diagram can help you understand what happens and why. Reread the story and identify causes and effects.

Cause ➔ Effect	
➔	
➔	
➔	
➔	

Comprehension

Genre
Science Fiction is a fantasy in which an invention involving science or technology affects historic or imaginary characters.

Analyze Story Structure
Cause and Effect
As you read, fill in your Cause and Effect Diagram.

Cause ➔ Effect
➔
➔
➔
➔

Read to Find Out
Which part of this story is science and which part is fiction?

The Gold Rush Game

by William F. Wu

illustrated by Cornelius Van Wright and Ying-Hwa Hu

Eric Wong looked at his new game on the computer screen. "Let's play." He clicked the button to start.

"The Gold Rush," his friend Matt O'Brien read out loud, as he rolled his chair closer. "What's that mean? I want to see it! Come on, I'm going first."

"I'm older," said Eric. "Besides, it's my game."

"Be nice." Eric's mom came up behind them. "We bought the game so Eric could learn more about the Gold Rush," she said to Matt. "His dad and I are tracing our family tree. Eric's great-great-great grandfather on his dad's side came to California from China during the Gold Rush, but we don't know much about him."

"Hey, look at the game," said Eric. On the screen, he saw steep, mountain slopes covered with tall, green trees. Some men wearing broad-brimmed hats rode horses along a muddy path, leading mules with bundles on their backs. Picks and shovels were tied to the bundles. Chinese men, with long, braided queues down their backs, squatted by a rushing river.

"Who are those guys?" Matt asked. "Are they looking for gold?"

"They might be," said Eric's dad as he came into the room. He held out a small piece of paper with two Chinese characters written on it. "This is the name of our ancestor who first came to California. I don't know Chinese, but my grandfather wrote it down for me when I was growing up."

Eric turned and looked. "What was his name?"

"Daido," his dad said. "I'll say it slower, 'Dye-doe.' It means 'Great Path.' That's a good name for a man who took a great adventure traveling across the Pacific Ocean to a new land. In Chinese, his family name would be given first. And so, he was called Wong Daido."

"Wong Daido," Eric repeated. "Yeah."

"Do you know how to write that?" Matt asked, looking at the name.

"No." Eric shrugged.

"We'll let you play your game," said Eric's mom. "Come on, dear." She and Eric's dad walked away.

"Look." Eric pointed to the screen. A miner wearing a broad-brimmed gray hat lifted a rock showing a button that said, "Press if you dare."

"I dare you," Matt said loudly.

"I'm doing it." **Annoyed**, Eric pressed the button.

669

Suddenly Eric and Matt found themselves standing in a narrow space between two large, tall rocks by the muddy road in the mountains, with trees towering over their heads. Miners and **prospectors** walked and rode past. Eric's heart beat faster with excitement, but he was also a little scared.

"What happened?" Matt asked. "This is creepy. Where are we?"

Eric smelled the scent of pine trees and kicked at the mud. "I think we're really in the Gold Rush. We went back in time!"

"Did you say, back in time?" Matt stared around them in shock.

"Come on." Eric walked up to the mysterious miner who had lifted the rock. "Do you know a man named Wong Daido?" Eric carefully pronounced his ancestor's name, remembering to put his family name first.

The miner laughed. Then he looked closely at Eric and Matt. "You're not from around here are you?"

"No, we're not," said Eric hoping the man wouldn't ask any more questions.

"Do you know how many people are in this area? We're on the Feather River upstream from Marysville, in the western foothills of the Sierra Nevada in California. Men came to find gold. We're called the Forty-niners because so many of us have come this year."

"What year?" Matt asked, his eyes wide.

"1849, of course," said the miner. He frowned. "Don't you boys know what year it is? Gold was discovered in this area last year. Now, Forty-niners are coming from all over America and lots of other places."

Cause and Effect
How did Eric and Matt find themselves back in 1849?

"How do they get here?" Eric asked.

"I came overland from the eastern United States by wagon train. A good friend of mine took a ship from the east coast south around Cape Horn at the tip of South America. From China, other men come on ships across the Pacific Ocean."

"But where do they live?" Eric asked. "I don't see any houses here."

"Marysville is a new town," said the miner. "It was started by miners and prospectors. But men also live in camps, sometimes together and sometimes on their own, while they look for gold." He pointed to the river. "But the best way to find a Chinese miner is to ask other Chinese miners."

Matt ran down to the edge of the river, where a Chinese miner squatted by the rushing water, swirling sand in a metal pan.

Eric hurried after him. "Hey, mister, is your name Wong Daido?"

"No." The man shook his head. Then he gave Eric a little smile and pointed downstream. "You see that man? His name is Wong."

Matt ran down the bank, but this time Eric ran, too. They stopped next to Mr. Wong together, near a big tree growing right beside the river.

"Are you named Wong Daido?" Eric asked.

Mr. Wong was a little younger than the other Chinese miner. His long, braided queue swung behind him as he looked up. "I am," he said, giving both boys a big smile. "Why do you ask?"

Eric was afraid to explain he and Matt had traveled through time from the future. He was sure Mr. Wong wouldn't believe him and might chase them away, so he changed the subject. "My name's Eric, and this is my friend Matt. Have you found any gold?"

"Not today. Some days I find enough gold to buy food that will last until the next time I find gold. I filed this claim so I have the right to pan gold here. The river washes gold dust downstream, so I catch river water, mud, and sand in this pan and try to find it." He moved the pan in a **circular** motion, so that water sloshed out with some of the sand. "Gold is heavy, so it stays in the pan."

"Wow," said Matt. "And the river's so fast."

"Don't you have to get sand from the bottom of the river?" Eric asked. "It looks really deep right here!"

"It's very deep here," said Mr. Wong. "The riverbank drops steeply from the edge of the water and the current's very fast. But I can take the sand and mud right here at the edge and pan it. And the water itself carries sand, even when it looks clear. On a good day, the water brings gold to me."

"Mine too," said Eric. "You're welcome."

"I thought I was going to drown. Everything I have dreamed about would have come to an end." He paused and looked down at the ground. "I came from a poor peasant village in southern China," Mr. Wong went on. "I hope to find some gold and send for a woman I love. We'll marry here and raise a family in America—at least, I hope so."

"Hey, that's good," said Matt. "Because—"

Eric jabbed Matt with his elbow and interrupted, ". . . because it's a good idea." He smiled, knowing that Mr. Wong's dream was going to come true.

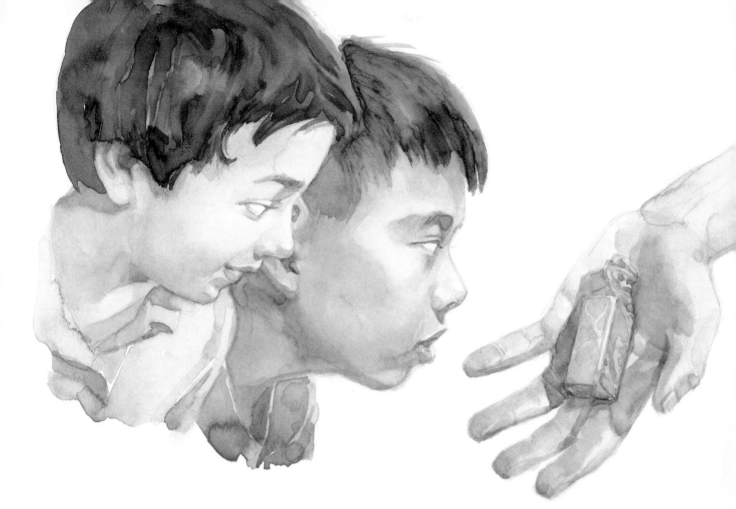

"I don't have much to offer in return for my life," said Mr. Wong. He reached into his pocket and pulled something out. "This is my chop."

Eric and Matt looked. It was a small piece of ivory, with unfamiliar shapes carved on the bottom. "What's it for?" Eric asked.

"I'll show you." Mr. Wong pushed the bottom into a smooth spot of mud next to the river. When he lifted it, three marks were in the mud. "That's my name, Wong Daido. I don't have any gold today. But I would like you to accept this as my gift. I will always remember you."

Eric took the chop. "That's very nice of you. Thanks."

"I should return to my camp and dry off," said Mr. Wong.

"I think we better go home, too," said Eric. "We enjoyed meeting you!" He carefully put the chop in his pants pocket.

"Thank you again for your help," said Mr. Wong. "Goodbye." He picked up his pan and walked away from the river toward the muddy road.

"How do we get back to our time?" asked Matt. "Maybe we should try to find those big rocks. But where are they?"

"Come on," Eric said to Matt. "I remember where they are. Maybe we'll find some kind of clue there that will help us get back." He led Matt back into the space between the two big rocks where they had walked out. Suddenly they were back in Eric's living room in front of the computer.

"Wow! It worked. Those rocks must be some kind of doorway into the past." Matt looked at the computer screen. "That's a great game!"

"Who's winning?" Eric's mom asked, as she and his dad came in.

"Mom! Dad!" Eric called out. "We went into the game and back in time!"

"Yeah," said Matt. "We met Eric's great-great-great grandfather!"

Eric's mom and dad laughed.

"I love the way these games build imagination while they teach history," said Eric's mom. "Isn't that nice?"

"Dad! He told us he filed a claim for his mine along the Feather River!"

"Well, I know from what I read in my grandfather's journal that Daido did file a claim. Let's see if we can find out if it was along the Feather River." Eric's dad moved to the computer and conducted an Internet search. After a while he looked up in surprise. "Wong Daido did file a claim in that area in 1849. I found a **reference** to it."

"Do you believe me now?" Eric asked.

"C'mon, Eric. Do you expect me to believe you actually went back in time?"

"No, I guess not." Eric felt a wave of **disappointment**, then suddenly reached into his pocket. "Maybe this will convince you!" He pulled out the chop. "Dad! Look at the name: Wong Daido." Smiling, Eric held it up.

On the chop, a little bit of gold dust from the river **glinted** in the light.

679

File a Claim with William, Cornelius, and Ying-Hwa

William F. Wu has liked history since he was a boy. During recess at school, he and his friend acted out famous historical events. William also enjoyed writing stories and poems. He first thought about becoming a writer when he was eight years old.

Cornelius Van Wright and **Ying-Hwa Hu** are a husband and wife team who have been illustrating books for more than 15 years. Cornelius studied art in New York City, while Ying developed her art skills in Taiwan and Minnesota. With such different backgrounds, the two try to combine their different cultures into each illustration for this story.

 LOG ON Find out more about William F. Wu, Cornelius Van Wright, and Ying-Hwa Hu at **www.macmillanmh.com**

Author's Purpose

What clues in *The Gold Rush Game* helped you to understand the author's purpose for writing this science fiction story? Did William F. Wu want to inform or entertain the reader? Discuss the evidence that led you to your conclusion.

Comprehension Check

Summarize

Summarize *The Gold Rush Game*. Who are the main characters? Explain what they are trying to do and what happens to them.

Think and Compare

1. What caused Eric and Matt to go back in time? Use your Cause and Effect Diagram to help you answer. **Analyze Story Structure: Cause and Effect**

Cause ➡ Effect
➡
➡
➡
➡

2. Reread page 670 of *The Gold Rush Game*. How do you think the **prospector** knew that the boys were not "from around here"? **Analyze**

3. How would you change the plot to include one of Matt's ancestors? Invent a character with traits that would fit into the story. **Synthesize**

4. Why is it important for people to learn about their family's history? Explain your answer. **Evaluate**

5. Read "In Search of Gold" on pages 664–665. How is Larry's experience similar to that of the prospectors in *The Gold Rush Game?* How is it different? Use details from both selections in your answer. **Reading/Writing Across Texts**

People came from all over—some from as far away as China. In 1850, a year after California became a state, there were 3,000 Chinese men living there—and another 22,000 on their way. One of the few women in gold rush country used the pen name "Dame Shirley." Shirley was a doctor's wife whose real name was Louise Amelia Knapp Smith Clappe. She spent a year living in rough mining camps along the Feather River and wrote letters filled with colorful information about the era.

In one letter, "Dame Shirley" described the way the miners spoke. She especially liked their figure of speech "seeing the elephant."

That meant "having a remarkable experience," nearly as remarkable as finding an elephant in the gold mines. In 1851 she wrote this about the gold miners: "I never could appreciate the poetry or the humor of making one's wrists ache by knocking to pieces gloomy-looking stones...."

Miners set up systems that dumped huge amounts of dirt and gravel into long wooden boxes. They poured in water to wash away everything but the heavier gold. By 1852, though, most of the easier-to-find gold had been discovered. Then miners began digging underground.

Some Californians became concerned about the **environment** when mud and trash washed into California's rivers. Lawmakers finally passed laws in 1854 that stopped much of this pollution. However, some effects are still visible even today.

Gold mining was popular until shortly after World War II, which ended in 1945. Although most of the gold is probably gone now, people still look for gold in the rivers of northern California. They dip a shallow pan in the river and swirl it around to wash out the dirt. A very lucky miner might find a few specks glinting in the bottom of the pan.

Connect and Compare

1. Look at the timeline on page 683. About how many years did the gold rush last? **Reading a Timeline**

2. Why do you think the earliest gold miners made no effort to protect the environment? **Evaluate**

3. Reread page 683 of this article and page 672 of *The Gold Rush Game*. How did the "49'ers" get to California? **Reading/ Writing Across Texts**

Social Studies Activity

Research gold prices. Find out how much gold was worth in each of the following years: 1950, 1960, 1970, 1980, 1990, 2000. Plot your data on a line graph.

 Find out more about gold at **www.macmillanmh.com**

My article for the school newsletter includes topic sentences and interesting details.

I summed up with a strong conclusion.

A Day at White Pines Forest

by Casey R.

The White Pines Forest is a great place to visit. If you like rivers and boating, you'll find lots to do. You can go boating on Muddy River in many different kinds of boats. People who like to swim can go to Colson Lake. Little kids can play happily on the lake's sandy shore.

There's plenty to do on dry land, too. You can hike and picnic among the pine trees. At the wildlife center, visitors can watch snakes slowly slithering around in their cages and hear owls hoot spookily. You will find great things to do at White Pines Forest.

Your Turn

Write a short magazine article about a special place to visit in your community. Write topic sentences and support them with details. In your details, describe the features of this special place and explain why it is worth visiting. Sum up with a strong conclusion. Use the Writer's Checklist to check your writing. Include photographs in your article.

Writer's Checklist

☑ **Ideas and Content:** Have I included the most interesting information about this special place? Did I use a **strong conclusion**?

☑ **Organization:** Did I start each paragraph with a topic sentence and then provide interesting supporting details?

☑ **Voice:** Will readers sense my enthusiasm?

☑ **Word Choice:** Did I use precise and colorful language to help my readers picture this place?

☑ **Sentence Fluency:** Did I vary my sentences?

☑ **Conventions:** Did I use *good* and *well* correctly? Did I check my spelling?

WILD
VISITORS

Talk About It

Why is this photograph of a peregrine falcon living in a big city surprising?

LOG ON Find out more about wild visitors at **www.macmillanmh.com**

The Country Mouse and the City Mouse

retold by Jeff Banner

One day Country Mouse invited an old friend from the city to visit her. Country Mouse welcomed City Mouse with a delicious meal of fresh barley and corn. City Mouse was very quiet, so Country Mouse asked her whether anything was wrong.

"I was just missing the city," she replied **wistfully**. "You must come visit one day. There are lots of good things to eat."

Country Mouse thought this was a very good idea, so a few weeks later she traveled to the city. City Mouse invited her friend for dinner at her favorite restaurant. Country Mouse followed City Mouse as she tiptoed quietly into a cupboard and listened.

"So, what are we doing?" asked Country Mouse.

"Shhh. We're doing a bit of **eavesdropping**," City Mouse whispered. "When the cook leaves for the night, we can help ourselves to that lovely bag of sugar over there."

A light went out, and it grew quiet. City Mouse nibbled a hole in the bag, and Country Mouse took the tiniest taste.

"I've never tasted anything so wonderful in all my life!" she cried.

Just then, the mice heard a **scuffling** sound coming from behind the cupboard door. "Run for your life!" screamed City Mouse.

"That's Esperanza, the cook's rotten cat," City Mouse explained when they were safe. "You don't ever want to make her **acquaintance**. One swipe from her claws and it's curtains. When she's asleep again, we can go back for more sugar."

But Country Mouse was too frightened to go back, so they went down to the basement instead. There they found a **jumble** of grain bags stacked randomly against the wall.

Country Mouse happily nibbled this and that. Then she saw something that made her mouth water—a hunk of cheese! Country Mouse was about to bite it when. . .

"STOP!" yelled City Mouse. "Can't you see that's a trap?" she said **scornfully**! "One nibble and that big metal thing comes crashing down."

Country Mouse was horrified. The city was not the safest, most **logical** place for a mouse to live—or visit! So Country Mouse went home and never visited the city again.

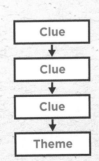

Reread for **Comprehension**

Analyze Story Structure

Theme In a fable the theme may be expressed as the moral. To identify the theme, think about the story structure. Think about what the characters do and say and what happens as a result. Finally, ask yourself, "What lesson, or moral, does the author want the readers to learn?"

A Theme Map can help you identify an author's theme. Reread the story to find the theme.

Clue
↓
Clue
↓
Clue
↓
Theme

Comprehension

Genre

Fantasy is a story with invented characters, settings, or other elements that could not exist in real life.

Analyze Story Structure
Theme

As you read, fill in your Theme Map.

```
┌──────────┐
│   Clue   │
└────┬─────┘
     ▼
┌──────────┐
│   Clue   │
└────┬─────┘
     ▼
┌──────────┐
│   Clue   │
└────┬─────┘
     ▼
┌──────────┐
│  Theme   │
└──────────┘
```

Read to Find Out

What happens when a country cricket winds up in a big city?

THE CRICKET
IN TIMES SQUARE

By George Selden

DRAWINGS BY *Garth Williams*

Chester

Tucker Mouse had been watching the Bellinis and listening to what they said. Next to scrounging, **eavesdropping** on human beings was what he enjoyed most. That was one of the reasons he lived in the Times Square subway station. As soon as the family disappeared, he darted out across the floor and scooted up to the newsstand. At one side the boards had separated and there was a wide space he could jump through. He'd been in a few times before—just exploring. For a moment he stood under the three-legged stool, letting his eyes get used to the darkness. Then he jumped on it.

"Psst!" he whispered. "Hey, you up there—are you awake?"

There was no answer.

"Psst! Psst! Hey!" Tucker whispered again, louder this time.

From the shelf above came **scuffling**, like little feet feeling their way to the edge. "Who is going 'psst'?" said a voice.

"It's me," said Tucker. "Down here on the stool."

A black head, with two shiny black eyes, peered down at him. "Who are you?"

"A mouse," said Tucker, "Who are *you*?"

"I'm Chester Cricket," said the cricket. He had a high, musical voice. Everything he said seemed to be spoken to an unheard melody.

"My name's Tucker," said Tucker Mouse. "Can I come up?"

"I guess so," said Chester Cricket. "This isn't my house anyway."

Tucker jumped up beside the cricket and looked him all over. "A cricket," he said admiringly. "So you're a cricket. I never saw one before."

"I've seen mice before," the cricket said. "I knew quite a few back in Connecticut."

"Is that where you're from?" asked Tucker.

"Yes," said Chester. "I guess I'll never see it again," he added **wistfully**.

"How did you get to New York?" asked Tucker Mouse.

"It's a long story," sighed the cricket.

"Tell me," said Tucker, settling back on his haunches. He loved to hear stories. It was almost as much fun as eavesdropping—if the story was true.

"Well it must have been two—no, three days ago," Chester Cricket began. "I was sitting on top of my stump, just enjoying the weather and thinking how nice it was that summer had started. I live inside an old tree stump, next to a willow tree, and I often go up to the roof to look around. And I'd been practicing jumping that day too. On the other side of the stump from the willow tree there's a brook that runs past, and I'd been jumping back and forth across it to get my legs in condition for the summer. I do a lot of jumping, you know."

"Me too," said Tucker Mouse. "Especially around the rush hour."

"And I had just finished jumping when I smelled something," Chester went on, "liverwurst, which I love."

"You like liverwurst?" Tucker broke in. "Wait! Wait! Just wait!"

In one leap, he sprang down all the way from the shelf to the floor and dashed over to his drain pipe. Chester shook his head as he watched him go. He thought Tucker was a very excitable person—even for a mouse.

Inside the drain pipe, Tucker's nest was a **jumble** of papers, scraps of cloth, buttons, lost jewelry, small change, and everything else that can be picked up in a subway station. Tucker tossed things left and right in a wild search. Neatness was not one of the things he aimed at in life. At last he discovered what he was looking for: a big piece of liverwurst he had found earlier that evening. It was meant to be for breakfast tomorrow, but he decided that meeting his first cricket was a special occasion. Holding the liverwurst between his teeth, he whisked back to the newsstand.

"Look!" he said proudly, dropping the meat in front of Chester Cricket. "Liverwurst! You continue the story—we'll enjoy a snack too."

"That's very nice of you," said Chester. He was touched that a mouse he had known only a few minutes would share his food with him. "I had a little chocolate before, but besides that, nothing for three days."

"Eat! Eat!" said Tucker. He bit the liverwurst into two pieces and gave Chester the bigger one. "So you smelled the liverwurst—then what happened?"

STRATEGY SKILL

Theme
What is the author's message about different types of characters becoming friends?

"I hopped down from the stump and went off toward the smell," said Chester.

"Very **logical**," said Tucker Mouse, munching with his cheeks full. "Exactly what I would have done."

"It was coming from a picnic basket," said Chester. "A couple of tuffets away from my stump the meadow begins, and there was a whole bunch of people having a picnic. They had hard boiled eggs, and cold roast chicken, and roast beef, and a whole lot of other things besides the liverwurst sandwiches which I smelled."

Tucker Mouse moaned with pleasure at the thought of all that food.

"They were having such a good time laughing and singing songs that they didn't notice me when I jumped into the picnic basket," continued Chester. "I was sure they wouldn't mind if I had just a taste."

"Naturally not," said Tucker Mouse sympathetically. "Why mind? Plenty for all. Who could blame you?"

"Now, I have to admit," Chester went on, "I had more than a taste. As a matter of fact, I ate so much that I couldn't keep my eyes open— what with being tired from the jumping and everything. And I fell asleep right there in the picnic basket. The first thing I knew, somebody had put a bag on top of me that had the last of the roast beef sandwiches in it. I couldn't move!"

"Imagine!" Tucker exclaimed. "Trapped under roast beef sandwiches! Well, there are worse fates."

"At first I wasn't too frightened," said Chester. "After all, I thought, they probably come from New Canaan or some other nearby town. They'll have to unpack the basket sooner or later. Little did I know!" He shook his head and sighed. "I could feel the basket being carried into a car and riding somewhere and then being lifted down. That must have been the railroad station. Then I went up again and there was a rattling and roaring sound, the way a train makes. By this time I was pretty scared. I knew every minute was taking me farther away from my stump, but there wasn't anything I could do. I was getting awfully cramped too, under those roast beef sandwiches."

"Didn't you try to eat your way out?" asked Tucker.

"I didn't have any room," said Chester. "But every now and then the train would give a lurch and I managed to free myself a little. We traveled on and on, and then the train stopped. I didn't have any idea where we were, but as soon as the basket was carried off, I could tell from the noise it must be New York."

"You never were here before?" Tucker asked.

"Goodness no!" said Chester. "But I've heard about it. There was a swallow I used to know who told about flying over New York every spring and fall on her way to the North and back. But what would I be doing here?" He shifted uneasily from one set of legs to another. "I'm a country cricket."

"Don't worry," said Tucker Mouse. "I'll feed you liverwurst. You'll be all right. Go on with the story."

"It's almost over," said Chester. "The people got off one train and walked a ways and got on another—even noisier than the first."

"Must have been the subway," said Tucker.

"I guess so," Chester Cricket said. "You can imagine how scared I was. I didn't know *where* I was going! For all I knew they could have been heading for Texas, although I don't guess many people from Texas come all the way to Connecticut for a picnic."

"It could happen," said Tucker, nodding his head.

"Anyway I worked furiously to get loose. And finally I made it. When they got off the second train, I took a flying leap and landed in a pile of dirt over in the corner of this place where we are."

"Such an introduction to New York," said Tucker, "to land in a pile of dirt in the Times Square subway station. Tsk, tsk, tsk."

"And here I am," Chester concluded forlornly. "I've been lying over there for three days not knowing what to do. At last I got so nervous I began to chirp."

"That was the sound!" interrupted Tucker Mouse. "I heard it, but I didn't know what it was."

"Yes, that was me," said Chester. "Usually I don't chirp until later on in the summer—but my goodness, I had to do *something*!"

The cricket had been sitting next to the edge of the shelf. For some reason—perhaps it was a faint noise, like padded feet tiptoeing across the floor—he happened to look down. A shadowy form that had been crouching silently below in the darkness made a spring and landed right next to Tucker and Chester.

"Watch out!" Chester shouted, "A cat!" He dove headfirst into the matchbox.

Harry Cat

Chester buried his head in the Kleenex. He didn't want to see his new friend, Tucker Mouse, get killed. Back in Connecticut he had sometimes watched the one-sided fights of cats and mice in the meadow, and unless the mice were near their holes, the fights always ended in the same way. But this cat had been upon them too quickly: Tucker couldn't have escaped.

There wasn't a sound. Chester lifted his head and very cautiously looked behind him. The cat—a huge tiger cat with gray-green eyes and black stripes along his body—was sitting on his hind legs, switching his tail around his forepaws. And directly between those forepaws, in the very jaws of his enemy, sat Tucker Mouse. He was watching Chester curiously. The cricket began to make frantic signs that the mouse should look up and see what was looming over him.

Very casually Tucker raised his head. The cat looked straight down on him. "Oh, him," said Tucker, chucking the cat under the chin with his right front paw, "he's my best friend. Come out from the matchbox."

Chester crept out, looking first at one, then the other.

"Chester, meet Harry Cat," said Tucker. "Harry, this is Chester. He's a cricket."

"I'm very pleased to make your **acquaintance**," said Harry Cat in a silky voice.

"Hello," said Chester. He was sort of ashamed because of all the fuss he'd made. "I wasn't scared for myself. But I thought cats and mice were enemies."

"In the country, maybe," said Tucker. "But in New York we gave up those old habits long ago. Harry is my oldest friend. He lives with me over in the drain pipe. So how was scrounging tonight, Harry?"

"Not so good," said Harry Cat. "I was over in the ash cans on the East Side, but those rich people don't throw out as much garbage as they should."

"Chester, make that noise again for Harry," said Tucker Mouse.

Chester lifted the black wings that were carefully folded across his back and with a quick, expert stroke drew the top one over the bottom. A *thrumm* echoed through the station.

"Lovely—very lovely," said the cat. "This cricket has talent."

"I thought it was singing," said Tucker. "But you do it like playing a violin, with one wing on the other?"

"Yes," said Chester. "These wings aren't much good for flying, but I prefer music anyhow." He made three rapid chirps.

Tucker Mouse and Harry Cat smiled at each other. "It makes me want to purr to hear it," said Harry.

"Some people say a cricket goes 'chee chee chee,'" explained Chester. "And others say, 'treet treet treet,' but we crickets don't think it sounds like either one of those."

"It sounds to me as if you were going 'crik crik crik,'" said Harry.

"Maybe that's why they call him a 'cricket,'" said Tucker.

They all laughed. Tucker had a squeaky laugh that sounded as if he were hiccupping. Chester was feeling much happier now. The future did not seem nearly as gloomy as it had over in the pile of dirt in the corner.

"Are you going to stay a while in New York?" asked Tucker.

"I guess I'll have to," said Chester. "I don't know how to get home."

"Well, we could always take you to Grand Central Station and put you on a train going back to Connecticut," said Tucker. "But why don't you give the city a try. Meet new people—see new things. Mario likes you very much."

"Yes, but his mother doesn't," said Chester. "She thinks I carry germs."

"Germs!" said Tucker **scornfully**. "She wouldn't know a germ if one gave her a black eye. Pay no attention."

"Too bad you couldn't have found more successful friends," said Harry Cat. "I fear for the future of this newsstand."

"It's true," echoed Tucker sadly. "They're going broke fast." He jumped up on a pile of magazines and read off the names in the half-light that slanted through the cracks in the wooden cover. "*Art News—Musical America*. Who would read them but a few long-hairs?"

"I don't understand the way you talk," said Chester. Back in the meadow he had listened to bullfrogs, and woodchucks, and rabbits, even a few snakes, but he had never heard anyone speak like Tucker Mouse. "What is a long-hair?"

Tucker scratched his head and thought a moment. "A long-hair is an extra-refined person," he said. "You take an Afghan hound—that's a long-hair."

"Do Afghan hounds read *Musical America*?" asked the cricket.

"They would if they could," said Tucker.

Chester shook his head. "I'm afraid I won't get along in New York," he said.

"Oh, sure you will!" squeaked Tucker Mouse. "Harry, suppose we take Chester up and show him Times Square. Would you like that, Chester?"

"I guess so," said Chester, although he was really a little leery of venturing out into New York City.

The three of them jumped down to the floor. The crack in the side of the newsstand was just wide enough for Harry to get through. As they crossed the station floor, Tucker pointed out the local sights of interest, such as the Nedick's lunch counter—Tucker spent a lot of time around there—and the Loft's candy store. Then they came to the drain pipe. Chester had to make short little hops to keep from hitting his head as they went up. There seemed to be hundreds of twistings and turnings, and many other pipes that opened off the main route, but Tucker Mouse knew his way perfectly—even in the dark. At last Chester saw light above them. One more hop brought him out onto the sidewalk. And there he gasped, holding his breath and crouching against the cement.

They were standing at one corner of the Times building, which is at the south end of Times Square. Above the cricket, towers that seemed like mountains of light rose up into the night sky. Even this late the neon signs were still blazing. Reds, blues, greens, and yellows flashed down on him. And the air was full of the roar of traffic and the hum of human beings. It was as if Times Square were a kind of shell, with colors and noises breaking in great waves inside it. Chester's heart hurt him and he closed his eyes. The sight was too terrible and beautiful for a cricket who up to now had measured high things by the height of his willow tree and sounds by the burble of a running brook.

"How do you like it?" asked Tucker Mouse.

"Well—it's—it's quite something," Chester stuttered.

"You should see it New Year's Eve," said Harry Cat.

Gradually Chester's eyes got used to the lights. He looked up. And way far above them, above New York, and above the whole world, he made out a star that he knew was a star he used to look at back in Connecticut. When they had gone down to the station and Chester was in the matchbox again, he thought about that star. It made him feel better to think that there was one familiar thing, twinkling above him, amid so much that was new and strange.

Theme
How does the author use his characters to express the theme?

On a Journey with George and Garth

George Selden wrote this story after he heard a cricket chirping in the Times Square subway station. Chester's whole story came to George immediately. The cricket reminded George of his home in the countryside where he used to live.

Other books by George Selden and Garth Williams

Garth Williams worked very hard to make the creatures in this story look and act like real people. First he started with an actual photograph of the animal. Then he drew and redrew until the animal seemed to have human qualities.

 Find out more about George Selden and Garth Williams at **www.macmillanmh.com**

Author's Purpose

Why did George Selden write *The Cricket in Times Square*? Was his main purpose to explain, entertain, or persuade? What details help you to know?

Comprehension Check

STRATEGY SKILL

Summarize

Summarize *The Cricket in Times Square.*
Tell about the main characters, the most
important events in the story, and the theme.

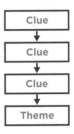

Clue
↓
Clue
↓
Clue
↓
Theme

Think and Compare

STRATEGY SKILL

1. New York City is filled with people from many different
   backgrounds and countries. What message do you think the
   author is sending by making a cricket, a cat, and a mouse
   his main characters? Use your theme chart to answer the
   question. **Analyze Story Structure: Theme**

2. Reread page 708 of the story. How do you think Chester feels
   about New York after he sees Times Square? Use story details
   to support your answer. **Analyze**

3. If you could be a character in the story, which character
   would you choose to be, Chester or Tucker? Explain your
   answer. **Apply**

4. Tucker advises his new **acquaintance** Chester to give the
   city a try. How would you decide if this is a good idea?
   Support your answer with details from the text. **Evaluate**

5. Read "The Country Mouse and the City Mouse" on pages
   690–691. How is Country Mouse's experience similar to
   Chester's on pages 701 to 704? How is it different? Use
   details from both selections in your answer. **Reading/Writing
   Across Texts**

Science

Genre

Editorials are articles printed in newspapers and magazines that express the opinions of the writer.

Text Feature

Advertisements are text and pictures that try to persuade consumers to buy a product.

Content Vocabulary

colony

echolocation

insecticides

The Chance of a Lifetime

by Patricia West

What words come to mind when you see or think of a bat? Creepy? Dark? Dangerous? People who know very little about this creature might answer in this way. Those who know bats would use words such as "fascinating," "amazing," even "beautiful."

All of us here in Austin have an incredible opportunity to take a first-hand look at the Mexican free-tailed bat. A **colony** of bats has settled under the Congress Avenue Bridge.

I urge all of you to come out to see these bats. They tend to come out around sunset. Depending on the size of a colony, bats can eat tens of thousands of insects during their nightly flights. That, my friends, is a lot of mosquitoes.

cont. on page 714

Advertisement

SKILL **Reading an Advertisement**

The purpose of an advertisement is to persuade people to buy a product. Look for ways in which the author motivates customers to come to Kramer's.

Our Best Bat House Just Went On Sale!

SALE!

Now Only $40.00
(Regularly $55.00)

Designed by the Bat Society
Slanted roof for better run-off
Weather-resistant red cedar
Made in the USA

Special: Hammocks—Up to 50% off!

Wheelbarrows—10% off when you bring this ad

For a limited time only. Sales end 6/30.

KRAMER'S LAWN AND GARDEN

555 Main Street, Cedar Park, Texas • (555) 555-5555

Open daily 10-6

cont. from page 712

Unfortunately, bat populations are falling all around the county. This decline is due to several factors. **Insecticides** have killed many bats. People have disturbed bat roosts. Sadly, people who mistakenly think that bats are dangerous or carry disease have intentionally destroyed them. Scientists, however, believe that fewer than one bat in 200 is sick. Sick bats are too weak to fly, so they rarely come in contact with people. We need to spread the word.

Dr. Markus Rivera, a scientist who studies bats, has some helpful advice to pass along. Here are his bat-viewing suggestions.

Tips on Viewing Bats

- Look for bats at dawn or dusk.
- Pick an open spot to see bats against the sky.
- Look for bats near water or streetlights.
- Never touch a bat.
- Do not disturb bats during the day when they sleep.

Did You Know?

Did you know that bats do not rely on their eyes when they fly and hunt insects? They use **echolocation**. They emit high-pitched sounds. When the sound waves bounce off objects and return to the bat's ears, it can tell how far away the object is.

Connect and Compare

1. What are some persuasive techniques used in the ad on page 713? Could a customer at Kramer's get 50% off all hammocks? Explain. **Reading an Advertisement**

2. If you want to watch bats, when and where should you look? **Analyze**

3. Think about the editorial and *The Cricket in Times Square.* What are some misunderstandings that people have about crickets? About bats? **Reading/Writing Across Texts**

 Science Activity

Research either bats or crickets. Draw a picture of one. Write three facts you learned in your research.

 Find out more about bats at **www.macmillanmh.com**

715

Write a News Article

School News

What ARE Those Birds?

by Matthew E.

Have you seen the big green birds on the telephone poles behind the school? Their messy nest has been there for at least three years, growing larger every year.

The birds are called monk parakeets, but they are a kind of parrot that originally lived in South America.

How did they get here? They are probably escaped pets. Bird experts think the parakeets like it here on the coast because it doesn't get too cold in the winter. Next time you're outside for recess, take a look at our monk parakeet colony.

I wrote a fact-filled news article about an interesting subject.

I included the "five Ws"— who, what, why, when, and where.

Your Turn

Write a news article about an animal outside its habitat. Choose a topic that is important or unusual—something that will interest your readers. Think about the "five Ws" as you research and write: *who, what, where, when,* and *why*. Make sure you answer these questions with facts. Use the Writer's Checklist to check your writing.

Writer's Checklist

☑ **Ideas and Content:** Did I pick an interesting topic and present facts, not opinions?

☑ **Organization:** Did I answer the questions "Who?," "What?," "Where?," "When?," and "Why?"

☑ **Voice:** When I read the article aloud, did it sound as if I used enough facts to support the topic?

☑ **Word Choice:** Did I use precise words?

☑ **Sentence Fluency:** Did my writing flow smoothly from one idea to the next?

☑ **Conventions:** Did I use *more* or *most* or other adverbs that compare? Did I check my spelling?

Talk About It

What do we gain from learning about the natural world around us?

LOG ON — Find out more about studying nature at **www.macmillanmh.com**

Discovering Nature's Secrets

Vocabulary

fossil

stumbled upon

paleontologist

inspected

Scorpion and damsel fly trapped in amber (above), and an Etruscan amber carving (below)

Amber: Nature's Time Capsule

About 30 million years ago, this tiny scorpion found trouble. It got stuck in some sticky stuff called resin. Over millions of years, that resin grew dryer and harder. Finally it turned into a material called amber. The scorpion remained perfectly preserved in a golden prison.

Amber is nature's time capsule. It forms a tight seal around whatever is trapped inside, protecting it from the effects of aging. Scientists have found insects preserved in amber that come from the time of the dinosaurs.

Several years ago, a scientist discovered an important amber **fossil**: three tiny flowers that were 90 million years old. Found in New Jersey, they are the oldest whole flowers ever seen.

Because amber is beautiful, people value it for reasons other than science. For centuries people have made jewelry and sculpture from amber. To the ancient Etruscans, who lived in what is now Italy, amber was as precious as gold. But not all amber is golden. Some is white, red, or green.

LOG ON Find out more about amber at **www.macmillanmh.com**

A Dinosaur Named Bambi

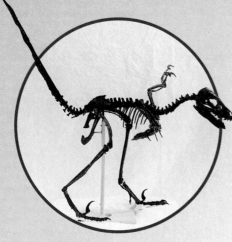

Bambiraptor had a long, stiff tail and long arms that could bend at the wrist. It may also have had feathers.

"This big ball of dirt rolled over, and I saw black bones in it," recalls Wes Linster, describing his astonishing discovery in 1994 at age 14. Linster was digging on a ranch near Choteau, Montana, when he **stumbled upon** the new dinosaur species. His family nicknamed the three-foot-long fossil Bambi because it was so small.

The fossil itself is the skeleton of a baby that lived 75 million years ago. It belongs to a dinosaur family that most scientists believe are the ancestors of birds.

Paleontologist John Ostrom first **inspected** the bones in 1995. "The skeleton is a jewel," he says. "I think it's one of the most valuable scientific specimens ever found in North America."

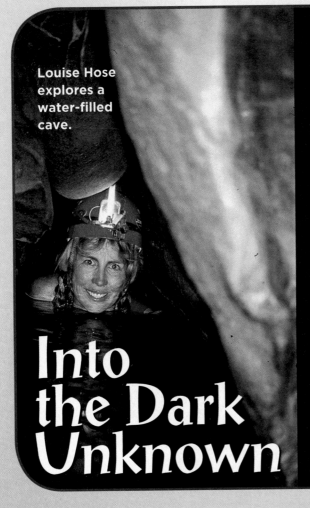

Louise Hose explores a water-filled cave.

Into the Dark Unknown

Louise Hose is a geologist and a speleologist, or caver. For the past few years, she has gone to Tapijulapa (tah•pee•hoo•LA•pa), Mexico, to map a cave. She and her fellow explorers found that it is full of animals that have adapted to life underground. There are vampire bats, spiders, and colorless fish and crabs in the cave's streams.

They also discovered something more amazing: colonies of microscopic living creatures that can survive in extreme conditions. Even with poisonous air and with no light, these creatures thrive underground. The living colonies drip down like a runny nose. They contain sulfuric acid, which can burn human skin. A photographer on the expedition named the slimy critters "snottites."

Meet a Bone-ified Explorer

Comprehension

Genre

A **Nonfiction Article** gives information about real people, places or things.

Monitor Comprehension

Make Generalizations

A generalization is a broad statement. It combines facts in a selection with what a reader already knows to tell what is true in many cases.

What does a paleontologist do next after she's discovered the largest and most complete Tyrannosaurus Rex fossils ever found?

722

Sue Hendrickson poses with a model of the foot of the Tyrannosaurus Rex she found.

As a little girl in Munster, Indiana, Sue Hendrickson always kept her eyes on the ground. "I was really shy and always walked with my head down," she says, "but my curiosity was strong." She often searched the ground for low-lying treasures. Hendrickson's interest in finding things turned into an exciting job. Now she is a field **paleontologist**. As a paleontologist, Hendrickson gets to spend a lot of her time exploring—and digging. Her searches for new discoveries have taken her to countries around the world.

Hendrickson became famous after making a gigantic discovery in August 1990. After a long day of digging in South Dakota, she **stumbled upon** one of the largest and most complete specimens of a T. rex skeleton ever found. "It was as if she was just waiting to be discovered," Hendrickson says. "It took 67 million years, but we finally got to her."

Finding the Fossil

How did this **fossil** hunter discover this ancient natural wonder? It all started with a flat tire. While others from her digging team went to get the tire fixed, Hendrickson decided to explore a nearby cliff with her golden retriever, Gypsy. She walked around with her eyes to the ground, as usual. Suddenly, she noticed a few pieces of bone. Then she looked up. She **inspected** the rocky cliffs above her head and saw three dinosaur backbones. She quickly headed back to the team to tell them about her exciting discovery.

Over a period of three weeks, the paleontologist and her team were able to uncover the huge dinosaur fossil. The team decided to name the dino fossil Sue, after Hendrickson. How does Hendrickson feel about finding Sue? "She is, I am certain, the greatest discovery I will ever make," she said.

Sue Hendrickson stands next to the skull and teeth of the T. rex skeleton before they were removed from the cliff.

724

Diving for Treasure

Hendrickson's adventurous spirit and curiosity about the past have taken her to extreme places to do her work. When she's not digging for bones, she's diving for sunken treasure. She has been working with a team in Egypt to find the palace of Cleopatra. The palace sank underwater during a fifth century earthquake. "Sharing these finds with the world is the biggest thrill," says Hendrickson.

Hendrickson also explored a 400-year-old sunken ship in the waters near the Philippines. The ship was called *San Diego*. It was a Spanish ship that was used for trade and battle. In 1600, the ship sank to the bottom of the South China Sea. Hendrickson was part of the team that helped make the *San Diego* famous again.

In 2004, Hendrickson joined a team of divers in Egypt to find an ancient sunken city. She also was part of a dive in Cuba to explore a ship that sank in 1714.

What advice does Hendrickson have for kids who want to get their fingers dirty? "Spend some time volunteering out in the field with professionals," she recommends. "And focus on school. It will equip you to learn on your own."

Sue Hendrickson explores an ancient shipwreck.

Think and Compare

1. What is a paleontologist?

2. What generalization can you make about Sue Hendrickson's life?

3. Do you think you would like traveling as much as Sue Hendrickson does? Why or why not?

4. What is the value of the discoveries—fossils in amber, "Bambi," "snottites"—described in these selections?

725

Test Strategy

On My Own

The answer is not in the selection. Use what you know to form your answers for questions 4 and 5.

Out on a Limb

A canopy crane lowers researchers from the Smithsonian Tropical Research Institute into the canopy of a rain forest in Panama.

Rain forests are one of Earth's last frontiers. They are filled with plants and animals that are rarely—if ever—seen by humans. According to one estimate, more than half of all life forms on Earth live in tropical rain forests. Some scientists believe there may be many millions more.

Scientists are now focusing on the forest canopy. The canopy is the highest part of the forest. It is a network of leaves, vines, and branches that forms a world within a world. It functions differently from other parts of the forest because of its height and exposure to sunlight. This world has been difficult to study because of the great height of rain forest trees. New techniques and equipment are changing that. The canopy crane is one important example.

The canopy crane is an ordinary construction crane equipped with a special platform. The crane lifts the platform above the treetops and then gently lowers it into the canopy. Scientists use the platform as a base of operations for their studies. One scientist described this experience as "like landing on the moon." Scientists agree that there is much to learn about this unique place that is right here on Earth.

Go On ▶

Directions: Answer the questions.

1. **Why are rain forests considered one of Earth's last frontiers?**

   A   Travel is prohibited in most places.

   B   Scientists have been unable to study many of the organisms that live there.

   C   The forest canopy keeps scientists out.

   D   Scientists have little interest in studying the plants and animals of the rain forest.

2. **What condition helps make the canopy different from other parts of the rain forest?**

   A   People do not live there.

   B   Animals cannot reach it.

   C   It is higher and receives more sunlight.

   D   It contains no plants.

3. **The canopy crane allows scientists to**

   A   work from a platform that has been lowered into the treetops.

   B   parachute into the canopy from above, like astronauts.

   C   remove trees more easily.

   D   avoid the dangerous animals on the forest floor.

4. **What do you think is the most interesting thing about the work of these scientists?**

5. **Do you think it is important for scientists to continue to study the plant and animal life in the rain forests of the world? Why or why not?**

Tip

Use what you know.

Write to a Prompt

Sometimes scientists must go to new and unfamiliar places. Write a personal essay about a time when you had to go somewhere new or face something new. Express your opinion about what you experienced.

I summed up my opinion in the last paragraph.

Change Can Be Good

I grew up in a small town. I knew just about every person there, and they knew me. I was very happy there. Why would I want to leave? Then one day my mother said we were moving. She had a great new job, in a city a thousand miles away.

The city was very different. I didn't know anybody. I didn't know my way around. We lived in an apartment, not a house. People spoke with a different accent. Even the food was different.

Well, I was miserable for about three days. Then I met my new neighbor, a kid my age. He introduced me to his friends. When school started, I met even more new friends. I learned my way around, and there was a lot to do. I decided I liked <u>most</u> of the food.

I still miss my old town and my old friends. But I can go back for a visit, so now I figure I have two home towns!

Writing Prompt

Some people welcome new experiences. Others like things to stay the same. Either way, we all have to face new things in life. Write a personal essay about a time when you had to face something new. Describe the situation, how you felt before, and how you felt after.

Writer's Checklist

☑ Ask yourself, who will read my essay?

☑ Think about your purpose for writing.

☑ Plan your writing before beginning.

☑ Use details to support your opinion.

☑ Be sure you state your opinion and give reasons for it.

☑ Use your best spelling, grammar, and punctuation.

AIRPLANES

My Brothers' Flying Machine

by

JANE YOLEN

paintings by
JIM BURKE

Award Winning Author

I was four years old when Papa brought home a little flying machine. He tossed it into the air right in front of Orv and Will. They leaped up to catch it.

"Is it a bat?" Orv asked. Or maybe it was Will.

When at last the "bat" fell to the floor, they gathered it up like some sultan's treasure, marveling at its paper wings, admiring the twisted rubber band that gave it power. I wanted to touch it, too, but they would not let me, saying I was too little, though I was but three years younger than Orv, to the very day.

When the "bat" broke, they fixed it together, Will directing Orv—with his busy hands—tinkering till the toy worked better than when Papa first brought it home.

Our older brothers, Reuchlin and Lorin, looked down on childish activity, but Will was not put off. He made one, and two, and three more "bats," each one bigger than the last. Orv was his constant helper. I stood on tiptoe by the table, watching them work.

Will shook his head. "On a much larger scale," he said, "the machine fails to work so well."

They both were puzzled. They did not know yet that a machine twice as big needs eight times the power to fly.

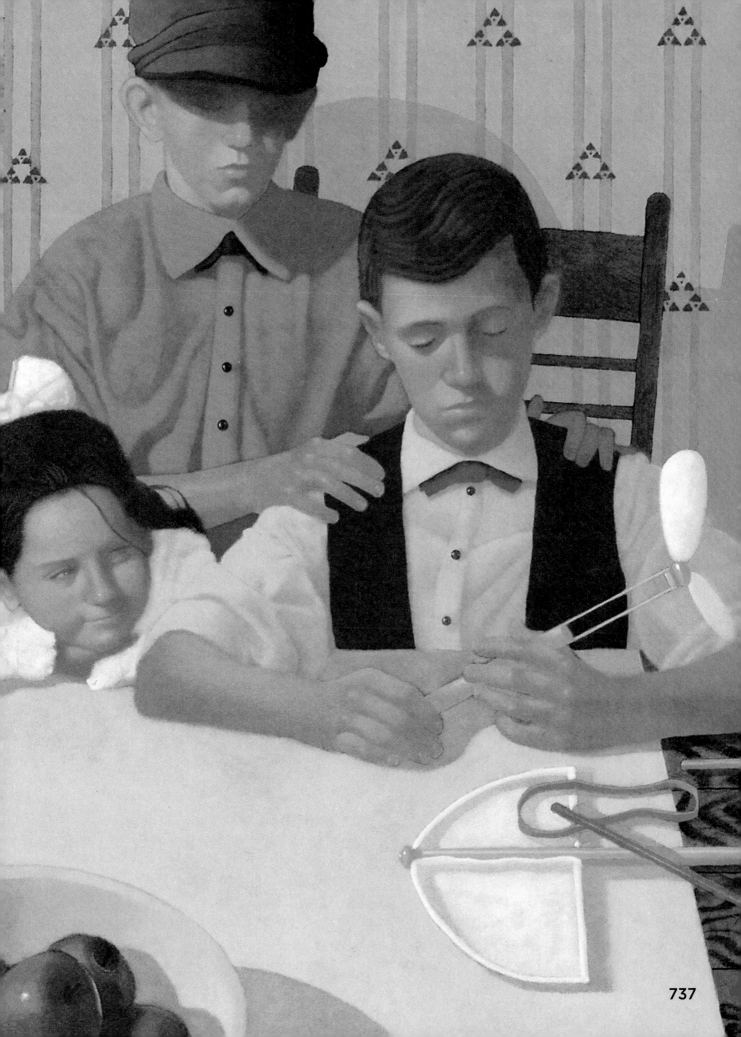

After that, Will built sturdy kites, which he sold to his pals in school. Orv made a printing press, with an old tombstone for a press bed, wheels and cogs from a junkyard, and the folding top of my old baby buggy that he had found in the barn. My, it made me smile to see it.

Papa and Mama **applauded** their efforts. Orv's press could print a thousand pages an hour. A printer from the great city of Denver came to visit and climbed under and over Orv's baby-buggy press. At last he laughed, amazed. "Well it works," he said, "but I certainly don't see how."

Orv and Will made many messes, but Mama never complained. She'd always been the one who gave them a hand building things when they were boys. Poor Papa. He knew God's word well enough, but not how to drive a nail.

When dear Mama died of tuberculosis, I took over her role: keeping the house, making the meals, and always giving the boys applause, even after I graduated from college and worked as a teacher.

The newspapers and magazines were full of stories about people trying to fly. Lilienthal, Pilcher, Chanute, MEN INTO BIRDS, the **headlines** read. I wondered if such a thing were really possible. Orv said: "insects, birds, and mammals fly every day at pleasure, it is reasonable to suppose that man might also fly."

Will wrote off to the Smithsonian for all their books and pamphlets on flight. He and Orv studied page after page. The first question they asked was: *How can we control the flight?*

They knew that a bicycle is **unstable** by itself, yet it can be controlled by a rider. *How much more control would an aeroplane need?*

Overhead, buzzards wheeled in the sky, constantly changing the positions of their wings to catch the flow of air. "If birds can do it," Orv mused out loud, "so can men." He seemed so certain, I began to believe it could be done. I began to believe it could be done by Will and Orv.

STRATEGY SKILL

Author's Perspective
What is the author's perspective about Will and Orville's sister? What role does Jane Yolen have her play in the story?

IRVING

MOUILLARD

O. LILIENTHAL

TRIGONOMET

They built their first aircraft right in the bicycle shop. I took over running the place, as Mama would have, so they might make their flying machine.

That first aircraft's wings spanned a full five feet. I measured it out myself. The craft was of pinewood covered with fabric and sealed with shellac. Like a kite, it was controlled by a set of cords.

When it was finished, Orv and I went off on a camping trip with a group of friends. While we were gone, Will did a sneak. He marched out to a nearby field and he flew the **glider**, watched only by some boys. The thing suddenly swooped down on them. The boys ate dust that day, I'll tell you.

Their first aircraft was a big kite. But a kite is not an aeroplane. So Will and Orv set about to build it bigger—sixteen or seventeen feet, large enough to carry a man but still open to all the elements.

Will lay facedown on the lower wing, showing me how he planned to fly. I tried to imagine the wind in his face, the dirt and grass rushing up to greet him like an old bore at a party.

"Is it safe?" I whispered.

He winked at me, smiled, and said, "If you are looking for perfect safety, sit on the fence and watch the birds."

Dayton, Ohio, where we lived, was not the place to fly the craft. Will and Orv needed somewhere with open spaces and strong, regular breezes. They thought about San Diego, about St. James, Florida, about the coasts of South Carolina and Georgia.

On December 17, a cold and windy day, the *Flyer* repaired and ready, they decided to try again. **Hoisting** a red flag to the top of a pole, they signaled the lifesaving station for witnesses. Four men and a teenage boy appeared.

The men helped them get the *Flyer* onto the starting track. Orv lay down on the lower wing, his hips in the padded cradle. Will shook Orv's hand.

"Now you men," Will called out, "laugh and holler and clap and try to cheer my brother."

The motor began: *Cough, cough, chug-a-chug-a-chug*. Orv released the wire that held the plane to the track. Then the plane raced forward into the strong wind and into history.

The boys sent a telegram home to Papa and me.

After that, the world was never the same. Many men went into the air. Women, too. I was not the first woman to fly. That honor went to the wife of one of our sponsors, Mrs. Hart O. Berg, with a rope around her skirt to keep it from blowing about and showing her legs. She flew for two minutes and seven seconds, sitting stiffly upright next to Will.

A Parisian dressmaker who watched the flight invented the hobble skirt, which for a short time was quite smart. Such is fashion.

But how I laughed when I had my turn at last, flying at Pau in France on February 15, 1909. Will took his seat beside me. Orv waved from the ground. The plane took off into the cold blue. Wind scoured my face till my cheeks turned bright red. Then I opened my arms wide, welcoming all the sky before me.

At last they settled on Kitty Hawk on the Outer Banks, a two-hundred-mile strip of sand with the ocean at its face and North Carolina at its back. Will called it "a safe place for practice." Only sand and hearty breezes. Only sun and a moon so bright Orv could read his watch all hours. I kept the store. Will and Orv kept the sky.

Weeks, months went by in practice. The boys sent me letters almost every day so that I might follow their every move. When they were home, I was in their closest confidence.

At Kitty Hawk they flew the aircraft with a man—and without one—but always controlled the craft from the ground. We had thought: *Stand on the shoulders of giants, and you are already high above the ground*, but success did not come as quickly as we hoped. Finally Will made a big decision: "We cast the calculations of others aside."

Back in Dayton they would start anew. This time when they left Kitty Hawk for home, when they left the wind, the sand, the mosquitoes that left lumps like hen's eggs, they came home with a new idea.

Author's Perspective
How does the author feel about the Wright brothers? Provide examples from the story to support your answer.

Now they worked dawn to dusk, so absorbed in what they were doing, they could hardly wait for morning to come to begin again. They built a small wind tunnel out of an old starch box and used a fan to make the wind. Then they built a larger tunnel.

They learned about lift and drag. They tried out many different kinds of wings. And three years, almost to the day, after Will had written to the Smithsonian, they were ready for *powered* flight. They built the *Flyer*, with a **wingspan** of just over forty feet.

Our friend Charlie Taylor made a twelve-horsepower engine for the *Flyer*, a motor both light and powerful. Gasoline was gravity-fed into the engine from a small tank just below the upper wing. The *Flyer* was so big—over six hundred pounds of aeroplane—it could not be assembled whole in our shop.

Back to Kitty Hawk they went at the tag end of September 1903, carrying crates filled with aircraft parts. It took weeks to put the *Flyer* together, weeks more to prepare for the flight.

Winter came blustering in early. It was cold in camp, each morning the washbasin was frozen solid, so they wrote in their letters. They kept fiddling, tinkering, changing things.

Finally, on December 14, they were ready. They flipped a coin to see who would be pilot. Will won, grinned, climbed into the hip cradle, and off the *Flyer* went, rattling down the sixty-foot starting track, then sailing fifteen feet into the air, where it stalled, crashed. But they were encouraged nonetheless. The telegram they sent to Papa and me read: *Rudder only injured. Success* **assured**. *Keep quiet.*

On December 17, a cold and windy day, the *Flyer* repaired and ready, they decided to try again. **Hoisting** a red flag to the top of a pole, they signaled the lifesaving station for witnesses. Four men and a teenage boy appeared.

The men helped them get the *Flyer* onto the starting track. Orv lay down on the lower wing, his hips in the padded cradle. Will shook Orv's hand.

"Now you men," Will called out, "laugh and holler and clap and try to cheer my brother."

The motor began: *Cough, cough, chug-a-chug-a-chug.* Orv released the wire that held the plane to the track. Then the plane raced forward into the strong wind and into history.

The boys sent a telegram home to Papa and me.

After that, the world was never the same. Many men went into the air. Women, too. I was not the first woman to fly. That honor went to the wife of one of our sponsors, Mrs. Hart O. Berg, with a rope around her skirt to keep it from blowing about and showing her legs. She flew for two minutes and seven seconds, sitting stiffly upright next to Will.

A Parisian dressmaker who watched the flight invented the hobble skirt, which for a short time was quite smart. Such is fashion.

But how I laughed when I had my turn at last, flying at Pau in France on February 15, 1909. Will took his seat beside me. Orv waved from the ground. The plane took off into the cold blue. Wind scoured my face till my cheeks turned bright red. Then I opened my arms wide, welcoming all the sky before me.

Soar with Jane and Jim

Jane Yolen was asked by her editor to write a book about the Wright brothers for the 100th anniversary of their first flight. Jane wanted her book to be different from all the other books about the Wrights. She did a lot of research, until she came across an interesting note about the Wright brothers' sister. Jane knew she had found her story.

Other books by Jane Yolen

Jim Burke has been an award-winning artist for many years, but this is his first book for children. Jim currently lives in New York City.

Another book by Jim Burke

LOG ON Find out more about Jane Yolen and Jim Burke at **www.macmillanmh.com**

Author's Purpose

How can you figure out Jane Yolen's purpose for writing *My Brothers' Flying Machine*? What clues tell you if she wanted to inform, explain, or entertain?

Comprehension Check

Summarize

Summarize *My Brothers' Flying Machine.* Explain who the main characters are and tell the most important story events in the order in which they happened.

Think and Compare

1. What makes this story about the Wright brothers different from other biographies you have read? Use your Author's Perspective Map and story details to answer the question. **Monitor Comprehension: Author's Perspective**

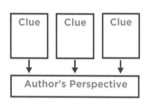

Clue	Clue	Clue
↓	↓	↓
Author's Perspective		

2. Reread page 744. How do you think Will feels about living in "perfect safety"? Use story details in your answer. **Analyze**

3. Imagine you are reporting on the Wright brothers' historic flight at Kitty Hawk. What would your **headline** and article say? **Synthesize**

4. Would the Wright brothers have succeeded without the support of their sister? Explain your opinion. **Evaluate**

5. What do you learn about the Wright brothers' first flight in "Take Off" on pages 732-733? What else do you learn from pages 748-750 of *My Brothers' Flying Machine?* **Reading/Writing Across Texts**

Poetry

A **Narrative Poem** tells a story. Some narrative poems have rhyming patterns, and some do not.

SKILL

Literary Elements

Repetition happens when a word or phrase is repeated throughout a poem.

Personification is a literary device in which human characteristics are given to an animal, thing, or idea.

Brave New Heights

I hear Amelia Earhart
took a plane
and flew it like a bullet
straight up through clouds
into an atmosphere
we can't see

and when the engine
cut
(the plane being pushed
as high as it would go)

> The first line of the poem is repeated later.

I hear Amelia Earhart
turned that plane
straight back
down into a blanket
of foggy cloud lying thick
and nearly to the ground

only with the clouds gone
could she pull back on the stick
the ground screaming in her face
Amelia tacked that plane
back into the sky
saving herself and breaking
another flying record
—*Monica Kulling*

> The phrase "the ground screaming in her face" is an example of personification. The poet describes the ground as if it were a human being.

Connect and Compare

1. If you were the poet, how else might you use personification in this poem? **Personification**

2. How is this narrative poem like a story? Tell about the poem's main character, the problem faced by the main character, and the solution. **Analyze**

3. Compare Amelia Earhart with the Wright brothers as they are described in *My Brothers' Flying Machine*. How are they similar? How are they different?
Reading/Writing Across Texts

 Find more about narrative poems at **www.macmillanmh.com**

Write an Interview

Writer's Craft

Important Details

Unnecessary details slow the reader down. A good writer includes only **important details** essential to the theme or story.

I included important details about Ann.

I took out the extra words I didn't need.

All About Ann

by Lisa B.

I interviewed my neighbor Ann Smith. She writes and illustrates children's books. Many of her books are about birds and flying insects. I asked Ann why that was.

"I've always wished I could fly," said Ann. "I guess that's why I make books about things that fly." Ann said she usually goes to the woods to watch birds and insects. On a pad of paper, she sketches them and carefully takes notes about what they do. She also reads a lot of books about animals that can fly.

I asked Ann what her next book will be about. She laughed and said, "It's about airplanes!"

Your Turn

Interview someone about his or her job. First prepare a list of questions. During the interview, ask these questions and write down the answers. Then use your notes to write one or two paragraphs. Start a paragraph by including the question you asked. Then include the person's answer. Use direct quotations whenever possible. Use the Writer's Checklist to evaluate your writing.

Writer's Checklist

☑ **Ideas and Content:** Did I include important details in my paragraphs?

☑ **Organization:** Did I start by introducing the person and telling what his or her job is?

☑ **Voice:** Will the reader get a clear sense of what this person is like?

☑ **Word Choice:** Did I phrase my questions in such a way that I got the information I was looking for?

☑ **Sentence Fluency:** Did I delete unnecessary words?

☑ **Conventions:** Did I use quotation marks around direct quotations? Did I check my spelling?

ANTS

Amazing Ants

by Tara Rosati

What do you want to be when you grow up? Perhaps an **astronomer** who studies the stars? Perhaps a scientist who **investigates** ants? Find out how interesting these insects are.

Social Insects

There are about 10,000 kinds of ants. Most are not **solitary** but live in groups called colonies. Ants are everywhere, but they prefer their **territory** to be in warm climates and never where it's very cold.

Communication among ants varies. Some tap on the outside of their nest to alert the ants inside that food or enemies are nearby. Other ants can make squeaking or buzzing sounds. Ants also make chemicals that other ants in the colony can smell. Each chemical communicates different information to the colony.

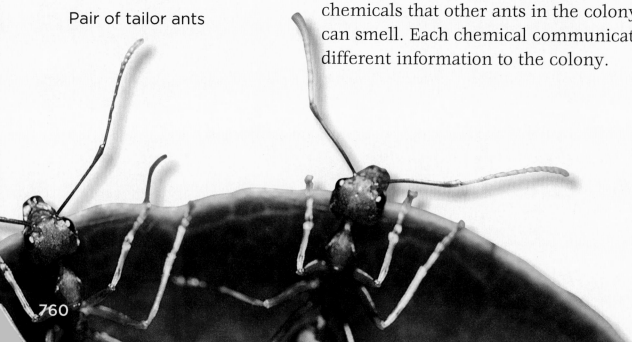

Pair of tailor ants

Dairying Ants

These ants got their name from the way they get most of their **nutrients**. Dairying ants "milk" insects called aphids. In exchange for the juice, dairying ants protect the aphids against other insects.

Some dairying ants are also babysitters. They keep aphids' eggs in their nests during the winter. Then when the eggs hatch, the ants place the baby aphids on plants.

Fungus Growers

Some ants are gardeners. They grow fungi that the colony can eat. These ants gather leaves, flower petals, and other things from outside the nest. Then they bring them inside to use as fertilizer in their fungi gardens.

Ant Survival

Ants have lived on Earth for a long time. They have been found in **prehistoric** pieces of amber. This is material that existed during the time of the dinosaurs! These tiny creatures have had to **overcome** many challenges in order to survive, and ants are here to stay.

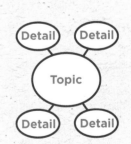

Black garden ant caught in sundew

Reread for **Comprehension**

Analyze Text Structure

Description Authors may structure the information they present in a variety of ways. A paragraph may define or classify. It may list examples using words such as *for example, such as, is like, include,* or *which shows*. It may also describe the characteristics of the subject.

A Description Web can help you identify text structure. Reread the article and use the chart to help you determine the text structure.

```
        Detail   Detail
            \     /
            Topic
            /     \
        Detail   Detail
```

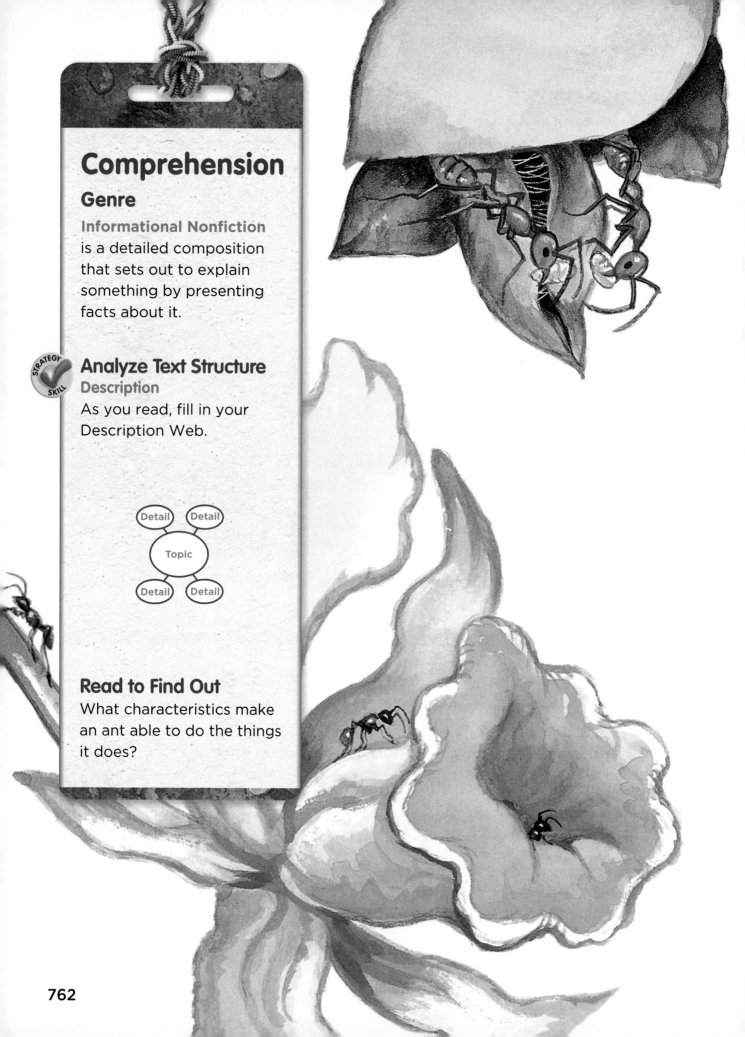

Comprehension

Genre

Informational Nonfiction is a detailed composition that sets out to explain something by presenting facts about it.

Analyze Text Structure
Description

As you read, fill in your Description Web.

STRATEGY SKILL

Detail — Detail
Topic
Detail — Detail

Read to Find Out

What characteristics make an ant able to do the things it does?

The Life and Times of the Ant

written and illustrated by

Charles Micucci

Masters of the Earth

Ants are one of the world's most important insects. They plow more soil than beetles, eat more bugs than praying mantises, and outnumber many insects by 7 million to 1.

Tunneling out of jungles and forests and into back yards on every continent except Antarctica, ants ramble on as if they own the Earth. Perhaps they do.

Ounce for ounce, an ant is one of the strongest animals on earth. An ant can lift a seed five times its weight, while an elephant can lift a log only one fifth of its weight.

Each year, the world's ants dig up more than 16 billion tons of dirt— enough to fill 3 billion dump trucks.

Ants are frequently compared with people because they live in social communities and work together to solve their problems.

Great Dynasties on Earth

Ants have been digging through dirt for more than 100 million years. Their dynasty stretches from the time of dinosaurs to today.

Today
People

65,000,000 B.C.
Ants

100,000,000 B.C
Dinosaurs

Friends in Low Places

There are more than a million kinds of insects. Most of them are **solitary** insects. Their survival depends on only one being—themselves.

An ant is different; it is a social insect. It cannot survive by itself for long periods of time. Ants need other ants to help build a nest, gather food, and protect themselves from enemies. This need for other ants is not a weakness but a strength that enables the ant to **overcome** its small size.

When an ant is threatened by a larger insect, it emits a scent called an alarm pheromone. Other ants smell the odor and rush to help.

STRATEGY SKILL

Description
In the second paragraph of "Friends in Low Places," what details help describe how ants are different from other insects?

Ant Talk

Successful teamwork requires effective **communication**. Ants express themselves by using four senses.

Smell

Ants emit pheromones that other ants smell through their antennae. These scents warn of danger, say hello to friends, and inspire fellow ants to work harder.

Touch

Ants tap one another with their antennae to announce the discovery of food and to ask for food.

Sound

When some ants are trapped in a cave-in, they rub the joint between their waist and abdomen to produce a squeaky sound that other ants "hear" through their legs.

Taste

Ants exchange food with other ants mouth to mouth. These ant "kisses" are a way to share nutrition and chemicals that says "We're family."

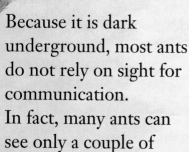

Because it is dark underground, most ants do not rely on sight for communication. In fact, many ants can see only a couple of inches, and some army ants are blind.

The Ant Family

Ants live in social groups called colonies. A small colony may contain only 12 ants, while a large colony overflows with more than 7 million ants. Each colony has three types of ants: workers, male ants, and the queen ant.

Worker Ants

Most of the colony's ants are workers. They are all female, but they do not lay eggs. Although they are the smallest ants, they do all of the chores: clean the nest, gather food, and defend the colony. When you see an ant dragging a crumb of food, you are looking at a worker.

Male Ants

All males have wings and can be seen for only a few weeks in the summer. They mate with the queen but do no work in the colony.

Queen Ants

The queen ant lays eggs and is the mother of all the ants. Young queens have wings, but old queens do not. All queens have large abdomens to produce eggs. Some queens lay millions of eggs per year.

How an Ant Colony Starts

After a hot summer rain, a young queen takes off on her mating flight. The queen flies into a cloud of male ants and mates in the air.

Afterward, all the males die, and the queen returns to the earth. She breaks her wings off by rubbing them on the ground.

Then she digs a hole in the soft, moist earth and starts laying eggs. She will never leave the nest again.

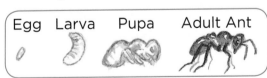

Egg Larva Pupa Adult Ant

During the next three months, the eggs develop through four stages: egg, larva, pupa, and adult ant.

After they have hatched, the first workers assume the duties of the colony. They search for food and protect the queen. As the queen lays more eggs, the workers enlarge the nest.

Inside an Anthill

Most ants build their homes underground. Ants dig by scooping dirt with their mandibles (jaws). As they chew the dirt, it mixes with their saliva to form little bricks. Then they pack the little bricks together to reinforce the tunnels. Finally, the ants carry the excess dirt outside with their mandibles, and it gradually forms an anthill.

Beneath the anthill lies the ant nest. Small nests have only one chamber just inches below the surface, while large nests may have thousands of chambers and may be as deep as twenty feet. All nests provide shelter from the weather and a safe environment for the queen ant to lay eggs.

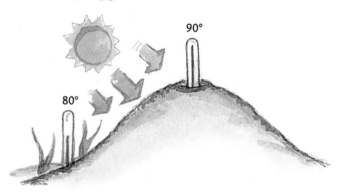

An anthill absorbs the sun's rays and transfers the heat down into the nest. An anthill can be ten degrees warmer than the surrounding area.

Ants often nest beneath a rock or log, which protects the nest and traps moisture in the dirt. Ants require moisture so that their bodies do not dry out.

Ants dig their nests deep enough to reach damp dirt. As air dries out the nest, they dig new tunnels into the damp dirt.

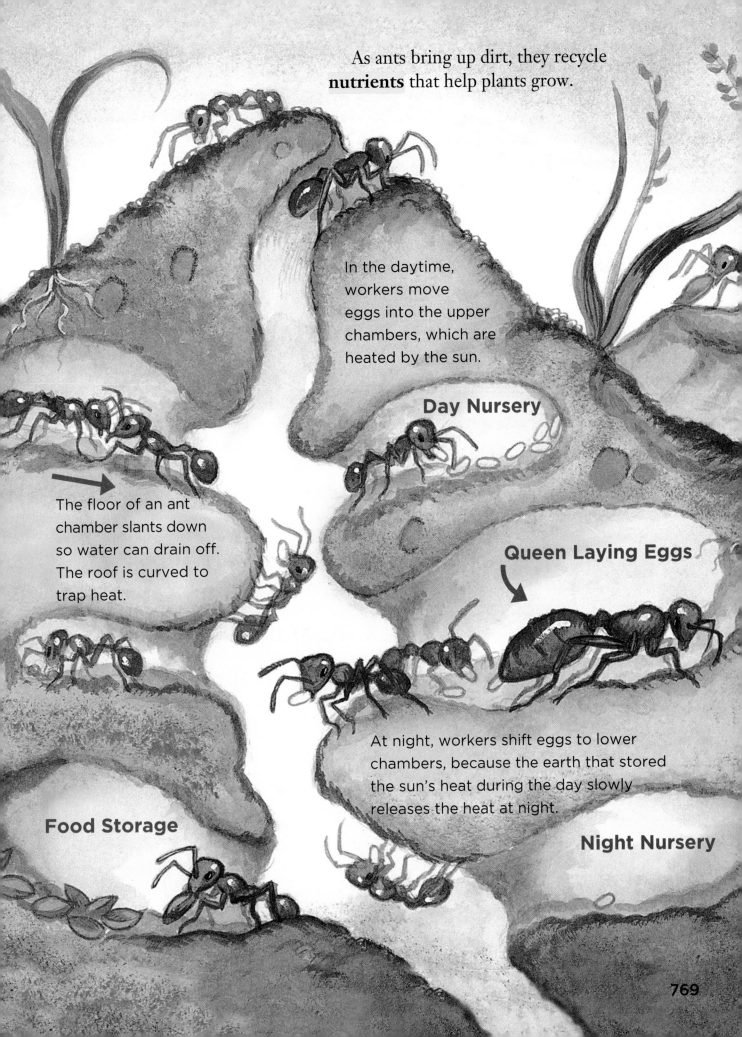

As ants bring up dirt, they recycle **nutrients** that help plants grow.

In the daytime, workers move eggs into the upper chambers, which are heated by the sun.

Day Nursery

The floor of an ant chamber slants down so water can drain off. The roof is curved to trap heat.

Queen Laying Eggs

At night, workers shift eggs to lower chambers, because the earth that stored the sun's heat during the day slowly releases the heat at night.

Food Storage

Night Nursery

A Life of Work

Ants begin their working lives by cleaning themselves. In a couple of days they start sharing food and licking each other. These food exchanges bond the colony together. There is no boss ant, but active ants usually begin doing chores and then other ants join in.

Younger ants work in the nest — tending the queen ant, feeding larvae, and digging tunnels. After a couple of months, the ants leave the nest to search for food. There is no retirement; worn out or battle-scarred, ants work until they die.

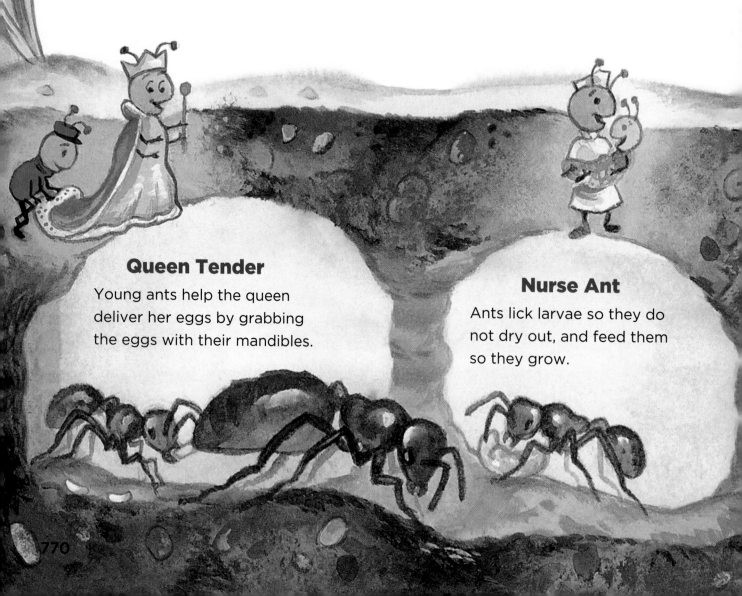

Queen Tender

Young ants help the queen deliver her eggs by grabbing the eggs with their mandibles.

Nurse Ant

Ants lick larvae so they do not dry out, and feed them so they grow.

Foragers

The oldest ants search for food. Most foragers search within fifty feet of the nest, but if food is scarce, they may travel thousands of feet.

Guard

When ants first leave the nest, they stand near the entrance, blocking strange ants from entering.

Tunnel Diggers

As the population grows, ants dig more tunnels for the increased traffic and new chambers to store the eggs and larvae.

Digging holes can be hard work. To remove a pile of dirt 6 inches high, 6 inches wide, and 6 inches long requires 500,000 loads of dirt.

771

Show Me the Way

Every warm day, foraging ants patrol the colony's **territory**. They are not just wandering; they are searching for food. When an ant finds food, she rushes back to the colony while laying a scent trail. It is the scent trail that leads the other ants to the food source.

Each forager moves out in a different direction. One of the ants discovers a cookie crumb. She **investigates** it with her antennae. Then she tries to drag it home, but it's too big.

So she rushes home to get help. Every couple of steps she bumps her abdomen against the ground and her scent gland releases an invisible vapor, which forms a scent trail.

Back inside the colony, the forager alerts other ants about the cookie by tapping them with her antennae. Suddenly, several ants rush out and follow the scent trail to the food.

Each of the new ants harvests part of the cookie and transports it back to the colony while laying a scent trail of her own.

Soon the vapors of the scent trail are so thick that many more ants join the harvest. As they return, the foraging ants share their feast with the ants inside the nest. Within twenty-four hours, every ant in the colony has tasted the cookie.

Harlow Shapley, an **astronomer** whose hobby was ants, tested their speed. He discovered that they run faster on hot days.

GRASS ROOT SPEED LIMITS

Temperature	78°F	85°F	92°
Speed (inches per second)	1	1³⁄₈	1⁵⁄₈

STRATEGY SKILL

Description
How does this table help describe how ants run on hot days?

773

Tunneling Through Time

Ants evolved from wasps more than 100 million years ago. They have been dodging footsteps ever since. As dinosaurs thundered above ground, ants dug out a home below. The mighty dinosaurs are long gone, but the little ant has survived.

Today, myrmecologists search for the secrets of the ants' long existence and how those traits may benefit our society. They study ant fossils in **prehistoric** amber and observe the daily habits of ant colonies.

100,000,000 B.C.
Ants dug tunnels under dinosaurs.

90,000,000 B.C.
Two ants were sealed in amber. Millions of years later, the amber was found in New Jersey.

65,000,000 B.C.
Some scientists think a giant meteorite crashed into Earth, killing the dinosaurs. But ants, which could hide underground, survived the disaster.

2000 B.C.
Aborigines in Australia ate the honey of honeypot ants. Their modern descendants call these sweet ants *yarumpa*.

400 B.C.
Herodotus, a Greek historian, wrote about ants that mined gold. Today, some miners sift through anthills to learn what minerals lie underground.

1500s–1800s
When Europeans conquered the Caribbean islands, their forts were frequently invaded by ants. They offered rewards and prayed to Saint Saturnin to stop the six-legged armies.

A.D. 1200–1300
Chinese farmers used ants to keep their orange trees free of insect pests.

1687
Anton von Leeuwenhoek, who invented the microscope, discovered ant eggs and pupae.

1991
Bert Hölldobler and Edward O. Wilson, two myrmecologists, won the Pulitzer Prize for their book *The Ants*.

1859
The biologist Charles Darwin wrote about ant intelligence and teamwork in his classic work *The Origin of Species*.

1880
Germany passed a law protecting wood ants because they kept trees free of pests.

2000
Scientists applied ant behavior as a model for computer networks. Computer systems based on ant behavior rerouted around problems quicker than previous systems did.

1890s–1930s
William Wheeler, one of America's first myrmecologists, traveled around the world collecting ants and ant fossils.

The tunnel of time continues for ants. Their hard work inspires people today, as it has for many centuries. Look down on a warm day and you will probably find an ant. Drop a piece of food . . . and an ant will probably find you.

The Life and Times of Charles Micucci

Charles Micucci often fills his nature books with amusing illustrations, just as he does in this selection. Once he even drew the planet Earth wearing red sneakers. Charles carefully researches his science topics. Sometimes he does experiments to help him write. When he was working on a book about apples, he planted 23 apple seeds and cared for them in his apartment.

Other books by Charles Micucci

LOG ON Find out more about Charles Micucci at **www.macmillanmh.com**

Author's Purpose

The Life and Times of the Ant is a work of informational nonfiction. What was Charles Micucci's purpose for writing it? What clues in the text or illustrations help you to know?

Comprehension Check

Summarize

STRATEGY SKILL

Summarize *The Life and Times of the Ant.* Include only the most important information in your summary.

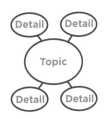

Think and Compare

STRATEGY SKILL

1. Use your Description Web to describe the inside of an anthill. Use story details in your descriptions. **Analyze Text Structure: Description**

2. Reread page 763 of *The Life and Times of the Ant.* Why do you think the author describes ants as "masters of the Earth"? **Analyze**

3. How could you use what you have learned about ants to **overcome** a problem? Explain your answer. **Apply**

4. How do ants keep nature in balance? Use details from the story to support your answer. **Evaluate**

5. Read "Amazing Ants" on pages 760–761. What did you learn about how ants get food that was not in *The Life and Times of the Ant?* **Reading/Writing Across Texts**

THE Ant AND THE Grasshopper

*retold and illustrated
by Amy Lowry Poole*

A LONG TIME AGO, in the old Summer Palace at the edge of the Emperor's courtyard, there lived a grasshopper and a family of ants.

The ants awoke every day before dawn and began their endless tasks of rebuilding their house of sand, which had been washed down by the evening rains, and searching for food, which they would store beneath the ground. They carried their loads grain by grain, one by one, back and forth, all day long.

The grasshopper liked to sleep late into the morning, rising as the sun stretched toward noon.

"Silly ants," he would say. "You work too hard. Come follow me into the courtyard, where I will sing and dance for the great Emperor."

The ants kept on working.

"Silly ants," the grasshopper would say. "See the new moon. Feel the summer breeze. Let us go together and watch the Empress and her ladies as they prepare for midsummer's eve."

But the ants ignored the grasshopper and kept on working.

Soon the days grew shorter and the wind brought cooler air from the north. The ants, mindful of the winter to come, worked even harder to secure their home against the impending cold and snow. They foraged for food and brought it back to their nest, saving it for those cold winter months.

Comparing the traits of the grasshopper and the ants will help you identify the moral.

"Silly ants," said the grasshopper. "Don't you ever rest? Today is the harvest festival. The Emperor will feast on mooncakes and sweet greens from the fields. I will play my music for him until the moon disappears into the smooth lake water. Come and dance with me."

"You would do well to do as we do," said one of the ants. "Winter is coming soon and food will be hard to find. Snow will cover your house and you will freeze without shelter."

But the grasshopper ignored the ant's advice and continued to play and dance until the small hours of the morning.

Winter arrived a week later and brought whirls of snow and ice.

The Emperor and his court left the Summer Palace for their winter home in the great Forbidden City. The ants closed their door against the ice and snow, safe and warm, resting at last after their long days of preparation.

And the grasshopper huddled beneath the palace eaves and rubbed his hands together in a mournful chirp, wishing he had heeded the ant's advice.

Connect and Compare

1. Identify the moral of this fable. Is this a good lesson to learn? Why or why not? **Moral**

2. What problem does the grasshopper have? At what point in the story is he aware of it? Does he solve his problem? **Analyze**

3. Think about *The Life and Times of the Ant*. How are the ants in this fable similar to the ants in that selection? How are they different? **Reading/Writing Across Texts**

 Find out more about fables at **www.macmillanmh.com**

Writer's Craft

Beginning, Middle, and End

Write a good **beginning, middle, and end** when you summarize an article.

Write a Summary

My Summary of "Gibbons"

by Luis M.

Gibbons are small apes that live in rain forests in Southeast Asia. They make their homes high up in the treetops. There they eat, sleep, and raise their babies. Gibbons eat fruit, leaves, insects, and sometimes even small animals.

Gibbons move around in the trees skillfully. They can travel through treetops at 40 miles an hour. Leaping from branch to branch, they sometimes jump 50 feet to another tree. These small animals are remarkable.

I read and took notes on an article about gibbons. Then I summarized the article. I began with a key fact.

I ended with a strong conclusion.

Your Turn

Choose a magazine or a news article, or a chapter from a nonfiction book. Take notes on the article. List the main ideas and the important details for each main idea. Then use your notes to write a summary with a good beginning, middle, and end. Use the Writer's Checklist to check your writing.

Writer's Checklist

 Ideas and Content: Did I include only the most important details in my summary?

Organization: Did I support the main ideas with a good beginning, middle, and end?

 Voice: Did I use my own words instead of copying?

Word Choice: Did I choose precise nouns, verbs, and adjectives?

Sentence Fluency: Are my sentences short and choppy? Can I combine any sentences with prepositions to make my writing flow better?

Conventions: Did I use capitalization and punctuation correctly? Did I check my spelling?

Test Strategy

Author and Me
The answer is not directly stated. Think about everything you have read to figure it out.

Diamonds for the Taking

by Lin Chen

Join the fun!

Come to Herkimer, NY, and prospect for diamonds!

Just a few taps of a hammer and hundreds of sparkling diamonds are yours for the taking

Don't miss out! No one goes home empty-handed.

Have you ever wondered what it would be like to be a prospector? What would it be like to tap rock with a hammer, hour after hour, in the hopes of discovering a glittering diamond?

Each year hundreds of people do just that in upper New York State. Herkimer County, New York, is the only place in the world where Herkimer diamonds can be found. Actually, they aren't real diamonds. They are natural quartz crystals with points at both ends.

Go On ▶

When true diamonds are taken from the earth, they need to be cut and polished to make them sparkle and shine. Herkimer diamonds come out of their rocky homes already shaped and polished by nature!

How Herkimers Began

Some 500 million years ago, a shallow sea covered parts of what is now New York State. Particles of rock and earth settled to the bottom of the water. Over millions of years, this sediment built up. The weight of the sediment on top pressed down on the bottom layers. Gradually, the layers of sediment turned into rock. Water seeped through pores in the rock and eventually became trapped in pockets in the rock. Over time, crystals formed in the pockets.

Long ago, the sea dried up. Glaciers and storms wore away the top layers of rock. This weathering exposed hidden crystals, and the first Herkimer diamonds came to light!

Native Americans in the area took their name from the gems. The local Mohawks were known as "The People of the Crystals."

Prospecting for Diamonds

There are no deep shafts in these "diamond mines." The mines are rocky, open pits. Safety comes first when prospecting for diamonds. The ground is rough and uneven. Prospectors are told to wear shoes or hiking boots, not sandals. Goggles are recommended as well. A rock chip in your eye can cause a serious problem!

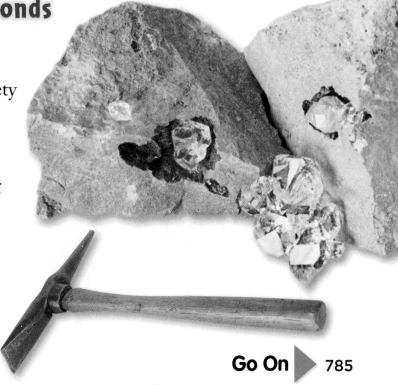

Some collectors just wander around, hoping to spot a diamond. Some sift through the dirt. Serious prospectors use crowbars, rock hammers, and heavy chisels. Most miners use hammers that weigh two or three pounds. Whatever the tool, the method is the same. They pound the rock until it breaks apart. If they're lucky, a crystal will be there.

The luckiest prospectors find pockets of crystals, rather than a single stone. These pockets can be as much as six feet wide and can contain thousands of crystals. Most pockets contain crystals in a wide range of sizes, up to eight or more inches long. Sometimes a crystal has a water bubble inside it. Even more unusual is a crystal with ancient plants floating in the water bubble. Twin crystals, double crystals, and smoky crystals are all possible as well.

Shouts of "I found one!" encourage other prospectors to keep working. If they keep at it, they may be lucky, too. If not, they can always buy a Herkimer diamond in the gift shop.

Go On ▶

Directions: Answer the questions.

1. How does the author feel about prospecting for diamonds?

A It is too hard to be worthwhile.

B It can be both fun and exciting.

C It is a waste of time and effort.

D It is dangerous and scary.

2. What is the author's purpose in writing this selection?

A to provide information about Herkimer diamonds

B to explain how to prospect for true diamonds

C to persuade people to visit New York State

D to compare true diamonds with Herkimer diamonds

3. Why would someone want to hunt for a Herkimer diamond?

A to pretend it's a real diamond

B to sell it for a lot of money

C for the challenge of finding one

D to give one as a birthday gift

4. What is one message the author wants to get across to readers?

5. Look back at the advertisement on page 784 of the selection. What is the purpose of this ad? Use details from the selection to support your response.

Writing Prompt

Imagine that you have been to Herkimer County to prospect for diamonds. Write a one-paragraph news story for the school newspaper about your visit and the discoveries you made there.

Glossary

What Is a Glossary?

A glossary can help you find the **meanings** of words in this book that you may not know. The words in the glossary are listed in **alphabetical order**. **Guide words** at the top of each page tell you the first and last words on the page.

Each word is divided into syllables. The way to pronounce the word is given next. You can understand the pronunciation respelling by using the **pronunciation key** at the right. A shorter key appears at the bottom of every other page. When a word has more than one syllable, a dark accent mark (ˈ) shows which syllable is stressed. In some words, a light accent mark (ˊ) shows which syllable has a less heavy stress. Sometimes an entry includes a second meaning for the word.

Guide Words

First word on the page   Last word on the page

Sample Entry

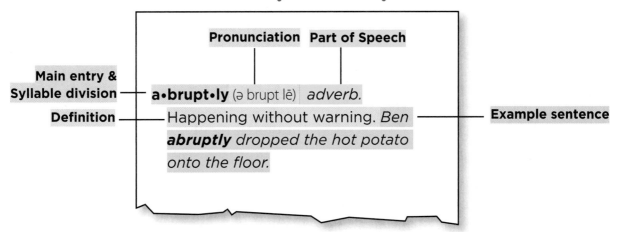

Pronunciation   Part of Speech

Main entry & Syllable division

a•brupt•ly (ə brupt lē)   *adverb.*

Definition

Happening without warning. *Ben **abruptly** dropped the hot potato onto the floor.*

Example sentence

Pronunciation Key

Phonetic Spelling	Examples
a	**a**t, b**a**d, pl**ai**d, l**au**gh
ā	**a**pe, p**ai**n, d**ay**, br**ea**k
ä	f**a**ther, c**a**lm
âr	c**are**, p**air**, b**ear**, th**eir**, wh**ere**
e	**e**nd, p**e**t, s**ai**d, h**ea**ven, fri**e**nd
ē	**e**qual, m**e**, f**ee**t, t**ea**m, p**ie**ce, k**ey**
i	**i**t, b**i**g, g**i**ve, h**y**mn
ī	**i**ce, f**i**ne, l**ie**, m**y**
îr	**ear**, d**eer**, h**ere**, p**ier**ce
o	**o**dd, h**o**t, w**a**tch
ō	**o**ld, **oa**t, t**oe**, l**ow**
ô	c**o**ffee, **a**ll, t**au**ght, l**aw**, f**ou**ght
ôr	**or**der, f**or**k, h**or**se, st**or**y, p**our**
oi	**oi**l, t**oy**
ou	**ou**t, n**ow**, b**ough**
u	**u**p, m**u**d, l**o**ve, d**ou**ble
ū	**u**se, m**u**le, c**ue**, f**eu**d, f**ew**
ü	r**u**le, tr**ue**, f**oo**d, fr**ui**t
u̇	p**u**t, w**oo**d, sh**ou**ld, l**oo**k
ûr	b**ur**n, h**ur**ry, t**er**m, b**ir**d, w**or**d, c**our**age
ə	**a**bout, tak**e**n, penc**i**l, lem**o**n, circ**u**s
b	**b**at, a**b**ove, jo**b**
ch	**ch**in, su**ch**, ma**tch**

Phonetic Spelling	Examples
d	**d**ear, so**d**a, ba**d**
f	**f**ive, de**f**end, lea**f**, o**ff**, cou**gh**, ele**ph**ant
g	**g**ame, a**g**o, fo**g**, e**gg**
h	**h**at, a**h**ead
hw	**wh**ite, **wh**ether, **wh**ich
j	**j**oke, en**j**oy, **g**em, pa**g**e, e**dg**e
k	**k**ite, ba**k**ery, see**k**, ta**ck**, **c**at
l	**l**id, sai**l**or, fee**l**, ba**ll**, a**ll**ow
m	**m**an, fa**m**ily, drea**m**
n	**n**ot, fi**n**al, pa**n**, **kn**ife, **gn**aw
ng	lo**ng**, si**ng**er
p	**p**ail, re**p**air, soa**p**, ha**pp**y
r	**r**ide, pa**r**ent, wea**r**, mo**r**e, ma**rr**y
s	**s**it, a**s**ide, pet**s**, **c**ent, pa**ss**
sh	**sh**oe, wa**sh**er, fi**sh**, mi**ss**ion, na**ti**on
t	**t**ag, pre**t**end, fa**t**, dress**ed**
th	**th**in, pan**th**er, bo**th**
<u>th</u>	**th**ese, mo**th**er, smoo**th**
v	**v**ery, fa**v**or, wa**v**e
w	**w**et, **w**eather, re**w**ard
y	**y**es, on**i**on
z	**z**oo, la**z**y, ja**zz**, ro**s**e, dog**s**, hou**s**es
zh	vi**s**ion, trea**s**ure, sei**z**ure

Aa

ac·ces·so·ries (ak ses´ə rēz) *plural noun.* Extra parts or add-ons that are useful but not essential. *We bought several* **accessories** *for our new car.*

ac·com·plish·ments (ə kom´plish mənts) *plural noun.* Successes; actions of which one can feel proud. *The parents stood and applauded their children's* **accomplishments** *at their elementary school graduation.*

ac·cuse (ə kūz´) *verb.* To say that a person has done something wrong or illegal. *I will not* **accuse** *someone of something unless I am sure.*

ac·quaint·ance (ə kwān´təns) *noun.* A person one knows, but who is not a close friend. *Carole is an* **acquaintance** *from camp.*

ac·ti·vist (ak´tə vist) *noun.* A person who believes in and actively supports a cause. *Rev. Dr. Martin Luther King, Jr., was an* **activist** *for peace and social justice.*

ad·vanced (ad vanst´) *adjective.* Beyond the beginning level; not elementary. *As a singer, Sheila was really* **advanced** *for her age.*

ag·ile (aj´əl) *adjective.* Able to move and react quickly and easily. *Bonita is an* **agile** *softball player.*

al·ler·gies (al´ər jēz) *plural noun.* Conditions that cause a person to have an unpleasant reaction to certain things that are harmless to most people. *My aunt has* **allergies** *in the spring when plants bloom.*

a·maze·ment (ə māz´mənt) *noun.* Great surprise or wonder. *To the* **amazement** *of the audience, the children played some difficult music perfectly.*

am·bu·lance (am´byə ləns) *noun.* A special vehicle that is used to carry sick or injured people to a hospital. *My neighbor once had to call an* **ambulance** *to take him to the hospital.*

an·ces·tors (an´ses tərz) *plural noun.* People in the past from whom one comes. *Your great-grandparents are some of your* **ancestors**.

an·cient (ān´shənt) *adjective.* Very old. *An* **ancient** *castle sat on the edge of a lake.*

an·noyed (ə noid´) *adjective.* Bothered or disturbed. *Kevin looked* **annoyed** *when his little sister came out to join the game.*

a·pol·o·gize (ə pol´ə jīz´) *verb.* To say one is sorry or embarrassed; make an apology. *Aaron said, "I'd like to **apologize** for being late."*

ap·plaud·ed (ə plôd´əd) *verb.* Showed approval for or enjoyment of something by the clapping of hands. *The crowd **applauded** the soldiers as they came off the ship.*

ap·pre·ci·at·ed (ə prē´shē āt´əd) *verb.* Understood the value of; was grateful for something. *The boss **appreciated** how much his workers did for the company.*

as·sign·ments (ə sīn´mənts) *plural noun.* Tasks that are given out or assigned. *The teacher gave us two math **assignments** for homework.*

as·sured (ə shùrd´) *verb.* Made certain or sure. *Our hard work **assured** the success of the festival.*

as·tro·naut (as´trə nôt´) *noun.* A person trained to fly in a spacecraft. *The **astronaut** will walk on the moon.*

Word History

Astronaut is made from the Greek words *astron* for star and *nautēs* for sailor (as in *nautical*).

as·tron·o·mer (ə stron´ə mər) *noun.* A person who works or specializes in astronomy, the science that deals with the sun, moon, stars, planets, and other heavenly bodies. *An **astronomer** will speak at the next science fair.*

at; āpe; fär; câre; end; mē; it; īce; pîerce; hot; ōld; sông; fôrk; oil; out; up; ūse; rüle; pùll; tûrn; chin; sing; shop; thin; <u>th</u>is; hw in white; zh in treasure.

The symbol ə stands for the unstressed vowel sound in about, taken, pencil, lemon, and circus.

au·di·tion (ô dish´ən) *noun.* A test or try-out for an actor or other kind of performer. *Mariana was nervous about her **audition**, but she played very well.*

Word History
Audition is formed from the Latin *auditio*, which means "a hearing."

a·void·ed (ə void´əd) *verb.* Stayed away from. *Butch **avoided** doing hard work.*

awk·ward (ôk´wərd) *adjective.* Lacking grace in movement or behavior; clumsy or uncomfortable. *Until Julio learned the steps, his dancing was **awkward**.*

Bb

back·ground (bak´ground) *noun.* The part of a picture that appears to be behind the rest. *I painted a bright figure against a dark **background**.*

bar·be·cue (bär´bi kū´) *noun.* A meal, usually meat, cooked outdoors over an open fire. *We had a great **barbecue** in the park.*

ba·yous (bī´ūz) *plural noun.* Slow-moving or stagnant streams, rivers, or inlets, especially in the southern United States. *We canoed through many quiet **bayous** during our trip.*

bliz·zard (bliz´ərd) *noun.* A strong windstorm marked by intense cold and blowing snow. *No one should try to drive in a **blizzard**.*

bluf·fing (bluf´ing) *verb.* Trying to fool people with a false show of confidence, courage, or knowledge. *Rory said he could fly, but I knew he was **bluffing.***

bor·der (bôr´dər) *noun.* A line between one country, state, county, or town and another. *A river runs along the **border** between the two states.*

boy·cotts (boi´kots) *plural noun.* Protests in which people refuse to buy from or work for a person, nation, or business. *The community plans **boycotts** of all the unfair businesses.*

Word History
Boycotts comes from Charles Boycott who was shunned by Irish farmers for his harsh actions against them.

brit·tle (brit´əl) *adjective.* Likely to break or snap. *Susan's fingernails became **brittle** and started to break.*

bum·bling (bum´bling or bum´bəl ing) *adjective.* Making clumsy mistakes. *The **bumbling** detective would never solve the mystery.*

Cc

cam·ou·flage (kam´ə fläzh´) *verb.* To hide or conceal by using shapes or colors that blend with the surroundings. *The chameleon is able to **camouflage** itself by changing the color of its skin.*

card·board (kärd´bôrd´) *noun.* A heavy, stiff paper used to make boxes and posters. *I like to store my small toys in shoe boxes made of **cardboard**.*

ca·reer (kə´rîr´) *noun.* A job or occupation pursued for all or part of someone's life. *My grandmother's **career** as a research biologist lasted for many years.*

cas·ting (kas´ting) *noun.* The process of choosing people for the different parts in a play or movie. ***Casting** for the new movie went on for weeks.*

at; āpe; fär; câre; end; mē; it; īce; pîerce; hot; ōld; sông; fôrk; oil; out; up; ūse; rüle; pùll; tûrn; chin; sing; shop; thin; this; hw in white; zh in treasure.

The symbol ə stands for the unstressed vowel sound in about, taken, pencil, lemon, and circus.

cau·tious·ly (kôˊshəs lē) *adverb.* In a careful way. *Because so many cars were coming, we crossed the street* **cautiously***.*

cir·cu·lar (sûrˊkyə lər) *adjective.* Having or making the shape of a circle. *The referee's arm made a* **circular** *motion as he blew the whistle.*

cit·i·zen (sitˊə zən) *noun.* A person who was born in a country or who chooses to live in and become a member of that country. *Carmine is an Italian* **citizen** *but often visits the United States.*

cli·mate (klīˊmit) *noun.* The average weather conditions of a place or region through the year. *Most deserts have a hot, dry* **climate***.*

clut·tered (klutˊərd) *verb.* Filled with a messy collection of things. *Val's bedroom was* **cluttered** *with all of her sports equipment.*

coax·ing (kōksˊing) *verb.* Persuading or influencing by mild arguing. *The instructor was* **coaxing** *young swimmers into the water.*

col·lage (kə läzhˊ) *noun.* A picture made by pasting paper, cloth, metal, and other things in an arrangement on a surface. *Once I made a* **collage** *of my day, and it was full of bright colors and cotton balls.*

Word History
Collage comes from the French word *collage*, from *colle*, meaning glue or paste.

col·o·ny (kolˊə nē) *noun.* A group of animals living together in the same place. *The noise from the penguin* **colony** *was deafening.*

com·mo·tion (kə mōˊshən) *noun.* A noisy disturbance; confusion. *We ran out into the hall to see what was causing the* **commotion***.*

com·mu·ni·ca·tion (kə mūˊni kāˊshən) *noun.* An exchanging or sharing of feelings, thoughts, or information. *Some forms of* **communication** *do not require speech.*

com·ple·ted (kəm plētˊəd) *verb.* Done, finished. *I could hardly wait until my brother* **completed** *his Thanksgiving project and we could all go to the movies.*

con·sid·er·a·tion (kən sid′ər ā′shən) *noun.* Thoughtfulness for other people and their feelings; something carefully thought about. *Leroy showed great* **consideration** *for his grandmother.*

con·sis·ted (kən sis′təd) *verb.* Contained; was made up. *The batter* **consisted** *of a cup of flour, one egg, and a cup of milk.*

con·sume (kən süm′) *verb.* To eat or drink. *Growing children can* **consume** *a lot of food.*

con·vinced (kən vinst′) *verb.* Caused a person to believe or do something. *The coach* **convinced** *the team they could win, and they did.*

cor·al (kôr′əl) *adjective.* Made of coral, a hard substance like stone made up of the skeletons of tiny animals. *We went snorkeling on the* **coral** *reef.*

crank·y (krang′kē) *adjective.* Cross or in a bad temper; grouchy. *Roni is always* **cranky** *before she's had breakfast.*

craters (krā′tərz) *plural noun.* Bowl-shaped pits or holes made by the impact of a meteorite. **Craters** *are easier to spot in the desert.*

criss·crossed (kris′krôst) *verb.* Went across, back and forth. *Grandma* **crisscrossed** *lengths of dough to make a pretty pie top.*

cur·rent (kûr′ənt) *noun.* A portion of a body of water or of air flowing continuously in a definite direction. *The lifeguard blew his whistle when he noticed that the* **current** *was taking the boys out too far.*

---

at; āpe; fär; câre; end; mē; it; īce; pîerce; hot; ōld; sông; fôrk; oil; out; up; ūse; rüle; pull; tûrn; chin; sing; shop; thin; this; hw in white; zh in treasure.

The symbol ə stands for the unstressed vowel sound in about, taken, pencil, lemon, and circus.

Dd

de·cayed (dē kād´) *adjective*. Having undergone the process of decomposition; rotted. *We walked past **decayed** stumps in the woods.*

de·mon·stra·ted (de´mən strā´təd) *verb*. Showed by actions or experiment. *The performer **demonstrated** great skill with both the piano and the drums.*

de·scen·dants (di send´ənts) *plural noun*. People who come from a particular ancestor. *My neighbors are **descendants** of a French explorer.*

des·per·ate (des´pər it) *adjective*. Very bad or hopeless. *I needed money, but I was not **desperate** for it.*

de·vi·c·es (di vīs´əz) *plural noun*. Things used or made for specific purposes. *You can choose from several kinds of **devices** for help in opening a can.*

di·ges·ted (dī jest´əd) *verb*. Broke down and absorbed food. *The snake rested while it **digested** the rat it had swallowed.*

di·rec·tor (di rek´tər) *noun*. The person in charge of a play, movie, or TV show. *The **director** called for a dress rehearsal over the weekend.*

dis·ap·point·ment (dis´ə point´mənt) *noun*. A feeling of being disappointed or let down. *Losing the match was a **disappointment**, but I still like tennis.*

dis·ease (di zēz´) *noun*. An illness. *Smallpox is the one serious **disease** that has been wiped out.*

dis·guised (dis gīzd´) *verb*. Changed the way something or someone looks to hide it or to look like something else. *The king **disguised** himself as a peasant and walked through the market.*

dis·gus·ted (dis gus´tid) *adjective*. Having a strong feeling of dislike. *I felt **disgusted** by the way the bully was treating others.*

diz·zy (diz´ē) *adjective*. Having the feeling of spinning and being about to fall. *Riding the Ferris wheel makes me **dizzy**.*

doc·u·ment·ing (dok´yə ment ing) *verb.* Making a record or collecting information. *The scientists took notes **documenting** their findings.*

dove¹ (dōv) *verb.* Plunged head first into water. *We watched as the woman **dove** perfectly off the board and into the deep pool.*

dove² (duv) *noun.* A medium-size bird of the pigeon family. *The **dove** cooed quietly on the window ledge.*

down·stream (doun´strēm´) *adverb.* Moving in the same direction as the current of a stream. *On a raft, it is easier to float **downstream** than to push upstream.*

dy·nas·ties (dī´nə stēz´) *plural noun.* Periods of time during which a line of rulers from the same family is in power. *Construction of the Great Wall of China took place from the Han to the Yuan **dynasties**.*

Ee

eaves·drop·ping (ēvz´drop´ing) *noun.* Listening to other people talking without letting them know you are listening. ***Eavesdropping** is not a polite thing to do.*

ech·o·lo·ca·tion (ek ō lō kā´shən) *noun.* A way to find out where objects are by making sounds and interpreting the echo that returns. *Bats rely on **echolocation** when they hunt for insects.*

ee·rie (îr´ē) *adjective.* Strange in a scary way. *We heard an owl's **eerie** hooting as we walked home in the dark.*

e·lec·tri·cal (i lek´tri kəl) *adjective.* Relating to the form of energy carried in wires for use to drive motors or as light or heat. *Dad carefully connected the **electrical** cables to the positive and negative terminals on his car's battery.*

Word History
Electrical comes from the Latin *electrum*, meaning "amber," because of amber's property of attracting other substances when rubbed.

at; āpe; fär; câre; end; mē; it; īce; pîerce; hot; ōld; sông; fôrk; oil; out; up; ūse; rüle; pùll; tûrn; chin; sing; shop; thin; **th**is; **hw** in **wh**ite; **zh** in treasure.

The symbol ə stands for the unstressed vowel sound in about, taken, pencil, lemon, and circus.

end·less (endʹlis) *adjective.* Having no limit or end. *The line of people seemed **endless**, and not everyone would get a ticket.*

en·dured (en dùrdʹor en dyùrdʹ) *verb.* Survived or put up with. *The workers **endured** the hot sun all day.*

en·ter·pri·sing (enʹtər prīʹzing) *adjective.* Showing energy and initiative; willing or inclined to take risks. *Brian, an **enterprising** young man, ran for class president and won.*

en·vi·ron·ment (en vīʹrən mənt) *noun.* Everything that surrounds an animal and affects it. *Polar bears have adapted very well to their cold **environment**.*

es·ti·mat·ed (esʹtə māʹtəd) *verb.* Judged or calculated, as of the value, quality, extent, size, or cost of something. *It is **estimated** that there are only 30,000 to 50,000 Asian elephants left in the world.*

eth·nic (ethʹnik) *adjective.* Being part of a group of people with religion, language, national origin, or some other background in common. *We went to World Food Day and sampled many **ethnic** foods.*

e·va·po·rate (i vapʹə rātʹ) *verb.* To change from a liquid or solid into a gas. *When heat makes water **evaporate**, the water seems to disappear.*

Word History
Evaporate comes from the Latin *evaporatus*, "to disperse in vapor," from *ex*, "out," and *vapor*, "exhalation."

e·ven·tu·al·ly (i venʹchü ə lē) *adverb.* In the end; finally. *We **eventually** got a DVD player because the good movies were not being released on video.*

ev·i·dence (evʹi dəns) *noun.* Proof of something. *People thought the knave stole the tarts, but they had no **evidence**.*

ex·as·per·at·ed (eg zasʹpə rātʹəd) *verb.* Annoyed greatly; made angry. *My dad got so **exasperated** helping with my math that my mom took over.*

ex·plo·ra·tion (ekʹsplə rāʹshən) *noun.* The act of traveling through unfamiliar areas in order to learn about them. *Remote-controlled vehicles are carrying out an **exploration** of the surface of Mars.*

ex·po·sure (ek spō′zhər) *noun.* The condition of being presented to view. *Each time the dog saw a new toy was counted as one* **exposure**.

Ff

fade (fād) *verb.* To become gradually weaker, fainter, or dimmer. *When a song ends, sometimes it will* **fade** *out.*

faint (fānt) *adjective.* Not clear or strong; weak. *A* **faint** *noise came from outside, but I couldn't see anyone.*

fam·ished (fam′isht) *adjective.* Very hungry; starving. *After a long day of running and swimming, the children were* **famished**.

flicked (flikt) *verb.* Hit or moved with a quick, light snap. *Fred* **flicked** *the fly off his face.*

flinched (flincht) *verb.* To draw back or away, as from something painful or unpleasant; wince. *When the door suddenly slammed, Myra* **flinched**.

fluke[1] (flük) *noun.* A chance happening; an accidental turn. *The substitute player's touchdown pass must have been a* **fluke**.

fluke[2] (flük) *noun.* The flat part of a whale's tail. *The whale smacked the water with its* **fluke**.

fool·ish·ness (fü′lish nəs) *noun.* The act of not showing good sense. *I wanted to race across the street, but my mom will not allow that* **foolishness**.

fos·sil (fos′əl) *noun.* The hardened remains or traces of an animal or plant that lived long ago. *The* **fossil** *we found had imprints of ancient seashells in rock.*

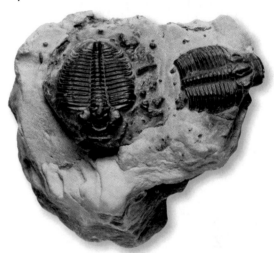

frag·ile (fraj′əl) *adjective.* Easily broken; delicate. *My toothpick ship is too* **fragile** *to take to show and tell.*

fu·els (fü′əlz) *plural noun.* Substances burned as a source of heat and power, such as coal, wood, or oil. *When the world runs out of fossil* **fuels**, *we will be forced to use alternate energy sources.*

at; āpe; fär; câre; end; mē; it; īce; pîerce; hot; ōld; sông; fôrk; oil; out; up; ūse; rüle; pu̇ll; tûrn; chin; sing; shop; thin; this; hw in white; zh in treasure.

The symbol ə stands for the unstressed vowel sound in about, taken, pencil, lemon, and circus.

Gg

gaped (gāpt) *verb.* Stared with the mouth open, as in wonder or surprise. *The audience gaped at the acrobats.*

gen·u·ine (jen´ū in) *adjective.* Sincere; honest. *My friends and I made a genuine effort to help kids new to the school.*

gli·der (glī´dər) *noun.* An aircraft that flies without a motor. *Riding in a glider can be exciting.*

glin·ted (glin´təd) *verb.* Sparkled or flashed. *Rays of sunshine glinted on the water.*

glis·ten·ing (glis´ən ing) *adjective.* Shining or sparkling with reflected light. *The glistening eyes of the children looked out from the stage.*

globe (glōb) *noun.* The Earth (as a shape). *Our globe is the home of billions of people.*

glo·ri·ous (glôr´ē əs) *adjective.* Having or deserving praise or honor; magnificent. *The autumn colors were just glorious.*

guard·i·an (gär´dē ən) *noun.* A person or thing that guards or watches over. *My older brother sometimes acts like my guardian.*

guide (gīd) *noun.* Someone who shows the way, such as on a tour or trip. *We followed the guide carefully along the narrow trails.*

Hh

hab·i·tat (hab´i tat´) *noun.* The place where an animal or plant naturally lives and grows. *A pond is a good habitat for frogs.*

Word History
Habitat comes from the Latin *habitare*, meaning "to dwell."

han·dy (han´dē) *adjective.* Within reach, nearby; easy to use. • **come in handy.** Be useful. *It's amazing how many times a dictionary can come in handy.*

harm·less (härm´les) *adjective.* Not able to do damage or hurt. *My dog looks mean, but really she is harmless.*

head·lines (hed´līnz) *plural noun.* Words printed at the top of a newspaper or magazine article. *The most important news has the biggest **headlines**.*

he·ri·tage (her´i tij) *noun.* Something that is handed down from previous generations or from the past; tradition. *Jazz is now a part of our country's cultural **heritage**.*

hi·ber·nate (hī´bər nāt´) *verb.* To sleep or stay inactive during the winter. *Bears eat a lot to get ready to **hibernate**.*

hi·lar·i·ous (hi lâr´ē əs) *adjective.* Very funny. *Kendra tells **hilarious** jokes.*

his·to·ri·ans (hi stôr´ē ənz) *plural noun.* People who study or write about history. ***Historians** can help us to understand the past.*

hoist·ing (hoist´ing) *verb.* Lifting or pulling up. ***Hoisting** logs out of the water, the men soon grew tired.*

i·den·ti·fied (ī´den´tə fīd´) *verb.* Proved that someone or something is a particular person or thing. *The fingerprints on the gold watch **identified** the butler as the thief.*

im·ag·es (im´ij əz) *plural noun.* Pictures of people or things. *The artist had painted large **images** of the people and animals she saw every day.*

im·mi·grants (im´i grənts) *plural noun.* People who come to live in one country from another. *Many **immigrants** come to the United States every year.*

im·pres·sive (im pres´iv) *adjective.* Deserving admiration; making a strong impression. *The track team won five races, which was their most **impressive** result all year.*

in·de·pen·dence (in´di pen´dəns) *noun.* Freedom from the control of another or others. *America gained its **independence** from Great Britain.*

---

at; āpe; fär; câre; end; mē; it; īce; pîerce; hot; ōld; sông; fôrk; oil; out; up; ūse; rüle; pull; tûrn; chin; sing; shop; thin; this; hw in white; zh in treasure.

The symbol ə stands for the unstressed vowel sound in about, taken, pencil, lemon, and circus.

in·jus·tice (in jus′tis) *noun.* Lack of justice; unfairness. *There are many tools to fight **injustice**, and everyone should know them.*

in·sec·ti·cides (in sek′ti sīdz) *plural noun.* Chemicals used to kill insects and other pests. *Some **insecticides** can reduce the number of mosquitoes.*

in·spec·ted (in speck′təd) *verb.* Looked at closely and carefully. *The official **inspected** our car and declared that it was safe to drive.*

in·spire (in spīr′) *verb.* To stir the mind, feelings, or imagination. *Nature can **inspire** some people to write poetry.*

in·sult (in′sult′) *noun.* A remark or action that hurts someone's feelings or pride. *Not to invite Marta to the party would be an **insult**.*

in·tel·li·gent (in tel′i jənt) *adjective.* Able to understand and to think especially well. *Mr. Lee asked an **intelligent** question.*

in·ter·fere (in′tər fir′) *verb.* To take part in the affairs of others when not asked; meddle. *My mom hates to **interfere**, but she often gives me good advice.*

in·ves·ti·gates (in ves′ti gāts′) *verb.* Looks into carefully in order to find facts and get information. *A detective **investigates** mysteries for a living.*

Jj

jeal·ous·y (jel′ə sē) *noun.* A feeling of envy of what a person has or can do. *Ken felt some **jealousy** when he saw Lin's new bike, but he got over it.*

jour·ney (jûr′nē) *noun.* A trip, especially one over a considerable distance or taking considerable time. *Ping made a **journey** to China to meet his grandparents.*

jum·ble (jum′bəl) *noun.* A confused mixture or condition; mess. *My room is a **jumble** of toys and books, so I have to clean it.*

Ll

leg·en·dary (lej′ən der′ē) *adjective.* Relating to a legend, or a story that has been handed down for many years and has some basis in fact. *Johnny Appleseed's efforts to spread the apple tree have become **legendary**.*

lim·it·ed (lim′i tid) *adjective.* Restricted, or kept within boundaries. *The menu had only a **limited** number of choices.*

log·i·cal (loj′i kəl) *adjective.* Sensible; being the action or result one expects. *When it rains, I do the **logical** thing and put my bicycle in the garage.*

loos·ened (lü′sənd) *verb.* Made looser; set free or released. *Brad **loosened** his necktie when the ceremony was over.*

lum·ber·ing (lum′bər ing) *adjective.* Moving in a slow, clumsy way. *Put a **lumbering** hippo in the water and it becomes a graceful swimmer.*

lurk (lûrk) *verb.* To lie hidden. *Many animals **lurk** in their dens to escape the heat of the day.*

Mm

mag·ni·fy (mag′nə fī′) *verb.* To make something look bigger than it really is. *Devices such as microscopes help to **magnify** small things.*

mas·sive (mas′iv) *adjective.* Of great size or extent; large and solid. *The pro wrestler had a **massive** chest.*

mi·cro·phone (mī′krə fōn′) *noun.* A device that converts soundwaves into electrical signals, which can then be recorded, broadcast, or amplified. *We couldn't hear the principal in the back of the auditorium because her **microphone** was broken.*

Word History
Microphone comes from the Greek words *mikros,* meaning "very small," and *phone,* meaning "sound."

mi·cro·scope (mī′krə skōp′) *noun.* A device for looking at things that are too small to be seen with the naked eye. *To see small cells in the body one needs to use a **microscope**.*

Word History
Microscope comes from the Greek words *mikros* meaning "very small," and *skopein,* meaning "to view or examine."

at; āpe; fär; câre; end; mē; it; īce; pîerce; hot; ōld; sông; fôrk; oil; out; up; ūse; rüle; pull; tûrn; chin; sing; shop; thin; <u>th</u>is; hw in white; zh in treasure.

The symbol ə stands for the unstressed vowel sound in about, taken, pencil, lemon, and circus.

midst (midst) *noun.* A position in the middle of a group of people or things. *"There is a poet in our **midst**," said the principal, "and we need to clap for her."*

mis·chief (mis′chif) *noun.* Conduct that may seem playful but causes harm or trouble. *The kittens were always getting into **mischief** when we weren't home.*

mis·un·der·stood (mis′un dər stŭd′) *verb.* Understood someone incorrectly; got the wrong idea. *I **misunderstood** the directions and did the wrong page for homework.*

mut·tered (mut′ərd) *verb.* Spoke in a low, unclear way with the mouth closed. *I saw he was mad by the way he **muttered** to himself.*

mys·te·ri·ous (mi stîr′ē əs) *adjective.* Very hard or impossible to understand; full of mystery. *The fact that the cookies were missing was **mysterious**.*

Nn

nat·u·ral (nach′ər əl) *adjective.*
1. Unchanged by people. *We hiked through **natural** surroundings of woods, streams, and meadows.*
2. Expected or normal. *The **natural** home of the dolphin is the open ocean.*

ne·ga·tives (neg′ə tivz) *plural noun.*
1. Photographic images made when film is developed. *The photographer looked at the **negatives** through the magnifier.* **2.** Words or phrases that mean "no." *We heard nothing but **negatives** in the report.*

ne·glec·ted (ni glekt′əd) *verb.* Failed to give proper attention or care to; failed to do. *I **neglected** to finish my science project and could not present it at the fair.*

non·vi·o·lence (non vī′ə ləns) *noun.* The philosophy or practice of opposing the use of all physical force or violence. *The demonstrators practiced **nonviolence** during the march on Washington.*

now·a·days (nou′ə dāz′) *adverb.* In the present time. *People hardly ever write with typewriters **nowadays**.*

nu·mer·ous (nü′mər əs or nū′mər əs) *adjective.* Forming a large number; many. *The mountain climbers faced **numerous** problems, but they still had fun.*

nu·tri·ents (nü′trē ənts or nū′trē ənts) *plural noun.* Substances needed by the bodies of people, animals, or plants to live and grow. *Sometimes we get ill because we are not getting the proper **nutrients**.*

nuz·zle (nuz′əl) *verb.* To touch or rub with the nose. *My dog will **nuzzle** me when he wants attention.*

Oo

o·be·di·ence (ō bē′dē əns) *noun.* The willingness to obey, or to carry out orders, wishes, or instructions. *It is important to show **obedience** to safety rules.*

Word History

Obedience comes from the Latin word *oboedire*, meaning "to hearken, yield, or serve."

op·por·tu·ni·ties (op′ər tü′ni tēz) *plural noun.* Good chances or favorable times. *School offers many **opportunities** to be involved in clubs.*

or·bits (ôr′bits) *plural noun.* The path in space of one heavenly body revolving around another. *When we studied **orbits** I learned it takes Pluto 248.53 years to go around the sun.*

or·phan·age (ôr′fən ij) *noun.* An institution that takes in and cares for children whose natural parents are absent or dead. *Martina had to travel to the Chinese **orphanage** to adopt her son.*

out·stretched (out′strecht′) *adjective.* Stretched out; extended. *His **outstretched** palm held the quarter I had dropped.*

o·ver·come (ō′vər kum′) *verb.* To get the better of; beat or conquer. *The team was able to **overcome** losing the lead to go on to win the game.*

at; āpe; fär; câre; end; mē; it; īce; pîerce; hot; ōld; sông; fôrk; oil; out; up; ūse; rüle; pùll; tûrn; chin; sing; shop; thin; this; hw in white; zh in treasure.

The symbol ə stands for the unstressed vowel sound in about, taken, pencil, lemon, and circus.

o·ver·crowd·ed (ō'vər kroud'id) *adjective.* Having too many people or things. *The small apartment was **overcrowded** with furniture.*

o·ver·heard (ō'vər hûrd') *verb.* Heard something one was not supposed to hear. *I **overheard** my brother planning a surprise party for me.*

o·ver·joyed (ō'vər joid') *adjective.* Very happy. *The whole team felt **overjoyed** when we won the soccer game.*

Pp

pa·le·on·tol·o·gist (pā' lē ən tol'ə jist) *noun.* A scientist who deals with fossils of prehistoric animal and plant life. *The **paleontologist** spoke to the class about the history of dinosaurs.*

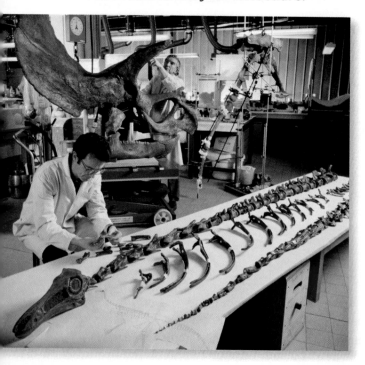

par·a·lyzed (par'ə līzd') *adjective.* **1.** Having lost movement or sensation in a part of the body. **2.** Made powerless or helpless. *The actress felt **paralyzed** by stage fright.*

part·ner·ship (pärt'nər ship') *noun.* A kind of business in which two or more people share the work and profits. *Janell, Pat, and Erik formed a gardening **partnership**.*

patch·work (pach'wûrk') *noun.* Something put together out of many uneven or varied parts. *From the air, the land looked like a **patchwork** of green and brown fabrics.*

pe·cul·iar (pi kūl'yər) *adjective.* Strange; not usual. *I had the **peculiar** feeling that I was being watched.*

pe·ri·od (pîr'ē əd) *noun.* **1.** A length of historical time. *The 19th century was a **period** of railroad building.* **2.** A mark of punctuation (.) at the end of a declarative sentence or an abbreviation.

per·sis·tence (pər sis'təns) *noun.* The ability to keep trying in spite of difficulties or obstacles. *Running a business requires **persistence**.*

phras·es (frāz'iz) *plural noun.* Groups of words expressing a single thought but not containing both a subject and predicate. *When I proofread my report, I made **phrases** into complete sentences.*

pol·i·ti·cians (pol´i tish´ənz) *plural noun.* People who hold or seek elected offices. *Four **politicians** were running for the one seat in Congress.*

pos·i·tive (poz´i tiv) *adjective.* Certain; sure. *I was **positive** I left that cookie right here on the counter.*

pow·wow (pou´wou´) *noun.* A North American Indian ceremony characterized by feasting and dancing. *People were selling wild rice and fry bread at the **powwow**.*

pre·cious (presh´əs) *adjective.* **1.** Having great cost or value. **2.** Held in high esteem; cherished. *Gold is a **precious** metal.*

pre·his·tor·ic (prē´his tôr´ik) *adjective.* Belonging to a time before people started recording history. ***Prehistoric** artists sometimes made cave paintings to tell a story.*

pre·serve (pri zûrv´) *verb.* To keep safe for the future. *My parents **preserve** some of my school papers every year.*

pro·claimed (prə klāmd´) *verb.* Announced publicly. *The principal **proclaimed** May 20 as the day for our annual class trips.*

pro·fes·sion·als (prə fesh´ə nəlz) *plural noun.* People who have an occupation that requires special training. *Engineers and architects are **professionals**.*

pros·pec·tors (pros´pek tərz) *plural noun.* People who explore an area for minerals, such as gold. *California was full of **prospectors** during the Gold Rush of 1849.*

pro·tes·ted (prō test´əd) *verb.* Complained against something. *When the workers lost their jobs, they **protested** to the union.*

Rr

raft (raft) *noun.* A kind of flat boat made of logs or boards fastened together. *Floating down the river on a **raft** is a nice way to spend a summer's day.*

---

at; āpe; fär; câre; end; mē; it; īce; pîerce; hot; ōld; sông; fôrk; oil; out; up; ūse; rūle; pull; tûrn; chin; sing; shop; thin; this; hw in white; zh in treasure.

The symbol ə stands for the unstressed vowel sound in about, taken, pencil, lemon, and circus.

re·al·is·tic (rē′ə lis′tik) *adjective.* Seeing things as they are; practical. *I dream of being a famous rock star, but I should also be* **realistic** *and stay in school.*

reef (rēf) *noun.* A ridge of sand, rock, or coral at or near the surface of the ocean. *Boaters have to be careful not to scrape against the* **reef** *below.*

ref·er·ence (ref′ər əns or ref′rens) *noun.* A statement that calls or directs attention to something. *The speech makes a* **reference** *to a play by Shakespeare.*

re·fresh·es (ri fresh′iz) *verb.* Restores strength and vitality to, as through food or rest. *Lemonade* **refreshes** *on a hot summer day.*

re·gion (rē′jən) *noun.* A geographic area whose characteristics are different from the others. *Nine of the original thirteen colonies can be found in the Northeast* **region.**

re·hearse (ri hûrs′) *verb.* To practice a song or play in preparation for public performances. *We have two weeks to* **rehearse** *before opening night!*

rep·tiles (rep′tīlz) *plural noun.* Cold-blooded vertebrates of the group Reptilia, which includes lizards, snakes, alligators, crocodiles, and turtles. *Most* **reptiles** *lay eggs, although some give birth to live young.*

re·spon·si·bil·i·ty (ri spon′sə bil′i tē) *noun.* The quality or condition of having a job, duty, or concern. *Taking care of the dog was my* **responsibility.**

risks (risks) *plural noun.* Chances of loss or harm. *Explorers were willing to take* **risks** *in the hope of discovering new lands.*

roamed (rōmd) *verb.* Moved around in a large area. *The grizzly bear* **roamed** *over a wide valley and the nearby mountains.*

roles (rōlz) *plural noun.* Characters or parts played by an actor. *Indira got one of the leading* **roles** *in the class play.*

ro·tate (rō′tāt) *verb.* To turn or cause to turn around on or as on an axis. *I had to* **rotate** *the image because the photo was upside down.*

rum·bling (rum´bling) *noun.* A heavy, deep, rolling sound. *The* **rumbling** *of thunder woke me up.*

Ss

sa·cred (sā´krid) *adjective.* Dedicated to or set apart for a religious use or purpose. *In ancient Greece, olive trees were* **sacred** *to Athena.*

sanc·tu·ar·y (sangk´chü er´ē) *noun.* A refuge for wildlife where predators are controlled and hunting is not allowed. *My friend runs a* **sanctuary** *for injured hawks and owls.*

scat·tered (skat´ərd) *verb.* Spread or thrown about here and there. *Practice balls were* **scattered** *all over the tennis court.*

sci·en·ti·fic meth·od (sī´ən tif´ik meth´əd) *noun.* The process used by scientists, in which a problem is stated, a hypothesis is formed, data are collected through observation or experimentation, and the hypothesis is proved or disproved by analyzing the data. *The crime lab is an essential ingredient in the detective's application of* **scientific method.**

scorn·ful·ly (skôrn´fəl ē) *adverb.* In a way that shows that something or someone is looked down upon and considered bad or worthless. *The critic spoke* **scornfully** *about the new artist's paintings.*

---

at; **ā**pe; f**ä**r; c**â**re; **e**nd; m**ē**; **i**t; **ī**ce; p**î**erce; h**o**t; **ō**ld; s**ô**ng; f**ô**rk; **oi**l; **ou**t; **u**p; **ū**se; r**ü**le; p**ů**ll; t**û**rn; **ch**in; si**ng**; **sh**op; **th**in; <u>**th**</u>is; **hw** in **wh**ite; **zh** in trea**s**ure.

The symbol **ə** stands for the unstressed vowel sound in **a**bout, tak**e**n, penc**i**l, lem**o**n, and circ**u**s.

scuf·fling (skuf´əl ing or skuf´ling) *noun.* The sound of feet shuffling. *When we heard* **scuffling** *from upstairs, we knew Grandpa had finished his nap.*

se·cure (si kyŭr´) *adjective.* Not likely to be taken away; certain or guaranteed. *verb.* To take possession of for safekeeping. *The police will* **secure** *the birdcage to use as evidence at the trial.*

seg·re·ga·tion (seg´ri gā´shən) *noun.* The practice of setting one racial group apart from another. *There are laws against* **segregation** *in public schools.*

se·lec·ting (si lek´ting) *verb.* Picking out among many; choosing. *I spend a long time* **selecting** *the right gift.*

self·ish (sel´fish) *adjective.* Thinking only of oneself; putting one's own interests and desires before those of others. *A second piece of cake sounded good, but I didn't want to be* **selfish.**

sen·si·ble (sen´sə bəl) *adjective.* Having or showing sound judgment; wise. *If you make a mistake, the* **sensible** *thing to do is apologize.*

shim·mer (shim´ər) *verb.* To shine with a faint, wavering light; glimmer. *The walls of the canyon began to* **shimmer** *in the rays of the setting sun.*

silk·en (sil´kən) *adjective.* **1.** Made of silk. **2.** Like silk in appearance. *Antonio wrote a poem about the girl's long* **silken** *hair.*

sky·scrap·ers (skī´skrā´ pərz) *plural noun.* Very tall buildings. *The city has many* **skyscrapers,** *and some of them are 50 stories high!*

slith·ered (slith´ərd) *verb.* To slide or glide like a snake. *When the snakes* **slithered** *across the ground, they hardly made a sound.*

snick·er·ing (snik´ər ing) *verb.* Laughing in a mean or disrespectful manner. *The children stopped* **snickering** *when their mother told them to be kinder.*

snor·ing (snôr´ing) *verb.* Making harsh or noisy sounds while sleeping. *The dog was* **snoring** *on the porch when I came home.*

snuf·fled (snuf´əld) *verb.* Breathed noisily because of partly stopped-up nasal passages. *Because of a bad cold, I* **snuffled** *all day.*

sol·i·tar·y (sol´i ter´ē) *adjective.* Living, being, or going alone. *For trying to escape, the prisoner was placed in* **solitary** *confinement.*

Word History
Solitary comes from the Latin *solitarius,* meaning "alone," lonely.

sores (sôrz) *plural noun.* Places where the skin has been broken and hurts. *My hands had* **sores** *after raking leaves all morning with no gloves on.*

spe·cial·ty (spesh´əl tē) *noun.* A special thing that a person knows a great deal about or can make very well. *Making quilts is my Aunt Lisa's* **specialty**.

strikes (strīks) *plural noun.* **1.** The stopping of work to protest something. *The workers threatened* **strikes** *if conditions did not improve.* **2.** Pitched balls in the strike zone or that a batter swings at and misses.

strut·ting (strut´ing) *verb.* Walking in a self-important way. *Marilyn went* **strutting** *around in her new boots from Italy.*

stum·bled (stum´bəld) *verb.* To lose one's balance, as by missing one's footing, stubbing one's toe, or tripping over an obstacle. • **stum·bled up·on** *verb.* To come upon something unexpectedly or by chance. *We* **stumbled upon** *the clues that would lead us to the treasure.*

sub·urbs (sub´ûrbz) *plural noun.* The areas around a city where people live. *Many people commute from the* **suburbs** *into the city.*

Word History
Suburbs come from the Latin *suburbium*—from *sub*— "under" and *urbs,* meaning "city."

sur·vey (sər vā´) *verb.* To view or examine as a whole. (sûr´və) *noun.* A comprehensive view. *A* **survey** *of the crime scene revealed three possible points of entry.*

sus·pi·cious (səs pish´əs) *adjective.* Causing doubt and mistrust; causing the feeling that something is wrong. *When my mom saw me by the cookie jar, I could tell she was* **suspicious**.

---

at; āpe; fär; câre; end; mē; it; īce; pîerce; hot; ōld; sông; fôrk; oil; out; up; ūse; rūle; pu̇ll; tûrn; chin; sing; shop; thin; this; hw in white; zh in treasure.

The symbol ə stands for the unstressed vowel sound in about, taken, pencil, lemon, and circus.

swal·lows¹ (swol´ōz) *verb.* Causes food or other substances to pass from the mouth into the stomach. *Kathy's sore throat hurts every time she* **swallows**.

Word History
Swallows comes from the Old English word *swelgan* with the same meaning.

swal·lows² (swol´ōz) *plural noun.* Several groups of small birds having a slender body and a forked tail.

Word History
Swallows comes from the Old English word *swealwe*, meaning "this bird."

swamp (swomp) *noun.* A kind of wetland in which grasses and shrubs grow on land almost permanently covered by shallow water. *Many endangered birds, such as the snowy egret, can be found in this* **swamp**.

swarms (swôrmz) *plural noun.* Large groups of insects flying or moving together. *When the hive fell,* **swarms** *of angry bees flew out.*

Tt

tan·gles (tang´gəlz) *plural noun.* Knotted, twisted, confused masses. *The garden hose had not been rolled back up and was full of* **tangles**.

tech·nique (tek nēk´) *noun.* A method or way of bringing about a desired result in a science, art, sport, or profession. *Part of Allison's* **technique** *in running is to breathe in and out on counts of seven.*

Word History
Technique comes from the Greek word *tekhnikos*, meaning "relating to an art or craft."

tem·ples (tem′pəlz) *plural noun*. Buildings used for the worship of a god or gods. *Visitors to Athens can tour many **temples** of the ancient Greeks.*

ter·ri·to·ry (ter′i tôr′ē) *noun*. Any large area of land; region. *My brother's **territory** for selling office supplies is in North Carolina.*

tes·ti·fy (tes′tə fī′) *verb*. To give evidence under oath in a court of law. *The woman took her place on the witness stand to **testify**.*

threat·ened (thret′ənd) *adjective*. Having a sense of harm or danger. *The dark storm clouds made the players feel **threatened** with a rain-out.*

tot·tered (tô′tərd) *verb*. Walked or moved with unsteady steps; rocked or swayed as if about to fall. *The baby **tottered** as she first tried to walk.*

tra·di·tions (trə dish′ənz) *plural noun*. Knowledge, beliefs, or customs handed down from one generation to another. *People of many cultural **traditions** live in the United States.*

Uu

un·con·sti·tu·tion·al (un′ kon sti tü′ shə nəl) *adjective*. Not in keeping with the constitution of the United States. *Segregation was declared **unconstitutional** by the Supreme Court.*

un·fair (un fâr′) *adjective*. Not fair or just. *Punishing all of us for the actions of my little sister seemed **unfair**.*

un·ions (ūn′yənz) *plural noun*. Groups of workers joined together to protect their jobs and improve working conditions. *Labor **unions** fight to get workers the safety equipment they need.*

u·nique (ū nēk′) *adjective*. Having no equal; the only one of its kind. *In many ways, the Everglades is **unique**.*

u·ni·verse (ū′nə vûrs′) *noun*. Everything that exists, including Earth, the planets, the stars, and all of space. *Many scientists spend their lives studying the wonders of the **universe**.*

---

at; āpe; fär; câre; end; mē; it; īce; pîerce; hot; ōld; sông; fôrk; oil; out; up; ūse; rüle; pùll; tûrn; chin; sing; shop; thin; <u>th</u>is; hw in white; zh in treasure.

The symbol ə stands for the unstressed vowel sound in about, taken, pencil, lemon, and circus.

un·sta·ble (un stā′bəl) *adjective.* Not settled or steady; easily moved or put off balance. *Although the raft looked **unstable**, it floated very well.*

un·sus·pect·ing (un′sə spek′ting) *adjective.* Having no suspicions. *The **unsuspecting** girls did not realize they were about to get sprayed by the hose.*

Vv

val·u·a·ble (val′ū ə bəl) *adjective.* Of great use, worth, or importance. *The excavation gave us some **valuable** new information about the settlers.*

ven·ture (ven′chər) *noun.* A business or some other undertaking that involves risk. *Rea's new **venture** was a carpet-cleaning service.*

ves·sels (ves′əlz) *plural noun.* Ships or large boats used to transport or carry over water. *The ocean liner known as the* Titanic *was larger than all other oceangoing **vessels** of the time.*

Ww

week·days (wēk′dāz′) *plural noun.* The days of the week except Saturday and Sunday. *We only go to school on **weekdays**.*

whirl·wind (whûrl′wind′, wûrl′wind′) *noun.* **1.** A whirling current of air that moves forward with great force. **2.** Anything resembling a whirlwind. *She moved about the apartment, packing like a **whirlwind**.*

wild·life (wīld′līf′) *noun.* Living things, especially the animals that live naturally in an area. *We saw lots of **wildlife** on our hike in the woods.*

wing·span (wing′span′) *noun.* The distance between the tips of the wings of a bird, insect, or airplane. *The **wingspan** of some hawks is five feet.*

wis·dom (wiz′dəm) *noun.* Good judgment and intelligence in knowing what is right, good, and true. *When I'm not sure what to do, I look to my grandpa's **wisdom**.*

Word History
Wisdom comes from the Old English word *wisdom*, from *wis*, meaning "having sound judgment, learned."

wist·ful·ly (wist′fəl ē) *adverb.* In a sadly longing way; yearningly. *My grandma looked at her wedding pictures **wistfully**.*

Acknowledgments

(Continued from Copyright page.)

"I Love the Look of Words" by Maya Angelou from SOUL LOOKS BACK IN WONDER. Copyright © 1993 by Tom Feelings. Reprinted by permission of Dial Books, a division of Penguin Books USA Inc.

"I Was Dreaming to Come to America" selected by Veronica Lawlor from I WAS DREAMING TO COME TO AMERICA. Copyright © 1995 by Veronica Lawlor. Reprinted by permission of Viking Press, a division of Penguin Books USA Inc.

"Into the Swamp" by Elizabeth Schleichert, photos by C. C. Lockwood. From RANGER RICK SEPTEMBER 2003 — INTO THE SWAMP. Copyright © 2003 by the National Wildlife Federation. Reprinted by permission of People and Nature: Our Future Is in the Balance.

"The Life and Times of the Ant" by Charles Micucci from THE LIFE AND TIMES OF THE ANT. Copyright © 2003 by Charles Micucci. Reprinted by permission of Houghton Mifflin Company.

"Light Bulb" and "Lightning Bolt" by Joan Bransfield Graham from FLICKER FLASH. Text copyright © 1999 by Joan Bransfield Graham. Reprinted by permission of Houghton Mifflin Company.

"Me and Uncle Romie" by Claire Hartfield, paintings by Jerome Lagarrigue. Text copyright © 2002 by Claire Hartfield, paintings copyright © 2002 by Jerome Lagarrigue. Reprinted by permission of Dial Books, a division of Penguin Books USA Inc.

"Mountains and plains" and "No sky at all" from AN INTRODUCTION TO HAIKU: AN ANTHOLOGY OF POEMS AND POETS FROM BASHŌ TO SHIKI. Copyright © 1958 by Harold G. Henderson. Reprinted by permission of Doubleday Anchor Books, a division of Doubleday & Company, Inc.

"Mighty Jackie: The Strike-Out Queen" by Marissa Moss, illustrated by C. F. Payne. Text copyright © 2004 by Marissa Moss, illustrations copyright © 2004 by C. F. Payne. Reprinted by permission of Simon & Schuster Books for Young Readers.

"My Brother Martin: A Sister Remembers, Growing Up with the Rev. Dr. Martin Luther King, Jr." by Christine King Farris, illustrated by Chris Soentpiet. Text copyright © 2003 by Christine King Farris, illustrations copyright © 2003 by Chris Soentpiet. Reprinted by permission of Simon & Schuster Books for Young Readers.

"My Brothers' Flying Machine" by Jane Yolen, paintings by Jim Burke. Text copyright © 2003 by Jane Yolen, illustrations copyright © 2003 by Jim Burke. Reprinted by permission of Little, Brown, and Company.

"My Diary from Here to There" story by Amada Irma Pérez, illustrations by Maya Christina Gonzalez from MY DIARY FROM HERE TO THERE. Story copyright © 2002 by Amada Irma Pérez, illustrations copyright © 2002 by Maya Christina Gonzalez. Reprinted by permission of Children's Book Press.

"Mystic Horse" by Paul Goble. Copyright © 2003 by Paul Goble. Reprinted by permission of HarperCollins Publishers.

"The Raft" by Jim LaMarche. Copyright © 2000 by Jim LaMarche. Reprinted by permission of HarperCollins Publishers.

"Roadrunner's Dance" by Rudolfo Anaya, illustrated by David Diaz. Copyright © 2000. Text reprinted by permission of Susan Bergholz Literary Services, New York. All rights reserved. Illustrations reprinted by permission of Hyperion Books for Children.

"The snow is melting" and " Winter solitude" from THE ESSENTIAL HAIKU: VERSIONS OF BASHŌ, BUSON, AND ISSA. Introduction and selection copyright © 1994 by Robert Hass. Unless otherwise noted, all translations copyright © 1994 by Robert Hass. Reprinted by permission of The Ecco Press.

"Snowflake Bentley" by Jacqueline Briggs Martin, illustrated by Mary Azarian. Text copyright © 1998 by Jacqueline Briggs Martin, illustrations copyright © 1998 by Mary Azarian. Reprinted by permission of Houghton Mifflin Company

"A Walk in the Desert" by Rebecca L. Johnson with illustrations by Phyllis V. Saroff from A WALK IN THE DESERT. Text copyright © 2001 by Rebecca L. Johnson, illustrations copyright © 2001 by Phyllis V. Saroff. Reprinted by permission of Carolrhoda Books, Inc.

"Wild Horses: Black Hills Sanctuary" by Cris Peterson, photographs by Alvis Upitis. Text copyright © 2003 by Cris Peterson, photographs copyright © 2003 by Alvis Upitis. Reprinted by permission of Boyds Mills Press, Inc.

ILLUSTRATIONS
Cover Illustration: Bandelin-Dacey Studio

18-19: Laura Watson. 20-37: (bg) Joe Cepeda. 39: Joe LeMonnier. 50-51: (bg) Wetzel & Company. 50-51: (tl) Laura Westlund. 52: (tl) Phyllis V. Saroff. 52-53: (bg) Wetzel & Company. 53: (tr) Phyllis V. Saroff. 54: (tl) Phyllis V. Saroff. 54-55: (bg) Wetzel & Company. 55: (tr) Phyllis V. Saroff. 56: (tl) Phyllis V. Saroff. 56-57: (bg) Wetzel & Company. 57: (tr) Phyllis V. Saroff. 58: (tl) Phyllis V. Saroff. 58-59: (bg) Wetzel & Company. 59: (tr) Phyllis V. Saroff. 60: (tl) Phyllis V. Saroff. 60-61: (bg) Wetzel & Company. 61: (tr) Phyllis V. Saroff. 64: (l) Phyllis V. Saroff. 66-67: (bg) Russell Farrell. 68: Daniel Del Valle. 76: Joe Lertola. 84: Kim Johnson. 86-101: Anna Rich. 105: Geoff McCormack/ Photo Researchers. 112-137: Jim LaMarche. 139: Joe LeMonnier. 142: Daniel Del Valle. 145: Viviana Diaz. 146: Paul Mirocha. 152-169: C.F. Payne. 158: (br) Daniel Del Valle. 180-201: Maya Christina Gonzalez. 206: Daniel Del Valle. 213,216: Rick Nease for TFK. 224-243: Rosalyn Schanzer. 246: Daniel Del Valle. 250: Ann Boyajian. 252-265: Nicole Wong. 270: Daniel Del Valle. 280-297: David Diaz. 298-301: Murray Kimber. 302: Daniel Del Valle. 303: Maryana Beletskaya. 308-323: Chris Soentpiet. 328: Daniel Del Valle. 329: Time Life Pictures/Getty. 346-367: Paul Goble. 372: Daniel Del Valle. 378-401: Mary Azarian. 402-403: Tina Fong. 404: Daniel Del Valle. 406-408: Argosy. 414-437: Mark Teague. 446: Lane Gregory. 448-463: Kristina Rodanas. 476: Rick Nease for TFK. 504-505: Jesse Reisch. 506: Daniel Del Valle. 512-529: Katherine Brown-Wing. 530-533: David Groff. 558-559: Robert Casilla. 560: Wetzel & Company. 564-565: David LaFleur. 566-585: Renato Alarção. 586-589: Courtesy Puddlejump Players. 590: Daniel Del Valle. 595: Rick Nease for TFK. 608-627: Jerome Lagarrigue. 628-629: Megan Halsey. 650-651: John Hovell. 652-655: Ande Cook. 656: Ernesto Burciaga/Alamy. 664-665: Greg Shed. 666-681: Ying-Hwa Hu & Cornelius Van Wright. 686: Daniel Del Valle. 690-691: Loretta Krupinski. 692-709: Garth Williams. 715: Argosy. 720: American Museum of National History. 734-753: Jim Burke. 754-755: Bandelin-Dacey Studios. 761: Paul Mirocha. 762-777: Charles Micucci. 778-781: (bg) Amy Lowry Poole. 782: Daniel Del Valle. 783: John Hovell. 788-789: Renato Alarção.

PHOTOGRAPHY
All photographs are by Macmillan/McGraw Hill (MMH) except as noted below:

16-17: Annie Griffiths Belt/CORBIS. 17: Nick Koudis/Getty. 36: (tl) Courtesy Johanna Hurwitz; (tc) Wetzel & Company; (bcr) WernerPhoto.com. 38-39: Vo Trung Dung/Corbis Sygma. 40: (tl) Keith Srakocic/AP; (br) Graeme Robertson/Getty. 41: Siner Jeff/ Corbis Sygma. 42: CORBIS. 43: Lew Robertson/CORBIS. 44-45: Michael & Patricia Fogden/CORBIS. 45: Alan and Sandy Carey/ Getty. 46: Jack Barrie/Bruce Coleman. 47: Dave Tipling/Alamy. 48-49: Bruce Clendenning/Visuals Unlimited. 49: Martin J Miller/ Visuals Unlimited. 51: (tr) Steve Warble. 52: (b) Brian Vikander. 52: Barbara Gerlach/Visuals Unlimited. 53: (tc) Richard Day/Daybreak Imagery; (b) Tom Bean. 54: (tc) Bayard A. Brattstrom/Visuals Unlimited; (b) Rob Simpson/Visuals Unlimited. 55: John Cunningham/Visuals Unlimited. 56: (tc) LINK/Visuals Unlimited; (b) John Gerlach/Visuals Unlimited. 57: Hal Beral/Visuals Unlimited. 58: Malowski/Visuals Unlimited. 59: John Gerlach/Visuals Unlimited. 60: (tr) Barbara Gerlach/Visuals Unlimited; (b) Joe McDonald/ Visuals Unlimited. 61: Tom J. Ulrich/Visuals Unlimited. 62-63: Bruce Clendenning/Visuals Unlimited. 64: Courtesy Lerner Publishing Group. 64-65: (bkgd) Martin J Miller/Visuals Unlimited; (bl) Barbara Gerlach/Visuals Unlimited. 65: (bc) Rob Simpson/Visuals Unlimited; (br) Steve Warble. 68: Michael Newman/Photo Edit. 69: Digital Vision/Getty. 70-71: William Smithey Jr/Getty. 72: Frank Staub/Index Stock. 73: Corey Rich. 74-75: Ken Wilson/Wildfaces. 77: Campbell William/CORBIS Sygma. 78: (cl) Galen Rowell/CORBIS; (bcl) Raymond Cramm/Photo Researchers; (bcr) Richard Kettlewell/ Animals Animals; (bl) Tony Arruza/CORBIS; (bc) W. Gregory Brown/ Animals Animals. 80: SuperStock/AGE. 81: (bkgd) Dian Lofton for TFK; (c) C. Squared Studios/Getty; (cr) Dian Lofton for TFK. 82-83: NASA/AP. 83: NASA/Getty. 85: Stock Trek/Getty. 100: (tl) Photo by Das Anndas. Courtesy Farrar, Straus and Giroux; (cr) Courtesy Anna Rich. 102: NASA. 104: Detlev Van Ravenswaay/Science Photo Library. 104-105: Chris Butler/Science Photo Library. 106: Rubberball/Getty. 107: Photodisc/Getty. 108-109: Steve Dunwell/Index Stock. 109: Jeremy Woodhouse/Getty. 110: John Beatty/Getty. 111: (cl) Jen & Des Bartlett/Bruce Coleman; (bkgd) Jim Brandenburg/Minden. 136: Courtesy Jim LaMarche. 138: CC Lockwood. 138-139: (bc) Edmond Van Hoorick/Getty. 140: CC Lockwood. 140-141: Sami Sarkis/Getty. 141: CC Lockwood. 142: Photodisc/Getty. 143: Christoph Burki/Getty. 148-149: Tim Shaffer/Reuters. 149: C Squared Studios/Getty. 150: